Behavior, Truth

and

Deception

**Applying Profiling and Analysis
to the Interview Process**

Behavior, Truth and Deception

Applying Profiling and Analysis to the Interview Process

Michael R. Napier

CRC Press
Taylor & Francis Group
Boca Raton London New York

CRC Press is an imprint of the
Taylor & Francis Group, an **informa** business

CRC Press
Taylor & Francis Group
6000 Broken Sound Parkway NW, Suite 300
Boca Raton, FL 33487-2742

Printed in the United States of America on acid-free paper
10 9 8 7 6 5 4 3 2 1

International Standard Book Number: 978-1-4398-2041-4 (Hardback)

Library of Congress Cataloging-in-Publication Data

Napier, Mike R.
  Behavior, truth and deception: applying profiling and analysis to the interview process / Mike R. Napier.
       p. cm.
  Includes bibliographical references and index.
  ISBN 978-1-4398-2041-4 (hbk. : alk. paper)
  1. Interviewing in law enforcement. 2. Criminal behavior, Prediction of. I. Title.

HV8073.3.N37 2010
363.25'4--dc22   2010009479

Visit the Taylor & Francis Web site at
http://www.taylorandfrancis.com

and the CRC Press Web site at
http://www.crcpress.com

It is difficult to select a few to single out for this dedication, especially when so many have had a major influence on your life. There are five important groups and several individuals that I want to recognize in this dedication.

To all the fine men and women in the FBI who through their personal and professional life have epitomized the FBI creed of fidelity, bravery, and integrity.

A special dedication is offered to the FBI's BSU, the NCAVC, the FBI's Crisis Management Unit, and the Critical Incident Response Group, all located at or near the FBI Academy, for offering their skills, talents, and public service to law enforcement, wherever their location, in the earnest hope of solving some of our most pressing, harmful, and demanding crimes.

To all the professionals in policing, and those in positions ancillary to policing, who strive to make American society safer and more humane and mitigate some of the harm and damage caused by those degenerate and deviant criminals who sometimes seem to roam with impunity.

To all victim's advocates and counselors who provide the caring and human touch and personal services to those who have suffered at the hands of those who violate.

Special thanks are in order to every member of the Academy Group who offered their wise counsel, support, and the opportunity to continue working in these areas.

On a personal level:

No one succeeds without family support and mentors. Throughout my entire career, my family has steadfastly stood with me and made personal sacrifices that allowed me to pursue my dreams and goals. Each member of my immediate family has made sacrifices to allow me to take advantage of opportunities for academic study and advancement, sometimes absenting myself for weeks at a stretch. Some of those trips included ventures into unsettled and unfriendly regions of lesser-developed countries that served to highlight their concerns. To each of them, I am thankful for their understanding, sacrifices, and encouragement.

Two mentors, who became fast friends, had an impact on my professional life through their availability and generosity.

Kenneth P. Baker's departure from this life this year left a hole in the lives of many. His legacy is the influence he had on many and his unfailing giving and caring.

Roy Hazelwood has touched the lives of many in law enforcement around the world. His efforts to educate officers about the true nature of sexual violence raised the bar of professionalism when dealing with offenders and victims alike.

Table of Contents

19 Legal Perspectives on Interviewing 275

JOHN C. HALL

Foreword

It was my great and good fortune to have been a part of the Federal Bureau of Investigation (FBI) family for nearly 28 years. Very early in my investigative career I was tasked with breaking a case involving industrywide corruption. The allegations included the bribery by plant owners of U.S. Department of Agriculture inspectors/veterinarians and meat graders. Many of these individuals had been targeted before but without any success. The investigation examined whether tainted, rotten meat was being approved for the school lunch program, meals for on duty troops, and for meat supplies for several federal agencies. Another aspect was that corrupt government employees were arbitrarily "grading" the meat into higher grades than was proper, thereby affecting the prices paid by everyone living on the West Coast and states bordering that area. During the inquiry it was learned that the owners were meeting regularly and, in a classic antitrust manner, fixing the prices for meat products in their very large service area. The end result of the investigation was the conviction of 89 individuals and corporations and the reshaping of the Los Angeles meat industry.

On the coattails of my successes as an investigator, I was provided with ample opportunities to obtain training in a variety of investigative areas. None was more fascinating than joining with a select cadre of agents who trained as "profilers" by the FBI Behavioral Science Unit (BSU). When the analytical and profiling units split from the BSU, I went with the analytical and profiling group, eventually headquartered off the FBI Academy campus. The exposure to the BSU research and instruction data provided a wealth of material to consume, digest, and apply to real-life dramas involving many, many areas of violent crime. My affiliation with the BSU led to a deep appreciation of interviewing techniques applicable to violent and evil offenders.

The National Center for the Analysis of Violent Crime (NCAVC) was established as the umbrella organization housing the behavioral science talent at the FBI Academy. The Crisis Management Unit selected me to join them after years of representing them in the field. I was trained as a "hostage negotiator" until we became "crisis negotiators." The unit provided regular and in-depth training, leading some of us to be selected to the FBI's high-profile unit designated as the Critical Incident Negotiating Team. This training into the deviant and disturbed minds of hostage takers and barricaded subjects meshed well with the BSU disciplines.

I was also fortunate enough to be selected to become a polygraph examiner, which entailed months of arduous training by the Department of Defense Polygraph Institute (DODPI). The bureau provided additional training and tutoring. This job with the FBI entailed tons of travel and the opportunity to be involved in nearly every major case in my area. The most stimulating part of administering polygraph examinations came from the pretest interview and then, if deception was indicated, the face-to-face interrogation. In this capacity, I racked up considerable experience in interrogating.

Each of my assignments came with reading material and expectations. It is this personal history that has shaped my interview/interrogation knowledge base, style, experience level, and arsenal of psychological weapons. I had the opportunity to receive interview training from FBI experts and from specialists outside the bureau. I also received interview-specific training from Reid and Associates, the Central Intelligence Agency (CIA), DODPI, and Avinoam Sapir's scientific content analysis course.

Experience, including instances of failure, is often the best instructor available, but closely following is the interaction with my peers and the sharing of ideas, concepts, and practical applications in the area of interviewing. Some of the best exchanges took place at the academy or at FBI and DODPI training sessions. Personal conversations with others having similar interests cannot be credited enough for stimulating my thought process. It is for all these reasons that I have discovered that often the line between personal discovery and stimulation from others blurs.

With recognition that an original thought is a rarity, I wish to express thanks and gratitude to several sources that had an impact on my interview philosophy and practices. From my family tutelage, my formal and informal education, and experiences in the private sector, a wealth of knowledge was garnered regarding dealing with people. I wish to specifically acknowledge Reid and Associates for adapting known psychological principles and existing police investigative knowledge into a highly useful and ethical interview program. My affiliation with the BSU and NCAVC of the FBI led to a deep appreciation of interviewing techniques applicable to violent and evil offenders. The views expressed here are certainly mine and do not necessarily represent the views or positions of the FBI. This education has continued through association with my learned colleagues at the Academy Group Inc. in Manassas, Virginia.

My good fortune continued postretirement by signing on with the Academy Group. This joint collaboration encompasses the finest collection of forensic behavioral science minds to be found anywhere. The Academy Group possesses many answers regarding the understanding of dishonest, violent, brutal, and sexually violent behavior; they allowed me to join them and from the beginning openly shared their expertise, time, experience, patience, and guidance.

My proofreaders, critics, and peer reviewers made invaluable comments and suggestions. Thanks Judy, Carolyn, Steve, and Perry.

This book includes the expertise of an incredible collection of personalities, experiences, and talent. This is truly a joint presentation of my personal choices for an interview "dream team." The readers are truly blessed with the opportunities to view a collection of approaches for interviewing and interrogating violent and sexually violent individuals. Many thanks are offered to each of the contributors.

Author

Michael R. Napier retired from the FBI after nearly 28 years of service and being assigned to the Albuquerque, Los Angeles, Oklahoma City, and Kansas City field offices and to the Critical Incident Response Group (CIRG) at the FBI Academy. At CIRG he was assigned to the Crisis Management Unit and the Behavioral Analysis Unit, both of which operated under the behavioral sciences umbrella known as the National Center for the Analysis of Violent Crime. Mike was a supervisory special agent in Los Angeles, Oklahoma City, and CIRG. He supervised organized crime and labor racketeering programs, white collar crime squads, and a program in the profiling and behavior analysis units. He was on the FBI's Critical Incident Negotiating Team, which was used for high profile cases both nationally and internationally. Mike also represented the Behavioral Science Unit as a field coordinator assigned to assist local, state, and national law enforcement agencies on difficult and unsolved cases in the area of violent crimes. He was also a certified FBI polygraph examiner.

Contributors

Susan H. Adams, Ph.D., a retired Federal Bureau of Investigation (FBI) agent, is a consultant in law enforcement communications. She has 28 years of teaching experience, and her areas of expertise include statement analysis, interviewing techniques, detection of deception, nonverbal communication, interpersonal communication, and behavioral styles. Dr. Adams has been a speaker at international conferences in Vienna, Prague, Edinburgh, Toronto, and Ottawa and at regional conferences throughout the United States. She addressed the American Association of Police Polygraph Examiners, the National Conference of FBI Polygraph Examiners, the FBI Behavioral Analysis Program, and the Annual Women in Federal Law Enforcement

Conference on the topic, "Statement Analysis: What Do Suspects' Words Really Reveal?"

As an adjunct instructor for the University of Virginia, Dr. Adams taught National Academy graduate courses and served as an interviewing instructor at the FBI Academy. Dr. Adams received her doctoral degree in human development from Virginia Tech. She also received the University of Virginia Jefferson Award for excellence in research. She has authored and coauthored numerous articles.

Richard L. Ault Jr., Ph.D. served in the U.S. Marine Corps and for 24 years was a special agent in the FBI. In 1994, he was the deputy chief of the Behavioral Science Unit (BSU) at the FBI Academy. He received a bachelor of science degree in psychology from Huntingdon College, Montgomery, Alabama; his master of arts degree in counseling and guidance from the University of Alabama; and his doctoral degree in counseling psychology and student development from the American University, Washington, D.C. Dr. Ault has lectured at Patrick Henry College on the psychology of espionage and indirect assessment in intelligence.

In the FBI, Dr. Ault worked criminal, organized crime, and domestic terrorism cases. He was assigned to the BSU from 1975 to 1994, where he conducted thousands of assessments of violent crimes and thousands of assessments for the intelligence community.

When he retired, Dr. Ault was placed on contract to the FBI as the pioneer member and senior advisor of the FBI's Behavioral Assessment Program in counterintelligence and counterterrorism. In July 2003, while working with the Office of the National Counterintelligence Executive, he was awarded the National Intelligence Meritorious Unit Citation for his assistance on the Robert Hanssen Damage Assessment Team. He has participated in damage assessments in numerous other spy cases and currently works as a consultant to the Defense Intelligence Agency. Dr. Ault is a vice president of the Academy Group Inc. He is a consultant to private industry, law firms, and federal, state, and local government agencies in all areas of violence and violent crimes.

John C. Hall is a retired FBI agent. A native of Kentucky and a graduate of the University of Louisville Law School, he served as legal counsel for the university for almost 2 years before joining the FBI in 1970. In the course of a 32-year career with the FBI, he served as an investigator in the Oklahoma City and St. Louis divisions. In addition to his investigative responsibilities, he served as the principal legal advisor, principal firearms instructor, and a member of the St. Louis SWAT team.

John served 1 year in the Legal Counsel Division at FBI headquarters in Washington, D.C. The last several years of his career were spent at the FBI

Academy, Quantico, Virginia, where he served in the prestigious legal unit as a legal instructor and later as the chief of the Firearms Training Unit. In the last assignment, he was responsible for the creation of the widely acclaimed Ammunition Testing Program of the FBI and supervised the transition of the FBI from revolvers to pistols. He has published numerous articles in the *FBI Law Enforcement Bulletin* on constitutional law, criminal procedure, and related topics. Nationally recognized as an expert in the legal and practical issues relating to the use of force by law enforcement officers, he coauthored a book on the use of deadly force by law enforcement officers, *In Defense of Self and Others*. He resides in Fredericksburg, Virginia. If I had paid John for all the times I sought out his vast knowledge on legal matters, particularly those concerning interviewing, he would be a wealthy man. John has the facility of being comfortable and at ease with himself and his circumstances. He is also an accomplished musician and vocalist.

Lt. Tracy Harpster has served with the Moraine Police Department in Ohio since 1984. He has worked as a street officer, undercover narcotics officer, sergeant, detective sergeant, and operations lieutenant. From 2002 to 2005, he was a task force director in the Ohio Organized Crime Investigations Commission, investigating large-scale RICO (Racketeer Influenced and Corrupt Organizations Act) operation, theft, money laundering, and gambling crimes. Lt. Harpster is a graduate of the 216th Session of the FBI National Academy, Quantico, Virginia, and worked on the FBI Joint Terrorism Task Force in Dayton, Ohio.

Lt. Harpster received a bachelor of science in criminal justice from Bowling Green State University and a master of science from the University of Cincinnati. His master's thesis examined the indicators of innocence and guilt of 911 homicide callers reporting the offense. The study analyzed verbal indicators to gain insight to homicide crimes and to explore pertinent issues during the investigation and the interview of the caller. Lt. Harpster has provided numerous presentations on the analysis of 911 calls in homicide cases at local, regional, and national conferences.

R. Stephen Mardigian served 31 years as an FBI supervisory special agent, regional field office program manager, violent crime assessor, and administrator for the FBI's National Center for the Analysis of Violent Crime (NCAVC). He has conducted detailed evaluations of violent crime cases for criminal justice agencies faced with the most baffling and vicious crimes. He participated in and directed NCAVC violent crime research projects such as the *Crime Classification Manual* and the child killer-infant abductor and serial rapist studies. He has provided investigative analysis on hundreds of cases involving homicide; sexual assault; child abduction and molestation;

arson; bombing; extortion; product tampering; stalking; workplace violence; domestic and international terrorism; and threat assessment.

Mardigian is currently the executive vice president with The Academy Group Inc., the world's largest privately owned forensic behavioral science firm. As a consultant to corporations, he specializes in providing human resources, employee assistance programs, security, corporate, and legal professions with behavioral threat assessments and analyses of aberrant and criminal behavior and incidents that affect workplace safety and security. He has lectured extensively in the United States and abroad concerning violent crime assessment, offender characteristics, and threat assessment. In addition, he has offered expert witness testimony on decisive crime analysis issues in state criminal trials.

Barry L. McManus, vice president of deception detection services of Abraxas Corporation in McLean, Virginia, joined the Central Intelligence Agency in 1977 with a degree in sociology as a staff security officer in the Office of Security after serving 5 years on the Metropolitan Police Department in Washington, D.C. He served on the West Coast and on the Director of Central Intelligence (DCI) protective staff with the former director of the Central Intelligence Agency, William Casey. On the staff, he spent most of his time abroad before finding his home in the Polygraph Division in November 1982, where he served the remainder of his agency career. He served in all Polygraph branches, worked as a line supervisor domestically, and served as office chief of an overseas polygraph office.

He returned to the excitement of the technical side of polygraph after some years in management and became an expert examiner and interrogator. To reach "expert" level in the operational field, an examiner must be thoroughly knowledgeable of the overseas environment and demonstrate superior competence in polygraph techniques. McManus took language training and other necessary training required of an overseas operator. In this role, he was involved primarily in support of the Directorate of Operations. His primary mission was conducting high-gain, high-risk cases. McManus has taken his role seriously. "When dealing with human lives, you have a major impact. You have to respect that responsibility."

McManus has extensive professional experience in the Middle East, Africa, Europe, and Latin America. His agency career has taken him to more than 130 countries. An associate professor in the Administration of Justice, Barry earned a bachelor of arts in sociology at Loyola College and a master of arts in organizational and security management at Webster University and is currently completing work on a doctorate of arts in higher education at George Mason University. He is noted for his contribution in supporting the fight against terrorism.

Peter A. Smerick has a bachelor of arts degree in political science from Pennsylvania State University and a master of education degree from the University of Virginia. In the 1960s, he served as a U.S. Army combat photography officer in Vietnam and a special agent for the Naval Investigative Service.

Smerick became an FBI special agent in 1970 and specialized in surveillance and crime scene photography. In 1976, he was promoted to the FBI Laboratory as a supervisory special agent and a questioned document examiner and examiner of photographic evidence. In 1985, Smerick was assigned to the FBI Academy as an instructor in forensic science and crime scene management techniques.

He became a criminal profiler and violent crime analyst (1988) for the FBI's NCAVC, where he focused on crimes of homicide, rape, child molestation, kidnapping, extortion, and product tampering and specialized in the assessment of anonymous and threatening communications. Smerick testified before both houses of Congress regarding his profile of David Koresh, leader of the Branch Davidians, during that group's 1993 standoff with the FBI in Waco, Texas. He currently serves as president and chief executive officer of the Academy Group Inc., Manassas, Virginia, the largest privately owned forensic behavioral science firm in the world.

Introduction to Behavior, Truth and Deception

Applying Profiling and Analysis to the Interview Process

1

MICHAEL R. NAPIER

Contents

Introduction

Welcome to a book devoted to interviewing and interrogating by law enforcement personnel. The book was written with the goal of making it functional and practical, with a hands-on perspective. You will not find a lot of theories and abstract presentations. You will spend your reading and contemplation time on aspects of interviewing intended to bring about admissions, if not confessions. This book contains several unique features that separate it from other books on like topics.

First, a primary concept for this book is to blend the lessons learned from criminal personality profiling and criminal investigative analysis and apply them to the best interviewing and interrogation practices for optimal results. One of the results of this approach is targeted subject interviewing (TSI) process. TSI provides an interview plan tailored to the vulnerabilities and psychological weaknesses of the suspect as revealed by the subject's criminal behavior and interaction with the victim. This method is illustrated through application to the crime of rape, child molesting, and homicide, but it can be utilized with any crime suspect.

A chapter that covers some cultural considerations when interviewing or interrogating persons with a Hispanic or Muslim heritage was written by Barry McManus, an expert in his field who gained his appreciation of these cultures from his extensive experiences with the Central Intelligence Agency (CIA), as both an agent and a polygraph examiner.

The famed Behavioral Science Unit (BSU) and National Center for the Analysis of Violent Crime (NCAVC) at the Federal Bureau of Investigation (FBI) conducted research into criminal thought processing, modus operandi, and ritual of many known offenders. Unselfishly, these "lessons learned" were freely disseminated to assist law enforcement in handling unsolved violent crimes. Many lessons were gleaned from extensive, detailed, and face-to-face interviewing of a variety of violent criminals. Dr. Richard Ault, R. Stephen Mardigian, and Peter Smerick, my colleagues, have consented to lend their nationally and internationally recognized expertise and to write on topics that enhance the thorough approach to interviewing the sexually violent criminal. I am also fortunate to have contributions by John Hall, a most respected legal talent for the FBI; Dr. Susan Adams, who taught officers at the FBI Academy how to get the most out of interviewing; and her linguistics research associate, Lt. Tracy Harpster. Sue and Tracy have provided great insight into how individuals structure their statements.

This body of work is provided to assist anyone who does criminal interviewing and interrogating in making these processes more productive and successful. The approaches in this book are aimed at not only the experienced investigator but also the officer understudying to be a detective, who will be well served by the techniques discussed.

Applying good interviewing practices is hard work, both mentally and physically. The practice of interviewing and interrogating is one of the most demanding and stressful endeavors an investigator will undertake. It can also be the most rewarding experience he* can have. Even with advances in the forensic sciences, it is still the interview and interrogation processes that solve crimes and place the case in the context a jury can understand. The work product derived from interviewing is the bow on the total investigative package forwarded to the prosecutor. A great deal rests on the shoulders of the officer who is undertaking the interviews of victims, witnesses, and suspects. Victims, parents, loved ones, and society are waiting for solutions to crimes that affect them directly or that occur in their environment.

As a general rule, an officer enters this combat at a disadvantage. Figuratively, he has one arm tied behind his back. The suspect in an interview, which may turn into an interrogation, has the cards stacked in his favor. Absent strong evidence from the crime scene or the laboratory or the interviews of witnesses, the suspect is the only individual who knows the "ground truth." The interviewer's job is to talk someone into feeling good about going to jail. The suspect interrogation "business" is demanding: At the conclusion of the interview or interrogation, there is only one winner.

The investigator is charged with protecting society and at the same time safeguarding the suspect's rights. The officer hefts the weight of his sworn duty while carrying the obligation of protecting all members of society, including those antisocial members who daily attempt to destroy society. He must walk a very fine line, which is sometimes not clearly defined in law or court decisions.

The line separating the rightful duties of an investigator from borderline or improper acts is a moving line as the interview process is dynamic. The line that separates proper conduct from prohibited conduct moves based on the words utilized, on developing case facts, and on the clash of two personalities with differing goals.

Every officer practitioner is guided, seemingly by an invisible hand, in each of his daily endeavors. That guidance comes directly from his internalized values. Those values express themselves in his attitude and his behaviors. It is refreshing to note the men and women who carry the shield are guided by the proper values that lead them to seek the opportunities to "protect and serve." Personal ethics invariably wind their way into the interview room.

---

* The male pronoun is used throughout this book for ease in reading and is not intended to be neglectful of the female gender.

Overview

Chapter 2: Answering Critics of Police Interviewing Techniques

It may be difficult to imagine, but there are some who are pleased when they can take from an investigator, sometimes for the thinnest of reasons, his hard-won confession. After he obtains the confession, they will use it to demean the officer and his investigative techniques. Some social psychologists would take away an officer's ability to interview suspects and would levy heavy penalties against the officer for his genuine and honest efforts to protect society. These experts are highly critical of police work.

Chapter 2 contains material that confronts their criticism and invalidates their challenges to valid and reliable confessions. Additional details are provided regarding the police and the most commonly used interview tactics.

Chapter 3: Psychology in Law Enforcement:
The Criminal Use of Fantasy in Violent Crimes

Basic, deviant, and sexual psychologies are briefly examined to expose the origins of offender motivation along with the thinking process of violent offenders. These data lay the foundation for understanding the sexually violent offender.

Chapter 4: Five Stars for Success and Some Relevant Thoughts

Several opportunities to improve interviewing effectiveness are outlined, including some vital thoughts on interviewer safety. An interviewer's personal traits certainly affect the outcome of the interviewing whether the interviewee is a victim, witness, or suspect. The best and worst qualities are discussed in this chapter. A detailed examination of how to reliably assess a person prior to a face-to-face meeting is presented.

Chapter 5: An Analytical Process for Crimes of Violence

The analytical methodology used by the BSU for cases that had ground to a halt is detailed. This process, called criminal investigative analysis (CIA), was used in preparation for analyzing a case generally or in preparation for drawing a criminal personality profile. The end result of the CIA was a clearer and more thorough understanding of the details and behavior involved in the commission of the crime.

Chapter 6: Indirect Personality Assessment

Prior to undertaking a suspect interview, the officer is obligated to know all he can about the individual. Indirect personality assessment is a technique for getting a jump start on finding out who that person is based on the evaluation of several close associates. That process will provide details useful in planning the contact and knowing which buttons to push.

Chapter 7: Interviewer's Verbal Strategies

Chapter 8: Nonverbal Communication

Two chapters are dedicated to the verbal and nonverbal process of interviewing. Most law enforcement personnel place considerable faith in interpretation of unspoken gestures. In many situations, there is an almost predictable dialogue and style of answering that will follow certain questions. The development of those words and signals can be coaxed along using questions designed to cause that dialogue to occur and be accompanied with anticipated and complimentary nonverbal gesticulations. You will find many details explaining how to get the most from an interview using questioning skills in specific ways.

Chapter 9: Interview and Interrogation Techniques

Many techniques are available to the officer when speaking with victims, witnesses, and suspects. Their power is dependent on understanding when and how to implement them. In suspect interviews, that strength is multiplied when the techniques are combined, restated, and pursued as a reasonable solution to an individual's dilemma of being the focus of a police inquiry. Many of these tactics are outlined and included in real case scenarios for illustration.

The various techniques, tactics, and strategies are explained, and the context in which they are most appropriate is examined. Most are suitable in any given situation but reach their peak of effectiveness in certain situations. The technique of "building up the question" and other delivery methods to heighten the impact of the techniques are explained.

The psychology and the psychological effect of individual tactics are explained to add to the understanding of when each is appropriate to include in the interview. Dividing and redividing the most usable techniques begin the development of an interview plan. One of the most successful but overlooked techniques is "reading minds" of suspects. The secret and power of that skill are unveiled.

An often-overlooked concept for maximizing the interview contact is reducing a suspect's confidence level. Like most interview and interrogation tactics, this process is done not in one bold stroke, but by chipping away at his belief that he can win the confrontation. Specific methods for reducing the suspect's confidence are provided.

Chapter 10: Interview of the Rape Victim and Rapist Typologies

The crime of rape is briefly examined from the viewpoint of both the victim and the offender. The behavior-oriented interview of the victim is an essential component of that knowledge, and the key to doing that interview correctly is detailed. This technique, advanced by Robert R. Hazelwood and Ann Wolbert Burgess, is addressed and illustrated regarding its value in obtaining a full understanding of the offender's motivation, methods, personality, and weaknesses. This foundation is vital to the TSI technique.

Chapter 11: Targeted Subject Interview: Interviewing the Rapist

When an interviewer can gear his approaches to a particular suspect's personal vulnerabilities, he is functioning at peak performance. The material in this chapter takes the officer to that point. Many of the objectives of the preceding chapters are drawn together in this chapter on the TSI process. The primary focus is on the violent crime of rape, but the techniques are easily extrapolated to any other crime, as illustrated in Chapters 15 and 16, on interviewing murderers and child molesters. There, the interviewer will bring forward what he knows about the crime based on several elements he has recognized through the investigative and analytical processes explained in preceding chapters. The goal is to find the weaknesses of the interview subject through his behavior in committing the crime. Using that knowledge, a subject-specific interview plan can be drawn. Any number of interview techniques may then be selected as best suited for attacking the subject's vulnerabilities.

Chapter 12: Recognizing and Investigating False Allegations of Rape

Actual false allegations of rape are believed to be few, but no statistical record keeping exists. Officers are urged to be deliberate when examining cases for indicators of false allegations. A methodology for making that determination is presented in this chapter. TSI application is explained.

Chapter 13: Using Statement Analysis in Rape Investigations

Too often officers become suspicious of various components of a rape victim's statement and anticipate that the case will be "unfounded." This chapter provides guidance regarding how to validate or refute those beliefs. Case examples are included to illustrate the varying degrees of personal needs a pseudovictim has in placing herself as the "victim" of a most brutal and intrusive act of violence.

Statement analysis is a methodology for examining the report of victims and is outlined and illustrated by case examples. The required officer skills for analyzing rape complaints are discussed at length to better assist in validating claims of rape.

Chapter 14: Is the Caller the Killer?
Analyzing 911 Homicide Calls

This chapter on statement analysis is drawn from original research into 911 phone calls. When utilized by the homicide investigator, he will be in a position to more astutely question witnesses and analyze the crime scene on his arrival. The goal is to distinguish valid, distressed callers from those made by a person who is criminally involved.

Chapter 15: Analyzing Homicide Cases
Preparatory to Suspect Interviews

This chapter is designed to provide an overview of homicidal behavior and the characteristics of men or women who murder. The intent is to provide not only a brief background that will lay out a course for conducting the investigation but also insight into the individual and his or her vulnerabilities in the interview and interrogation situations. The TSI technique is explained in relation to homicide interviews.

Chapter 16: Child Molesters and Pedophiles

This chapter provides a brief glimpse at the types of offenders to detail a basic understanding of child molesters and to guide an interview process. Methods of targeting suspects in child-molesting cases for substantive interviews by using suspect weaknesses and vulnerabilities based on their crime behavior are detailed.

Chapter 17: Interpersonal Stalking:
Characteristics of Predators and Prey

Stalking is a crime of terror. It is often intended to strike fear in the mind of the victim in efforts to control nearly every feature of her life. It is an often misguided and sometimes deadly practice of individuals with a mental illness. This insidious crime is examined for offender motivations and practices.

Chapter 18: Cultural Considerations for Interviewing

Policing in America is quickly evolving with the influx of immigrants and the dynamics of "world politics" now being focused on many places in this country. The specialist writing this chapter on the Hispanic and Muslim cultures does not intend to make the reader an expert, but he or she will be made aware of certain culturally derived behaviors that may guide the interview. The thrust of what the proficient investigator must know when interviewing individuals from the Hispanic or Islamic cultures is addressed.

Chapter 19: Legal Perspectives on Interviewing

Never before in the history of criminal investigations has "toeing the line" been more critical. An expert with many years of experience instructing police officers and FBI agents in the ins and outs of the law guides the reader through many legal challenges. This complex set of data will be reduced to understandable proportions. The courts, contrary to popular opinion, have historically been permissive and reluctant to hinder police interviewing efforts due to the critical role they play in guarding against chaos. The information in this chapter will assist the reader in doing the job correctly and by the rules.

Appendix

Several of the tools suggested throughout this book are described in some detail, but there is no substitute for seeing the actual item. Those pieces are reproduced and included in the Appendix to provide a clearer illustration of "how to do it."

Answering Critics of Police Interviewing Techniques*

2

MICHAEL R. NAPIER

Contents

Introduction

There is a body of serious criticisms by non-law-enforcement individuals—social psychologists—that should be regarded as a blessing in disguise. We can "go to school" on these assertions and accusations to become better interviewers. These critics urge serious sanctions against the interview process and the officer, sometimes on the merest of assumptions and technicalities. These social psychologists would like to impose, among other things, the requirement that all interviews and interrogations be recorded from start to finish. This allows them the luxury of judging the officer's efforts at their

---

* A prior version of this chapter was coauthored with Dr. Sue Adams and is published in Napier, M.R., and Adams, S., Criminal Confessions: Overcoming the Challenge, *FBI Law Enforcement Bulletin*, November 2002: 1–6.

leisure and without experiencing the stress and pressure of live contact. They may then apply their judgments, which are made while they are not under the same stresses or time constraints as the officer. They would hold the officer accountable for the merest of errors or a slip of the tongue, sometimes applying an interpretation unintended by the officer.

Take the following example, which occurred in a country with a similar legal foundation to that of the United States. It illustrates how innocent remarks can be exaggerated and leave society unprotected. Is it too farfetched to see, as I do, a similar turn of events in the United States?

Case 2.1

An officer, on the complaint of a young girl, was attempting to interview her father regarding his alleged molestation of the girl. At the outset, the officer explained the purpose for the interview, and the father objected saying, "I don't want to talk about that." The officer responded, "You must, don't you see? We must understand what has happened." The subsequent confession of the father was rejected because the officer erred when he said, "You must." The court interpreted this to mean that the interview was compulsory. Structurally, and with intent to do his duty, that was not the intent of the officer.

This type of development presents a catch-22 for law enforcement. Although officers would become accustomed to being audio recorded or filmed in the learning curve period, the confession rate will drop. That is what happened in England when the "must record" rule was implemented. Case 2.1 illustrates how simple **human errors** can be dissected, twisted, and taken out of context. This is particularly a concern given the trend toward our jurisprudence system becoming noticeably populated by activist judges who sometimes rule according to personal views and not the law. This trend becomes more disconcerting when the antipolice, antiauthority, antiresponsibility acceptance sentiment is factored into the mix. The Massachusetts Supreme Court ruled in the recent past that if a confession is not recorded and only the testimony of the officer regarding the circumstances of how the confession came about is presented, **the jury may take a negative inference about the credibility and truthfulness of the testimony**. An officer's sworn testimony need not be accepted in contrast to that of a defendant. This ruling came close to stating that all officers' testimony is tantamount to perjury.

With the advent of police patrol units being equipped with secure video and sound recorders, will it become the standard of the police community also to equip detective cars with recorders? Will all interviews be conducted at police headquarters? That arena changes some of the legal groundwork that currently governs detention, custody, and interviewing standards.

Following this type of reasoning and judicial atmosphere, recording confessions as an offensive measure may become the best defense for policing. But where is the line drawn? Assume that only the confession portion of the interview or interrogation is recorded, what will happen if a suspect blurts out a confession when the recorder is not running? Will it become necessary to record all interviews, even of victims and witnesses? Who will absorb the added costs for recording equipment and storing and retrieving tapes? What happens when a recording is made in good faith, but somehow the electronic ether devil garbles it or loses its traceability? How will the community be served with all the possible glitches and snafus that can beset the best, most sincere, and most honest efforts of the officer who only wants to protect and serve?

Until those developments are in place, the officers of each community will labor in the belief that they can and will make a difference in a world increasingly filled with evil hearts and minds. All of the complaints of our critics can be negated by the officer's adherence to fundamental and established interview and interrogation techniques.

Proving False Confessions Can Occur

At a college level, students are selected for important research. The testing will conduct an experiment using a standard keyboard. The test controllers explain that the student is to strike the specified key on their command. They are told never to touch a particular key, as it will erase the main computer's entire memory. As the controllers call out the keystrokes and the student complies, all goes well until they speed up their demands for specific keys to be struck. At some point, they will call out a key located next to the forbidden key. The student will strike the correct key, but the computer will react as if the forbidden key was hit, and the computer shuts down. In the ensuing confrontation, some students have admitted to striking the forbidden key, thus establishing that an innocent person can be tricked into a confession.

Now, mentally compare that situation to a police interrogation of a subject suspected in a rape and murder. The "test" simulations do not hold up well. Nonetheless, critics will extrapolate these examples and suggest that the likelihood of false confessions is a widespread threat.

Are there bad apples in policing? Undoubtedly. There are a few rogues who occasionally surface to the embarrassment of all the rest. Without exception, I have found the police population in American law enforcement to be populated with dedicated, talented men and women of integrity. Investigators are of a solemn mind-set when they swear to uphold the Constitution, which involves identifying, charging, and prosecuting criminals by working within an ethical framework.

Let us be honest. Under certain conditions, some people with an inadequate personality can be unintentionally cowered and then provide a false confession, even to brutal and grotesque crimes. Those unintended and unplanned results can be avoided, and the information that follows instructs on the precautions that will not allow a confession to be contested.

Criticisms by Social Psychologists

Social psychologists have been recognized in several courts and have testified against the techniques utilized by most police interviewers in the United States. Their testimony has been accepted in criminal and civil cases. Examination of some of their critiques has led me to the conclusion that there is some merit in what they say.

Critics use the term *coercive* to describe police interviewing tactics, claiming that certain tactics result in a false confession. The critics' position is hampered by their difficulty in identifying with certainty the number of confessions obtained through coercion (Cassell, 1997). It is imperative to obtain an accurate representation of the false confessions obtained under police questioning; ongoing research is attempting to address this need (Jayne and Buckley, 1998). Even if each alleged false confession were indeed false, the occurrence of alleged false confessions, when viewed in the framework of the millions of suspect interviews conducted annually, is statistically miniscule.

The criticism of law enforcement interview tactics can be distilled into five primary complaints. Each criticism can be addressed through the application of a corresponding interview principle. The application of these corresponding principles will enhance the suspect interview processes, lead to clearly valid statements, and strengthen confessions that are not otherwise suspect. When regularly used, these principles will illustrate the good faith efforts of police when identifying suspects and obtaining constitutionally admissible confessions.

Criticism 1: Noting and Interpreting a Suspect's Behavior

One censure of police procedures stems from the way police select their primary suspects. The critics assert that the police rely too heavily on their observations of suspect behavior in the interview room. As the interview progresses, the police allegedly select a suspect for more intense scrutiny through their interpretation of his behaviors. Critics allege that officers are not qualified to make those judgments, and that the techniques they use are neither scientifically valid nor reliable. By placing credibility on their "hunches" and "on-the-spot reading" of a suspect's verbal and nonverbal responses to questioning, they may end up improperly focusing on the wrong person. As part of their claim that officers are not qualified to make correct decisions, they cite their failure to distinguish between responses made under the stress of police scrutiny and deceptive responses (Ofshe and Leo, 1997a). The critics continue by claiming that behaviors such as the inability and failure to look the officer in the eye are heavily relied on and, in the officer's mind, take on the weight of evidence. They note that the precautions in place are inadequate to protect the innocent from unreasonable investigative focus (Leo and Ofshe, 1997).

Principle 1: Let the Facts Speak for Themselves

Often, particularly in the early stages of an investigation, there may not be any evidence clearly pointing the way to a logical suspect. The investigators are then left with their investigative experience and history of dealing with known deceivers and the criminal element in general. They have "gone to school" by reading deceptive behaviors through real-world experiences, not the theories of social psychologists. The police investigator knows that his gut instincts are for lead purposes only and must be compared with the evidence as it accumulates as the investigation plays out. In that context, he knows that facts govern instincts. If the investigative hunch or supposition does not square with known facts, always follow the facts.

In his book *The Gift of Fear*, Gavin de Becker (1997) offered several interesting observations about our intuition and hunches and criticized us for not being more in tune with our inner guidance system, which has proven to be highly reliable. This should be required reading for the population most likely to be victimized.

Criticism 2: Personal Vulnerabilities

Social psychologists correctly point out that certain individuals possess traits that cause them to be overly susceptible to police interrogation techniques. Their susceptibly may arise from many sources, but the end result is that it may lead them to confess falsely (Ofshe and Leo, 1997b). At one time, the American Psychological Association described many of these traits as involved with inadequate personality disorder, and the term aptly described the behaviors the police encounter. The "inadequate personality" just was not up to the task of maneuvering through life with ease. Others who may be vulnerable to the pressures inherent in being interviewed in a police setting are the youthful, unsocialized, and immature person; those with low or borderline IQ or mental handicaps; a person in bereavement due to personal loss; individuals with language barriers; a person in the midst of serious drug or alcohol withdrawal; someone who is excessively fatigued; and the illiterate, socially isolated, or inexperienced with the criminal justice system (Gudjonsson, 1992).

Individuals possessing traits like these are believed to lack sufficient strength of "personality," making them more readily subject to poor decision making and mental dullness and to following the suggestions of others.

Principle 2: Interview before You Interrogate

To get the most from an interview requires advance planning. Unless exigent circumstances are present, competent investigators have learned to invest time in the initial information-gathering process (Vessel, 1998). By learning details about all aspects of a suspect's life and lifestyle, subsequent problems can be avoided. If the suspect is reported to have low intelligence, not only check school records but also determine his social functioning ability. Does he have below-normal intelligence but a reputation for being street smart? To what language level does he respond? What are his language difficulties or drug use patterns? How does he function in the real world? As noted by one master of interrogation, although the suspect may have below normal intelligence, he may also possess "a PhD in social intelligence" or what police officers call "street smarts" (Holmes, 1995).

Vulnerable qualities do not give a free pass to anyone or eliminate an interview with that individual. Vulnerabilities such as reduced mental capabilities, the inability to withstand pressure, bereavement, and the like may increase suggestibility and require special care in use of questioning techniques. Place his reported vulnerability in context and then adjust individual pieces of the interview plan to accommodate his frailties. Fully document any adaptations. Design the interview plan to meet specific word use levels. In the plan, design specific word usage to determine if the suspect understands questions at your normal questioning level and make a note of that. List the words used and how he responded to illustrate his comprehension.

Case 2.2

A prepubescent female suddenly disappeared from a public street while on an errand to a store. A 29-year-old man became a suspect, and through solid police work he also became a suspect in a similar incident involving a prepubescent female 10 years prior. His conviction for one of the murders was based on a confession. He was certified at an early age by Texas as being intelligence handicapped. However, carefully gathered background information indicated that he was capable of dealing with life and living alone. Based on this knowledge, no language adjustments were felt to be necessary. Later testimony clearly indicated that he understood each question and responded appropriately. Challenges to his multiple confessions were denied.

The initial, low-key interview phase can be designed to obtain "norming" information about how the suspect normally responds both verbally and nonverbally. It is also an opportunity to gather information *from the suspect* about his education, language ability, and difficulties in life.

Criticism 3: Statement Contamination

Another current criticism that may be at least partially valid is that police inadvertently contaminate confessions through reliance on questions that contain crime scene data and investigative results (Gudjonsson, 1992). This flaw may be amplified when the investigator uses crime scene or investigative photos in the questioning process. There is likelihood that these procedures might in fact "educate" the suspect (Zulawski and Wicklander, 1998) by providing knowledge that the suspect simply parrots back, especially if he is attempting to escape intense interrogation pressure. The result is that the suspect appears to offer a valid confession.

Case 2.3

A 13-year-old female was raped, murdered, and decapitated. A 16-year-old male was questioned as an alibi witness for the man who was subsequently convicted of the crime and sentenced to life in prison. During the questioning of the alibi witness, the police became suspicious of his personal involvement in the crime. Eventually, he provided a description of the crime and pointed out crime scene details indicative of his direct involvement in the murder and decapitation. The investigators were persistent, and the youth provided an explanation of how he knew incriminating details. He reported that while being questioned an investigator sorted through crime scene pictures attempting to locate a specific picture. The suspect stated: "When he switched ... the pictures real quick, I saw what was happening before them pictures [the pictures selected for the investigator's specific question] ... he says, Where you think the body was? But when he was switching them, I saw where the body was. ... Then he says, where is the head part. ... Anybody's going to know where a person's place is when they got the big, yellow thingy around the water thing, the toilet. They had that caution thing [crime scene tape] all around there." This youth was identified as possessing an IQ of about 70.*

---

* Parenthetical emphasis and clarifying comments added. In keeping with this investigative team's reputation for professionalism and integrity, the charges against the alibi witness were subsequently dropped in the interest of justice.

The investigator may be asked later to recite the questions he asked and to demonstrate how the suspect answered. Good note taking will serve the officer well should that happen.

Principle 3: Preserve the Evidence

To avoid contaminating a suspect's admissions and to avoid unnecessarily revealing investigative knowledge, an investigator should initiate the criminal involvement phase of questioning by using only open-ended questions. Open-ended questions avoid the pitfalls of leading or informing a suspect. They begin with phrases such as "Describe for me …," "Tell me about …," and "Explain how …." These questions force the suspect to commit to a version of events instead of simply agreeing with the investigator. Open-ended questions make it difficult for a suspect to lie successfully because the suspect may provide a wealth of information in this free narrative form (Gudjonsson, 1992). The first generation of follow-up questions should also be open ended.

If, however, a suspect decides to lie, the open-ended question provides him a forum. This aspect of the open-ended question technique is a bonus for the investigator, becausee every lie told forecloses avenues by which the suspect may later try to defend himself (Zulawski, 2002).

To be effective, the answers to the open-ended questions must be received without judgment, reaction, or interruption by the investigator. Not interrupting takes willpower. By allowing the suspect to tell his story without interruption, the investigator fulfills the basic purpose of an interview: to obtain information. The investigator gains the bonus of locking the suspect into a position (Holmes, 1995). The verbal position chosen by the suspect may contain information that later becomes evidence of guilt or provides a connection to the crime, the crime scene, or the victim.

The greatest asset derived from initiating the interview with open-ended questions is that the questioning process has not been contaminated. The investigator has not educated the suspect to the details of the crime or subsequent investigation and thereby has preserved the evidence. After listening to the narrative responses to the open-ended question, the skilled investigator will probe with additional open-ended questions, saving direct, closed questions for the end.

Criticism 4: Creating a False Reality

The police are alleged to use techniques that create a false reality for the suspect by limiting his ability to reason and to consider alternative options (Ofshe and Leo, 1997a). The criticisms are as follows: The police intentionally present only one side of the evidence or options available to the suspect, namely, the options that benefit only the police. Once the suspect accepts a narrowed option, he is coerced by inferred benefits, such as avoidance of a premeditated murder charge in favor of describing the crime as an accident. The obvious benefit of accepting this proffered lesser alternative leads the suspect to be coerced into a false confession out of fear of police and prosecutorial prowess.

Principle 4: Adjust Moral Responsibility

Critics may lose sight of the fact that the role of the interviewer is to question suspects, not to provide legal counsel (Caplan, 1985). It is also not the investigator's purpose to provide options so the guilty suspect may conceal his criminal involvement.

Experienced investigators are familiar with the following aspects of confessions:

1. Confessions are not readily given.
2. Full confessions originate with small admissions.
3. Guilty suspects seldom tell everything.
4. Most offenders are not proud of their violence and recognize that it was wrong.
5. Guilty suspects omit details that cast them in a harsh, critical light.
6. Offenders usually confess to obtain a position they believe to be advantageous to them (Holmes, 1995).

Astute interviewers utilize rationalization, projection, and minimization to remove barriers to obtaining confessions. These are the same techniques that the suspect uses to justify and place the sometime-abhorrent behaviors in terms that salve the suspect's conscience (Napier and Adams, 1998). Thus these psychological techniques serve two purposes: They allow the investigator to safeguard society by identifying guilty suspects, and they provide face-saving opportunities to make it easier for the suspect to confess.

These techniques initially downplay the suspect's culpability by omitting provocative behavior, blaming others, or minimizing actual conduct. It may be necessary to suggest that the suspect's criminality was an accident (Jayne and Buckley, 1998) or the result of an unexpected turn of events, events that were perhaps provoked by the victim. The investigator's goal is to obtain an admission or to place the suspect near the scene or with the victim. The practiced interviewer uses the initial admission as a wedge to open the door to additional incriminating statements by refining his techniques and by using all the case facts to point out the flaws and insufficiency in the original admission. The goal is to obtain a fuller, more accurate description of the suspect's criminal behavior. Deputy Chief Perry Gilmore, of the Amarillo, Texas Police Department, is one of the most astute instructors on police interviewing that I know. He tells the analogy of getting a confession as being a hurdle, and the officer's job is to get over the small hurdle first. After clearing the first hurdle, the officer reruns the race, with a raised hurdle representing the obtaining of all the details.

It is an unrealistic solution to suggest that an investigator should be so restrained that he stops an admission of guilt in a homicide case to debate whether a suspect is a premeditated or spontaneous murderer. The final disclosure of case facts and laboratory results can provide the details to reveal the most likely version of events.

Criticism 5: Promising Coercive End-of-Line Benefits

Perhaps the most serious assertion is that investigators move into clearly coercive territory when giving clear and substantial identification of end-of-line benefits to confession. The coercive aspect is derived from the investigators' statement that to remain silent will lead to greater penalties, but that confessing to a minimized scenario will be rewarded (Ofshe and Leo, 1997b). The investigator may openly suggest that the suspect will be punished with the most serious charge available if he does not consent to the generously offered lesser interpretation of his actions (Ofshe and Leo, 1997a). It is contended that interviewers will blatantly and precisely state the suspects' expected penalty in unmistakable terms, such as the death penalty versus life imprisonment or life versus 20 years. In a like vein, it is offered that investigators may threaten harm via investigation or prosecution of a third party, such as a wife, brother, or child, if the lessened scenario is rejected. These tactics are accurately suggested as so coercive that they make an innocent person confess.

Principle 5: Use Psychology versus Coercion

The interview and interrogation system whose components are generally recognized as the most widely used and adapted in the United States follows the limitations imposed by the ethical standards as well as the dictates of the courts (Inbau, Reid, and Buckley, 1986). The courts in the United States have generously allowed investigators the breadth of creativity in interviewing suspects. Successful interviewing does not hinge on coercive techniques, as talented investigators have a ready reservoir of productive, acceptable, and psychologically effective techniques. Blatant statements by investigators depicting the worst-case scenario facing a suspect who does not accept a lesser responsibility are coercive and unnecessary. In general, these statements follow the pattern of "Look, first-degree murder carries a life sentence, but if this was an accident, manslaughter only means 10 to 20 years." Or "If you don't cooperate, I am personally going to prove your brother was up to his eyeballs in this murder. He will go down hard." Statements of this type are clearly coercive and less effective than the use of the psychological techniques of rationalization, projection, and minimization.

There is, however, a distinction between blatant statements and subtle references offered for interpretation as the suspect chooses. Suspects engage in a self-imposed personal decision-making process that incorporates their life experiences, familiarity with the criminal justice system, and their time-tested psychological processes of rationalization, projection, and minimization. Suspects may explain reasons for the crime (rationalization), blame others (projection), or lessen their culpability and express remorse, even if unfelt (minimization). Guilty suspects thereby attempt to describe their criminal acts as understandable in a manner that places them in a better position to obtain the desired lenient treatment. They eagerly listen for any opportunity to look good. The investigator is not responsible if the suspect chooses to offer an explanation of guilt that places him in what he perceives as a favorable position. The investigator achieves part of his goal for the suspect must admit culpability to achieve this desired and perceived position. It is then the responsibility of the investigator to accept the admission, return to the basics of the investigation, and obtain a statement that comports to the reality of the crime.

The most secure confession is anchored by corroboration. Some suspects may not readily provide information to support their involvement in a crime for fear of exposing the true nature of their evil acts. However, corroboration by a suspect by providing "holdout" information, details that are known to only a select few, solidifies a confession. Evidence linking details such as the location of the body, the weapon, or the fruits of the crime provides a superior foundation for protecting a confession from being retracted or otherwise successfully questioned in court.

Principle 6: Allow Suspects to Maintain Dignity

A final principle is offered not in response to a criticism, but as an underpinning to the entire interview process. All individuals are naturally entitled to personal dignity and self-worth. Convicted felons have explained that they would be more likely to confess to an investigator who treated them with respect and recognized their value as a person (Zulawski and Wicklander, 1998). Allowing suspects to maintain dignity, even in adverse circumstances, is not only professional but also increases the likelihood of obtaining a confession.

Ethics and Interviewing

Without intending to sound pious, I believe every officer is oriented to and infused with the belief that when he interviews suspects he must give his best legal effort for the victims, survivors, and society. What ethics apply to law enforcement interviewing? The answer is that, at a minimum, officers must know and respect the law and be dedicated to finding the guilty as well as the innocent.

Although organizations are built from the ground floor up, their values flow in both directions. The concept of professionalism for the investigator begins with basic duties and carries through to a legal responsibility—providing sworn testimony in open court. How an investigator approaches interviewing and interrogation may be viewed as symbolizing the ultimate reflection of the professional values of a department. "Casual values" are translated into a "casual attitude," which is translated into matching behavior. Vigilance to the highest policing values must be reflected in all aspects of policing but nowhere are they more important than in the interview room and in presenting the investigative product of the interview.

Bibliography

Caplan, G. M. Questioning Miranda. *Vanderbilt Law Review* 38(6) (November 1985): 1417–1476.

Cassell, P. G. Balanced Approaches to the False Confession Problem: A Brief Comment on Ofshe, Leo, and Alschuler. *Denver University Law Review* 74 (1997): 1123–1143.

de Becker, G. *The Gift of Fear.* Boston: Little, Brown, 1997.

Gudjonsson, G. *The Psychology of Interrogation, Confessions and Testimony.* Chichester, UK: Wiley, 1992.

Holmes, W. D. Interrogation. *Polygraph*, 24(4): 237–258 (1995).

Holmes, W. D. *Criminal Interrogation.* Springfield, IL: Thomas, 2002.

Inbau, F. E., J. E. Reid, and J. P. Buckley. *Criminal Interrogation and Confessions,* 3rd ed., Baltimore, MD: Williams & Wilkins, 1986.

Jayne, B. C., and J. P. Buckley. Reid and Associates. Winter 1998. http://www.reid.com/critics-research.html.

Leo, R. A., and R. J. Ofshe. The consequences of False Confession; Deprivations of Liberty and Miscarriages of Justice in the Age of Psychological Interrogation. *Annual Meeting of the Law and Society Association Meeting at St. Louis, Missouri, May 30, 1997.* Law & Society Associaton, 1–71, 1997.

Napier, M. R., and S. H. Adams. Magic Words to Obtain Confessions. *FBI Law Enforcement Bulletin* 67(10) (October 1998): 1–6.

Napier, M. R., and Susan Adams. Criminal Confessions: Overcoming the Challenge. *FBI Law Enforcement Bulletin* (November 2002): 9–15.

Ofshe, R. J., and R. A. Leo. The Decision to Confess Falsely: Rational Choice and Irrational Action. *Denver University Law Review* 74 (979) (1997a): 1051–1122.

Ofshe, R. J., and R. A. Leo. Social Psychology of Police Interrogation: Theory and Classification of True and False Confessions. *Studies in Law Politics and Society* 16 (1997b): 189–251.

Vessel, D. Conducting Successful Interrogations. Ott, J., Ed. *FBI Law Enforcement Journal* 67(10) (October 1998): 11–15.

Zulawski, D. E., and D. E. Wicklander. *Practical Aspects of Interview and Interrogation.* 2nd ed. Boca Raton: CRC Press, 2002.

Zulawski, D. E., and D. E Wicklander. Special Report: Interrogation: Understanding the Process. *Law and Order* (July 1998): 83–90.

Psychology in Law Enforcement
The Criminal Use of Fantasy in Violent Crimes

3

MICHAEL R. NAPIER

Contents

Introduction

Let's keep this simple. It is well established that people behave according to the way they think, i.e., their acts follow previously entertained ideas. We behave along the lines of what we think. The thought always precedes the act. This concept has guided the Behavioral Science Unit (BSU) and the National Center for the Analysis of Violent Crime (NCAVC) at the Federal Bureau of Investigation (FBI) in their analysis and profiling efforts. Their research has staunchly validated this concept.

Psychology may be viewed as a person's mind controlling his behavior. By being forewarned via a "read" of the offender's behavior in the crime, the officer can appreciate how an offender's behavior expresses who he is, why he is offending at this place and time, and how he selected his victim for the criminal acts. This knowledge serves as a system to guide how a particular crime is investigated and how the suspect should be handled in an interview and interrogation setting.

A word with which we are all familiar is *personality*. It reflects our value judgment of a person based solely on his exterior appearance and behaviors. Offenders are often skilled at concealing aspects of who they truly are and what their value systems are. However, in the commission of a crime for which he does not anticipate being caught, the offender releases his hidden nature via his criminal behavior and in his interaction with the victim.

The BSU and NCAVC have demonstrated that an offender's personality, including the hidden component, is imprinted on a crime scene. For the rape victim, it is indelibly imprinted on her conscious and unconscious memory. The proper processing of a crime scene may capture most of the behaviors employed during the offense and provide a basis for taking a read on the personality of the lawbreaker. To be clear, behavior is left at a crime scene and can be read for the traits of the criminal, which in turn will be used by the investigator for guidance in each aspect of his investigation.

Self-Esteem Influences Criminal Acts

How a person views himself and all his personal qualities lays the foundation for his self-esteem, the hard core of personality. The extent to which he sees himself as competent, valid, valued, and acceptable to society will set the stage for his ability, or lack of ability, to communicate meaningfully, to interact in socially acceptable ways, and to relate to others. Self-concept determines how a criminal will behave.

Consider that a rapist only has three methods for gaining control of a victim. One is smooth talking and using a con approach to trick the victim. To use the con, he must have self-confidence. On the other hand, consider the rapist who uses the surprise method of gaining control of a victim, which involves laying in wait for a victim or entering her residence under cover of darkness. His confidence in his ability to interact face to face with the victim most likely at its very lowest point; therefore he rejects other methods and reverts to behaviors with which he is comfortable, all in keeping with his self-esteem. The third option of the rapist is to immediately administer disabling force sufficient to stun the victim, possibly knocking her unconscious, so that she does not have any ability to cope with the assault. This method is called a blitz attack.

An offender's level of self-esteem governs the timing of his assault, his verbal and physical strategies, and the levels of his sexual violence. In many instances, confirming data can also be drawn from an interviewee through questioning by using carefully chosen questions and by carefully listening to his responses. Any interview should include 30 to 45 minutes of preliminary questioning and conversation preceding the guilt phase of questioning.

Mental Illness and Psychoses

The concepts of sanity and mental illness are largely misunderstood by most people due to a lack of any real life contact with mental illness. However, there are a significant number of people in the general population who are mentally impaired. Those who are out of touch with reality may be diagnosed as experiencing hallucinations or delusions. Someone with hallucinations has one or more sensory perceptors impaired, and as a result "senses the presence" of things that others in his environment do not share.* Delusions are thoughts and beliefs that are clearly wrong but are believed to be correct by mentally impaired individuals. Hallucinations and delusions present themselves as a psychosis or a loss of contact with the real world. Psychotic individuals are those who have a major mental illness, such as some form of schizophrenia or bipolar impairment. These individuals generally do not present the major crime problem faced today.

Psychopathic Personality

The criminal population is comprised of many types of people with varying degrees of mental health. Hard-core criminals consistently have some type of minor mental distortions called *personality disorders*. Those with a "criminal personality," often called psychopaths or sociopaths, populate the U.S. criminal class. Evidence suggests that up to 80% of all confined males have antisocial personality disorder (First and Halon, 2008). Others have some or many of the same traits but with insufficient strength to be diagnosed as having a psychopathic or sociopathic personality disorder. There are many differences in those terms that are recognizable to the trained psychologist, but for law enforcement purposes the two are generally regarded as the same population.

The term *psychopathic* (not to be mistaken for psychotic) involves traits and characteristics believed to be present from birth (i.e., they are inborn qualities). The person considered a sociopath is believed to have the same

---

* Hallucinations can affect any of the five senses, but hearing is the most often reported type of distortion. These individuals hear things, usually someone speaking to them and imparting information that affects their behavior, when in actuality no such contact is made. Thus they are out of touch with reality.

indistinguishable traits as a result of environmental factors (i.e., his family upbringing and socioeconomic realities in his formative years, etc.).

In *Without Conscience, the Disturbing World of the Psychopaths Among Us*, Robert Hare, (1999), a worldwide authority on psychopaths, presents this disorder in easily understood layman's terms. Utilizing Dr. Hare's guidelines and other sources, the following discussion involves traits and characteristics commonly associated with the psychopath.

Psychopaths are often hard to recognize until you look at their criminal acts. They are skilled at blending into their environment. Hare (1999, p. 103) quoting a *Wall Street Journal* article, took note that bankers stated that a psychopathic swindler "should be compelled to wear a bell around his neck," to serve notice of his presence and the potential danger he presented.

A true psychopath or individual with a criminal personality is devoid of the ability to empathize with the plight of the victim or the victim's terror or suffering. He recognizes their expressions of pain and degradation, but they are abstract to him. His emotional sensors are disconnected. He is sharp enough to know when and which emotional expressions are in order and can mimic them when it is to his advantage. This ability is captured when Hare (1999, p. 54) takes note of a comment made by the wife of a murderer when she said he "led a kind of paint-by-numbers emotional life…". Hare also cites psychologists J.H. Johns and H.C. Quay, who stated that psychopaths "know the words but not the music."

They are con men, with the capacity to be glib about almost any subject. According to one of Hare's (1999, p. 40) subjects: "I lie like I breathe, one as much as the other." In interviews, every word they utter should be questioned, dissected, and subjected to follow-up questioning.

For all his failures, the psychopath has an exaggerated view of himself, seeing only success or setbacks caused by the irresponsible acts by others. Loss and failure are never his fault. He projects blame onto everyone and anyone. He thinks only of himself and has no loyalty to his criminal confederates. There is only number 1 to consider as he views the rest of the world as "givers," present only to gratify him. He lives by his own rules.

Case 3.1: Burning Alive

A coed in her early twenties was rescued from her dormitory bed by a fireman responding to an alarm. The fire was limited to her room, in particular to her bed and the area immediately adjacent to it. She was found lying on the bed, badly burned from the area of her breasts to just below her pubic area. An attempt had been made to disable the smoke detector and to jam the sprinkler system with clothing. It was determined that she had been alive when she was set afire but had also been beaten, suffocated, and raped both anally and vaginally. Semen was recovered. In addition, she had three small and insignificant puncture wounds on her neck that produced a minimal amount of bleeding. She died a day later due to the severity of the burns.

The evening of her assault, she was intoxicated and was ejected from a fraternity party. She was driven to her dormitory by a designated driver and his friend. The friend remained behind to ensure that she got into her dorm and was okay. Obviously, he became a prime suspect. He initially agreed to a police interview, but did not show up. Subsequently he was interviewed and denied to the police that he had any connection to the young woman. His version of the event went through many alterations, ranging from having consensual sex with her and leaving her safe and sound in her dorm room to a statement implicating his friend, who became the second suspect.

Eventually, the police would determine that the first suspect had lied about his whereabouts at specific times and had arranged for a friend to lie to support his alibi. Ultimately, however, he confessed to following the orders of the second suspect in the commission of the crime. He alleged that the second suspect had beaten and suffocated the young woman, stopped the assault long enough to put on a condom, and then raped her vaginally and anally. Suspect 2 ordered Suspect 1 to repeat the rapes but without a condom. Suspect 2 reportedly threatened Suspect 1 and his family if he did not comply, although he could not provide the threatening language.

For Suspect 1, the police interviewers brought in "bait ploys" of having found his fingerprints in the dorm room and of having a videotape from the dorm showing him entering her room. These techniques swayed his stories and led him to confess and implicate Suspect 2. Because of the manner in which his final version of events had evolved and likely his generally elusive nature, he was asked to take a polygraph, to which he agreed.

When he came in for the polygraph, he immediately wanted to leave. He was cajoled to take the test and countered by offering to take the police to the murder weapon if they would allow him to visit his grandmother. He also offered to show the police where Suspect 2 had concealed items stolen from the victim's dorm room. Suspect 1 was escorted to his grandmother's as that was where the items were hidden. Some quantity of costume jewelry was recovered, but no murder weapon was found. Suspect 1 immediately admitted that he, not Suspect 2, had stolen the jewelry. The police then began the investigation of Suspect 2, forgetting about the polygraph exam for Suspect 1.

Suspect 2 adamantly denied any involvement, offered an alibi and proof of the alibi, and voluntarily provided blood for a DNA test. He also acted in many ways expected of an innocent party. He vouched for the designated driver as someone who would not commit this type of crime; he flatly denied that his fingerprints could be in her room as he had never been there, and refuted the assertion that he had been captured on videotape entering the victims' room. He offered to view the video to show that it was not him on the film and convincingly challenged the officer's assertion that many people had identified him on the tape. He did not attend that school and was not known by name by the number of students who were reported to have identified him. Nonetheless, he was arrested, but he was quickly acquitted by the jury.

The officers made several errors in conducting their investigation, but the primary error was that they did not recognize Suspect 1 as a psychopath or sociopath. The first remarkable clue that was not recognized or was grossly discounted was that the guilty party was willing to focus a fire on the sexual parts of a living victim's body and attempt to disable the smoke detector and sprinkler system. The impact of those behaviors was not only the severe injuries to the victim but also willingness to burn down an entire dormitory occupied by young women for the sole purpose of escaping detection. He personified a psychopath or sociopath, whose key characteristics include the ability to lie convincingly and often, to have no remorse, to do anything to protect himself, and so on. In addition, the police fell for his line about taking them to the murder weapon. What murder weapon? The victim had suffered blunt force trauma to her face from being hit with fists, had been suffocated with a pillow that remained in her room, and had died from the burns. There was no murder weapon. There also was no polygraph. Score one for the psychopath.

Similar to the focus of an infant who is concerned only with his bodily needs, Hare (1999, p. 58) states the psychopath or sociopath thinks along the line: "I did it because I felt like it." He can be highly impulsive, acting without forethought or a complete plan, or conversely, he can have very detailed plans. Which scenario is being followed will relate to his criminal experience, intelligence, and imagination.

The psychopath is also characterized by his total lack of guilt or remorse for his capacity for brutality and devastation of another human. This trait may show up in early questioning about areas that would generate an empathic or emotional response in others. His response may be noted as remote, flat, or given in a monotone. Case 3.1 provides a good example of psychopathy or sociopathy confounding a police investigation.

Dr. Stanton Samenow has vast experience with the criminal population based on his many years at St. Elizabeth's Hospital in Washington, D.C. He published his observations in *Inside the Criminal Mind* (1984). He was clear that incarcerated criminals are first and foremost rational, not mentally ill, and they make the choice to be a criminal.

Modus Operandi, Rituals, Fantasy, and Paraphilias

To more fully appreciate a discussion of these topics, Figure 3.1 depicts the linkage of modus operandi (MO), fantasy, ritual, and paraphilias.

Modus Operandi

The term *modus operandi* is likely as old as is the art and science of investigating. In its basic form, MO has three purposes. All offenders have an MO because those behaviors assist them in successfully completing the commission of their crimes while protecting their identity and assisting in their escape. An MO is used because it incorporates techniques that work. The MO is learned behavior that may be expanded and altered with added criminal experience, thought, and contact with other criminals. It is a thought-driven process containing only the basic behaviors for success in their chosen criminal activities.

Rituals

The term *ritual* is used in the sense of repetitive behaviors and has no relevance to satanic worship or practices. When the crime behaviors within an MO are no longer satisfying to a criminal, some will go in search of new behaviors that they believe will be fulfilling and satisfying. By definition, the new behaviors go beyond those necessary to commit the sex crime. These added dimensions are expanded within the framework of fantasies and are shaped by incorporating the three core behaviors. In the fantasy-based search for stimulating and arousing new behaviors, the offender will consider and rehearse verbal, physical, and sexual strategies. For analyzing the behavior of a sex offender, the examination of physical acts is focused on those physical behaviors that will knowingly hurt the victim. The new, enriching behaviors become repeated practices known as rituals. The rituals are incorporated into their criminal sexuality. Because he has tailor-made the rituals for himself, they become relatively static and unchanging.

Paraphilias

The rituals may become sexual practices that are condemned by the larger society and therefore are considered deviant sex acts or *paraphilias*. There is

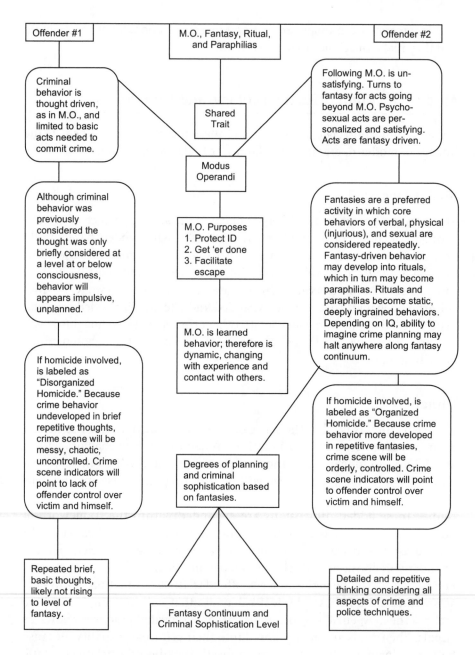

Figure 3.1 Analysis of offender psychology.

a long list of paraphilias, including exhibitionism (flashing), pedophilia (preferred sex partner is a child), sexual sadism (sexual arousal is derived from victim's responses to torture), voyeurism (peeping), transvestitism (males dressing in female clothes to enhance sexual arousal), and others.

Paraphilias are defined as follows:

Recurrent, intense, sexually arousing fantasies, sexual urges, or behaviors generally involving non-human objects to cover the paraphilias of fetishism and transvestic fetishism); or the suffering or humiliation of oneself or one's partner (to cover the paraphilias sexual sadism and sexual masochism), or children or other nonconsenting persons (to cover the paraphilias pedophilia, frotteurism, exhibitionism, and voyeurism). (First and Halon, 2008)

Paraphilias are often necessary for an individual to be aroused and to function sexually. Paraphilias may be of such strength that impulse control is difficult, which may lead to "needy" mistakes. Males are more commonly affected by paraphilias by a ratio of 20 to 1 (WebMd Medical Reference, 2003). This is likely one of the stronger reasons for the near absence of documented female pedophiles.

Paraphilias are so deeply ingrained into the sexual practices that some features of the afflicted individual's sexual acts are nearly predictable as they are behaviors generally associated with each paraphilia. The repeating of the ritual aspects of paraphilias has been successfully utilized in securing search warrants, convincing the court of the high likelihood that contraband would be present, and in defining the areas where such materials and evidence would be kept. Understanding paraphilias is a powerful investigative tool, as is knowing when to expect their absence.

The Criminal Use of Fantasy in Violent Crimes

"Every second of the night I live another life." These words from the song "These Dreams" by Heart were not intended to be about fantasies, yet they reflect several significant facets of criminal fantasies. Some criminals spend their nights fantasizing about their criminal acts or going trolling in the hope of finding the opportunity to give life to their fantasies. Some criminals live an alternate life through their fantasies and their criminal behavior, which breathe life into their mental machinations. Fantasies are a way of life for many sexual criminals.

In a private conversation with Roy Hazelwood, a foremost authority on sexual violence, we agreed that the role of fantasy is one of the critical factors in appreciating how an offender's behavior is shaped. We also agreed that fantasy is not properly respected for its profound effect on crime scenes, victim selection, and overall shaping of criminal conduct.

The significance of fantasy was first introduced to me in classes taught at the FBI Academy by the BSU, in case studies examined as part of the analytical learning process, and in various conversations with FBI personnel. Its true impact was felt, however, by looking at real-life acts of violence, sometimes severe violence. Understanding fantasies is essential for comprehending how brutal someone can be to another human being.

Fantasies separate the human mammal from other mammals by allowing us to be sexually aroused through an internal stimulus that operates separately from instinct. Such arousal patterns are learned behaviors. Observation of crime scenes where a fantasy has played out or deduction from significant behavior left imprinted on a scene may allow an analyst to separate one criminal offender from another as the fantasy-driven behavior becomes individualistic. Fantasies are normal behavior. There is nothing deviant in having fantasies; however, some fantasies are deviant.

Imagine (or draw) a line on a sheet of paper from left to right, and the line becomes a continuum. Criminal fantasies occur along a continuum. The continuum begins on one end with the person having repeated and *underdeveloped thoughts*. Depending on how adept one is at fantasizing, the experience may be just a single thought that is situationally repeated over and over (i.e., the husband in an argument with his wife has a thought flash through his mind such as "next time she does this, I am going to get the butcher knife and … "). When a similar situation arises, the same, or a similar, thought is briefly repeated. He does not process, examine, or expand on that basic thought. Should he act on those repeated thoughts, the crime will appear unplanned, and he likely will not be prepared for the results. The crime will appear spontaneous and messy, and abundant evidence will most probably be left for the crime scene techs.

The other end of the spectrum is defined as the person having a repeated and *detailed thought pattern*. The more sophisticated criminal will repeat his fantasies until he has either reached a point at which the fantasies are satisfying and fulfilling and/or he has worked his way through all the possible mistakes he could make and all the police responses he can imagine. Some fantasies may be replayed several hundred times.

How far along the continuum an individual moves is dependent on his ability to imagine. Imagination is noted as a function of intelligence. The more intelligent the offender is, the further he will likely move to the point of denying police evidence. The closer to the "repeated, detailed thinking" end of the continuum, the more likely he will be attuned to police investigative procedures and will attempt to deny the police any scraps with which to work. Therefore, fantasies, besides shaping the offender's behaviors, affect his criminal sophistication. Because not every sex criminal is equally bright, the criminal planning and sophistication of offenders in general will fall into position at various places along the fantasy and criminal sophistication continuum.

Experiencing Fantasies

The person who devotes a lot of time to criminal fantasies will likely move from having brief and repeated thoughts to a point at which the thoughts are experienced with images being formed within the fantasy. They will see in action what they have only thought in abstract and transient words. From that foundation, they may become aware of the feelings, emotions, and arousal associated with the behaviors imagined in the fantasy. Fantasies can develop from the images and feelings to a point at which an internal dialogue is included much as would be found in a play.

Case 3.2

In a *Dateline NBC* show in 2006, the infamous killer BTK, Dennis Rader, was filmed describing the development of his violent fantasies. Rader compared the progression of his fantasies with the production of a "picture show." He reported that he would lie in bed and think about his targeted victim. Once the victim became a fantasy to him, he would loop the story line over and over, thinking about how he would abduct and murder her. He wanted to be the producer and director of the picture show, which became his template for the crime. Rader was determined to follow through on the criminal activity no matter what it cost him. He stated that the fantasy would be enacted with a victim one way or another.

When Rader was interviewed by the Wichita, Kansas, team of police detectives, he was asked about his fantasy regarding a specific victim he had abducted and whose dead body he had carried into his church to pose for photographs. Rader repeated his mantra of how the fantasy was going to take place no matter what; that is, whether she was dead or alive. The power of the fantasy can become so all consuming that it drives the behavior of the criminal. In describing the power his fantasies had over him, Rader commented that he could neither stop his fantasies nor control them. He added that it was like the fantasies were in the "driver's seat."

Case 3.3

Richard Grissom Jr. was convicted of abducting, raping, and murdering three young women. Their bodies were never recovered. Regarding the murder of a fourth young woman whose body was mutilated post mortem, it was noted that her condominium had been cleaned after the crime. Not only was the crime scene vacuumed, but also the vacuum bags were removed from the scene. Grissom was never charged with this brutal homicide but was a very strong suspect. This scenario illustrates the efficiency with which a criminal may commit a crime when he has taken his fantasies to the far end of the continuum.

Do Fantasies Cause Violent Crime?

Do fantasies cause people to be violent? The short answer is "No," but they do play a distinct role in creating and shaping the nature of the violent acts committed. It is well understood that our learned sexual behavior is a part of our sexual personality, which governs our sexual stimulation or arousal. The mind controlling sexual behavior is the psychosexual aspect of arousal and accounts for a far higher percentage of individual arousal than either the instinctual or physiological components combined. Fantasies may be called daydreams, but they are, in any case, a mental function that creates pathways from our thought to our overt behaviors. Roy Hazelwood, in personal conversation, called fantasies a "mental rehearsal for a desired event."

Those desired events swirl around the core behaviors of verbal strategies, inflicting injurious harm, and the offender's choice of sexual acts. All three core behaviors are coordinated in fantasies and are assigned a sequence for use as the "play" develops.

Bibliography

Andreasen, Nancy C., and Donald Black. *Introductory Textbook of Psychiatry*. 2nd ed. Washington, DC: American Psychiatric Press, 1995.

Ault, Richard L., and James T. Reese. A Psychological Assessment of Crime Profiling. *FBI's Law Enforcement Bulletin* 49(3) (March 1980).

Wichita, Kansas Police Department. Criminal Interview of Dennis Rader, aka BTK. Wichita, Kansas: Wichita Police Department, 2006.

Deaver, Jeffrey. *The Sleeping Doll*. New York: Simon and Schuster, 2007.

Depue, Roger L., and Joyce M. Depue. To Dream, Perchance to Kill. *Security Management* (June 1999) 66–69.

Douglas, John E., and Alan E. Burgess. Criminal Profiling: A Viable Investigative Tool Against Violent Crime. *FBI Law Enforcement Bulletin* 55(12) (December 1986): 9–13.

Douglas, John E., Ann W. Burgess, Allen G. Burgess, and Robert K. Ressler. *Crime Classification Manual*. 2nd ed. San Francisco: Jossey-Bass, 2006.

Douglas, John E., Robert K. Ressler, Ann W. Burgess, and Carol R. Hartman. Criminal Profiling from Crime Scene Analysis. *Behavioral Science and the Law* 4(4) (1986): 401–421.

Gabbard, Glen O. *Psychodynamic Psychiatry in Clinical Practice. DSM-IV*. Washington, DC: American Psychiatric Press, 2005.

Hazelwood, Robert R., and Janet I. Warren. The Sexually Violent Offender: Impulsive or Ritualistic. In *Practical Aspects of Rape Investigation: A Multidisciplinary Approach*, edited by Robert R. Hazelwood and Ann W. Burgess, 97–112. Boca Raton, FL: CRC Press, 2001.

Napier, Michael R. Interviewing the Rapist. In *Practical Aspects of Rape Investigation: A Multidisciplinary Approach*, edited by Robert R. Hazelwood and Ann W. Burgess, 123–137. Boca Raton, FL: CRC Press, 2009.

Napier, Michael R., and Kenneth P. Baker. Criminal Personality Profiling. In *Forensic Science: An Introduction to Scientific and Investigative Techniques*, edited by Stuart H. James and Jon J. Nordby, 531–550. Boca Raton, FL: CRC Press, 2002.

Napier, Michael R., and Kenneth P. Baker. Criminal Personality Profiling. In *Forensic Science: An Introduction to Scientific and Investigative Techniques*, edited by Stuart H. James and Jon J. Nordby, 615–636. Boca Raton, FL: CRC Press, 2005.

Oldham, John M. Personality Disorders: A Brief Historical Review. FOCUS: *Journal of Lifelong Learning in Psychiatry* 3(3) (Summer 2005): 372–382.

Ressler, Robert K., and Ann W. Burgess. Violent Crime. Edited by Thomas J. Deacon *FBI Law Enforcement Bulletin* 54(8) (August 1985): 18–25.

Ressler, Robert K., Ann W. Burgess, and John E. Douglas. *Sexual Homicide; Patterns and Motives.* Lexington, MA: Lexington Books, 1988.

Ressler, Robert K., John E. Douglas, A. Nicholas Groth, and Ann W. Burgess. Offender Profiles: A Multidisciplinary Approach. *FBI's Law Enforcement Journal* 49(9) (September 1980): 16–20.

Samenow, Stanton. *Inside the Criminal Mind.* New York: Times Books, 1984.

Five Stars for Success and Some Relevant Thoughts

4

MICHAEL R. NAPIER

Contents

Setting the Stage for Success

Let us examine five concepts that set the stage for interviewing success. In my career, I conducted perhaps thousands of interviews, and looking back I found five constructs that often determine the outcome of police interviewing. Success may be obtainable without each of the five or any one of the five, but collectively they make the process work in favor of the officer and therefore in favor of society. The five key elements are, in order of importance:

1. Interviewer traits
2. Specific and detailed knowledge of the crime
3. Knowledge about the person being interviewed

4. Being practiced in the art and skills of interviewing and interrogating
5. Being in a position to arrange the proper contact setting.

Collectively, these five items also prepare the officer for another critical element: defending his interview product in adversarial proceedings.

Interviewer Traits

The success or failure traits of an interviewer are likely to determine the outcome of the interview or interrogation. The personal traits and characteristics of the interviewer will either enhance or diminish the likelihood of success; therefore they fall into two categories: success traits or failure traits. This element is mentioned first because good personal qualities may overcome other disadvantages. This topic is developed further in this chapter under the caption "Qualities that Shape Successful Interviewers."

Knowledge of the Crime

With possession of detailed knowledge of the crime, an interviewer will know which tactics fit best and use his interviewing personality to meet his goals. Without a solid basis provided by being well schooled in all of the aspects of the case as it has developed and a reliable interview plan, including tactics and strategies, the officer cannot be prepared.

Knowledge of the Interviewee

Having an extensive knowledge of the person being interviewed provides a road map to reach the goal of obtaining an admission or confession.

Who is this person who needs to be interviewed? How does he fit into the crime scenario? Beyond those broad questions, a more basic question is, **Who** is he, the real person? Often the question of who the individual is will not be answered until the interviewer takes the time to size him up. If properly instituted, the interview process requires a "getting-to-know-you" period more extensive than asking for his name, address, date of birth, and so on. An officer must ask a series of relevant personal questions long before jumping into the meat of the case with this specific person.

Beyond searching the department's computer for reference to the person, or checking the National Crime Information Computer (NCIC) or the Career Criminal History (CCH) files, an officer will be better prepared by taking the necessary and prudent step of checking Google or his favorite search engine. Individuals of any stripe of honesty are impressed when something pertinent about them, their family, or their life is dropped into a conversation. By this,

I am not referring to remarks that drag in prior police contacts, which are delivered in a manner that is received as petty or an attempt to intimidate. Use information that indicates you know him. If the interview is worthy of being conducted, take the time to do it correctly.

If a check of records indicates that a person has been a suspect, interviewed, charged, or tried on a criminal matter, it is vital to have all those details before commencing an interview on a new matter. Talk with other officers who have dealt with him under similar circumstances. Find out how he handles being interviewed by an investigator: Is he cooperative or hostile? Did he lie or avoid addressing a subject? Did he confess or plead guilty? Which interview techniques were used successfully or unsuccessfully?

Interview and Interrogation Skills

A working knowledge of interview and interrogation practices, especially when delivered in combination with positive personal qualities, places the interviewer on the inside track to success. How well honed are the officer's interviewing skills? By definition, those talents include the ability to interact with people from differing social strata. Included in the definition is the practiced knowledge of interview strategies, tactics, and techniques. The word *practiced* is intended to convey more than knowing how to interview. It means having walked the walk. There is no substitute for sharp skills made sharper by doing the job. Every "routine" interview is an opportunity to plan and execute interviewing skills that will be called into play when "the big one" comes along. The contents of this book provide the "how to" information that may be carried into every interview. See the discussion of interviewer qualities that follows for additional comments.

Interview Setting

Knowing how to select and arrange the most conducive setting to help maintain control of the interview process while providing for personal safety is often neglected as a factor contributing to success or failure. Being comfortable when interviewing means more than being confident and talented. Comfort is also obtained by familiarity—not only familiarity with the items discussed but also knowledge about the benefits of the interview location. An experienced officer is required to conduct interviews in every type of situation, and sometimes the setting is not optimal. Even those on-the-spot locations may be improved when the interview is one on which a case rests.

Most officers are most successful when conducting an interview on their home turf, but that is sometimes not possible, so make the most of what you have. One of the essential criteria is to find privacy for the officer and for the interviewee. An officer's chance of getting the most relevant information is proportional to the amount of privacy in the interview setting. Get away from distractions.

No matter what the location, the first consideration, even above privacy, is the officer's safety. Ensure an open route to safety should the person become aggressive. Do not get pinned in or cut off from a partner; interview one person at a time. This is true even for victims and witnesses. Keep your weapon on the side opposite the other person. Do not get distracted by your radio or cell phone. Arrange those items so that your strong gun hand is as free as possible.

Interview Room Amenities

If the interview is to be conducted at the police station, the officer should scout out the area to determine its condition and to arrange the fixtures so they are more conducive to effective contact. If the interview is being conducted indoors at a location where the officer may reasonably establish some control over the facility, he should execute the same efforts. Every reasonable effort should be made to make the area conducive to the officer's safety. Never assume that a person who may only be a suspect is not capable of violence simply because of a position he holds or because of his civic-minded reputation.

Some of the rooms assigned for interviews also serve other functions, including a private area for reading or having lunch. I always conducted the 2-minute drill during which decisions were made about whether ashtrays would be visible. For years, I told little white lies, claiming that smoking in federal buildings was forbidden. This was long before that prohibition became a fact. The exact truth was that smoke was an eye irritant for me, and I did not want to put up with it. A lit cigarette can also be a weapon that can take away your sight.

Some interview rooms are equipped with a telephone because of the multipurpose usage of the room. It was my practice to hide the telephone in a drawer or under a desk after removing the wall connector. I believe in the concept of "out of sight, out of mind." I did not want a telephone present to remind a person that he could contact an attorney.

An important part of the 2-minute drill is to arrange the chairs and desk or table in specific ways. In my interviews, first the suspect was provided a chair that did not allow him a view of anything distracting. I wanted him to concentrate on me, not on a calendar or a partially erased chalkboard in which he could lose his thoughts while I was making a pitch. I also wanted to deny him the use of any furniture except for a chair. If my choice of chair was not present at the beginning, I would seek out a chair that either had four legs or runners and no wheels. If he was going to move away from me, I wanted it to take a bit of effort so that I could assess what topics caused him to want to put some distance from me. The chair should not be equipped with arm rests as that forces a suspect to make a decision regarding how he is going to use or arrange his arms. I also wanted a specific chair that I could politely instruct him to take, thereby establishing some degree of control immediately on entry into the room.

If a second officer was to participate in the interview, I would explain my goals and purposes for the interview. We would agree on certain ground rules, such as whether he was to participate or if he was to participate but leave certain topics for me to present. Hand signals were also worked out so that he could remind me of something important that was just said to ensure that I had not missed it. This was accomplished by a simple tug of his ear. He could also roll his hand to indicate that I should pursue a topic because he believed that more information was obtainable. The list of signals is nearly bottomless. The second officer is ideally seated off to one side of the interviewee and slightly behind him. This allows him to observe the interviewee and to give me signals. Ideally, the second officer is also in the best position to take notes.

On the few occasions that juveniles were interviewed when the parents could insist on being present, I always spoke privately with the parents before entering the room. My goal was to influence them to waive their right to be present as they would likely feel a need to speak up at some point and would make it more difficult for their child to make admissions after having denied everything to them. If they insisted on being present, my next goal was to get them to agree to a seating arrangement similar to the one described for the second agent. I would give them a clear, but edited, version of what was going to happen during the interview. They were cautioned regarding what it meant if, on a critical question, their child turned to them as saviors and pleaded with his eyes for their intervention. I was clear about what would constitute indicators of truthfulness or deception.

Qualities that Shape Successful Interviewers

Investigators can find myriad interviewing schools with each supporting different approaches to the process. In reality, there is a somewhat limited set of tactics and techniques available to officers. There is, however, room for creativity in how and when those tactics come into play.

There is a caution that needs to be understood in adopting anyone's "system" or formula for interviewing. Interviewing successfully is highly individualized. The best interviewers have a natural talent for communicating. Absent a full set of those innate skills, an otherwise talented officer can train himself to marry the skills he does possess to the legally permissible tactics available to him. In this merging of talent and tactics, a customized interviewing personality will emerge.

I have found that the skills must be internalized by the investigator. He must massage them, change them, and make them his own. Mimicking another investigator's successful style and approach may lead to utter failure because the other officer's "suit doesn't fit," which will come across as being a fraud. The same holds true when trying to replicate lessons presented in interview seminars. The information is of good quality, but it must be individualized to match the user's talents.

I have often been asked to prepare an interview scenario to be used by another officer in his case. It does not matter how well the plan is drawn; if it requires skills and talents the officer does not possess, it is most likely going to fail.

There are some interviewing devices available that may be unsuitable for some officers. Their usage simply does not fit, and some investigators cannot make them work. Take things from each set of specialized training programs, test them several times in actual interviews, and incorporate those that are successful and discard the techniques that do not work.

Beyond using the best techniques for his interviewing personality, there are several other personality qualities needed for success. When I survey law enforcement attendees at my interviewing seminars for their view of the qualities that distinguish good from great interviewers, several aptitudes are invariably mentioned. The first and second required qualities are rarely recognized.

He adapts interview and interrogation techniques to his personality.
He displays an attitude of a seeker of truth.
He is patient. Quality interviews require an investment of time.
He is persistent. He hangs in until he gets through the trivia and gets answers to the questions he asks.
He intentionally paces each stage of the interview.
He is prepared with an interview plan drawn in advance.
He has acute listening skills in the "on" position.
He is prepared to change his attitude and demeanor just as a chameleon changes color.
He can convincingly be encouraging and understanding while adjusting his demeanor to challenging, incredulous, and questioning.
He has the ability to converse at all levels, from the street to the executive office.
He can bury personal beliefs and bias with each person interviewed.

Each skill mentioned works well in a set, not as a standalone talent. The interviewers perform at their absolute best when their talents and approaches are incorporated in and built around the first and second most needed qualities: sincerity and finding the roadblock.

The successful interviewer is an actor who can "bleed sincerity" (Inbau, Reid, and Buckley, 1986) when selling his product, even when he has said the same lines many times before. If he repeats those words by rote, in a monotone, he will come off sounding like a carnival huckster. The interview subject will be on alert for the next trick or rigged approach. The officer will likely be called on to sell concepts that slightly or totally border on truthful. To do so without the "feel" of sincerity is to condemn his pitch. Remember, the officer's efforts are geared to making prison and fines sound appealing.

Likewise, the truly talented investigator, as an adjunct to the pacing process, is probing for personal attitudes and values that reveal the vulnerabilities of the witness, victim, or suspect. When they are known, the interviewer will know how well the person accepts or rejects responsibility, how he defends his offensive acts, and what are his roadblocks to confession. Once recognized, the roadblocks can be skirted or minimized. The roadblocks for some are personal considerations such as publicity, exposure, and failure to meet the expectations of an intimate or a coworker or perceived family values. A good preinterview, before asking if he did the crime, is when these values will more likely be discovered.

Just as there are positive qualities that make success more likely, an investigator can possess negative qualities that severely lessen the opportunities to succeed. Beyond just reversing the positive qualities, the following interviewers have other negative qualities that lead to failure:

They rush the process.
They do not absorb and assess what has just transpired in the interview.
They allow their anxiety to show and govern the contact.
They lack confidence in themselves and their talents.
They lack an interview plan and "fly by the seat of their pants."
They have a low skill level regarding the proper use of permitted techniques.
They go out of their way to avoid gentle and professional confrontations.
They are gullible and too readily accept nonanswers and glib comments.
They do not control the interview process from start to finish.
They cannot demonstrate the proper attitude and demeanor for the situation.

The Miranda Warning

Chapter 19 on legal perspectives on interviewing presents a clear and well-articulated account of legal procedures affecting law enforcement interviewing and interrogating. One of the many important messages made in this chapter by John Hall, FBI legal instructor (ret.) deals with when to cease advising someone of his rights. If the message is clear that the person is not going to talk, stop advising the full set of rights and do not present the options to have an attorney present. If an officer goes the whole distance and the suspect indicates that he wants an attorney, any future interviewing cannot be attempted without involving the attorney. The only exception is if the suspect initiates contacting the authorities directly without the attorney. If the advice of rights ends before noting the "right" to an attorney or before the suspect asserts that he wants the presence of an attorney before answering questions, the police may reinstitute an attempt to question the offender directly.

It is my experience that officers administer these cautions unnecessarily. This abundance of caution may in the future cause the courts to impose stricter rules citing what has become "standard police practices" of giving the cautions when they are not required. The investigator should ask himself if providing the "Miranda warning" is required given the circumstances of the contact.

An overlooked tactic that would be effective in many interview situations is the oral or conversational presentation of the Miranda warning. The text of all the cautions required by the Supreme Court's *Miranda* decision may be woven into a conversation at any point during the contact as long as it is done at least by the time the custodial requirement kicks in. Therefore, all the rights could be provided casually and orally long before ever talking about any criminal involvement.

The required cautions may also be spaced over a period of time. These statements of rights may be done in a casual, offhand manner. This type of tactic should be reserved for special situations. Nonetheless, the timing and presentation of the Miranda cautions are legitimate interview and interrogation tactics. As a reminder, the statement of the cautions themselves must be all inclusive of those adopted by the Supreme Court.

However presented to the suspect, the Miranda cautions need not be an elaborate production. In situations and settings that do not require the advice of rights, an investigator may call attention to the absence of the advisement as a tactic to obtain more information from someone who may be a suspect.

The Miranda Rights Form

The existence of the Miranda rights form serves as a reminder that the cautions should be precise and all inclusive. Some departments require that a suspect initial after each statement of each right. The courts have not required that formality, and they have not required the use of a printed form or a signature signifying a waiver of the rights.

I would encourage an investigator to do several things with the Miranda rights form. First, the portion of the form that can be filled out in advance should be completed before the arrival of the suspect. This sends a subtle signal that the officer is prepared for his interview.

In addition, as a testimonial point, I recommend that the suspect be given the original form so that he is literally "given his rights." I strongly recommend that the suspect then be requested to read some portion of the form. This allows the officer to assess the reading capabilities of the suspect and to design a subsequent interview in accordance with his assessment. This process also tips the officer regarding the education and language level of a suspect and how a written statement must be prepared. After the formal process of advising a suspect of his rights and obtaining of the waiver, the form should be withdrawn and placed in a folder, which is then placed out of view of the suspect. There is a reason for the saying "out of sight, out of mind."

Some Miranda forms do not require beginning or ending times for the advisement. This allows an option for the investigator, who may note those times at the appropriate locations on the form even though they are not required. Those times may also be noted in the interview log. The length of time between the presentation of the rights and asking for a "knowing waiver" should be sufficient to convince a reasonable person that the waiver was considered and a rational waiving occurred. An officer should time his reading of the Miranda form and adjust his reading speed to demonstrate his careful advisement and the waiver-of-rights procedure. If extra time was used to explain any portion of the form, the times **must** indicate it. "Tick marks" may be made at any word or concept for which additional explanations were provided to ensure an understanding of the Miranda rights.

The End Game

The end game in interviewing and interrogating is the successful presentation in a courtroom of the fruits of that process. A professional officer is continually asking himself, "If I do this or say this, how will it play out in court? How will someone who does not know or appreciate what I do to protect them feel about my techniques and procedures?" Therefore, at the beginning of an interview and throughout the process, **"think prosecution."**

The Interview Log

In the not-too-distant past, officers were regularly required to maintain an interview log for each interview and interrogation. This log notes the events occurring within the interview contact. Each significant occurrence is noted, and the time of the occurrence is also posted to the log. The identity of the officer is also recorded by each occurrence. Items recorded in the log include the administration of the Miranda warning, any request made by the person being interviewed, all accommodations made to the subject of the interview (i.e., the offer or acceptance of restroom privileges, drinks, food, telephone calls, etc.).

One purpose of the interview log is to record the fairness and personal considerations afforded the interviewee. Using the log to testify will strengthen an officer's credibility should he testify that the listed amenities (courtesies) were actually afforded to the individual. It will also reflect the sequencing and timing of events within the context of the interview.

Tape Recording Interviews

There is an old adage that when a lawyer cannot attack the evidence, he will attack the officer personally. That is one of my concerns about any requirement to fully tape record all interviews from start to finish. While I continue to have many misgivings about the abuse to which tape-recorded interviews can be subjected, I have come to the belief that law enforcement officers should undertake a preemptive strike by recording the admissions or confessions portions of interviews. The same is true when all that is obtained from a suspect is a series of far-fetched denials that will in the end serve the prosecution. It will take some adjustment by officers to record, especially video record, interviews. When teaching, if the subject of recording interviews comes up, I often detect two things: a fear by officers because of a genuine concern that they will make a slight misstep that will be misinterpreted and a genuine discomfort from being filmed.

For consideration, it is suggested that at a minimum only the admission or confession portion of the interview be recorded. Using the following points, law enforcement may stave off the requirement that all interviews be recorded from start to finish:

1. After obtaining admissions, confessions, unseemly denials, the officer may make a recording of those statements. At the outset, record vital details to include the date, time, those present, and that an advice of right was given, if required. Get the subject's assent that he knows he is being recorded. If there is any concern that the suspect may recant or otherwise get cold feet if the recording process takes too long, the exact list of rights may be recorded individually after the admissions or confession is recorded. If the suspect has refused to sign the waiver portion of the Miranda form, record his acknowledgment of the rights and that he waived the rights but elected not to sign the form.

2. On the recording, briefly explain the interview process up to that point and request that the suspect confirm that the officer has not misspoken. On the recording, clearly and unequivocally ask the suspect to indicate any statements made by the officer that do not match his recollection or information.

3. The officer should recount the precise admissions or confession, pausing to obtain periodic agreement from the suspect. Initially, record just the pertinent points if there is concern that the suspect may become difficult or has been reluctant in making his statements.

4. When all the details of the confession have been recorded, return to the advice of rights and obtain concurrence of their prior presentation by recounting each right and the suspect's agreement that he waived them.

5. Record the usage of open-ended questions to demonstrate the lack of contamination. Record the question and then the response, including initial lies or corrections to prior statements. It is in the officer's best interest to be able to verify the use of open-ended questions by recording them in his interview plan, personal notes, and so on. This will take planning before the interview commences.

6. Periodically remind the subject to disagree if necessary and provide a statement of any and all accommodations (i.e., meals, drinks or refreshments, opportunities to use the bathroom, etc.) made. All of these should also be mentioned in the interview log.

7. Obtain agreement that no promises or threats have been made and that the statements are made voluntarily.

8. Expect and prepare for a challenge regarding having only recorded portions of the interview. Having the repeated concurrence of your proper handling of the interview in the suspect's own words is a large benefit.

9. Most of these points can be recorded on a 3 × 5 card and used to organize the recording and ensure that each point is made.

If an entire interview is being recorded, without making a production of the statement, a person should be advised that the interview may be monitored or recorded. This statement should be found in the officer's notes and on the interview log. It may also be included on the recording.

A properly equipped interview room will have the video camera located unobtrusively and not on a tripod right in front of the person. An officer should never point out the location of recording devices. The camera's red light should be disconnected or covered. These precautions are attempts to minimize the tendency for some suspects to play to the camera or have the camera become a distraction.

On the other side of the recording an interview coin, the following positive aspects are noted:

To protect the confession, the officer must present a professional demeanor.

The voluntary use of specific, approved, or standardized techniques will be documented.

Evidence of preparation or lack of preparation for the interview will be evident.

It will be clear that attempts were made to avoid contaminating a statement.

If a videotape is made, the jury may see the subject's nonverbal gestures.

The jury may also hear attempts by a subject to evade direct, incriminating questions.

The jury may be "educated" in advance regarding what is the typical behavior of truthful and deceptive persons.

Officers' Note Taking

Some suspects become nervous and guarded if they see an officer write down something after they have answered a question. If two officers are involved, the note taker may be seated to one side and slightly behind the suspect. Note taking may become less significant, especially on major cases, if the officer has an interview plan with specific questions properly formatted and prepared in advance. When those questions are asked, the officer will later be able to recall the answer if technical data are not involved. Besides a tick mark to show that the question was asked, a brief note of a key word or two in the answer should be a sufficient memory jogger. By using the paraphrasing technique, an officer will give back in summary form what the suspect has told him on essential topics, thus embedding that information in his memory. Note taking may be held off until after the essential elements of the case have been covered and the answers reinforced by paraphrasing.

Second-Chance Interviews

Should a second confrontational interrogation be necessary, the suspect has earned a psychological advantage. Because he "won" on the prior attempt, his psychological mind-set and confidence in beating the interrogator are increased, so he will likely hold out longer. This scenario indicates several points the professional should keep in mind.

Interviewing in the early stages of the investigation is critical. Before much of the investigative results are in, and prior to the development of a solid suspect, all interviews must be thorough. When handled properly, the early interviews of seemingly innocent individuals often develop details that are damaging to that individual when he becomes the focus of the investigation. Part of the definition of *thorough* at this stage is to inquire, in a casual or offhand manner, if the person has intentionally withheld information or is more involved in the crime than he has related. These may be explained as "must-ask" questions that will be posed to everyone, but they become the web that entangles the suspect down the road. Every lie told closes a door through which the suspect cannot reenter without damaging his position.

Interviews ending on a rancorous note add to the effort the officer applies to the subsequent interrogation. It is my personal experience that there is only a rare need for the investigator to raise his voice, pound on the table, or swear. If he is armed with the proper elements of psychological persuasion, he can accomplish more by asking the right question properly timed. By engaging in shouting matches, arguments, and theatrics, he demeans himself in the eyes of the suspect and reveals the depth of his investigative position and the extent of his confidence when confronting that person. When he is arguing, the officer is not discussing the crime elements or moving the investigation forward. In the early going, the officer is engaged in a tug of war, and his goal with each contact is to move the "rope" inch by inch to his side of the line.

Bibliography

Deaver, Jeffrey. *The Sleeping Doll.* New York: Simon and Schuster, 2007.

Gudjonsson, Gisli. *The Psychology of Interrogation, Confessions and Testimony.* Chichester, UK: Wiley, 1992.

Hess, John E. *Interviewing and Interrogation for Law Enforcement.* Cincinnati, OH: Anderson, 1997.

Holmes, Warren D. Interrogation. *Polygraph* 24(4) (1995): 237–258.

Holmes, Warren D. *Criminal Interrogation.* Springfield, IL: Thomas, 2002.

Inbau, Fred E., John E. Reid, and Joseph P. Buckley. *Criminal Interrogation and Confessions.* 3rd ed. Baltimore, MD: Williams and Wilkins, 1986.

Inbau, Fred E., John E. Reid, Joseph P. Buckley, and Brian C. Jayne. *Criminal Interrogations and Confessions.* 4th ed. Sudbury, MA: Jones and Bartlett, 2004.

Vessel, D. Conducting Successful Interrogations. Ott, J., Ed., *FBI Law Enforcement Journal* 67(10) (October 1998): 11–15.

Yeschke, Charles L. *The Art of Investigative Interviewing.* Boston: Butterworth-Heinemann, 1997.

Zulawski, David E., and Douglas E. Wicklander. *Practical Aspects of Interview and Interrogation.* 2nd ed. Boca Raton, FL: CRC Press, 2002.

An Analytical Process for Crimes of Violence*

5

MICHAEL R. NAPIER

Contents

> The ideal reasoner would, when he has once been shown a single fact in all its bearing, deduce from it not only all the chain of events which led up to it, but also all the results which would follow from it.
>
> **Sherlock Holmes**

Case 5.1

A young white female was assaulted and murdered in her middle-class townhome in a Midwestern city. Her body had been displayed in a manner to shock and to offend. She had been subjected to unspeakable brutality, both antemortem and postmortem. Her killer had repeatedly "carved" on her chest, and the letters "W H O R E" were visible. The carving tool was the bolt protruding from the leg of a disassembled table found at the crime scene. A sharp cutting instrument was used to inflict postmortem wounds. She had been strangled with a ligature, bound, and anally assaulted with a foreign object. Her body had been "cleansed" with a facial cream. A handwritten note had been placed on her pubic mound suggesting that the murder was a payback to her employer, a judge, for a sentence handed down on the offender. No material consistent with the ligature marks on the body was found inside the residence. Liquid dish soap had been forced inside her vagina and anus. Great care was taken in the anal insertion of an unbroken lightbulb. There was no evidence of a

---

* A prior version of this material was published in: Napier, M. R. An Analytical Process for Crimes of Violence, Sutton, A. R., Ed., *Magazine of the FBI National Academy Associates* (FBI National Academy Associates) 6(4): 18–25, July/August 2004.

physically forced entry to the residence, and the offender likely spent up to
5 hours with the victim. The victim's telephone answering tape had been
removed, and the residence revealed signs of someone recently vacuum-
ing the upstairs carpet. No foreign fingerprints of value were located.

What can the discerning investigator find in this scene that will allow
him to deduce the offender's personal traits, leading to his identification,
arrest, and conviction? What has the offender revealed to the investigator
about himself through his crime behaviors? Has he revealed his motivation,
identity, age, race, and prior relationship with the victim?

If assigned this case, would you first theorize that this offender was likely
a white male, mid-to-late twenties, with a prior, likely sexual, relationship
with the victim? Would you surmise the offender's name would be found in
the personal belongings of the victim? Would your conjecture include that
the offender's probable motive had not initially been homicide?

Analytical Background

> It has long been an axiom of mine that the little things are infinitely the
> most important.
>
> **Sherlock Holmes**

Prior to commencing an analysis, of necessity, the investigator will perform
a detailed inventory of the crime scene. In the inventory of tangible items,
each piece of physical evidence, its location, and its location in relation to
other pieces of evidence and fixed reference points are noted. The inventory
will also focus on the behaviors associated with the type and placement of
the evidence. It will also reveal evidence that would rightly be expected to be
present but has been removed. The investigator should be asking himself why
this evidence is located at this spot.

The operative concepts in performing an analysis in any violent crime are
to (1) conduct an analysis of individual items to discern behavior patterns,
(2) consciously keep the investigator's mind open to any possibility, and (3)
make analytical adjustments as new information is developed.

From examining many hundreds of sexually violent crimes and a
close association with the Behavioral Science Unit (BSU) and the National
Center for the Analysis of Violent Crime (NCAVC) of the Federal Bureau
of Investigation (FBI), I have learned several analytical points that can aid
greatly in placing new investigations on a firm footing and a path to success. The primary focus of this chapter is on the analysis of the behaviors
of the offender and the victim as they intertwine during the commission of
violent and sexually deviant acts.

Absent processing the crime scene and obtaining reliable forensic results from the laboratory, nothing has more of an impact on the proper foundation and course of an investigation than the ever-evolving process of analyzing the crime from first discovery to successful prosecution. Interviews of surviving victims, witnesses, and suspects are affected by the original analysis of the crime scene. Hand in hand, they set the course of the investigative strategy. Experienced investigators will confirm that the original analysis is unlikely to resemble subsequent analyses simply because of the new evidence or information gleaned as the investigation progresses.

The meaningful examination of behavior-indicating evidence left at the crime scene should be a skill of first rank for investigators, an act that is second nature to him. Once the investigator has developed the talent of recognizing and assessing the criminal's behavior, he will quickly appreciate the significance of that behavior as it has an impact on the quality of the interpretation of the total crime scene.

The thought of undertaking an *analysis* may be intimidating, because the term is suggestive of commencing an elaborate academic undertaking. In its elemental form, analysis is the scrutiny of *every known piece* of the puzzle to envision the completed picture (Rabon, 2003). The emphasis is on "every known piece," as the smallest details often tell the tale.

In sexual assaults, the examination of the minutia is for the purpose of finding a pattern of behaviors that reveals criminal sophistication, use of ritual (Hazelwood and Warren, 2001), or the exercise of behaviors that are intended to express or demonstrate the offender's search for power or his degree of anger. This aspect of the analysis relies heavily on the surviving victim recounting her behaviors and those of the offender (Hazelwood and Burgess, 2001).

Similarly, the purpose of analysis in a sexual homicide is to find a pattern of behavior reflective of the offender's methodology, use of or absence of ritual, criminal intelligence, and systematized approach to the victim and the crime. Hazelwood and Douglas (1980) selected two words to classify homicide offenders: organized and disorganized. Through research, Ressler, Burgess, and Douglas (1988) determined that offenders actually fell into one of three categories: organized, disorganized, or "mixed."

People generally behave in ways with which they are most comfortable and therefore in keeping with their personality (Hazelwood and Burgess, 2001). Accordingly, if a person's crime behavior can be observed and interpreted, certain attributes of that person may be surmised. When these attributes are combined with research findings about various categories of offenders, the "read" behaviors can assist in guiding the investigation and interviewing processes as well as development of a suspect. What a person does (behavior) and how that behavior is brought into play in the crime are most likely guided by the offender's goal, that is, his motive. Therefore the early analysis of the crime behavior may identify the offender's motivation in selecting a particular victim and explain why he exhibited specific behaviors with that victim. With that accomplished, a suspect or suspect profile may be developed early in the investigation.

It is a personal belief that most people have desires and thoughts about themselves that they hold secret from all but their closest associates. Perhaps such secrets are never related to anyone. An offender is more likely to feel sufficient anonymity when committing a crime that he unleashes the hidden side of his personality. These heretofore secret fantasies are identified by reading the scene and can be of immeasurable value in interviews of former sexual partners and the suspect himself.

The Three-Step Analysis Process

To find answers to questions like those posed above, the recommended analysis process is simple and involves a pencil-and-paper exercise. The process may seem cumbersome until it has been used several times, on any type of case, and has become second nature to the officer. A word of caution: Do not allow yourself to become sloppy or short circuit the process. If this is done, the incorrect end product of analysis will cast the entire investigation off course. Every significant piece of case data, no matter how small, needs to be considered and evaluated for confirmation that the analysis of each individual investigative product points in the same direction.

Begin by dividing a sheet of paper into three columns. The heading of the first column is "Behavioral Act," the second column is headed "Why Done," and the third column is "Analysis."

In column one, each separate piece of crime scene and investigative product will be listed individually and examined one at a time. In column two, directly across from that single entry in column 1, the officer is asked to list every reason he can think of as to why an offender would have committed that act. His job is to keep his mind open and to not omit any conceivable reason. The last step is to use column 3, and the officer should search his investigative knowledge data base from all of his prior training, education, and experience. In column 3, he is to list across from each item in column 2 his decision as to what each piece of the investigative puzzle means and how it fits into the overall crime. In column 3 the officer should use simple and basic terminology to indicate the impact and interpretation of every item in column 2.

The search in this process seeks a pattern of similar concepts or terms in each column 3 for every behavioral act in column 1. That pattern, if found, will summarize the offender's thought process, criminal sophistication, basis for victim choice and relationship to the offender, and motivation. If a

Table 5.1 Three-Step Analysis Process

Behavioral Act	Why Done	Analysis
1. Door kicked in	1A. Insufficient knowledge of victim (victimology), i.e. how she would react to con approach or other attempts to gain entry.	No or little planning. Limited knowledge of victim?
	1B. Tried con approach but failed.	Not behaviorally comfortable with verbal skills.
	1C. Offender not under rational/self-control.	Not rational. Unprepared.
	1D. Offender is impulsive.	Sloppy. Not prepared. Little self-control in this situation.
	1E. Offender under influence of drugs, alcohol.	Anger has been building. Reduced rationality.
	1F. Offender is under influence of extreme anger or rage.	Anger situational? Or targeted toward victim? No plan for situation or crime. Unsophisticated. Not organized.

pattern is not found the officer should (1) check his use of the process, perhaps utilizing a neutral party to verify his conclusions and/or (2) consider the possibility of the mixed pattern as indicative of two or more offenders whose behaviors are being revealed. This process is shown in Table 5.1.

The first entry for most items in column 2 should reflect the investigator's knowledge of the victim, as the victim's personality and reaction to the crime influences the offender's subsequent behaviors.

From this brief example, the interpretation of column 3 is that the offender is underprepared, disorganized, impulsive, and not under personal restraint. Other possible conclusions is that he lacks the ability to confront women face to face, is continually angry (possibly with women in general), came to victim with a purpose that victim rejected before admitting offender, and so forth.

As each piece of behavior is examined in column 1 it is expected that the conclusions and analysis in column 3 will result in similar findings, thereby providing a basis for commencing or continuing the investigation.

Analysis and Victimology

The term *victimology* is a known concept and is well established in the law enforcement and psychological communities (Schlesinger, 2003), but some investigators may not appreciate the benefits drawn from obtaining a full description of the victim's lifestyle (Napier and Hazelwood, 2003). Obtaining personal information regarding the victim's associates, alcohol or drug use, security consciousness, sexual practices, assertiveness, and so on should begin with the first witness interviews. It is a confidently held belief that what is known about the victim will help explain the crime scene, assist in understanding victim selection, improve the ability to determine offender motivation, and serve as a backdrop for testing the officer's crime scene reconstruction theories. In short, victimology aids investigators in focusing their inquiries. According to Lt. Kenny Landwehr, Wichita, Kansas, Homicide Unit, victimology is the second most important part of an investigation after the processing of the crime scene (*Manhunt in the Heartland*, Pie Town Productions, The Learning Channel, 2000).

In Case 5.1, many of the likely initial theories would prove out in the end; however, some critical thoughts would be considerably off the mark, as made clear by the later development of the victim's personal history and lifestyle. The sexual interest of the criminal in this victim is unquestioned, but his behaviors go beyond interest to expressions about the victim's overall sexuality, an indication that he was more than a casual acquaintance. In homicides, the historic pattern is that crimes are predominantly committed intraracially (i.e., whites assaulting whites, blacks assaulting blacks, etc.) (Schlesinger, 2003). In this case, the victim's dating habit of several years was to date black male athletes exclusively. Combining these data with the suspected closeness of the victim and offender, it would now be postulated that this killer was likely a black male athlete. The assumption that people date within their age range is also generally accurate (Schlesinger, 2003). Following this line of thinking, the offender's age would be estimated in an age range bracketing the age of the victim.

Analysis and the Organized or Disorganized Offender

The table leg, liquid soap, cleansing cream, paper, pen, and vacuum cleaner were items owned by the victim. With the exception of the dismantled table leg, most are common household items that could be relied on by an offender as likely to be found in any female's residence. This brings into question whether the offender assumed their presence, feeling no need to bring them to the scene. Or was his initial intention something entirely different from the homicide, which may have escalated from a rejection of his sexual advances? The answers to those pieces of the puzzle will be determined from the overall analysis of the crime scene.

The data could be misread as suggestive of a disorganized mind or an unprepared offender. To the contrary, some significant items were provided by the offender, and he took other actions within the crime scene that strongly suggest a substantial degree of ability to think on his feet. The offender removed the audiotape, binding materials, and a sharp cutting instrument from the scene. He likely used the victim's vacuum cleaner to clean up after himself and removed the debris and bag. He attempted to stage the scene by writing a note to misdirect the investigator's focus to people sentenced by a judge who was the victim's employer (Napier, 2004).

One of the hallmarks for analyzing homicides is the amount of evidence related to the offender's degree of control over the victim and the extent to which he had prepared for the crime. Although the offender presumably came to the victim for reasons other than homicide, he was able to quickly equip himself with binding materials of sufficient value to him that they were removed from the scene. (When arrested, the offender was attempting to meet a potential victim and had a complete "kill kit" in the trunk of his car. He had abandoned a similar kit when he fled the location of three homicides for which he was later convicted. The kit consisted of a pellet gun that simulated a real revolver, box cutter, duct tape, knives, and a spool of nylon rope.) The liquid soap would most likely have been used to conceal a sexual assault. The vacuum sweeper marks on the floor and the absence of the vacuum bag combine with other crime scene data to indicate an offender who would be labeled as organized.

Case 5.1 illustrates several analytical points: (1) Offenders tell many things about themselves by the behaviors they leave behind; (2) motives may be revealed by a careful examination of crime scene behaviors; (3) what is missing from a scene is important; and (4) victimology information is essential.

Additional Analytical Points

Case 5.2

In a small southern town, an elderly black female was strangled to death in her residence with a belt believed to have been hers. The handle of an umbrella was inserted vaginally near the time of death. The umbrella was absent the material cover and supporting ribs, exposing a pointed tip. A second umbrella was present and fully intact. One breast was partially uncovered, and she was nude from the waist down. There was no evidence of penis penetration. Her face had been covered with a pillow from the scene. A jar of generic petroleum jelly was beside the body, and photographs indicated the presence of petroleum jelly on her thighs. Beside the jar of petroleum jelly was a working desk-type lamp that was missing its shade. Her pants and panties had been cut off, likely with a pair of scissors, with the cuts beginning at the leg cuff and moving upward, across the crotch portion and through the waist. A partially eaten orange and orange peel were found in and beside a waste can. Her residence was somewhat unkempt but in keeping with the victim's personal habits. While there was no evidence of forced entry, her front door was locked, and the outside screen door was closed. A cinder block that she always placed against the screen door to hold it closed when she left was nearby but not used to hold the screen door closed.

What analytical principles apply in Case 5.2? Many of the same principles exhibited in Case 5.1 are appropriate in Case 5.2; however, other principles may also be observed. This offender left impressions of many of his personal characteristics through his crime scene behaviors. My interpretation of the crime scene behavior was that he was sexually inexperienced but sexually curious. This was evidenced by the victim's bare breast, exploratory insertion of the umbrella handle, the use of the petroleum jelly, and the need for the presence of a light nearby so that he could see what he was doing and observe the female body's response to his behaviors.

Did the offender bring the metal umbrella to the scene for the purpose of sexually exploring the victim? Victimology again reveals many details that assist the investigator. According to her victimology, she used a grocery cart to collect aluminum items that she sold at a recycling location. It was likely the victim had picked up the partial umbrella during her routine collection of aluminum. This analysis is supported by the offender's other weapon, a belt used as a ligature, which was also from the scene. The seemingly impromptu use of weapons of opportunity is one indicator that the motive for the initial contact was not a sexual assault and homicide. By using the handle portion of the umbrella and the table lamp, the offender clearly indicates his sexual inexperience, which is also suggestive of social inexperience, both characteristics of a loner.

When examining a scene, the investigator may observe a point at which the offender faced behavioral choices in the commission of the assault. Those choices reflect alternate behavior paths. Given the principle that behavior reflects personality, choosing one behavioral path over another provides more in-depth insight into the offender's personality. In Case 5.2, although the vaginal insertion of the umbrella handle is a graphic display of sexual curiosity, it is not anger-based behavior. This aspect of the crime is consistent with other characteristics that also feature low-level violence. Had the offender been angry with this female victim or women in general, he most likely would have chosen to insert the sharper, pointed end of the umbrella to display his anger and hatred. This offender's behavior was sufficiently bizarre to be suggestive of a mental impairment. This descriptor, coupled with other traits derived from an analysis of the scene, led to his identification. He confessed to this homicide and to a prior double homicide of a young mother and her infant child. Both had pillows placed over their faces.

Investigators should keep in mind that offenders make behavioral choices during their crimes. The options selected speak of their personality and are reflective of their motives, criminal sophistication, and socialization.

Case 5.3

Four adult males were discovered at the same scene, a state-owned shooting range used by deer hunters for sighting their rifles. Three of the victims sustained through-and-through gunshot wounds of a caliber consistent with a hunting-type firearm. In examination of the scene, blood in front of the shooting bench directed the investigators to drag marks that led to the discovery of two bodies loaded in the back seat of one of the victim's vehicle. Left at the scene were two firearms owned by the victims. One firearm was inside the car with the bodies, and the other was on the shooting bench. The body of the third victim, an unarmed state game warden, was located on the brass-casing-strewn parking area behind the shooting bench. The pockets of these three victims were turned out, and the offender took several hundred dollars. The fourth victim, although wounded, had an opportunity to flee a short distance before he fell down a ravine. He was executed from the roadway above but was not searched for valuables.

Case 5.4

The bodies of a male and female were found near a sandy beach maintained by the federal government. The recreation season had ended. The concession stand was closed, and the parking lot was barricaded. Both victims were in their early twenties and had been executed with gunshots to the back of the head. The male was completely dressed, but the female was nude, and her body was possibly posed in a sexually suggestive position. She had also sustained a penetrating but nonfatal gunshot wound to her face. They had been missing for several days prior to their discovery by a young man jogging on the beach as part of his conditioning program prior to joining the military. He was accompanied by his dog, who explored the area where the bodies were located and did not return, causing the owner to search for him and find the bodies.

These cases are presented to illustrate that seemingly random killings may be the result of some environmental cue or stressor recently experienced by the offender. In Case 5.3, Victims 1 and 2 were lifelong friends but did not know Victims 3 and 4. Victims 3 and 4 had met just the morning of their murder. Both groups were visiting the range as a matter of chance. Victims 1 and 2 stopped by to adjust the sights of their rifles before joining their wives to start a vacation. Victims 3 and 4 were on a spur-of-the-moment guided tour. Seemingly, there was no obvious motive to kill any of the victims because there is little logic in committing an armed robbery on victims at a shooting range. That these victims had considerable cash on their persons was an unforeseeable and an unpredictable occurrence.

Case 5.4 involves two young victims who had just met the weekend of their deaths and had no known prior association with the area of the crime. Most probably, they were just two young lovers who stopped for a private late night walk on the beach.

Cases 5.3 and 5.4 share the randomness of their occurrence, which was precipitated by personal stressors experienced by their murderers. In Case 5.3, the offender was facing constant financial pressures, which were made more intense by being laid off work that day. On his return home, he discovered his wife loading their truck with personal belongings. She announced their separation. This offender, similar to others, did not feel empowered to strike out at the source of his frustration but chose instead to kill four people who were unknown to him. He went to the shooting range full of rage and ready to vent that rage on anyone who appeared. Money was important to him, but robbery was unequivocally a secondary motive. He scored a financial gain beyond what he could have imagined before the murders.

In Case 5.4, the shooter had attended church earlier in the evening, where he had been subjected to 2 hours of insults and taunts by his girlfriend, who was late in her term of pregnancy. Her friends joined in deriding the boyfriend for his failure to marry her as promised and for having a second girlfriend who was also pregnant. The humiliation he experienced was on his mind when he escaped to the beach to be alone. At the beach, he spotted the young, amorous couple, and he returned to his vehicle to obtain his weapon. The convergence of three parties who were unknown to each other led to two of them being executed.

An investigator should be alert to and in search of a triggering cue that began the offender's movement to violence.

Conclusion

In policing, daily conversation and trading opinions about the most recent violent crime is as common as coffee and donuts. This give and take is the testing ground of investigations. I would venture a judgment that such discussions are healthy and essential to crime solutions. Keep in mind that an analysis is also called an opinion, and everyone is entitled to develop one. The element that distinguishes differing analyses is the case details found in support of each theory. So, this admonition is offered: Evidence leads and trumps.

A commonly heard basis for discarding or minimizing crime information is the expression, "I wouldn't have done it that way." The investigator who approaches an analysis of crime from this perspective will be fooling himself. He is substituting his values, fantasies, and criminal knowledge for those of the offender. It is more reliable to assume the part of the offender, guided by the behaviors left at the scene or with a surviving victim, and role-play or reenact the crime. To make this process more beneficial, the inclusion of information about the victim and the victim's likely reaction to the offender's acts is essential.

Role-playing is the process of crime reconstruction. At critical decision points in the conduct of the investigation, it is recommended that a crime reconstruction be undertaken. Like the theorizing already discussed, the crime reconstruction is a dynamic function and should be ongoing with the inclusion of additional investigative results. One of the purposes of the reconstruction is to attempt to sequence the events as they occurred, thereby walking in the footprints of both the offender and the victim. Forensic findings and the investigator's knowledge and experiences are valid inclusions in the reconstruction. The purpose for reconstructing a crime is to use all the small pieces to see the whole picture and to test the investigator's analytical theories. Reconstruction may include trying out a theory with others familiar with the case and allowing them to play devil's advocate and find unexplained evidence or errors in the analysis. If the overall picture and the analysis are congruent, the behavioral analysis is more likely correct.

Bibliography

Hazelwood, Robert R., and Ann W Burgess. *Practical Aspects of Rape Investigation: A Multidisciplinary Approach.* 3rd ed. Boca Raton, FL: CRC Press, 2001.

Hazelwood, Robert R., and John E. Douglas. The Lust Murderer. *FBI Law Enforcement Bulletin* (April 1980) 18–22.

Hazelwood, Robert R., and Janet I. Warren. The Sexually Violent Offender: Impulsive or Ritualistic. In *Practical Aspects of Rape Investigation: A Multidisciplinary Approach*, edited by Robert R. Hazelwood and Ann W. Burgess, 97–112. Boca Raton, FL: CRC Press, 2001.

Napier, M. R. An Analytical Process for Crimes of Violence. A. R., Ed., *Magazine of the FBI National Academy Associates* (FBI National Academy Associates) 6(4): 18–25, July/August 2004.

Rabon, D. *Investigative Discourse Analysis.* Durham, NC: Carolina Academic Press, 2003.

Ressler, Robert K., Ann W. Burgess, and John E. Douglas. *Sexual Homicide; Patterns and Motives.* Lexington, MA: Lexington Books, 1988.

Schlesinger, Louis. *Sexual Murder: Catathymic and Compulsive Homicides.* Boca Raton, FL: CRC Press, 2003.

Indirect Personality Assessment

RICHARD L. AULT JR.

Contents

Primary Goal

The primary goal of the forensic use of behavioral sciences, as practiced by the Federal Bureau of Investigation (FBI) for many years, is to understand how the criminal or other potential target perceives his or her environment to provide law enforcement or the intelligence community with practical advice to solve their specific problems. In this chapter, the "target" is any person in whom we have an interest, for whatever reason, such as the suspect of a crime, potential informant (asset), person of interest in an official investigation, and so forth.

In practice, this goal is achieved by reviewing the best-available information about the behavior of the target and using that information to arrive at a conclusion about that individual's motivations. This methodology includes a technique called indirect personality assessment (IPA). IPA and criminal investigative analysis and/or crime scene assessment have been used by the FBI since 1975 to assist law enforcement and intelligence agencies. The techniques that are used are based on research and experience in the field of forensic behavioral sciences.

The purpose of the IPA technique is to form opinions about a person's actions (or sometimes the actions of several persons) based on knowledge of that person's observed behaviors. One great mistake in any sort of investigation is the failure of an investigator, intelligence officer, or analyst to uncover as much information as possible about the person of interest in whatever case he or she is investigating. This chapter is intended for investigators, intelligence officers, case officers, and case agents—a whole group of those who need and use IPA for their craft. Therefore I refer to the officers as *investigators* and the IPA specialist as an *assessor*. Sometimes, sloth or distraction deflects us from uncovering the information we want and need. Sometimes, we simply think we know it all, having worked with "these types" for so many years. In any case, we are cheating ourselves, our profession, and those who trust us to do a professional job when we do not try to obtain as much accurate, reliable, and valid information as possible. Shreds, tidbits, scraps, minutiae, all types of information help inform the assessor who conducts the IPA for you, the investigator.

What Is IPA?

IPA is an investigative technique that uses the behavioral sciences to provide answers to questions the investigator must ask, but cannot always ask, the target. That is why this particular technique is called *indirect*. Assessment is described as judging the worth or importance of something. *Personality* is defined as that which constitutes, distinguishes, and characterizes a person as an entity over a period of time. It is a total reaction of a person to his or her environment (*Dorland's Illustrated Medical Dictionary*, 1981). In the behavioral sciences, and in this particular application of IPA, *assessment* is the use of behavioral science tools in a variable process to arrive at information of use to our case. In behavioral science research and psychology, we discuss two main types of assessment: *direct* and *indirect*. There are other, broader, terms used in research, such as *qualitative* and *quantitative*, but these attract conflicting attempts to define them. I stick with direct and indirect as acceptable terms.

Direct assessment is useful and is certainly used when possible. It is the use of such techniques as face-to-face interview, standardized personality tests, close surveillance, or any other means by which we do not care whether the target knows what we are doing. Frequently, but certainly not always, the information we get can be somewhat more accurate and reliable than information we obtain through indirect methods.

Indirect is just what it says. In science, some measurement uses tools we call "unobtrusive." That is, the observations are made without alerting the target to the fact that we are making them. Unobtrusive measures are indirect measurement (or assessment), and they are, for the most part, carefully screened by the scientists to ensure that there is ethical and legal constraint.*

---

* But this is not always the case. A sociologist named Laud Humphries conducted some research a number of years ago on homosexual behavior in public restrooms. He later published a book, *Tea Room Trade* (1970), in which he discussed his methodology, including violations of most existing ethical tenets of research, arousing major condemnation by academia.

In the "real" world of criminal or intelligence work, we are constrained by legal issues but at times excoriated for what is perceived by the more academic souls as violating ethical guidelines. Probably, this is accurate. We can do things that violate *their* ethics. But in the real world, ours is a different mission, and there are organizations in existence—such as the courts, our own executive branch, legislative fiat—that provide the appropriate direction that limits what we can do to gather information and the type of information we can gather.

Indirect assessment includes the specialty of gathering information through an intermediary agent. We are doing indirect assessment any time we ask a trusted friend who their favorite mechanic is or where they prefer to shop for vitamins. Indirect assessment, then, is nothing particularly new. And, as you have noticed, it can be combined with direct assessment, such as when you take your car to that favorite mechanic and he or she ruins your transmission (thereby providing considerable insight about the mechanic). In our work, we are using indirect assessment but applying specialized information (the tools of the behavioral scientist) to arrive at answers for the questions facing the investigator, such questions as the following: Who would do such a thing as this? How do we question this person to get a confession? Or, in intelligence work: How do we recruit this person? What sort of problems will we have handling this person if we do recruit him or her? How do we ease this person out of our system—that is, "retire" the target from being our asset without psychological trauma for him? This continues for a multitude of questions that require knowing the type of personality traits the target may have. In fact, the process of IPA is set forth in its label: We gather information indirectly about the target to form a judgment regarding what sort of personality characteristics the target has and what sort of weaknesses, or strengths, we can exploit to enhance our chances to interact with that target successfully.

Note again that the dichotomy between direct and indirect is not a fixed chasm. There are times when information may be obtained directly for use in a predominantly indirect assessment, for example, using "pretext" calls or the use of "sting" operations—called "false-flag" operations in the intelligence community. Another example is the use of some standardized personality tests commercially available to qualified individuals. For example, one such test is called the NEO Personality Inventory, Revised (NEO PI-R) (Costa, 1994, 2003). It is a personality measurement device that assesses aspects of five major personality characteristics along with six traits from each personality characteristic. The NEO has a form, called Form R, that allows observers such as spouse, peers, or experts—if they are acquainted with him—to rate the target. The use of Form R by an expert assessor can often enhance the IPA results. There are so many information-gathering techniques that there is considerable diversity in the methods used by disparate intelligence-gathering forces: criminal investigators, intelligence officers, and the like.

IPA involves applications of behavioral science techniques, but it is not an immovable format. It is based on application of principles derived from science, but it is also an art form that relies on the experience of the behavioral science practitioner. The primary "instrument" of the assessor is any technique* that provides the investigator some insight into the behavior of the target.

How Do We Implement IPA?

It is always desirable that the experienced investigator do all he or she can to gather information for the assessor. There are few fixed rules in this technique, with each professional preferring his or her own approach. However, there are several guidelines that seem to make the IPA outcome a benefit time after time. First, bear in mind that IPA is simply a tool in the tool belt of the investigator. There is no reason the assessor should try to "take over the case." Unlike profiler shows in TV series or in movies, the IPA is a specialty, and the assessor, who should know a great deal about the specific techniques in the environment in which they operate (i.e., criminal investigations, intelligence activity, operational techniques, etc.), is there to help those personnel assigned to handle management of the case or operation. The assessor is not the boss.

Second, like most tools, IPA is a specialty that requires a background (preferably a graduate degree) in behavioral science, with forensic experience involved as well. The lynchpin skill in the assessor's tool kit is psychology, preferably heavy on the clinical or counseling side. Personally, I would not demand solely a license in clinical psychology because very little of what an assessor does requires a license and because clinical psychology is only a part of the background experience an assessor needs. As mentioned, experience in forensic work as well as knowledge of the particular career field in which the assessor works will provide a starting point in the training of an assessor.

Third, an IPA is labor intensive. It requires that an assessor review available information and be able to ask for more and more specific information. It takes a great deal of time and, in the end, may not produce much more information about the target than already exists. Often, an experienced assessor can speak to such an outcome early in the assessment. It would be fair to say at this point, however, that not all is lost if the outcome is little additional

---

* Just to keep from repetition, assume that in any cases mentioned here the techniques discussed will be legal and within standard ethical principles.

information. The more the investigator gathers information about the target, the more he will learn. The more he knows about the target, the better is the bedrock of information to inform his decisions in the matter.

With enough information gathered about a target, the assessor may well be able to answer several questions about the process of the case. However, generally the assessor will set out to answer only one specific question (such as one of those set forth here). The assessor will gather information sufficient for him or her to form a conclusion (if possible), and that information will be oriented to the main question.

How Does IPA Get Its Information?

Gathering the kind of information needed for an assessment requires the usual tools of investigation, some of which were mentioned in the previous discussion. The tools include, but are not limited to, interviews, use of established assets (informants), examination of seized evidence, monitoring of communications, surveillances, pretext elicitation, false-flag operations, and review of existing records, whether official (like medical, arrests, court, etc.) or nonofficial (like personal letters provided by reliable, cooperating witnesses or trash covers).

There are some established techniques that still help the investigator in the process of ensuring that reliable information is gained from whatever interviews the investigator conducts. An older, somewhat outdated, article about IPA suggested several guidelines for interview techniques that are still useful (Ault, 1995): (1) Ask the same question of many sources. (2) Determine how the source knows the information. (3) Determine when the source learned the information. (4) Determine how long the target has exhibited the described behavior. These steps ensure that the information we receive about a target has some relevance to the IPA process.

In addition, there is a section appended to this chapter that contains one version of a list of questions of the type that should be asked by investigators in interviews. Various assessors place emphasis differently on their own "pet" information from questionnaires to draw conclusions. But, there are only so many questions that assist in the process. Most of those questions are attached here. Even so, there may be more that have proven useful to you. Do not discard them if they are not presented in this chapter.

It has been shown time and again throughout the years it has been used by FBI and FBI assessors that the IPA can be of great benefit to the investigator. The results of the process can provide an investigator with alternative solutions to problems he or she faces in the course of handling a case. In fact, the proven value of the technique over the years is such that to ignore IPA is to ignore an important asset.

A sample IPA questionnaire is provided at the end of this chapter, but it has been minimized, and some questions and topics have been removed to fit the space available. This form has undergone numerous revisions and is readily adaptable to specific types of inquiry, such as assessment in workplace violence situations.

Application to the Criminal Interview

In large law enforcement departments, the detective may be able to obtain the services of an in-house professional assessor with the required education and experience to assist in drawing conclusions based on all the compiled case data. Other investigators may have to rely on their own training, experience, and good judgment to assess how the indirect personality material can best be used to determine a target's vulnerabilities.

Perhaps a few examples may highlight the process. After the initial step of gathering the information and reviewing it, some themes may be readily located by combining specific pieces of information. For example, the following IPA form deals with a target's functioning in relationship to those who have exercised power and control through his life. The questioning about his dealings with his parents, coworkers, the military (if applicable), and authority figures such as law enforcement may provide data that can be combined for guidance in the type of officer who does the interview and the approaches he takes. If the target has difficulties with authoritarian leaders, the officer may grumble a bit about his bureaucracy while in the rapport-building phase. These same data may be used with the mind-reading and the planting-seeds techniques, by the officer, relating to the target (suspect) that a prior offender had difficulties in dealing with authority and describing how that trait shaped the current offender's crimes, just as is found in the crime being investigated. The investigator may add that her tough-minded and authoritarian sergeant has told her that every technique possible will be tried in this case, even though the results will point toward the offender (planting seeds). The IPA form lists, for example, how the traits of rebelliousness, rationality, practicality, and neatness (orderly) may be used to match the traits of a good suspect while providing guidance to interviewing approaches.

The protocol also covers indicators of anxiety and stress during all time periods of the target's life. If the anxiety is a new feature or noticeably increased around the time of the crime, these situations are often accompanied by the target having sleep and appetite difficulties; that combination of current traits could provide guidance in multiple phases of the interview. If, for example, the violent crime has "disorganized" features, that aspect is consistent with that type of offender. The sloppy, disoriented offender is susceptible to empathic approaches, including, perhaps, themes and the techniques of mind reading and planting seeds. The final page of the IPA assessment questionnaire has a list of traits such as loner, disorderly, nervous, and insecure that may form a pattern applicable to the example.

Alternatively, if the crime being investigated is an "organized" homicide, the questionnaire may reveal traits that correspond with the manner in which a target approaches the maintenance and care of his vehicle are in general keeping with that type of offender. That offender also is more prone to respond to the production of evidence that may be in hand or made plausible by bait/dangle questions and the planting of seeds.

Amended Indirect Personality Assessment Questionnaire*

The following questions have been developed to gather information about the personality and behavior of a particular individual. Data provided will be utilized in formation of an assessment of the individual's personality and potential behavior. The accuracy of the assessment is enhanced by and dependent upon the quality and quantity of facts provided. Assessment(s) often supply valuable insight for use during personal interviews.

Instructions: These questions should be posed to multiple individuals who have personal knowledge of the Subject. Answer as many questions as possible, providing narrative answers (rather than simple yes/no answers) to enhance the overall assessment. If more space is needed, write on the back of the paper.

* From The Academy Group, Inc., a forensic behavioral science company. Consultation/ Training/Research/Investigations.

Individual Filling Out Form	
Name	Position
Part I: Family History	
1.	Subject's full name
2.	Subject's date of birth
3.	Subject's place of birth
4.	Arrest history (if applicable)
5.	What was the socioeconomic status of family when Subject was growing up?
6.	Number of brothers. Number of sisters.
8.	Subject's place in birth order?
9.	Are both parents still living? Mother Yes ☐ No ☐ Father Yes ☐ No ☐
	If parents are alive, where do they live? Mother Father
	If deceased, when did they die? Mother Father
10.	Describe the nature of Subject's relationship with parents (close, distant, other)?
	Was Subject's relationship with parents always this way? Please explain.
12.	Which parent was dominant?
13.	Was either parent absent, ineffective, or inconsistent when Subject was growing up? Explain.
14.	What date(s) are significant to the Subject? For example, anniversaries, birthdays, date of death, etc.
15.	What religion, if any, did the family practice? To what degree?
17.	Is Subject currently religious? To what degree?
18.	Where does Subject currently reside (address, type of dwelling, neighborhood and community setting)?
19.	Who does Subject live with (name, age, relationship)?
21.	Does Subject have friends or acquaintances? How many of each does Subject have?
23.	Has Subject ever belonged to any groups or organizations (when, name of group, position held by Subject)?

24.	Does Subject express distrust of any person, organization, or group? If so, please explain.
	Part II: Physical Characteristics and Appearance
29.	Does Subject have any distinguishing marks, scars, or tattoos? If yes, describe.
30.	Is Subject self-conscious or proud of these characteristics? Please explain.
31.	Does Subject have any mannerism or gestures that stand out (nervous habits, changes in voice patterns when nervous, upset or angry, etc.)? If so, describe.
32.	Does Subject do anything to change or camouflage any of the characteristics or mannerisms noted in questions 27–30? If yes, explain.
33.	What is your overall impression of Subject's appearance (excessively neat, sloppy, dirty, etc.)?
	Part III: Health
34.	What is Subject's current state of health? Has it changed recently?
36.	Has Subject noticeably gained or lost weight? If so, describe.
37.	Subject exhibited, been treated for, or had a history of mental health problems?
38.	Is there a history of mental health problems in Subject's family? If so, describe.
39.	Does Subject use alcohol or drugs? Yes ☐ No ☐ If yes, has this increased/decreased recently? Increased ☐ Decreased ☐ No change ☐
	Is Subject's use of these substances normal/excessive?
41.	What are Subject's sleeping habits (early or late riser, night or day person, sleeps more than normal)?
42.	Have there been any recent changes in Subject's sleeping habits? If yes, describe.
	Part IV: Education
43.	What is the highest level of education Subject has achieved? When and where?
44.	If school was not completed, why not?
	Part V: Employment
49.	Is Subject presently employed? If yes, what type of work? What skill level?
50.	Name of company where Subject is employed. How long with this company?

51.	Describe Subject's work performance (tardy, absent, lazy, efficient, professional, etc.).
52.	Does employment require Subject to interact with coworkers, supervisors, subordinates or the public? If yes, describe.
53.	What is the nature of Subject's occupation (type of job, skill level, etc.)?
	Part VI: Marriage and Children
57.	Is Subject currently married or in a common law relationship? If yes, for how long and to whom? Please describe relationship.
58.	Is marriage important to Subject? If yes, why?
59.	Does Subject have marital problems? If yes, describe.
61.	How many times has Subject been married? If married more than once, to whom, when, and how long?
62.	Does Subject have children? If yes, with whom, ages, gender, and who has custody?
	Part VII: Hobbies and Leisure
65.	Does Subject have any special talents or skills? If yes, describe.
66.	What does Subject do in his spare time?
68.	What type of reading, movie, or video material does Subject read or view?
70.	Does Subject play any games or sports? If yes, describe.
71.	What does Subject spend money on?
72.	Does Subject own a vehicle? Describe make, model, condition, how well maintained, etc.
	Part VIII: Behavior and Personality
73.	Knowing what you know about Subject, how would you describe him or her (warm, sincere, loner, macho, decent, angry, happy, distant, etc.)? Please explain.
75.	What failure has Subject experienced (marital, financial, career, etc.)?
76.	What is important to Subject (family, status, money, possessions, sports, other)?
78.	Does Subject display emotion? If yes, give examples.
79.	What makes Subject happy? What makes Subject sad? What makes Subject angry?
82.	Is Subject a risk taker? If yes, give examples.

83.	Is Subject truthful? If no, under what circumstances does he or she fabricate lies?
84.	Does Subject have a sense of humor? If yes, explain.
85.	Does Subject use profanity? If yes, to what degree?
86.	Does Subject handle stress well? If no, explain.
87.	In addition to how Subject relates to coworkers and supervisors, how does he deal with others in positions of authority, including officers in the military, if he served, teachers and the principal in school, law enforcement, and others who hold positions of power?
90.	How you would describe Subject's temperament?
91.	What is Subject's opinion of himself?
92.	How many close friends does Subject have?
94.	Does Subject own weapons? If yes, describe.
95.	Has Subject ever talked about harming himself or ever attempted suicide?
96.	To your knowledge, has Subject ever been violent? If yes, describe.
97.	Has Subject ever talked about or bragged about hurting others?
98.	Has Subject ever threatened others?

Part IX: Narrative Description
Please use this space to add any other information that would aid in understanding Subject's personality. Add another sheet of paper, if necessary.

Personality Characteristics						
Circle the appropriate number which most closely represents subject's personality.						
Introvert (reserved)	1	2	3	4	5	Extrovert (Outgoing)
Loner (prefers to be alone)	1	2	3	4	5	Social (enjoys company of others)
Self-centered ("me" oriented)	1	2	3	4	5	Concern for others
Passive (submissive)	1	2	3	4	5	Aggressive (dominant)
Emotional (lead with the heart)	1	2	3	4	5	Rational (lead with the head)
Mood swings (seesaw emotions)	1	2	3	4	5	Even tempered (consistent emotions)
Disorderly (sloppy)	1	2	3	4	5	Orderly (neat)
Irresponsible	1	2	3	4	5	Responsible
Rebellious (risk taker)	1	2	3	4	5	Conservative (conformist)
Vindictive (gets even)	1	2	3	4	5	Forgiving (lets bygones be bygones)
Nervous (anxious)	1	2	3	4	5	Calm (laid back)
Pessimistic (glass half empty)	1	2	3	4	5	Optimistic (glass half full)
Rigid (uncompromising)	1	2	3	4	5	Flexible (easygoing)
Dependent	1	2	3	4	5	Independent
Idealistic	1	2	3	4	5	Practical
Insecure	1	2	3	4	5	Confident
Manipulator	1	2	3	4	5	Straightforward

Bibliography

Ault, R. L., Jr., and R. Hazelwood. Indirect Personality Assessment. In *Practical Aspects of Rape Investigation: A Multidisciplinary Approach*, edited by R. R. Hazelwood and A. W. Burgess, 205–218. New York: CRC Press, 1995.

Ault, R. L., and J. T. Reese. A Psychological Assessment of Crime Profiling. *FBI's Law Enforcement Bulletin* (March 1980).

Costa, P., McCrae, R. *NEO Personality Inventory, Revised (NEE PI-R)*. Lutz, FL: PAR Psychological Assessment Resources, Inc. 1994, 2003.

Dorland's Illustrated Medical Dictionary. Philadelphia: Saunders, 1981.

Humphreys, L. *Tearoom Trade: Impersonal Sex in Public Places*. Chicago: Aldine. 1970, 1975.

Interviewer's Verbal Strategies

7

MICHAEL R. NAPIER

Contents

Case 7.1

FBI Agent Jim Norman: Do you know why we are here?
Timothy McVeigh: That **thing** in Oklahoma City, I guess.

In Minneapolis a number of years ago, I met with retired FBI (Federal Bureau of Investigation) agent Jim Norman, who had played a pivotal role as the overall case agent, or lead investigator, in the investigation of the anarchist bombing of the Alfred P. Murrah Building in Oklahoma City by Timothy McVeigh. He related that he was sent to interview McVeigh and take him into federal custody after he had been stopped by the Oklahoma Highway Patrol for driving without a license plate and wearing a concealed Glock pistol under his jacket. The former agent explained that he wanted to get McVeigh's attention and to test him for indicators of guilt and guilty knowledge. To do that, he had McVeigh brought into a room and, sitting across from McVeigh, asked the question in Case 7.1.

McVeigh's answer is a classic response that strongly indicates involvement in a crime because his word choice about himself as the offender is nondescript and minimized and does not reflect on the reality of the bomb or the horror of the crime. This approach is encouraged by both Reid's Behavioral Analysis Interview system (Inbau et al., 2004) and Warren Holmes (Holmes, 1995).

Several authors have supplemented instruction and tips received from various sources about the verbal techniques available to interviewers of victims, witnesses, and suspects. Some of the verbal tactics discussed in this chapter were acquired by experience, but others were learned from formal training and reading materials provided by Reid and Associates, the FBI, the Central Intelligence Agency (CIA), and the Department of Defense Polygraph Institute. Other tips were collected in personal conversations from others in the field of investigations. The officer truly dedicated to mastering the interviewing process is encouraged to consult the sources cited at the end of each chapter.

Asking the correct question, with the appropriate style, and recognizing the most likely response from an innocent person or one who is involved in a crime may set the stage for establishing the officer's confidence and forcefulness in further questioning. With a crime the magnitude of the Oklahoma City bombing, anyone not involved in the crime would use phrases such as devastating, unbelievable, terror beyond belief, a crime against humanity. Only someone needing to provide distance from crime or to salve their conscience would refer to it as "that thing."

Many of the most effective questions that can be put to victims, witnesses, or suspects have grown into non-law-enforcement folk tales passed from one generation to the other. They involve human nature as witnessed by generations on generations. For example, my mother told me that liars cannot look you in the eye or stand up straight. Likewise, I was advised that people are more likely to praise themselves than to demean themselves with personally unkind statements or labels. She also instructed that, "It is not always what you say to someone, but how you say it." I and many others have found that advice to be right on the mark, as well as an effective interviewing guide. Experience has validated that advice.

Case 7.2

As the supervisor of the bank fraud squad in Los Angeles, I took a call from one of the largest banks in southern California. It came in at almost 5:00 p.m. on a Friday evening. The bank official advised of the discovery that several hundred thousands of dollars were missing from the bank's vault. That was not a situation that could be put off until Monday morning. It does not require a strong imagination to realize that I was not going to be popular when I sent most of my squad to the bank on a Friday night during the infamous Los Angeles rush hour traffic. A senior agent was designated to report back as soon as he understood the circumstances of the case. When he called, he advised: "The manager of the branch was waiting at the door for us, and the first thing he said was that he was glad to see us because he had a thief in his employ and wanted him caught." The agent was highly experienced and did not require guidance, but I offered that the interview of the manager could be placed on hold because he was not a likely suspect. My decision was based on the manager's use of the word "thief, a demeaning term" and proved to be correct.

This chapter focuses on questioning victims, witnesses, and subjects. The material is divided into various sections, such as that dealing with an officer's attitude and demeanor, question formation, question type and style, dangle questions, and undermining a suspect's confidence in himself.

Freshness and Sincerity

In my estimation, the number one personal quality of a successful interviewer or interrogator is the ability to project an aura of sincerity through each step of the process. I am in agreement with Inbau et al. (2004) that the interviewer must "bleed sincerity." His credibility will be established in part by the interviewee's assessment of his reliability, knowledge, professionalism, and genuineness. If he shows signs of hypocrisy or untruthfulness when gathering background information or indicating an interest in the interviewee as a person, the interviewer's personal credibility will be in tatters. This will happen long before he must rely on that credibility when making his "pitch." Sincerity is the foundation for all tactics and strategies involving interview procedures.

Along with sincerity, the signals sent or gestures made by the interviewer must have the "feel" of freshness. Messages sent by the officer will likely be dead on arrival if they lack the impression of originating with that person and have the feel of crispness and sparkle. The burden on the investigator is to make his sales pitches and themes seem fresh, new, and original even though he has used them time and time again. He must be like a stage actor at the end of the season, making each pronunciation as genuine as it was on opening night.

Necessary Groundwork: Structuring of an Interview

When I teach interviewing to a law enforcement audience, I often pose the question, "When you are doing an important or critical interview, how many minutes pass before you ask a suspect if he is involved in the crime?" The typical answer is less than 10 minutes. This approach shortchanges the interview process, case solution, and professional investigating. Long before asking the "did-you-do-it question," a considerable amount of time should have been devoted to getting to know and understand the qualities of the person being interviewed.

Some investigators, particularly early in their career, find confidence and comfort by utilizing a system for initiating an interview. It is strongly urged that the criminal interviewer impose a discipline on his process rather than wander through the interview jumping frome one topic to the next. It is more beneficial to the investigation when the process is paced in a logical order because interviewing can be a stressful and demanding undertaking, but it does not need to be. A steady pace allows time to observe the characteristics of the person, consider the current answer, and think ahead to the series of questions. The officer has many particulars to notice. One should be whether the interviewee is patient, confident, rehearsed, genuinely cooperative, able to look you in the eye, or in possession of techniques by which he accepts or defers personal responsibility. By using an interview template, the detective forces disclosure of more than basic information and will uncover the interviewee's interview strategy and personal traits. If reading the nonverbal channel of communication is planned, the subject is placed in a position where he gives up those behaviors in a nonconfrontational and less-stressful procedure. From that context, they become the yardstick for measuring truthfulness and deception later in the contact.

By having an established format, there are several benefits. First, because he has "been there, done that," he is at ease at a time when he is being evaluated by the interviewee for his confidence and competence. Having a tried-and-true routine adds polish to his manner. The set routine also ensures that all pertinent points are covered and not overlooked.

Most significantly, he is forced to spend time getting to know the person before him, and he establishes a basis for evaluating the interviewee over the course of the contact. As with most paperwork generated in an inquiry, the background format, found in the Appendix (Structuring an Interview), is discoverable by a defense attorney. The upside is that it also may be used as a powerful testimonial tool. It is a memory enhancer and may also validate specific information obtained or the basis for decisions and conclusions made throughout the interview.

Attention is called to the Structuring an Interview form in the Appendix. The material on the form has to sound as if it comes from the personality of the officer to have a ring of validity. Therefore, like all other interview techniques, it should be edited to fit the individual officer's personality and speaking mannerisms. The form is somewhat encoded, so it is difficult for someone to steal a meaningful glance at it. In that eventuality, it also contains data covering more situations than any one particular interview, so the interviewee will not know which topics have been chosen to be asked. A small tick mark or underlining a first letter of a word may serve to remind the officer of those items intended to be used in a particular context. Table 7.1 contains an explanation of the form.

The form is divided into three sections so that the interview will flow over a range of topics as each sector becomes more aggressive and more directly focused on the crime. The sections are labeled "Personal History Section," "Transition to Crime Specifics," (see Table 7.2) and the "Interview Plan." Those divisions need not appear on the actual form used. The form may be retyped to suit the officer.

Many of the first items, particularly in the personal history portion, are predictable and routine, and no further comment is necessary. Each topic listed has a purpose, one not likely understood by the interview subject. Some questions may form a basis for choosing themes or pitches to be utilized later. Some are there to assist in probing the nature of the individual.

Case 7.3

As an example of how an inquiry about their employment was used in cases of thefts from federally insured banks, I inquired of each suspect whether employees were allowed to bring a purse and coat to their teller stations. They usually were allowed to bring personal items to their stations. In the confrontational stage, this knowledge was combined with the projection technique, and the message was brought home by asking a series of questions: "Who knows the most about protecting money, you or the bank?" "Don't you see that they made it too easy for this loss to occur? It is almost like they set you up." "You agree, don't you, that if they had used proper security you would never have taken that final step?"

Interview Flow

The structure of an interview generally should flow smoothly from one segment to another. The exception is when transitioning to the guilt phase, which features accusatory questions. A slight pause should be used to separate the

Table 7.1   Explanation of the Structuring an Interview Form

Personal History Section	Starts at top of form and ends with "Results Prior Invest."
Transition to Crime Specifics	Begins with "Your role this crime" and ends with "How would U have done it?"
Interview Plan	Immediately follows the Transition section.
V W S	Circle correct subject status: Victim, Witness, Suspect.
M S D W E	Marital status choices: Married, Single, Divorced, Widowed, Engaged.
Spse/FmrSpouse	Represents attempt to engage in discussion about the spouse or former spouse and some situations naturally encountered between couples to see if he uses projection or minimization to explain problems in the relationship.
Mom/Dad—Spent Time—Know Diff	Is nonthreatening to innocent but raises character questions in the guilty. "Did your parents spend time with you explaining things that you must do because they are 'right' and things you should never do because they are 'wrong'?" Likely answer is "Yes," which prompts the question, "Do you understand the issue today [theft, rape, homicide, etc.] would be wrong?" "So, you do know the difference between right and wrong? Right?"
Pass On?	This phrase is connected to preceding item. Reinforces concept of right and wrong by asking if he is passing to his children the values of right and wrong. If affirmative answer is received, it can serve as foundation for questions later when comparing the standards set for his children regarding specific situations (i.e., tell the truth, take responsibility, etc.). He is then asked, "Do you expect more of your 8-year-old than you do of yourself?"
Employment and Rate/ Problems	Request subject to rate his employer and ask if he has any problems at work. Question designed to get disclosure of how subject handles authority issues and other problems, use of RPMs (rationalizations, projections, and minimizations), and so on. If issue is internal theft, can provide theme of "If only they had [treated you right, provided health care, etc.], you would never have done ____."
Military Svc/MOS/ Discharge/Problems	Was he in the military? How did he handle authority? Was he ever reprimanded? MOS means his assigned area of training. Regarding discharges, some will claim "medical" or normal discharge, which prompts inquiry regarding what those terms mean and whether they were honorable discharges.
Med Hist. Opinion Current Health	Designed to obtain data for defending admissions and confessions later because he did not declare problems that would interfere with interview situation.
Mental Hist. Counseling—Nervousness	As above. Determine if ever had counseling for any issues, such as anger control, marital issues, and so on.
Today—/Medication/ Sleep/Nrm/Alcohol/ Narco/Drugs	As above. What is his functioning status on date of interview? Was his previous night's sleep normal? If not, why not? Is he worried about the interview? This provides areas to explore.

Table 7.1 Explanation of the Structuring an Interview Form (Continued)

Tell Me About Self, Sports/ Leisure/Like Yourself/Why	Aims for self-disclosure by asking personal question. How does he spend his time? Does he like the person he is? Why or why not?
Rate-Truthful%/Honest/%/ Who Do You Admire?	Questions are not a challenge to the innocent but may raise internal issues with the guilty. This is a request to have subject rate himself. Note two places to rate himself regarding truthfulness using scale of 0 to 100. It may be advantageous to challenge **any** answer given. "Are you telling me you are 100% truthful on every issue?" Or, "Are you telling me you are only 70% truthful?" Followup with, "Let me ask again using the standard of truthfulness on important issues because you know today's issue is important." This inquiry sends a signal that the interview is going to be thorough, and questioning his answer may cause some internal distress in a deceptive party. It is revealing of this person, but also of American society, regarding whether anyone is admired. If they have personal idols, inquire about qualities that make them worthy. Ask later, "Do you measure up to your idol's values of honesty and truthfulness?" This may generate internal "conscience."
Ever Involved Any Criminal Situations?	Any involvement in prior criminal acts raises issues of predisposition regarding crime under investigation. Do not be surprised that disclosure is not forthcoming.
Results Prior Invest.	How did he handle his prior criminal situation? Did he plead guilty? Was he convicted (after spending money on an attorney)? Did he confess?
Upsets in Life Last 6 Mo./ Year	This question probes for difficulties in his personal life that could have acted as a "triggering cue," propelling him into the criminal acts.
Interview Plan rows: Important Topics; Names, Dates, Players; Techniques	Interviewing can be a high-pressure situation. The prompts serve as reference to case data. The "techniques" column may contain coded references to ploys planned for some part of the interview (e.g., GC/BC could represent use of good cop/ bad cop scenario or a question about possibly being on a video surveillance tape from the crime scene area).

preceding nonconfrontational segment from the confrontational phase, in which the questions are stronger and more personal. In the accusatory phase, the demeanor and attitude of the officer is going to change, and the pause will lay the groundwork for that change.

Experienced interviewers recognize the role of momentum in the interview, but more importantly in an interrogation. Momentum keeps the process rolling along with few pauses that allow for the subject to mull over options while keeping the pressure on him for an admission or confession. Maintaining momentum should be a high-priority technique for the police officer. The

Table 7.2   Transition to Crime Specifics

Question or Comment	Likely Verbal Responses
What was your role in this crime?	T: Expect an immediate and emphatic denial of any involvement. Look for nonverbal honesty gestures. D: It is likely the question will be met with a delayed answer, which will consist of a weak denial.
Do you have an alibi for when this occurred?	T: "Absolutely! Do I need one? I was at … ." D: The question is answered with a question: "When was it again that this happened? I think I was … ."
How do you believe this crime happened?	T: "It seems to me that it required … [planning or some expertise or was simple]." D: It is likely he will attempt to distance himself from this crime by denying any speculative thoughts.
What was your reaction when you heard of _____ crime?	T: "I was shocked and thought that whoever did this should have to pay the highest price." D: "I thought it was just another person acting out for personal gain. It was just another crime" [adjust to severity of crime, murder vs. financial].
I have a long list of people to talk with. How do you feel about being interviewed today (at this location, by the police)? FU: How do you feel about being chosen for this interview?	T: "This is really a bad time. I am in the middle of an audit, but if I can help, ask away. Let's get it done." D: "This is really a bad time. I am in the middle of an audit. You guys are really great, real professional, and do a fine job" [flattery].
Who is the most likely (type) person to do this?	T: "A depraved maniac must have done it; a normal person would never do this sort of thing." D: "Someone who has a bit of a problem and needs some help did it" [adjust to crime, i.e., someone who has a problem with the company or management].
Why would someone say you are the doer of this crime?	T: "They would have to be absolutely crazy and wrong. I have no association with crime or criminals. This will be verified as you investigate." D: "Someone has a grudge against me. Likely, they are the one who did it" [adjust to type of person being contacted, i.e., criminal associate vs. person with positive reputation].

Table 7.2   Transition to Crime Specifics (Continued)

Question or Comment	Likely Verbal Responses
Is there anyone you believe would absolutely not do the crime?	T: "There are several people above suspicion. Tom, Dick, Harry [etc.] would never stoop to this sort of thing." D: "How would I know? It could be anyone" [attempts to keep the suspect population as large as possible so he does not standout].
What should happen when the person is identified (or if it is a false report)?	T: "Hang them or at least prosecute them. They have caused a lot of people major headaches [an innocent person could have gone to jail]" [harsh]. D: "It depends on why they did it. Probably they have problems, need counseling, go easy on them" [soft, generous].
Motive: Why would someone do this crime?	The question is similar to the one regarding the type of person, so expect similar answers.
Opportunity: Of everyone you know, who most likely had the best chance to do this _____? (name crime)	T: "This had to be an inside job, someone who works there [or knew her]. I would have a look at Larry, Moe, and Curly." D: "Beats me. It could have been anyone who was out that night [or needed money]."
Means: Talent to do the crime. In your opinion, was this a difficult _____ (name crime) to do? From your associations, who would have the ability to get this done?	T: "I would guess that it took some skill and knowledge to peel that safe. That is who I would look for—someone with that knowledge or who had done it before." D: "Hell, I don't know. Likely, any fool could have done this thing" [will keep suspect pool large and uses minimizing term, soft word].
Would you trust this person in the future?	T: "No! Steal from me once, you will steal again." D: "I believe people who make simple mistakes like this should be given a second chance. It's in the Bible."
What will investigative results show about you?	T: "We don't need to wait for those results, but they will show that I am clean, uninvolved, and honest, not a lowlife like this thug." D: "Who can say? People like to tell stories about me, and they always exaggerate and tell only the worst possible things. The final report will likely be way off the mark. I hope it shows that I did not do this thing."
Bait: Choices for bait may be as follows: We may have you on video; we may have found your fingerprints; someone saw you; other evidence was found connecting you to this crime.	T: "It is not possible for you to have me on video or have my fingerprint from the crime scene. I was not there when this crime happened." D: "Let me think. I may have touched something when I was there before this thing went down, and I was over there earlier in the day" [changed story].

Table 7.2　Transition to Crime Specifics (Continued)

Question or Comment	Likely Verbal Responses
If a financial audit is done, what will it show about how you spend money?	Expect same type of answers as with polygraph and hypnosis questions.
If my supervisor wants you to take a polygraph, are you willing? FU: What will results be when you are asked questions about you doing the crime? FU: Ask the same questions but substitute use of hypnosis instead of a polygraph.	In my experience, both the truthful and the deceptive will generally agree to take the polygraph. Fewer will agree to hypnosis. This is a good and valid question to ask even where polygraphs are forbidden by law. It is the follow-up question, literally asked within seconds of the first, that indicates who should continue under suspicion. D: If the involved individual initially agrees, he will, upon asking of follow-up question, immediately backpedal, providing excuses why he cannot take the test, for instance, "I have sinus problems and take three Tylenol tabs a day"; "Don't you know those aren't admissible?"; "I will need to check with my attorney"; "I don't really believe in them."
Do people steal from the company? FU: What is the easiest way to steal?	T: "Some few probably do, but most of these people are totally honest. You might check out … ." D: "Heck, everybody steals one time or another. It seems like it would be easy, something everyone could figure out."
How would you have done it?	T: "I would not have done it. But, from what I know from the paper and some gossip, it seems that a diversion was needed and it took more than three people." D: "I have no idea how these things are done. I am not an investigator. That's your job to figure this out."

D, likely deceptive response; FU, follow-up or alternative question; T, likely truthful response.

interview form/plan will assist with meeting this goal. When momentum is lost, it may be necessary to restart an interview from ground zero.

Case 7.4

At the request of a local police department I was interviewing a suspect in a multiple murder case. Having spent several hours with the suspect over two prior contacts, we knew each other well by the time the third interview began. This final contact occurred on a Saturday in the interview room in the investigations unit. A large, clearly visible sign was posted by the interview room forbidding smoking. The sign bore the commander's name. As luck would have it, the commander was in the office on this

Saturday. After a long period of reworking information uncovered in the prior interviews, this contact progressed with the aim of obtaining new data. The subject had been incarcerated for a while and had few opportunities to smoke. Following a long period of interviewing, he asked if he could smoke. Mindful that progress was being made, I put him off with a promise that he could smoke "in a little while." He made some interesting and helpful statements, but following those, he renewed his request for a smoke. Again, he was put off with the same promise. More pieces of guilty knowledge were provided, but he again asked for a smoke. This time, he was adamant and threatened to end the interview. I consulted with the investigator, and he asked his commander. The commander's response was an inflexible and unequivocal, "No!" It was then necessary to secure the elevator and transport the prisoner to a caged area from which he could not escape. He was allowed to smoke a couple of cigarettes. Once back in the room, all momentum had been lost, and he acted as if he had never spoken to me before. To this day, I wonder what might have been gained for the price of a cigarette during the interview. The case remains unsolved.

Stimulating "Readable" Behavior

In a criminal inquiry, additional anxiety beyond that inherent in an interview by authorities should be introduced in phases. The questions used in the Personal History section of the Structuring an Interview form should, by design, not generate noticeable anxiety in the interviewee. The questions employed in the Transition to Crime Specifics should cause some tension only in a guilty person, or one with guilty knowledge, because they are related to their crime. These questions are not threatening to an innocent party. The Interview Plan segment is confrontational and accusatory, which will be stressful for a subject who was involved in the crime. As the tension and stress increase, a criminal target is more likely to unconsciously seek relief by displaying nonverbal indicators of deception. The truthful person generally should not be threatened by any of the questions, absent defensiveness caused by the officer's demeanor, attitude, and tone of voice.

The autonomic nervous system (ANS) exists for several reasons. Of interest to the policeman is its function in protecting a person. When an individual feels threatened and anxious, certain body functions take on a protective mode without conscious instructions. One of the observable changes is when the tension seeks outlet in the form of nonverbal gestures. In the automatic search for escape from the tension and anxiety, a person will have sensations, likely below the level of awareness, that will require a physical output (e.g., movement of the eyes and limbs, touching the nose and face). These physical changes and responses are reliably known to result in almost predictable movements. The physiological importance for the interviewer is that he may create these conditions by asking questions that stimulate the ANS in the deceptive person, causing physical responses that are time honored, inborn, and readable.

Observers of human behavior (Inbau et al., 2004) have correlated those innate physical (nonverbal) reactions to verbal responses resulting from the same stimulus. The stimulus is the calculated choice of questions that threaten the deceptive person. For the interviewer, this means he has two channels in which he may see and hear nearly predictable results stimulated by his questions. This awareness of needing to track multiple tasks is demanding, but being forewarned regarding the likely responses from a deceptive or a truthful party makes the task easier.

It has long been understood in law enforcement circles that suspect interviewing should include, at a minimum, questions involving a person's means to commit the crime, his motive for engaging in the criminal acts, and whether he had the opportunity to be where the crime was committed. Holmes (1995) cited two additional areas for exploration. One is evidence connecting questions that explore potential confirmation that links the subject to the crime, the crime scene, or victim. Another is the topic of the subject's character, which includes his prior history of criminal behavior, his thoughts or plans for conducting criminal acts, or his predisposition for crime.

Using those five question topics, a number of other areas have been developed around the behaviors and elements of the crime. They are designed to probe for weaknesses or lies within the suspect's story and to cause him to change his statements or recant them entirely. Their use also has the benefit of forcing a person to choose how far he will verbally distance himself from the crime or the other players. They are designed to create a decision point for the interviewee, generate readable tension and stress in those attempting to deceive, and provoke verbal responses that are aligned with those expected of liars. They are built on a long-established history of police interviewing, and many have a solid psychological basis. Briefly stated, they place the interviewer in charge of the course of the inquiry and create verbal and nonverbal clues that can be read and interpreted.

An investigator with some imagination can conjure an entire array of questions to accomplish these goals. However, the questions are set forth in some books on interviewing (Holmes, 1995; Inbau et al., 2004; Zulawski and Wicklander, 2002). Some examples of these questions are contained on the Structuring an Interview form. Realize that no call of whether someone is truthful or deceptive can be made on any isolated verbal or nonverbal response. Reliability is gained by observing repeated similar signals that may be seen as a pattern of conduct under similar questioning.

Speculation

Regardless of the topic, people like to know what is going on in their community. They are interested in events that touch on their lives, even if only indirectly. People generally like to know secrets. When a crime occurs near a person's geographic location, the area of their residence, or place of employment, or to a friend or family member, their interest is piqued. People will ask questions about it, read the newspaper, or watch TV for information about the event and actively engage in speculation about the who, where, what, and why of the event. It is human nature. Speculation questions call for the interviewee to share with the officer their thoughts on what was done, by whom, and why it was done. Some will relate that they do not gossip or concern themselves with the business of others. If a potential suspect refuses to reflect about a crime, it may be because he has no need to ponder the issue: He may well know the answer. The refusal to speculate does not by itself reflect deception or lack of cooperation with a police investigation, but it should raise a red flag.

Delivering the Question

How a question is presented has an impact on the way an officer is viewed and how the interviewee responds. People, including those who want to assist the police, are often acutely attuned to the manner in which an officer goes about his questioning process, It seems this is especially the case with those who have a relationship with the victim, which would naturally cause them to be included in the early suspect pool (i.e., parents of missing children, spouse or boyfriend of a murdered or missing victim, or the businessman whose shop was robbed of an insured item). This is even more prevalent today, when there is more generalized distrust of authority and of the police specifically. If a person perceives prejudice, an attitude of superiority, a belief of guilt, or that the interview is only a formality since conclusions have already been made, his response will reflect his belief about the officer's sincerity, open-mindedness, and level of hostility toward him personally.

Should the officer display any of these traits, he will likely see escalating hostility in the responses from even the most cooperative person. The officer, seeing this hesitation, hostility, or resentment, may read it as a reluctance to cooperate or, worse, as evidence of deception. From that point forward, the interview will contain an escalation of reactions. In these circumstances, an officer may develop an ever-increasing feeling that he is being deceived by the interviewee, who is now looking more and more like a valid suspect. In reality, the officer has guided the escalating defensiveness by his original projection of suspicion or guilt.

The professional officer always checks the wording of his questions, his tone and inflection of voice, and how his words have an impact on the person being interviewed. A false reading of deception may be avoided by carefully planning how to approach each individual to ensure that there is no misunderstanding about the content and intent of each question. Those suspicions by an interviewee not only may affect the answer the officer receives to a particular question but also the answers he receives on all subsequent questions. Remember, it is not only what is said, but also how it is said.

Building Up to a Question

The following technique should not be overdone, as that will diminish its effectiveness. The interviewer should select only a few significant questions for this special treatment. By properly building up to those questions, the officer is ensuring that he has gained the subject's attention to the importance of the question. The buildup eliminates bluntness and incorporates the goal of a smoother delivery. A proper buildup includes three points. First, the officer places an emphasis on his qualifications in policing in general and in the area of specialization, such as homicide or sex crimes. Second, he provides two or three sentences about why the question is of significance to the interviewee. Last, he educates the person about the relevance of the question. While procuring the subject's attention, the officer should be carefully observing how the subject is reacting to each question.

Case 7.5

"Tom, I have been in policing for more than 15 years and investigating the specialized area of sexual violence for many of those years. I have learned that few areas of a criminal investigation of this type are more important than the scientific certainty of [computer-read fingerprints, DNA, or ballistic examinations]. In this case, we have the good fortune to have material that is being examined by forensic experts, and the results may well nail this case down. With all that in mind, will you voluntarily provide blood for scientific examination? That is your best bet to prove you are not involved in this case." An innocent party is most likely to readily agree to this. A questionable suspect may say he has concerns for privacy, sterility of the instruments, possible scientific error, his propensity to faint when he sees blood, or other excuses. Should a strong suspect balk at providing the material, a sales pitch around the value of cooperating and trying to earn some credit for being big enough to take responsibility for his criminal behaviors can be made along with the reminder that a court order may be obtained to get the item at issue.

This example may cause the guilty party to become concerned that he has overlooked some physical evidence, the possibility of a witness, camera surveillance, and so on. This may make him susceptible to verbal strategies that play on what aspects of the investigation are pending but may reveal his involvement. Bait or dangle questions also serve this purpose and are discussed below.

Question Formulation and Structure

Questioning a person is not an exercise in wasting time by just going through the motions. Questioning has a goal of obtaining information. The significance of some of the information sought may not be known at the specific moment an open-ended question is asked. How a question is structured may limit the amount of data received or even encourage a person to omit information. The omitted information may include areas that are not, at that point, known to be relevant. The use of an open-ended question is the best tool for obtaining most of the information available.

While no constitutional or lawful mandate exists requiring specific question types be used in criminal interviews and interrogations, the courts will react to the types of questions and question sequencing used. The courts may be positively impressed with a tactic and its results, or they be unhappy with the methods used. The court will nearly always be receptive to defense claims of improper questioning, planted data, or the suggestive or unduly leading question. Claims of officer contamination of the data pool via a question's format or structure are hard to offset.

Case 7.6

In a case of alleged child molestation, the responding officer interviewed a parent, who related her daughter's allegation of victimization by a man delivering furniture to the residence. After the officer understood the essential elements of the allegation, he next interviewed the young child. His opening comments to the child were intended to be reassuring and encouraging of a truthful answer to each of his questions. However, unwittingly, he subtly contaminated the interview by providing the following instruction to the child: "All I want you to do is tell me just what you told your Mom about what the man did."

The inclusion of the word *just* limits the parameters of his inquiry, denying any interest in additional information. He also prohibits the child from correcting any exaggerations or untruths that may have been communicated privately to the parent, thereby locking the child into only her original statements. His question opening the criminal subject should have been along the lines of the following: "Tell me the man who delivered the furniture."

The same open-ended question structure will well serve an investigator in nearly every type of inquiry. While the following instructions will seem easy to implement, the reality is that real effort by the officer is required.

The purest form of questioning without contamination is to ask open-ended questions. Until the habit of doing this is established, it requires alertness and discipline. One of the easiest allegations to make about the police interview product, either an admission or a confession, is to accuse the officer of supplying information that will later be claimed to have originated from the subject. The allegation of statement contamination is one of the most difficult for an officer to defend. His strongest defense is to demonstrate that no contamination came from the structure and content of his inquiries because he used open-ended questions.

His ally in this defense is to have written his critical questions in advance to demonstrate that they are free of corrupt words. A proper location for recording these details is in his interview plan and his report of the interview. The questions and answers may also be used within a written confession. By such solid planning and the utilization of those basic techniques, allegations made in adversarial proceedings can be defeated. This procedure is more effective than simply asserting the purity of the questions without anything to back up the claim, or to claim any contamination was inadvertent.

Open-ended questions begin with specific phrases, such as the following. "Explain how you were in the park on Friday night." "Describe the events at the park Friday night." "Tell me about what happened in the park Friday night." Note three things. First, the sentence is structured as a demand, not as a question ("explain …"; "tell me …"). Second, nothing in the statement gives away any investigative detail. Also, the question does not focus only on the storyteller as it would if the question was, "Tell me about what *you did* Friday night at the park."

Sapir (1992a,b; 1998) instructs his students in his scientific content analysis (SCAN) seminars that he can pick up a transcript of an interview or deposition, casually ruffle through the pages without reading any words, and identify who "won" the question-and-answer contest. If he sees short questions and long answers, the questioner won the contest. He calls it his

5%/95% theory. The question should make up 5% of the exchange, and the answer should constitute 95%.

Open-ended questions should be the question form (5%) because they call for a broad narrative from the person answering. A person intent on lying when discussing a substantial area of questioning will strive to keep his story tightly wound, providing the fewest details to remember and defend. The open-ended question throws a monkey wrench in his plans. They force early decision points for the interviewee, whether a victim, witness, or suspect. The interviewee has to decide whether to answer or not. The second decision point is, if they are going to answer, how much of the truth will they divulge. Also, if they answer, the questions require them to give up extensive data that they then have to keep track of and try not to contradict later. It is likely that some of the details they were planning on concealing will be revealed in the first interview or in the second or third rounds of questioning used to clarify their first version. This is best done by using only open-ended questions.

The open-ended question also provides an unwitting interviewee the opportunity to "leak" some detail that may reveal a greater depth of knowledge than was intended. Using their own words, the astute interviewer will latch on to those slipups and ask additional questions to determine what a specific word or phrase meant to the speaker. If the person intends to be deceptive, the open-ended question provides him that opportunity. Any lie told becomes a powerful weapon in the hands of an interviewer as those lies weaken the interviewee's position and deteriorate his confidence in putting one over on the interviewer. When used properly, a collection of lies can be made to "feel" like hard evidence. When telling lies, the interviewee also provides the opportunity to observe his traits when under the stress of lying. His stress level will increase when he is giving up information he would prefer to keep to himself. Added stress and anxiety increase the likelihood of more pronounced indicators of deception.

Questioning Format

The following is a simple, five-step process for interviewing and interrogating. The first step, which is in accordance with Sapir's program, (1992a,b; 1998) is to ask a broad, open-ended question that is really a command, such as "Tell me about Friday night." This shifts the burden to the interviewee as he must quickly decide how to answer and at what point to begin his story. If he questions where to begin his story or what topics he should include, no aid should be afforded to him. Let him decide all of the content of his statement. It is of no value if the statement has been tailored by any guidance provided by the interviewer. As Holmes (1995) stated, only the person interviewed should fill in any "voids" in his statement as those voids may be used later as an opening to obtain additional data.

Next, without assistance, correction, or interruption, the subject is allowed to tell his story, selecting the starting point, issues, and personalities included or omitted and the termination point. Some officers find these moments of silence difficult to handle. They often feel a need to interject themselves into the subject's narrative when he misstates some data or when it includes points the officer wants to cover at some other point. Let him tell his story uninterrupted. Interruptions are rude, carry a sense of judgment, and appear to be a play for power in an attempt to establish a position of dominance by the officer. Interruptions tend to signal the person to curtail or shorten his story, omitting information he may have intended to provide.

It is recommended that the officer provide a summary of the points following the subject's recitation. This allows the subject to correct misperceptions or incorrect statements and to amend his report. Or, the officer may pose the same question differently, requiring the subject to retell his narrative. Either way, the individual has committed himself to a position. In doing so, he has closed other avenues and approaches to that topic.

Should clarification be required because of obvious errors (e.g., times, street names, business locations, etc.), the interviewer should clarify them by again using an open-ended question dealing with only the part that needs clarification. For example, "Tom, tell me again about how you arrived at the park on Friday night." Once the statement is in its final version, the officer should use the paraphrasing or summarization technique described as a way of locking the person into his statement. Once the information is provided, the officer may move to additional topics, which will be explored via other open-ended questions.

All through the answers to each open-ended inquiry, the interviewer should intentionally adopt an attentive posture and a poker face. No reaction is allowed when obvious lies are told or the person slips up and unwittingly provides significant data. The official attitude projected by the officer should be one of a neutral seeker of the truth, one who is collecting data for future use.

Once it seems that the interviewee has fully answered each open-ended question and has been afforded the chance to correct any murky areas or mistakes, and the interviewer has recited his paraphrased summary, the data are to be documented. If serious omissions, lies, or suspected discrepancies are included in the statement, they should be documented as presented, and a notation should be made to rework that topic as the interview ends. If corrections are made later, those should also be recorded immediately following the written report of his original statement and introduced by proper phrases, such as "Later, the subject recanted [changed, altered, and amended] his statement to now say ... ."

Bait/Dangle Questions

Bait questions are also known as dangle questions. The names are derived from the questions' "dangling" possibilities before a suspect or because the question "baits" a suspect to change his story. There are many examples of individuals hearing what they want or expect to hear but not what is said. This can assist in the police interview. Bait questions are constructed carefully and with specifically chosen words, i.e., "Charlie, what if a new witness comes forward and identifies you as being at the scene?". They can also plant ideas about what may be discovered as the investigation progresses, allowing a subject to develop a fear that he will be identified or evidence will be found linking him to the victim or crime scene. Such concerns may make other questioning techniques more viable and lead to a confession. The bait question is a central part of the "mind-reading" technique discussed elsewhere.

Case 7.7

In the investigation of an abduction and murder of a young woman, a series of bait questions was used; the questions were instrumental in obtaining oral and written confessions, which included a map to the location of the victim's body. I was part of an FBI contingent assisting local and state authorities in the investigation, which had developed strong suspicions but not a single piece of evidence regarding the offender's identity. While the suspect was in custody on another charge, the director of the state investigative agency requested me to develop an interview plan. The plan was implemented by me and agents from the state. The subject was advised of his Miranda rights at the outset of the contact, and he provided a signed waiver. He was asked some very general questions about the missing woman, including whether he had ever given her a ride in his truck. He stated that she had never been in his truck, and further that he would speak with the agents but did not really want to talk about her. His denial, coupled with a series of dangle questions, proved to be his undoing. The interview plan called for general conversation, smoking cigarettes, and drinking Coke. During those activities, a few assertions about how the investigation of her disappearance and murder was being conducted were to be briefly mixed in and then dropped. The latter part was accomplished via bait and dangle questions.

Bait and dangle questions often begin with a "what-if" scenario in which the subject's attention is drawn to procedures and potentially discoverable evidence. Case 7.7, the questions and statements concentrated on trace evidence and other forensic evidence that was described as likely to be discovered. Some of the dangle questions were as follows:

"What will be your position if a single hair from the victim is discovered when your truck is processed? Oh, by the way, we found
your truck."

"Do you know how much blood is needed for testing to prove someone's identity? You know that even when someone has tried to
clean up their vehicle, they always miss someplace, such as under
the 'rolls' in the seat cover."

"How much interest will the victim's family have in the prosecutor
giving you a break as long as they do not have their daughter
back?"

On the second contact with this offender, he began by saying that
he was going to provide a complete statement. It is my contention that
the confession directly stemmed from the murderer considering all the
avenues and conclusions of the yet-to-be conducted investigation via
bait questions. The subject decided it was in his best interest to get some
"credit" by giving to the family the remains of their daughter.

Soft Words

Wordsmithing calls for carefully selecting words that are not offensive and
do not remind the interviewee of his failures or of the negative side of his
offenses. Soft words avoid mention of the penalties he faces if he takes responsibility for his behavior and admits what he did. It helps to soften the words
used when questioning and when making a sales pitch to do the right thing.
This involves substituting words that minimize the deeds (i.e., assault versus
rape, improper taking versus stealing, getting wild versus out of control, etc.).
The better approach is to refer to the incident as "that thing." I have never had
a person who did not know the incident and the details to which I was referring. I saw a news story about a famous baseball player who was caught, once
again, in possession of crack cocaine. One of his friends and fellow team-
mates was interviewed and only referred to "that thing that happened." If
that is how a person's friends would refer to a serious criminal act, that is the
way the interviewer or interrogator should also speak.

Case 7.8

Along with a police officer, I interviewed a boy in his late teens who was
the suspect in a series of arson fires that were becoming progressively
more dangerous. In the multihour interview, many incidents were discussed, but not one time were the words *fire* and *arson* used. The questions were structured as, "Remember that thing that happened over on

Oak Street? Remember how you started it using available material such as leaves and newspapers? Remember how it got out of hand, and you banged on the door and warned the woman inside? You should get credit for likely saving that woman's life." Note that the sales pitch also said something positive about the suspect.

Being calm while interviewing and interrogating is more effective than shouting, cursing, or slamming hands or papers on the table. Generally, little if anything is accomplished by this type of bravado. There is room for some theatrics when a specific point needs to be made, but only when it is planned. The officer should use control, reason, and practicality.

An attempt should always be made to say something positive about the subject of a criminal interview. This is important enough that a positive quality should be provided even if it has to be made up. People will speak more freely with someone who is nice to them. Do not overdo it and keep the comments of praise general.

Job of the Interviewer and the Interrogator

When functioning in the interview phase, the investigator's assignment is multifold. He should go out of his way not to alienate anyone and to get the most information possible. Some of that information may become evidence later when the case data is fleshed out, as the significance of a statement early in an investigation is often not known at that point. Information obtained in this phase locks a person into a position, and it is difficult for them to later change that position when new data are discovered, creating holes in his statements. In that regard, interviewing lays the foundation for a case; it determines how it will unfold and which investigative paths are most viable. This form of data gathering often assists in placing suspects in order from the most likely to the least likely. Again, the demeanor and attitude of the investigator in order to obtain the most, and the most reliable, facts is important.

When information obtained in the interview phase conflicts with other known data and a person becomes the focus of an inquiry, the interviewer morphs into an interrogator. Shifting gears from conversational to confrontational should be separated by a brief moment or two so the contrast is not severe. Now, the job description changes from that of obtaining data to challenging and validating information. By definition, interrogation is confrontational and accusatory, but there are other dimensions to this interrogation concept than just grilling a suspect.

The interrogator's primary job is to make admissions and confessions easy, painless to give, and to "feel" like the natural thing to do. This is most readily accomplished by way of RPMs as delivered within themes. This conclusion is so firmly held that the reverse is also a valid principle: Failure to use RPMs can make it difficult for an offender to confess.

For further examination of RPMs and the reasoning phase, a brief definition of terms is in order:

> *Rationalization* involves a person mentally reworking an entire scenario and arranging his role in a more favorable manner. He contrives to come up with "explanations" that satisfy him while hiding his true behaviors. For example, the police are called to a domestic situation after a woman has hit her spouse in the head with a lamp. The rationalized version as told by the spousal "victim" was that this was a sudden, uncalled-for attack. His story will not mention that he had been criticizing her all weekend with demeaning comments about her appearance, sexual abilities, and housekeeping skills.
>
> *Projection* is the attribution to another person or institution as the cause of an incident. It is always the fault of someone else. A bank teller told me she stole because of the lax security measures that invited theft. In the HBO documentary, *Murder: No Apparent Motive*, Edmund Kemper repeatedly cast blame for his serial killing of young coeds on his mother. He stated that he murdered the coeds because his mother worked for the university, and because of the way she raised him. He added a story about giving a ride to two hitchhiking women. They tried to provide him with directions to where they wanted to go. The directions were contrary to what he knew as the best way to get to their destination. Their directions would take them to the location where he had murdered two other women. His statement was, in effect, "If I follow their directions, they will take me to their death." Had he killed them, it would have been their fault.
>
> *Minimization* is an attempt to make the person's acts less serious to minimize their responsibility. With minimization, the acts seem less significant. In another bank teller theft situation, the employee may say that she stole the missing money, but it was only a small amount compared to all the money available to her for stealing.

As any crisis negotiator knows, the interviewer should not introduce rational ideas into his sales pitches early in the confrontational phase. In his attempts at reasoning with an offender, the interviewer is selling the position that now is the best time to clear up matters, and that there are benefits to confessing. With a serial murderer, I reasoned that the offender had, as in a poker hand, certain assets that he could cash in. In that case, his asset was the locations of the bodies of his victims. As noted in Chapter XX, the police interrogator presents only those matters that favor the rationale he is encouraging. He is not obligated to point out any liabilities associated with his theme or sales pitch.

RPMs and themes are the most powerful tool available to the interviewer turned interrogator. Themes may be divided into two categories: emotional and rational. The first category applies more to the use of rationalization, minimization, and projection as they appeal to hoped-for results and are not totally rational. The rational approach involves reasoning with a subject regarding why his defensive position will not work or why now is the best time to clear up the matter as opposed to waiting until attitudes against him harden. Examples of both types are contained in the Appendix.

For the investigator to appreciate how to use themes and RPMs, he should first understand the common reasons people confess. There are several reasons why a suspect would decide to confess, but there are two primary reasons. The first deals with a person who has some remorse or regret for what he has done. Many will try to display that emotion, but I am in agreement with Holmes's (1995) statement that this attitude applies to very few. More have regret, but the sorrow is primarily because they made mistakes and got caught.

The reality is that most people confess because of the options presented to them by the interviewer. Those options are couched in RPMs and themes, and the offender perceives that his offenses will be met with some degree of understanding, compassion, and leniency because of the way he designs his confession. The design of his confession is comprised of statements that minimize his foul deeds or project responsibility for his criminality on others. It is because of the interviewer's sincerity and delicate use of various techniques that the offender comes to believe he will get lenient treatment.

In fact, he is fully aware of how he should be treated by the criminal justice system that he is attempting to manipulate for leniency. In their search for ways to mitigate, improve, or avoid their rightful punishment, offenders will buy into concepts built into RPMs and themes. The officer, having demonstrated his sincerity in offering up modified scenarios, is also selling the belief that he can be trusted by the offender to be compassionate, understanding, and may tone down the offender's dark secrets.

In the case example of the murder of a young woman, the offender was asked "How much interest will the victim's family have in the prosecutor giving you a break as long as they do not have their daughter back?" Without any additional exploration of this concept, the offender interpreted the question as indicating that the family of the murdered victim would be extremely grateful for the recovery of their loved one. As he offered his confession to anally raping and murdering the victim and then hiding her body in an isolated field, he solicited the interviewer's assistance in assuring that her mother would be present and testify at his sentencing. He fully expected that his gesture of returning the body would earn him credit and stir the family to speak in favor of a lessened sentence. His horrid and senseless criminality instead motivated the victim's family to initiate a successful campaign to reinstate the death penalty in that state.

Magic Words: RPMs and Themes

What I intend to convey with the terminology of "magic words" is that some carefully chosen and strategically implemented words and phrases will lead to the best opportunity to obtain a confession. There is no literal "magic," but certain words and phrases can do amazing things. The magic words come in the form of RPMs, themes, stories, and a reasoning process that favors the police. The use of these techniques is both psychological and logical.

One of the suspected patterns validated through research conducted by the Behavioral Science Unit of the FBI in the late 1970s and into the 1980s was that violent and sexually violent criminals work through a decision-making process. Based on their criminally inclined thought pattern that takes place prior to the commission of a crime, they invoke a rational decision-making paradigm. It occurs lightning fast and is employed when they encounter life situations that meet the outline they have already decided will be featured in their crime of choice. In brief, the criminal has already considered his crime long before he actually commits it. The consideration may be highly elaborate or very simple, but he has thought about it.

The criminal mind utilizes this brief mental process prior to the crime as he believes it protects him and is an asset. This is especially true of the criminal located at any of several points along the fantasy continuum as it progresses from left to right. He sees his thought process as increasing his chances of going undetected while fulfilling his criminal needs.

As explained by Hazelwood (personal conversation), the offender's thought process involves five sequential steps. When presented with the opportunity to commit a crime based on his prior idea or concept, the mental review kicks in automatically. The deed is always preceded by the thought. The criminal has a criminal thought, but its expansion from a brief thought into a detailed criminal plan does not always take place. Some remain at the point of having just a brief thought (i.e., "rob a store"). Others will move along the fantasy continuum, exploring along the way various strategies that are fulfilling and geared to being successful. Their travel along the continuum will stop at a point determined by their imagination and ability to reason. Each point on the continuum represents a degree of criminal planning and sophistication by which he will explore how the crime will involve a police response. For self-protection, to the extent he is capable, he will try to plan the crime to eliminate evidence for the police to collect. Some offenders do not have the ability to think very far ahead or in detail, and they remain intent on committing the crime with a bare minimum of thought. At any rate, the prior criminal thought and its develop-ment are the first step in his thought pattern.

With the idea of the crime in his mind, he will evaluate the circum-stances for indicators of how it will benefit him. Asking "What is in this for me?" is an assessment of why he wants to commit the crime. This question is quickly followed by: "If I do this now, what will it cost me?" In Step 3 he considers the details of the crime and questions whether he will be identified or harmed, and the risks presented by his criminal behavior. Step 4 is when he reconciles Steps 2 and 3. He searches for a balance between benefits and costs and decides whether it is a go or no-go situation.

Knowing about each of the first four steps is valuable to the interviewer; however, Step 5 is the most critical to understand. It is in Step 5 that he justi-fies to himself why it is okay for him to commit the crime. If it is a robbery that is planned, his justification may be that the owner already makes more than he needs or that insurance will soften his loss. Internal thefts are deemed acceptable because of insurance or prior mistreatment by the company, or because they "owe" him more than his salary for all his hard work. In sexu-ally motivated crimes the offender may calculate that it is okay because "she is just a woman, and he is a man," or the victim represents women, who he hates in general. Many other justifications can occur to any criminal, but the important point is that he justifies his act before he does it. If given the opportunity in the early phase of interviewing, a suspect will likely "leak" how he handles stress and seeks to justify all of his errors, mistakes, or bor-derline criminal acts. How does he get through each day with his ego intact? His choices are to accept responsibility for what he has done or to use RPMs. The criminal will jump to the RPMs. Which method he uses in his everyday life is the one that he will choose to validate his criminal behavior.

When the interviewer provides questions that allow a suspect to reveal his secret pattern of excuses, he has found a major piece of his approach to the suspect. Knowing this pattern suggests which excuses for the crime the interviewer will present with sincerity to the criminal while attempting to get him to connect the dots of his relationship to the crime, the crime scene, or the victim. The suggested justifications will center on RPMs and be presented as themes. The goal is to make these validations palatable and to garner the criminal a position that earns special, lenient treatment. He can be sold these rationalizations because **the same thoughts occurred to him before he ever committed the crime.** The interviewer will have turned the criminal justifi-cation assets into liabilities.

A brief list of themes is included in the Appendix and is intended only to stimulate an interviewer's thinking about possible themes. The best themes come from topics reflecting human nature to which the criminal mind can relate, but they will also generally revolve around RPMs. As an example, read the theme about the rock in the shoe. It not only involves minimization but also invokes the reasoning process, suggesting to the criminal that he needs to take another look at what he has actually done and see it as a less serious matter. The new perspective will be presented as one that the interviewer, society, and the criminal justice system can more readily accept and partially excuse. This acceptance comes full circle to the position of justification he chose prior to committing the crime.

The RPMs and themes have the following qualities:

They are consistent with and compatible with today's legal standards.
They remove psychological obstacles to a suspect making a confession.
They provide a vehicle to connect the suspect with the victim or the crime.
They initiate the process of leading to full confession.
They indicate the worst qualities of the offender that can be stated so they can be understood and excused.
They say something positive about the offender.
They begin with a scenario that aids the offender to protect his self-esteem and "save face."

It is important to understand what *saving face* means and how important it is in obtaining confessions. Saving face means allowing the suspect to initially tell a story in a way that makes him look as good as possible. While doing this, he may be connecting himself to the victim, the crime scene, and the crime. The story puts a "good face" on what happened and allows a guilty party to salve his conscience.

In a murder case, I allowed without challenging a suspect to claim that prior to murdering the victim he armed her with a deadly weapon. There was a prior connection between them, and she could identify him. According to his confession, he placed a large industrial screwdriver in her hands and told her that only one of them could survive. At first, I thought this statement was a lie. On reflection, however, I concluded that it likely had some semblance of truth. The victim was not a violent person and in her state of shock after her rape was incapable of using this potentially deadly weapon. The overall effect of this part of his story was that it allowed him to internalize the justification that he killed her in self defense. The other particulars of his confession made it clear that legally the homicide was planned and committed without compassion. Self-defense was not a viable option; however, it made his giving the confession easier, and his version was included in the written report of the interview.

An example of face saving by saying something relatively positive about a suspect is to say something like "I believe you have never done something like this before" or, to paraphrase Holmes (1995), "This represents a failure of judgment, not a failure of character."

RPMs and themes are constructed with soft words and delivered gently. Strong statements with psychological implications do not need to be delivered with harsh tones for their greatest impact. The "feather touch" means using a delivery method that has the subject feeling as if the interviewer has touched his psyche by tickling it with a feather. The impact is such that he is aware that the question's "feather" has touched his psyche, and the interviewer knows his true nature. He subtly becomes aware that this knowledge held by the interviewer will make it difficult to defend himself from the officer's tactics to obtain a confession.

Some people in policing feel that interviewing that is not loud, demeaning, and personal is not effective. They equate a gentle professional attack method with weakness. Likewise, some officers believe that not immediately challenging a lie told by a suspect allows the person to believe that he has put one over on them. In reality, the approach most disturbing to a suspect is the professional, calm path using questions delivered in a firm manner. Lies are often more important to the interview results when not immediately challenged but collected and challenged en masse, thereby taking on more significance and potentially the feel of evidence.

Of equal importance is what RPMs and themes do *not* do:

They do not violate legal, moral, or ethical standards.
They do not change legal responsibility for a criminal act.
They do not change the reality of who is the criminal and what he did in his crime.

The following scenario is an exception to the rule of using minimization techniques without changing legal responsibility.

Case 7.9

The Los Angeles Sheriff's Department investigated the possible homicide of a young woman who stayed in a hotel and had apparently gone out her eighth floor window. As they focused on a coworker as a suspect, they suggested that he had been responsible, but that her fall had been an accident. He agreed that it had been an accident and went on to state that he was going to commit suicide. Policy forbade further questioning and required an immediate arrest, followed by placing him on a suicide watch. As the case was left at that point, the officers unintentionally had altered the degree of criminality with which the suspect could be charged.

Case 7.10

Similar to Case 7.9, I conducted a subject interview involving the disappearance and possible murder of a young infant. After a long period of interviewing, the female suspect said she wanted to use the restroom. As she rose from her chair, I rose with her, maintaining eye contact, and said, "Kathy, this was an accident, wasn't it? You did not mean for it to happen." She replied, "Yes." On her return from the restroom, we worked on the details surrounding the baby's death. She never wavered from her version of accidental death, but today, as she awaits execution, her reported details of how the death occurred are notably different from what she related that day. She provided unbelievable details to support her claim of accidental death. I suggested that after the infant had fallen from her arms and hit his head she implemented her cardiopulmonary resuscitation (CPR) training and tried to save the baby. She added her own specifics by claiming she tried CPR for over an hour, despite an integral part of her story being that a phone was within inches of her position. This detail was included in the written statement and illustrates how saying something positive about a suspect can pay off for an investigator.

Test of Commitment and Scenario Evaluation

After a career of encouraging people to tell a straight story and sometimes confess to a crime, I have found that a reliable rule of thumb in evaluating stories is whether the scenario measures up to a comparison with what is natural and normal. Most human events closely follow that yardstick. On occasion, the officer may find a contrary example that must be closely questioned and scrutinized, but almost all things happen in logical or explainable ways.

Sapir lectures in his SCAN course that the teller of a true story must have commitment to its details. Similar positions are taken by Reid and Associates (2004) and Zulawski and Wicklander (2002). The test of commitment by the interviewer to his story must be passed before accepting a version of events from a witness, victim, or suspect. Part of what is being evaluated is the storyteller's confidence in or commitment to the truth of what he has related. A major function of the police interview and interrogation is to detect the offender's confidence and commitment level to each statement. When flaws are found in the commitment of the interviewee to his story, close questioning will cause it to unravel and create a basis for challenging the truthfulness of the person.

I am fond of Sapir's recommended procedures (1992, 1998). He suggested that after the person has told the story and all points have been clarified, some seemingly natural questions should be asked. The purpose of the following series of questions is to validate the person's commitment to his story.

In substance, the interviewer's inquiries are a series of questions, such as "Now that you told me these things, should I believe your story?" There is only one correct answer: Yes. Answers that indicate editing, omissions, or deception are, "I think so," "That is for you to decide," or "That is not my decision."

After that question is answered, the interviewer may ask, "Can you give me one reason why I should believe you?" To this second follow-up question, the answer reflecting commitment is something like "Because I told you the truth." Answers that indicate guilt include "I have no reason to lie" or "Why would I lie?" Note that neither one of these statements answers the question directly.

Sapir (1998) suggested that those two questions may be followed by asking, "What would you say if it was later determined that you lied?" A truthful person will likely give an unequivocal response along the line of "Impossible," "That can't happened because I told the truth," or "You would be wrong." Responses indicating deception include "What do you want me to tell you?" or "What can I say?"

The SCAN course also has a visual technique for getting to the same point. In this procedure, a line with arrow points on each end is drawn on a sheet of paper. At the left end, the number 0 is placed, and the number 100 is placed at the right end. The sheet of paper is laid in front of the interviewee, and he is advised that 0 indicates that he has told a completely untruthful story, and 100 indicates that he has told nothing but the truth. He is asked to place his finger on the line at a point that represents how much truth he has told. Where he places his finger is irrelevant. What is significant is the length of time it takes him to decide where to place the finger. Any hesitation indicates that deception and editing has taken place in his statements. A thorough examination of his version of events then follows to determine what is and what is not truthful.

Final Truth

The job of every interviewer and interrogator is to secure and document admissions and confessions. One method of doing this is to paraphrase the details provided by a subject, or to have a second officer witness the entire interview. In today's suspicious atmosphere in which law enforcement is not given unqualified deference or heard in a courtroom with the assumption of unquestioned integrity, all critical techniques and interview results need firm documentation. The strong suggestion is made that every admission and confession be documented, even when it is clearly not a complete, straightforward, and honest statement of responsibility. Lock the subject into his version of events. The lock-in does not have to contain every formal requirement or use formal legal language. It can be a signed note containing the date, time, place, parties involved, the subject's vital declarations, and the subject's signature and those of the witnesses. This may sound cavalier, but it is not because the more casual documentation does not end the interview or interrogation. Take the best you have and commit it to writing.

After a brief pause, including time to review the just-created document, any prior notes, and perhaps consultation with another officer, the primary interviewer can re-open the interview or interrogation. A brief statement is made by the officer to indicate that the signed statement just will not fly because it does not comport with known crime details. The search for the complete signed statement is not over until the investigator has a document or recording containing every known and significant detail of the crime.

The first signed statement is used as a wedge, and the officer engages in a monologue that includes a listing of defects and flaws in the original statement. In effect, the officer is undoing all of the RPMs and other techniques that were used to induce the subject's cooperation. Now, the investigator is selling a tougher position that calls for the subject to take more responsibility for what he did. The target of the interview may grant some of the points and dig into a position that is now closer to the known truth. Document that position and return to the interrogation. Repeat this procedure until the best possible statement has been obtained. Confessions rarely come in one full outpouring of information from a suspect; they are usually obtained incrementally. Some suspects will never tell all of the details no matter what the interrogator does or says.

Validation

Whenever possible, some pieces of the crime scene, criminal behavior, or investigative results should be held as confidential and not shared with the media. This holdout data should be shared generally within the department on a "need-to-know" basis. The purpose of holdout information is to have a few things only the offender can know. Questions about the topic of the holdout information will either reveal false confessions or substantiate a true confession.

Case 7.11

In a large Midwest city, young female children were being abducted, molested, and then returned to almost the same location where they were enticed into the car. A consistent description of the abductor/molester began to emerge from the children. He was described as a young black male with a highly distinctive hairstyle. The hairstyle included the sculpted outline of the city's skyline. This information was selected as the holdout data. The city where these crimes were repeatedly occurring is crisscrossed and circled with a network of major interstate highways.

The analysis of this series of molestations concluded that the offender was a local resident and not someone who exited one of the interstates, molested the children, and then reentered an interstate to leave the city. The profilers requested that the holdout information be made public, as its distinctive nature would generate an identification of the offender. An appeal was made to the chief of police, who recognized the value of the advice and ordered the holdout data released. Immediately, several calls were received that identified the same man as the offender. He was picked up and interviewed, and he confessed to each of the abductions and molestations. Sometimes holdout information is unique and is of more value when it is made public.

While holdout information is valuable in validating confessions, it is only one aspect of that process. Whenever a confession is taken, it must include detailed descriptions of the crime being investigated. The details sought include the names of any associates or partners, all information about the victim, the location of the victim's remains if applicable, details of verbal exchanges if the victim is a survivor, location of the crime, weapons used, the current location of the crime proceeds, and any other details pertinent to the crime. These details are essential so that they may be tracked down for a number of reasons, including the validation of the subject's confession. This procedure is invaluable in offsetting any attack on the confession at a later date.

Bibliography

Deaver, Jeffrey. *The Sleeping Doll.* New York: Simon and Schuster, 2007.

Ekman, Paul. *Emotions Revealed.* New York: Holt, 2003.

Gudjonsson, Gisli. *The Psychology of Interrogation, Confessions and Testimony.* Chichester, UK: Wiley, 1992.

Hess, John E. *Interviewing and Interrogation for Law Enforcement.* Cincinnati, OH: Anderson, 1997.

Holmes, Warren D. Interrogation. *Polygraph* 24(4) (1995): 237–258.

Holmes, Warren D. *Criminal Interrogation.* Springfield, IL: Thomas, 2002.

Inbau, Fred E., John E. Reid, and Joseph P. Buckley. *Criminal Interrogation and Confessions.* 3rd ed. Baltimore, MD: Williams and Wilkins, 1986.

Inbau, Fred E., John E. Reid, Joseph P. Buckley, and Brian C. Jayne. *Criminal Interrogations and Confessions.* 4th ed. Sudbury, MA: Jones and Bartlett, 2004.

Jayne, Brian C., and Joseph P. Buckley. Interrogation Alert! Will Your Next Confessions Be Suppressed? *The Investigator* (Winter 1998): special edition.

McManus, Barry L. *Liar.* Leesburg, VA: Global Traveler, 2008.

Napier, Michael R. Interviewing the Rapist. In *Practical Aspects of Rape Investigation: A Multidisciplinary Approach,* edited by Robert R. Hazelwood and Ann W. Burgess, 123–137. Boca Raton, FL: CRC Press, 2009.

Napier, Michael R., and Susan H. Adams. Magic Words to Obtain Confessions. *FBI Law Enforcement Bulletin* 67(10) (October 1998): 1–6.

Napier, Michael R., and Susan Adams. Criminal Confessions: Overcoming the Challenge. *FBI Law Enforcement Bulletin* (November 2002): 9–15.

Rabon, D. *Investigative Discourse Analysis.* Durham, NC: Carolina Academic Press, 2003.

Reiman, Tonya. *Power of Body Language.* New York: Pocket Books, 2007.

Sapir, Avinoam. *The LSI Course on Scientific Content Analysis.* Phoenix, AZ: Laboratory for Scientific Interrogation, 1987.

Sapir, Avinoam. *The LSI Annual Advanced Workshop on Scientific Content Analysis.* Phoenix, AZ: Laboratory for Scientific Interrogation, 1992a.

Sapir, Avinoam. *LSI Advanced Workshop on Scientific Content Analysis.* Phoenix, AZ: Laboratory for Scientific Interrogation, 1998.

Sapir, Avinoam, *LSI Scientific Content Analysis Newsletter Anthology.* Phoenix, Arizona: Laboratory for Scientific Interrogation, 1992b.

Shuy, Roger W. *The Language of Confession, Interrogation and Deception.* Thousand Oaks, CA: Sage, 1998.

Vessel, D. Conducting Successful Interrogations. John Ott, Ed. *FBI Law Enforcement Journal* 67(10) (October 1998): 11–15.

Yeschke, Charles L. *The Art of Investigative Interviewing.* Boston: Butterworth-Heinemann, 1997.

Zulawski, David E., and Douglas E. Wicklander. *Practical Aspects of Interview and Interrogation.* 2nd ed. Boca Raton, FL: CRC Press, 2002.

Nonverbal Communication

8

MICHAEL R. NAPIER

Contents

Introduction

Some do not accept as valid the use of nonverbal gestures for assessing the truthfulness or deception of an individual, while others accept that reading as gospel. Observing and evaluating nonverbal gestures is not a pure science. Because of the prevalence of its usage in police interviewing, the rationale for nonverbal communication needs to be placed in a workable context. Interview and interrogation experts who provide guidance in nonverbal interpretation are in general agreement regarding which signals to consider, and to their overall meaning. For specific details, consult the work of the authors cited in this chapter.

As described in Chapter 2, the early evaluation of a suspect's verbal and nonverbal behavior has been cited as a critical element of the abuse of police power. The complaint is undoubtedly valid in certain instances when the rules were not followed or there was an overeagerness to identify a particular suspect. That "rush to justice" taints the good work of so many other officers who play by the rules and obtain solid results.

Decisions made regarding nonverbal gestures and truthfulness can be well grounded when there is complementary evidence. To strengthen the accuracy of using nonverbal behavior, certain rules must be followed. The overall decision on truthfulness should consider the person's verbal responses simultaneously with his nonverbal gestures. Following all the rules is important. That said, the rule of confirmation by consistency is the rule that best positions the officer to make a useful decision on truthfulness.

As much as 70% of the meaning of communicated message is from the nonverbal channel of communication. Therefore, nonverbal communication is significant to the evaluation process and to the real meaning of the total message (Inbau et al., 2004).

Primarily consideration will be given to only two channels of communications, the verbal channel and the nonverbal channel. A person may more easily control his verbal channel. Some make their living by communicating and are well practiced in controlling both channels. Leading that group are lawyers, politicians, salespeople, actors and actresses, newscasters, commentators, the clergy, and so on. Some hardened criminals have also mastered the skill of controlling their physical behaviors when speaking.

Validation of Nonverbal Gestures

Most people do not have an interest in focusing their talents in this area and therefore are not skilled at practicing deception. Some of the research into nonverbal communication tends to support the contention that those signals are not consciously controlled. Ekman (2003) studied aboriginal tribes who have not experienced TV, movies, or the presence of outsiders and recorded examples of facial expressions that are universal. The facial expressions of those untouched by the "modern" world match or are closely aligned with the way the rest of us record and display our emotional reactions to happiness, fear, anxiety, stress, and concern.

Per Reiman (2007), the study of body language is a scientific undertaking dating back several hundred years. For over a century, scientists have validated the "fight-or-flight" reaction of humans when they perceive a threat. Scientific processes have validated changes in blood pressure, breathing patterns, pupil dilation, and perspiration, among other signs, when humans believe they are in danger.

This scientific validation of certain nonverbal signals as inborn and common to all humans along with the ability to demonstrate physiological changes provide some basis for the use by law enforcement of nonverbal gestures as deception illustrators. Even without that support, officers over the years have found that suspects and liars handle themselves in telltale ways that confirm their suspicions of deception. For the officer on the street, an even stronger endorsement of reading people comes from its use by their opponents, the bad guys of the world. They live on the street and it is a matter of survival for them to get the correct reading on the people around them, everyone from "the man," to their victims, to their competitors who would rip them off. Reading people is a proven way of life for some. Undercover officers must do the same and "go to school" on how the criminal handles his day-to-day matters.

The autonomic nervous system (ANS) has the primary function for self-defense measures that humankind needs available in the split-second recognition of a threat. The ANS, programmed by centuries of experience, internally generates alarms calling for responses. Facing questions about sensitive issues, or the perceived need to lie, sets off those alarms and causes stress. That anxiety seeks an outlet. Ekman (2003) stated that the altered physiology that requires some physical movement to relieve the stress gives birth to physiological changes and physical movements that are seen as nonverbal gestures. The survival of humans relies on the ANS warning system.

Relief for the stress and anxiety caused by lying comes from body movement. The desire to run, flee, clutch a weapon, and generally to defend the self are presented by miniaturized movements. People do in miniature what they would like to do full blown if they were not constrained.

Our parents grew up understanding the nonverbal phenomenon. I learned from my parents and grandparents many of the techniques used for spotting liars, deceivers, and generally untrustworthy individuals. They told me repeatedly not to trust someone who cannot look you in the eye when speaking, or to be watchful of someone who cannot proudly hold his or her head up or stand up straight when dealing with you.

The Federal Bureau of Investigation (FBI) and others confirmed the importance of nonverbal gestures in communications in their early training for hostage negotiations and interviewing skills noting the words of communications specialist Paul Watzlawick: "One cannot not communicate." The instructors also repeated the observation Henry Wadsworth Longfellow made before the turn of the nineteenth century in *The Hanging of the Crane*: "He speaketh not and yet there lies a conversation in his eyes" (Longfellow, 1875. pp. 29–30).

Stimulating Behaviors

As with verbal responses from suspects, nonverbal signs may be stimulated by proper questioning. The process of stimulating verbal and nonverbal responses provides the officer simultaneously with two channels of communication to evaluate.

The most effective environment is created by stimulating the behavior with an inquiring and nonaccusatory attitude. The stimulating questions must come before any accusatory questioning. The goal is to generate the natural (unstressed) response capabilities of the person when he is not put in a threatening situation.

The process for evaluating nonverbal communications in conjunction with verbal responses has rules to follow. Seven of those rules are reviewed here.

1. The setting: The observation perspective of the officer should be from an eye-to-eye position. The person being observed must be seated away from other furniture, in a chair without wheels or armrests. Those features allow the subject to move in the chair if he chooses or to move the chair itself while requiring him to determine what he is going to do with his arms, hands, and legs. The absence of a table ensures that his entire body may be observed at once. One signal of deception is for the subject to hold his head in the palm of his hand for long periods. This is more visible when there is no furniture a subject may use to support himself physically or psychologically.

2. Yardstick for comparison: The initial observations of the person's natural habits must be made prior to asking any questions that are confrontational. The goal is to establish how he handles his body movements and his physical and verbal attributes while he is being his "normal self." The Structuring an Interview form (see Appendix) contains many topics to be presented for discussion by the subject to allow ample opportunities for him to display both his verbal and nonverbal standard of behaviors. For instance, if the individual demonstrates that he has the capacity, or ability, to look the interviewer in the eye while providing nonthreatening background information, that ability may then be used to gauge his eye usage when the questioning moves to an accusatory format.

3. Timing: As with reading polygraph tracings, only the behavior that is stimulated by a question may be considered for evaluating the person's nonverbal movements. On recognizing the threat contained in the police question, the deceptive subject's body will go into a defensive mode. Immediately after the initial reaction to the threat, the body struggles to return to its normal functioning level.

Any nonverbal behavior occurring immediately prior to asking a question cannot be included in the assessment because it is not stimulated by the question. Likewise, because the body returns to its normal levels of functioning, any nonverbal gesture made after about 5 to 7 seconds cannot reliably be attributed to the question and is therefore discarded.

4. Consistency: The accuracy of the read on nonverbal behavior is greatly enhanced when the verbal response assessment and the nonverbal evaluation both come to the same conclusion. The appraisal of truthfulness on a single crime issue question is further supported when both communications channels are in agreement over the span of several crime-related questions. Reid and others agreed that consistency serves as a strong foundation for making the call of truthful or deceptive (Inbau et al., 2004). When, in conjunction with verbal responses considered as indicators of deception, the interview subject repeatedly uses nonverbal gestures such as touching his eyes, nose, earlobes, or lips; barricade gestures; grooming gestures; scratching; moving away from the investigator; and so on, consistency is found for deciding he is deceptive (Inbau et al., 2004).

5. Poker face: An officer's ability to make accurate decisions is hindered when his facial gesture reveals his conclusion on a relevant question. Likewise, he harms his position if he verbalizes his conclusions by saying, "I know you were untruthful because I saw you look away." A facial reaction or a verbal declaration alerts a suspect to the technique and will cause him to concentrate on avoiding his natural responses when lying. Concentrate on the observations and keep a poker face.

6. Case facts: Always make the call of deception within the context of known investigative case facts. It is a tactical error to conclude that a person is deceptive solely on the reading of a person's behavior, and caution should be used in making the decision. Such observations may justify more aggressive investigative inquiries, but it is risky to confront someone only on that basis. If the case facts are "soft," utilize the verbal and nonverbal analysis with caution. Most errors are of the "false-positive" type by which a person is thought to be deceptive when in fact he is truthful.

7. Present behaviors: An officer is restricted to considering only behaviors that he observes and not those he anticipates that his questioning will stimulate. Do not downgrade your assessment of a person because a behavior was expected and did not occur. Evaluate only those behaviors that are present.

Procedures

As part of the interview plan, a steady, measured pace should be pursued. The pace should be sufficient to allow an officer the opportunity to concentrate on asking one question at a time and then afford him time to digest the answer and accompanying gestures. To rush from question to question does not allow a solid basis for concluding if a person is truthful.

As pointed out by Reid and colleagues, one of the two communications channels must be evaluated first; appraise the verbal response because it the easiest for a subject to control (Inbau et al., 2004). The officer should review the oral answer by asking himself, "What did I just hear? What words were used? Did he really answer my question?" Once he has scored the verbal statement, he then considers what he observed with regard to nonverbal gestures. If his evaluation on both is the same, he has the beginning of the reinforcement or consistency he seeks. If, however, differing conclusions are reached for both channels, he should rethink his evaluation of the verbal response. This clearly indicates that the nonverbal channel is likely to provide more reliable guidance.

The Slow Vertical Flick

The procedure for capturing nonverbal gestures is relatively easy, but it does require regular practice until it becomes automatic. With a little practice, an officer may use a slow vertical flick of his eye to quickly take in a subject from head to toe. This flick of the eyes takes a fraction of a second, and most probably will not even be noticed by the interviewee. The secret to its use is twofold. An officer should time the vertical flick during the asking of a question and during its answer. The officer will need to repeat the procedure several times during both phases to capture any movements stimulated by the question. That will satisfy the timing issue of reading nonverbal gestures. Also, the officer is aided by his ability to pace the process, allowing himself the opportunity to observe and assess the gestures.

The officer is also assisted in reading nonverbal gestures by having closely observed the interviewee during the early, nonthreatening phase of the contact. From those observations, he will know which gestures are the favorites of the subject. Knowing what to be looking for will greatly aid in being able to spot the changes in short order.

Some Nonverbal Gestures

Barriers

Given that the origin of many nonverbal gestures stem from our need to survive, it should be no surprise that some deal with physical protection. The crossing of legs and arms is intended to cover our vulnerable midsection from an attack. Those needs carry over to fears having little to do with a physical attack. The protective covering of our vulnerable organs takes place when the person has a generalized fear because he has lied. He is not worried about a physical attack, but he gears up just the same because of real concerns about his well-being after lying.

Concealing

The same lie, or any other deception, may also trigger the need to hide parts of his face, such as the mouth, eyes, and forehead. These physical movements are generated due to the stress from possibly being discovered lying. While they may be viewed as protective gestures, there also is likely a deeper psychological significance to them. The message is that a deceiver cannot look the deceived in the eye or must hide his eyes because they will give away his deception. While instructing at the FBI Academy, Joe Koulis, a Chicago psychologist, illustrated the mouth-covering gesture by saying it was as if the person was attempting to prevent the lies from escaping while trying to shove them back down his throat.

Eyes

The use of one's eyes is believed by many to be a true indicator of whether a person is truthful. If I were to select only one observable nonverbal gesture to concentrate on for that determination, it would be how a person engages his questioner with his eyes. If the interviewee conceals his eyes with sunglasses or a hat pulled down low, he raises the question of whether the covering is intentional because he knows that the eyes will give away his deception. When appropriate, ask that the item be removed. Should the polite request be refused, the question has very likely been answered. By holding his head down and rubbing his forehead and eyebrows, the liar is shielding his eyes so they cannot be seen and evaluated.

The general belief is that the truthful examinee will want to concentrate on the questioner by way of determining the nature of each question because he will have no forewarning regarding what will be asked. Therefore, he will likely engage the officer by maintaining an eye-to-eye stance for most of the questioning. He will behave in the same manner when answering, but his gaze may not be eye to eye for his full answer. The truthful person's focus will be on the officer during most, if not all, of his answer as a demonstration of earnestness, sincerity, and honesty.

The criminal has no doubt regarding what the probable questions will be, so his attention will be focused on his answer. Once he becomes aware of which of the expected questions is being asked, his eyes will not be on the officer. Most likely, he will be looking away, concentrating on how to answer. The culprit most likely will start his answer by briefly looking at the officer but will quickly break eye contact for fear of being detected in the lie. Many liars will sneak a quick glance back at the officer on completion of the lie to measure the reaction to determine if he got away with the deception. If a subject believes his lying on a particular question was successful, his accompanying nonverbal gestures may be absent when the same area is touched on again.

Touching

There is a tendency for a person in the midst of lying to feel a compulsion to touch his eyes, face, nose, upper lip, or earlobes or to rub his face, especially during an answer. Reiman (2007) noted that touching the nose is one of the gestures most commonly associated with deception. She also explained that when a sense of anxiety from lying sets in, our blood pressure increases, causing the soft tissue in the nose to swell. In turn, that swelling produces a tingling sensation that we address by touching or scratching the area. The officer, knowing that these gestures occur, can be watchful for them, particularly while observing a suspect answering a question.

Posture and Moving in Chair

How would an officer know if the posture adopted by an interviewee is significant? By watching his physical attributes during the nonconfrontational questioning, he can take measure of the person. Attempting to deceive is a heavy burden on most people, and the person who slumps during the interrogation phase may be doing so because the combination of the "felt" weight of the burden and the "felt" need to become smaller and less observable affects his posture. The honest person does not bear a burden because he has confidence in the truthfulness and integrity of his answers.

Positioning Subject's Chair

Case 8.1

My police officer partner and I were requested to review a videotaped interview of a serial murder suspect that had been conducted by two sheriff deputies. The murders were especially grizzly as the prostitute victims were strangled, their body cavities filled with gasoline, and they were set on fire. The suspect was seated in a chair that had no arms. His entire body was easily visible to both officers. Near the end of the interview, the second officer, a female, leaned forward slightly to ask a question. Instantly, the suspect threw his head back, hitting the wall with a loud bang. It was clear that the suspect had problems with women and was a viable suspect in an investigation involving murders in which the offender demonstrated the same propensity.

Early in the video, the original position of the suspect's chair was further from the wall. He had quietly over time moved further and further from the interviewers. It is wise to provide room behind the suspect's chair to allow him to move and nonverbally demonstrate his emotional state about the pointed questions being asked. The attempt to distance himself from his questioners was the miniaturization of his desire to remove himself from the questioning. The flinging of his head into the wall sent a visible signal regarding proven techniques to be employed in any subsequent interview. It was suggested that the same team conduct any subsequent interview, but the next one should contain some staging by the officers. The plan was for the female to attempt to take the lead position away from the male officer and for him to react in a disapproving way. He was then to correct her on a fact or two and on her style of questioning. Eventually, she was to gather her papers and leave the room in a huff. The male officer would then attempt to bond with the suspect on the basis of their supposed similar feelings about women.

Any suspect's chair should start out positioned in such a way as to force him into an eye-to-eye alignment with the officer. Innocent suspects are not fearful of the officer because they are confident that they had no involvement in the crime, and their innocence will be shown. Reid et al.'s terminology for this is "frontal alignment" (Inbau et al., 2004). I refer to frontal alignment as remaining face-to-face with the questioner. Because of the innate desire to protect oneself when threatened, individuals who are lying will often turn sideways to the officer, as if giving an officer the "cold shoulder." Besides protecting his vulnerable center mass, this move will likely be accompanied by breaking eye contact, as the person is no longer face to face with the officer. Not remaining eye to eye is often seen as an indicator of deception.

A subject may turn his chair to one side to break eye contact, or he may move his body to one side while the chair remains in the same alignment. The person will turn in the direction of his preferred location (i.e., out of the room). The chair movement of a truthful person is most likely to be negligible.

No Single Gesture or Word

One of the cautions necessary for anyone relying on nonverbal readings is not to make a decision based on a single word or gesture (Inbau et al., 2004). If a gesture or phrase that is generally regarded as indicative of deception or truthfulness is noted but not repeated, it can be considered a coincidental "stray" expression. An experienced officer will understand that there can be some variations in any suspect's demeanor. For gestures and phrases to assist in making the call of truthfulness or deception, they need to be consistently used in response to a topic and to occur frequently enough to be regarded as a pattern.

Anxiety

One of the criticisms of police interview tactics is the claim that police officers are unable to distinguish between normal anxiety and the anxiety that is generated because of fear of detection. The first type of nervousness exists just because the person is being contacted on a serious matter by a law enforcement officer. The distinguishing feature is that the apprehension of someone who is hiding information or guilt does not fade as it does with the truthful subject on realization that the contact does not present a threat. The guilty and deceptive are at risk the entire time they are with the officer; therefore, the tension remains with their demeanor.

Proximity

Proximity is the measure of distance between two people. The "intimate" distance required by an individual is a personal comfort choice but is generally regarded as 12 to 16 inches. Less than that is likely to generate discomfort and anxiety in Americans. An officer should check the level of anxiety in the interviewee and ensure that it is not due to an invasion of his personal space. Different cultures often have different perceptions as to amount of personal space that is appropriate.

Personal space is an important consideration because the truthful person is more likely to lean forward when listening or speaking. He is not fearful of getting close to the interviewer because the interviewer does not present a threat. This usually cannot be said of the deceptive person. The forward lean is symbolic of interest and a willingness to assist, which are not the characteristics of the deceptive. Should the officer close the gap between himself and a valid suspect, he should expect discomfiture and possibly movement away by the subject. It does not require very much forward movement of the buttocks in a chair to change the proximity of a subject's head in relation to the interviewer's head. This slight movement may be sufficient to provide comfort to the deceptive interviewee and the movement may be regarded as a withdrawing from the interview.

Grooming Gestures

Nervous mannerisms, grooming gestures, and shifting postures are just some of the nonverbal gestures that reflect anxiety and result from attempts to mask stress (Hess, 1997). These gestures are not necessary movements but are done solely to relieve tension. Grooming gestures include picking imaginary lint from clothing, repeatedly adjusting jewelry and glasses, smoothing a moustache, running hands through scalp hair, wringing hands, or picking and chewing fingernails.

Breathing

Interviewers can determine truthful behavior such as breathing rate by observing the interview subject during periods when asking routine and nonthreatening questions (Hess, 1997). Breathing is one of the key components of a polygraph, and it may be utilized visually by an officer. The signal for the officer to watch for is a cessation of breathing called *apnea*. Holding of the breath may occur involuntarily as an indicator of deception. Apnea can be brief or of a longer duration. Being cautious in calling someone deceptive, the officer should concentrate on apnea of a few seconds timed to the asking of questions concerning guilt and up to a few seconds after an answer is provided.

Response Latency

Response latency is the time lapse from the end of a question to the beginning of the answer. In a U.S. National Security Agency research project, the average response latency of a truthful subject was 0.5 second, while the deceptive subject's response latency was three times as long at 1.5 seconds (Inbau et al., 2004). This detail assists in validating the theory that a liar will hesitate briefly before answering a question to determine whether to edit the answer or to configure the answer so it meets information furnished previously.

Bibliography

Coates, G. *www.wanterfall.com*. www.wanterfall.com (accessed February 3, 2008).

Deaver, Jeffrey. *The Sleeping Doll*. New York: Simon and Schuster, 2007.

de Becker, Gavin. *The Gift of Fear*. Boston: Little, Brown, 1997.

Ekman, Paul. *Emotions Revealed*. New York: Holt, 2003.

Gudjonsson, Gisli. *The Psychology of Interrogation, Confessions and Testimony*. Chichester, UK: Wiley, 1992.

Hare, Robert D. *Without Conscience*. New York: Guilford Press, 1999.

Hess, John E. *Interviewing and Interrogation for Law Enforcement*. Cincinnati, OH: Anderson, 1997.

Holmes, Warren D. Interrogation. *Polygraph* 24(4) (1995): 237–258.

Holmes, Warren D. *Criminal Interrogation*. Springfield, IL: Thomas, 2002.

Inbau, Fred E., John E. Reid, and Joseph P. Buckley. *Criminal Interrogation and Confessions*. 3rd ed. Baltimore, MD: Williams & Wilkins, 1986.

Inbau, Fred E., John E. Reid, Joseph P. Buckley, and Brian C. Jayne. *Criminal Interrogations and Confessions*. 4th ed. Sudbury, MA: Jones and Bartlett, 2004.

Longfellow, Henry W. *The Hanging of the Crane*. Boston: James R.Osgood, 1875.

Napier, Michael R. Interviewing the Rapist. In *Practical Aspects of Rape Investigation: A Multidisciplinary Approach*, 123–137. Boca Raton, FL: CRC Press, 2009.

Napier, Michael R., and Susan H. Adams. Magic Words to Obtain Confessions. *FBI Law Enforcement Bulletin* 67(10) (October 1998): 1–6.

Napier, Michael R., and Susan Adams. Criminal Confessions: Overcoming the Challenge. *FBI Law Enforcement Bulletin* (November 2002): 9–15.

Ofshe, R. J., and R. A. Leo. Social Psychology of Police Interrogation: Theory and Classification of True and False Confessions. *Studies in Law, Policies and Society* 16 (1997) 189–251.

Rabon, D. *Investigative Discourse Analysis*. Durham: Carolina Academic Press, 2003.

Reiman, Tonya. *Power of Body Language*. New York: Pocket Books, 2007.

Shuy, Roger W. *The Language of Confession, Interrogation and Deception*. Thousand Oaks, CA: Sage, 1998.

Vessel, D. Conducting Successful Interrogations. *FBI Law Enforcement Journal* 67(10) (October 1998).

Yeschke, Charles L. *The Art of Investigative Interviewing*. Boston: Butterworth-Heinemann, 11–15, 1997.

Zulawski, David E., and Douglas E. Wicklander. *Practical Aspects of Interview and Interrogation*. 2nd ed. Boca Raton, FL: CRC Press, 2002.

Interview and Interrogation Techniques

9

MICHAEL R. NAPIER

Contents

Introduction

Interviewing is often seen as the most complex and the most intense piece of investigating. When interviewing moves into interrogation, it can be the most stressful part of investigating, as much hope for the final outcome of a case rests with the interrogator and his skills. Interviews and interrogations are dynamic, which adds to the excitement of being in the investigative hot seat. When things go as planned, interviewing and interrogating can also be most rewarding to an officer. These endeavors are not scientific; they are mostly art form. Some officers excel at investigating; others stand out at interviewing. Those not naturally gifted at interviewing can hone their skills. This chapter is intended to assist interviewers at all skill levels.

The discussions that follow should be considered in connection with those in Chapter 7. An interview turned into an interrogation is similar to a contest of "tug-of-war" in that the rope represents incriminating information, and each side wants to own it and have the most information on their side. The subject does not want to disclose the information, and the police interviewer covets all the information pertinent to the inquiry. At the outset, the subject knows all the details; therefore he has most of the rope on his side. An officer is purpose driven and will not be satisfied without "winning" by obtaining every piece of crime information possible. Moving the rope to the officer's side takes time. As confessions are made one piece at a time, the officer's patience is vital to the process. Every inch of rope that crosses to the officer's side undermines the confidence of a criminal suspect. It also builds internal tension, which may be reflected in more pronounced and readable nonverbal gestures.

Interrogation is a personal contest between the officer and the suspect with only one winner. The first opportunity to engage in a confrontational interrogation is the best opportunity for the officer to score a home run. If he does not, his next-best option is not to dig a hole so deep that he, or the next officer to give it a try, cannot get out of it during the subsequent contact. That is why each officer is encouraged to use a lighter approach so as not to alienate the interviewee. If the first round is a draw or, worse, a failure, the options open to the police are limited. The location and setting of the contact can be changed or someone more knowledgeable in interviewing skills can be substituted, but the facts of the case and the suspect's position within the case facts cannot be changed. The most rational alteration is for a second interviewer to man the controls in the next round. The presence in the second interview of the first primary officer will only remind the subject of his prior success.

Case 9.1

In the aftermath of the Oklahoma City bombing by Timothy McVeigh, I was assigned to the Special Incident Operations Center (SIOC) to represent the analysis and profiling unit. SIOC is a situation room at Federal Bureau of Investigation (FBI) headquarters manned by specialists from various FBI disciplines. A call came in from agents seeking guidance on interviewing Terry Nichols, McVeigh's co-conspirator. They had been looking for McVeigh, and Nichols approached the FBI.

The agents had been interviewing Nichols for a period of time and, given the magnitude of the crime, were under considerable pressure. As the interview hit a bad spot, they would switch to a fresh agent from the interview team. This had occurred a few times before I was called. I provided several tips about the best procedures in that type of situation. The most meaningful was for the most skilled interviewer to be selected, place him in control of the interview, and leave him, sink or swim, to the end of the interview. Rotating interviewers in the midst of the interview was counterproductive.

Switching control of an interview between partners who began the inquiry together is acceptable when the first primary officer is not succeeding or a suspect indicates a preference for the second officer. Those situations, and the one with Nichols, are about the only times a change of primary interviewer is appropriate unless the change is part of a more elaborate, complex interview plan that includes such staging.

The Interview Plan

Implementation of interview and interrogation techniques begins with the formulation of an interview plan. The plan will include all of the strategies and tactics intended to be used. However, foremost in the interview plan are security concerns, which are often left unconsidered.

Case 9.2

A startling example of lack of consideration of a security plan occurred in San Bernardino, California, following the arrest of a man who had just tried to murder a police officer. The subject had been stopped for a traffic violation. After stopping for the officer, he fired his .45-caliber handgun, hitting the officer in the stomach before speeding away. Other police units responded to the "officer down" call, and some pursued and arrested the felon. An immediate search of his car and the shooting scene failed to locate his handgun. Once under arrest, the shooter was taken to a police interview room for interrogation. He was seated in the room, treated courteously, and provided a bottle of water. The entire matter was caught on camera, and the officer in charge is observed repeatedly checking his cell phone and turning his back to the subject. His attitude appears to be blasé, and the final chapter in this story clearly shows that the subject had not been searched or had not been adequately searched. After the officer exits the room for some purpose, the subject reaches under his shirt, removes the .45-caliber handgun, and commits suicide. This scene could have been much worse as several officers could have been murdered. Officer safety is the first consideration when drawing an interview plan. See the Appendix for the strategy checklist.

The interview plan is similar to an architect's blueprint. It is a depiction of the course the interview will take, but it is flexible enough to accommodate last-minute any adjustments dictated by unexpected events. The unexpected event will likely be the reaction of the interviewee to the questions asked. Those responses must be considered in advance and plans drawn regarding how they will be handled. A security concept is called *red teaming*, in which interview plans are dissected for weaknesses, and then a plan is devised to see if the original procedures have flaws. Important interviews should be red-teamed to anticipate how an interviewee may react to certain phrasing and crime-specific questioning.

The plan's purpose is to ensure that proper question phrasing and sequencing are used, that all points are touched on, and to list the tactics to be implemented. See the Structuring an Interview discussion in Chapter 7. The form is located in the Appendix.

Goals

Within the concept of an interview plan are the goals for the interview. These may be unstated in the plan, but they are never far from the consciousness of the interviewer. Good interviewers are driven to get to the bottom of the matter. In criminal subject interviews or interrogations, this means nothing less than obtaining a full confession. That is the goal, but it is not realistic to expect it will be reached each time. The officer can sometimes win the tug-of-war by getting a statement that is contrary to scientific findings or so outrageous as to be totally unbelievable, or just get more rope on his side than the subject was able to protect. Not every interrogation is launched from a position of strength in which there is scientific evidence identifying the perpetrator. Those interviews or interrogations are the real challenges. When the crime scene and case facts are clear, winning is easier. In other situations, a good interview plan improves the chance of success.

In some situations, just tying the person to the scene, the victim, or some piece of physical evidence is a victory. Some of the tactics discussed in this chapter deal with how to present accusations when no evidence exists to back up the confrontation, and situations when your best ally is a miscue by the subject.

The end goal of any interview should be its successful presentation in the courtroom before a jury who will decide the fate of those charged and who will scrutinize the techniques utilized by the investigating authority. Therefore before the contact begins and throughout the interview and interrogation process, the interviewer's guideline is to "think prosecution." This concept involves preparing the interview to pass the jury and the judge test, realizing they may not be receptive to some of the efforts to secure a confession.

U.S. Courts and Law Enforcement

Courts at every level in the United States have historically been generous to law enforcement, realizing that those officers are the line that separates safety from chaos. Across the board, law enforcement bodies have been strong adherents to the rules, but there have been, and will always be, rogue officers. To avoid being labeled as such, an officer may follow the interview template laid out in Chapter 2.

There are many inquiry options left open deliberately by the courts, including few prohibitions on an officer lying to a subject. While lying is an open topic, I strongly recommend that its use be held in abeyance except in unusual circumstances. Lying as a tactic is properly labeled making "tactical" statements and should be so noted in the interview plan. My experience is that lying is not usually required because well-phrased questions will get the same, if not better, results. Should the interviewer ever be caught in a lie, it is difficult or impossible to regain authoritarian status in the eyes of a suspect. The items discussed next have received the stamp of approval from various court decisions when they are used moderately.

Special Care Questioning

The topic of special care questioning is one of the five critical elements that lead to successful interviews as outlined in Chapter 1. Special care questioning involves the interviewer making adjustments in accordance with the interviewee's particular features or circumstances. Before beginning to interview someone, an attempt should be made to become somewhat familiar with that individual. This process is included in the Structuring an Interview format, which has suggestions to be used at the front end of the questioning process. One critical area of inquiry is to determine if the interviewee is a likely candidate for special care questioning.

Should information exist that the person presents mental or social adjustment difficulties or lifestyle impressions that cause him to stand out, an effort must be made to get the details and flesh out those ideas *before* conducting the interview. Some recent negative personal experiences or conditions such as mental retardation, death in the family, and learning disabilities require special care questioning as illustrated in Chapter 2. If the facts and circumstances warrant this precaution, the officer must document the procedures taken so the individual is not overwhelmed, to adjust language to the appropriate level, and generally to accommodate the condition of the individual. Without making the required adjustments, the interview product may be challenged or found to be unreliable.

Privacy for Effectiveness

There is no substitute for a private location for getting an interview off on the right foot. Privacy may determine whether an interview meets its goal of obtaining all the information available. Since a person, whether a victim, witness, or a subject, is being asked to disclose personal matters, they deserve the consideration of having privacy. The idea of privacy takes on two separate dimensions.

I have observed a number of interviews involving victims and witnesses being interviewed together. This violates a cardinal rule calling for all efforts to eliminate contamination. It also may cause the parties to provide less information than they would have because of the presence of another person. Parents, spouses, good friends, and others close to the heart of an investigation must be interviewed separately. One parent may know things about a daughter that has not been shared with the other parent, perhaps for good reason. The wife may believe in the innocence of her husband but feel the investigators need to know of his temper or why he acts in certain ways, but will not provide such data in the presence of the spouse. While believing in another's innocence, some may not want to tell about an act or omission by that person that could be interpreted as that individual being somehow responsible for an unfortunate chain of events ending in the death of a child or another person. These disclosures are highly unlikely to be made if both are party to the other's interview. Not only do good investigative habits call for private interviews, but also the courts will frown on cross contamination from one witness to another. The separation procedure fosters the feeling of being able to admit mistakes, errors, or guilt.

Combine that privacy attribute with Holmes's, and others', strong statement that the police setting provides a psychological advantage to the officer because of his control over the environment (Holmes, 1995). The precinct setting places a suspect out of his element and within the officer's comfort zone. A suspect's home may not be a safe place for the contact.

An officer should consider that interviewing a suspect in his home or office affords the subject many opportunities to take advantage of diversions to avoid discussing the pertinent topic. Any diversion lessens a person's concentration on the officer's interview thrust. The possible diversions are many and range from ringing telephones, coworkers dropping in, a boss who wants to know why the police are in his facility, to children running wild or otherwise being a nuisance.

Things to Avoid: Natural Interview Enemies

One interviewing technique is to consciously avoid certain pitfalls. There are four errors that may be readily avoided, and doing so could tip the balance in an interview. As indicated throughout this book, demeanor slips by an interviewer can be costly. The projection of honesty, integrity, balance, fairness, and sincerity are essential. How would you react to an interview when the interviewer projected contrary qualities?

The lack of an interview plan reflects a "fly-by-the-seat-of-your-pants" attitude and a cavalier approach to an already demanding job. Just because an officer has done other similar interviews does not forgive the need to plan each interview. The absence of a plan is a negative approach to interviewing.

Hand in hand with the lack of an interview plan is an officer losing control of himself. The interview aspect of investigating is the center cog in case resolution. An officer may not get all the information available from a person on the first contact. He should strive to avoid leaving himself in a poor position at the end of the first contact.

Last, some of these flaws occur when an investigator rushes into and through an interview. A planned, steady pace allows the avoidance of errors that occur when an interview is hurried from. Ceding some control by interviewing on the turf of the interviewee may cause an interview to be rushed, interrupted, or terminated abruptly.

When Will They Confess?

A confession is an investigative prize resulting from a properly drawn and implemented interview plan containing a strategy and a variety of tactics aimed toward that goal. To get to the point of themes and reasoning, it is imperative that a suspect be allowed to deny his involvement and provide a basis for his innocence (Inbau, Reid, and Buckley, 1986; Inbau et al., 2004). Pressure generated by the need for a suspect to make the denial will build internally and obstruct the officer's use of various tactics until the denial is vented. From that point, the interview or interrogation should be comprised primarily of a monologue by the interviewer containing arguments about why the person's resistance is a "lose-lose" situation. The solo presentation couples the lose-lose sales pitch with themes emphasizing alternatives that cast the subject in a better light, a light that does not shine brightly on his failures and ultimate responsibility for the crime. A subject must see a benefit to confession, and a confession usually involves an attempt by a suspect to place himself in the best position to receive leniency and better treatment. Only then will an officer win the tug-of-war.

Interview before You Interrogate

Pointing out that an officer should conduct an interview before jumping into an interrogation would appear to be an obvious point. This concept is highlighted, however, because some do not allot enough time to secure the benefits of a proper interview, to wit, securing knowledge about the person, his involvement in the crime, or his normal behaviors while being interviewed. There is a great deal of advantage to be gained by interrogating only after a thorough interview.

First, with limited knowledge of how the case will unfold, early interviewees may later develop into viable suspects. By interviewing them in a professional, nonjudgmental manner, information is obtained that will not be gained if, or when, they are interrogated. This information may prove to be their undoing, as early on they may disclose information that will later close avenues of escape, locking them into a fixed position made untenable by later investigative developments. There are few more powerful tools in interrogating than to confront someone with their own words that indicate guilt. Remember, interviewing embodies more than fact finding. When properly executed, it is influenced by intangibles such as the officer's attitude and demeanor. Any true interview must feel like an interview, not something harsher.

Interrogation should be reserved until there is a foundation of data justifying the combative and confrontational nature of an interrogation. Even then, an interview is recommended before going head-on into a confrontational mode. Allow the person to reveal how he handles stress, his personalized methods for answering nonaccusatory questions, and his alibi or role in the crime. In other words, establish a yardstick by which to evaluate reactions when the questions become more threatening and hostile.

Must-Ask Question

If we did not know prior to the now-infamous O.J. Simpson debacle, it is clearly imprinted on our memory that every interview of a potential or likely suspect must contain the "Did you do it?" question. Never pass on an opportunity to ask the question when interviewing anyone possibly connected to the investigative issue. This can be done nicely, professionally, but without apology (Sapir, 1987, 1992a,b, 1998). Explain that it is a routine question required by your quest for thoroughness. An innocent party will appreciate the officer's attention to investigative detail. The question may be phrased in many ways, such as "Do you have any involvement in this _____? Just so we are clear, you did not do this, don't know who did it, and you are not concealing from me any facts about this matter? Is that correct? These are questions I must ask, ground I must cover."

Pacing an Interview

An interview should move at a steady and regulated, but not plodding, pace. This allows time to hear and digest what has just been said, to evaluate the way the statement was delivered, and to absorb the impact of the statement in relation to known case facts and prior statements. An interview should have an open time frame, not constricted by a preset termination time. The tendency to rush when conducting important interviews is one of the most significant enemies of proper interviewing. Plan every interview by dividing it into sequential segments and handle each portion fairly and thoroughly.

Controlling the Interview

The saying "he who controls wins" is certainly applicable in interviewing. The interview plan should include consideration of how to obtain and maintain control of the person considering his social and political stances and his role in the inquiry. The first step for an officer in controlling the interview is to be in control of himself throughout the duration of the contact.

This can be done more effectively using a psychological approach than with dramatic and rude behavior. For instance, when a person is escorted into the interview room, it should already be arranged in a setting most favorable to the interviewer. By politely and professionally indicating which chair is assigned to the interviewee, the interviewer sets the tone of being in charge. This may be done by simply stating, "Mr. Jones, that chair with the brown seat back is for you. Please sit there." This considerate, polite, and professional approach sends a quiet psychological message of, "I am in charge, and I am telling you what to do. This is my interview." Including "Mr." and "Please" cost the interviewer nothing but often has a payback. If the person chooses to move his chair or adjust the setting, he should be corrected immediately, and the setting should be restored.

Most of the time, a table in the interview room is an obstacle to good interviewing. If there is a table in the setting, the officer should preempt it as his workspace and not allow the suspect to use any part of it. Controlling the table is integral to controlling the interview.

Often, a person who expects to be interviewed will prepare a shield to hide behind and will use it to deflect questions and the officer's authority. Sometimes, these barriers are as simple as a title or their attire. People seek power in every way possible. For some, wearing a custodian's outfit complete with his name, position, and company logo becomes a badge of authority and power. That uniform may be the only power he has in his life. This shield must be psychologically neutralized to take away his confidence and inclination to resist the officer. Without taking on airs of superiority, if the interviewee is a lower-level employee, the officer may have him describe his duties, the limits of his authority, and layers of supervision over his position.

One method of maintaining control is to pace the interview through a predetermined structure favoring the interviewer. There is power and control in being the person to ask the questions, thereby controlling the process and the interviewee. Another method is in choosing whether to elevate or diminish a person's status by including or excluding a title in front of his name. People who are important witnesses may be referred to formally as "Mr." or "Mrs." Individuals who are perceived to have low self-esteem may be induced to be forthcoming by using the same treatment. Likewise, the reverse process of omitting a title may increase the standing of the officer who uses his title and rank, at least initially.

Case 9.3

I was asked to assist in an investigation by polygraphing and interviewing "the Reverend John Thompson." The case agent provided a brief on the case and continually referred to the subject by his title and full name. The agent was requested to introduce me to the subject, but not to introduce the minister to me, thereby eliminating any referral of his title. To no one's surprise, when he came in to the office for the interview, he was fully adorned with ministerial emblems. The challenging aspect of this interview was the request that the reverend be interviewed immediately following his appearance before a federal grand jury. This presented an extra hurdle to overcome. The request was not only to obtain a confession but also to get the confession that would include an admission to perjury, which was fresh on his mind. I believe I achieved my goals in part because never, from introduction through hours of questioning, was the subject referred to by anything other than his first name.

Staging an interview can be used to build up the image of the interviewer. The staging may be accomplished by having other officers defer to the interviewer, call him "sir," interrupt the interview with an urgent message from the chief, or pass a note to him with an apology for the interruption but with the added reference that the note was urgent and for his eyes only. Likewise, the selected office or interview room may contain the officer's name and indicators that it is reserved only for him. His title may be enhanced, such as "Special Officer in Charge—Operation Skylight."

The Use of Lies

Smart liars attempt to keep their version of events tightly wound, hence the emphasis on the use of open-ended questions in Chapter 7. With a brief, closely knit story, the suspect has less to keep track of and less is available for challenge. Making the challenge of determining truthfulness more difficult, the skilled liar usually blends the lie with some partial truth. Even in the presence of the partial truth, some traces of the edited or altered material are often left intact (Sapir, 1987, 1992a,b, 1998).

Exposing a subject's lies is a commanding tool in the hands of a skilled interviewer and interrogator. Even more influential is to choose the most opportune time to unveil the exposure. Spotting lies is an inexact art form. Reliability in making the call of someone being truthful or deceptive is increased when verbal and nonverbal observations and indicators both point in the same direction. When both channels of communication repeatedly show indicators of deception on the same or similar topics, each may be regarded as confirmatory of the deception judgment. I believe nonverbal gestures are fairly reliable indicators of truthfulness or deception, especially when proper rules are followed.

By resisting the temptation to immediately point out the detection of a lie, the interviewer may bolster a suspect's confidence, which in turn may encourage the telling of additional lies. The interviewer gains an advantage by saving the revelation of lies until the use of themes and reasoning tactics are placed in play. When confronted with a bundle of lies, a skilled interviewer can make them take on the feel and substance of evidence against the subject. By using role reversal in the reasoning phrase, the interviewer may relate that he will testify at the subject's trial before the offender has his opportunity to testify. The officer may then add that he intends to relate that the suspect made inappropriate statements to him on several points, even one or two times on minor topics. Then, he will ask the suspect to stand in the shoes of a juror and consider how much the juror will believe his statements when he has already learned that the offender is misleading even on minor points. This tactic may be used as a wedge to move the offender closer to admitting he lied on the relevant issues, which may then be construed as an admission. When used correctly, this ploy by the officer may severely undercut the confidence of a subject. Destroying a suspect's confidence is one of the major goals for an interrogation.

When a suspect lies or utters serious misstatements and these are used collectively to challenge him, expect to see less adamant and less forceful denials of the criminal issues.

Two additional points must be made about situations involving a suspect who lies. First, document every statement that contains a lie. If the lie is later cleared up, show the original lie and then record the version that is claimed as the truth. As the final outcome of an investigation is uncertain, this record will likely be helpful at trial time. The record of deceit may be sufficiently significant to keep the offender from taking the stand to testify on his behalf.

Second, strive never to call a person a liar. It is one of the most personal attacks you can make on a person's character. If the term *liar* is bandied about in the interview, it becomes more and more difficult for a person to confess. A smart subject may declare the interviewer to be insulting when all the offender wanted to do was come in and assist the police. He may then terminate the interview and blame the investigator. He will use this excuse down the road to refuse to again "cooperate."

With a similar goal, some suspects may also attempt to get under the officer's skin and anger him sufficiently to start an argument. This effort to challenge the officer's professionalism and get him to lose his temper may then be used to justify the offender terminating the interview, stating "I don't have to put up with abuse or those kinds of comments." He can make it appear as if the termination was the fault of the officer. Such diversions are usually best left unacknowledged, and the last unanswered question is repeated to keep the interview on track.

Instead of name calling, the same message can be delivered to the suspect by saying, "I don't understand... ," or "Tell me again how ...," or "Are you certain that... ." He will get the message that the officer is not buying his line, and that he has been caught. This is also a tactic for helping to save face.

Using Props

The term *props* is derived from the theater's use of various items to enhance the setting of and the dramatic message of a scene. If appropriately chosen, they can be an effective adjunct in the interview room. Like most pieces of the interviewing puzzle, props come with certain rules for their usage. A prop can be almost anything pertinent to the crime under investigation, but it must be possible for the police to have that item in their possession. If the item is not believable under the circumstances of the known case facts, the officer's credibility may be stretched or challenged. It is best if props are not designed to shock or overwhelm a suspect by displaying graphic and brutal depictions of a crime scene. The suspect is most likely not proud of what he has done, and such a display will only cause him to recoil or withdraw from the interview.

If the suspect is a person who would enjoy reliving his brutality, the officer is well advised not to reward him by showing graphic depictions. A strong caution is also issued against the display of crime scene photos, as they may inadvertently "educate" a person, who then recites in his false confession what he had seen and this is mistaken as validation of his confession. So, props can be just about anything, and they must be believable.

Case 9.4

I was consulted on a case involving the mysterious disappearance during the night of a 2-year-old female child from a room also occupied by her parents. The child's body was found, and a medical examination indicated a sexual violation at the time of her death. An analysis was provided to help pinpoint a suspect. Once a suspect was identified, a new analysis included a strategy for affecting his postoffense behavior. When the police were ready to confront this individual, they contacted me and laid out their interview plan. The plan included using a pair of underwear in a clear plastic baggie and placing it in plain view. The problem with this portion of the plan was that none of the child's clothing had been recovered; therefore the prop failed the test of being possible and believable. Had the interview gone forward as planned, it would have been doomed to failure from the point the prop was introduced. It is likely that the interviewer's credibility would have never recovered from this error.

Guarding an interviewer's credibility must be an integral part of any interview plan. Recovery from an honest mistake is difficult, but the recovery from an elaborate and ill-conceived tactic is often impossible.

Case 9.5

I was asked to polygraph and interview a high-ranking government official based on his claim that he received a note rolled up inside his morning newspaper. The note threatened his family if he did not pass over certain highly classified materials to which he had access. From the outset, no one was able to contact his family members to verify their safety, and the claims were regarded as a possible attempt to cover his murder of the entire family. He was adamant in refusing to identify their "safe location" even to the FBI. His physiological responses to all relevant questions about the note strongly indicated deception. During the ensuing interrogation, a copy of the note was repeatedly placed within his line of sight. It was repeatedly swept away by the government official without even the slightest examination. This was taken as a valid indicator that he did not need to see or examine the note because he had written it. This was confirmed when he confessed to having written the note because of personal problems. It was verified that he had indeed sent his family to stay with others for their "safety."

Case 9.6

I assisted in the investigation of the murder of a 10-year-old female, and when the suspect was identified, he was interviewed in a room that was "staged" with several different props. One of the props was a dress from the little girl, which was hung directly in his line of vision. The victim's clothing had not been recovered, so the police officer assigned to undertake the interview and interrogation and I made reference to the dress and told the suspect that the dress belonged to the victim, but it was not the one she was wearing when she disappeared. It was identified as having been hung in the tent used by individuals assisting the police in searching for the victim early in the investigation. The suspect fit that description. The intent for the dress to be placed in his line of sight was to remind him of what had occurred with the victim and to take him psychologically back to the time of the abduction, rape, and murder. He confessed to that crime and to another similar murder.

These case examples illustrate how the effectiveness of props can be increased when they are merged with the interview setting.

Some items used as props may be totally fictional, but they still must meet the rules set forth in this chapter; that is, if a prop suggests that there has been a wiretap, it must be possible to have had a wiretap. This usage of props requires more imagination and great care in how the officers refer to the props. This is a more delicate usage of props because police credibility is more likely to become an issue. In the setting described regarding the murder of a 10-year-old girl (Case 9.6), additional props were included. Also used were file cabinets with the drawers bearing large labels that bore the name of the suspect, his likely coconspirator, and other titles, such as evidence and official reports. The file cabinets contained only reams of blank paper.

Case 9.7

In a Florida community, the police developed a viable suspect for a series of rapes. Before conducting an interrogation, they decided to bolster their evidence indicating the suspect's guilt by creating two sets of DNA laboratory reports, which concluded that his DNA was found inside the victims. To pull this off, they secured blank laboratory report forms from the state police laboratory and from a private laboratory specializing in DNA testing. During the interview, they confronted the suspect with his guilt and the statement that they could conclusively prove his involvement. This was disputed by the suspect until the falsified DNA reports were shown to him one at a time. With this "uncontestable evidence" against him, the suspect confessed. The case was appealed, and the use of the made-up laboratory forms was challenged. In this case, *State v. Cayward*, the Florida Supreme Court ruled **"It may well be that a suspect is more impressed and thereby more easily induced to confess when presented with tangible, official-looking reports as opposed to merely being told that some tests have implicated him."** The court concluded that the officers had taken the use of props a step too far. The opinion indicated that to have only made reference to the existence of the laboratory reports would not have been offensive, but the presentation of the forms overwhelmed the suspect and made him unable to defend himself. The court was clearly concerned with how the false documents would be identified in court proceedings years later after the officers were retired or deceased. In summary, the court concluded that well-staged and carefully presented evidence using only verbal suggestions of their existence was acceptable but a confrontation with the actual falsified report was too overpowering.

It is acceptable to use a sealed, nontransparent paper grocery-type bag, and any item may be placed inside to give the appearance of substance. Evidence tape or sticker should also be positioned on the bag. The bag is then placed within sight of the suspected culprit and in a location that he will have to crane his head to view it clearly. It should not be placed directly in front of him. The more time the individual spends looking over the bag or the more he asks questions about the bag's contents, the stronger the indicator of guilt. Should questions be asked about the item, it will create additional internal tension for the guilty suspect and likely make his nonverbal gestures more pronounced. An innocent person would not be concerned about the presence of the "evidence bag."

Dealing with Crying

Crying by a suspect can be a difficult behavior to handle, particularly when the interviewer and the suspect are both men. Crying by a suspect may be viewed as having one of two meanings. For many suspects, male or female, crying may be a test for the interviewer. It can be an attempt at manipulation. It may be a probe to see how far the interviewer will push the suspect. If the suspect is crying, the topic being discussed likely deals with some aspect of their guilt. The suspect wants to see whether the interviewer will ease off or avoid the topic that caused the crying. If the officer can be intimidated with crying, how much resolve will he have on other issues?

Another possible reason for a suspect to cry is genuine remorse either for the criminal act or for having been caught. If the remorse is genuine, the interviewer is most likely a short step away from a confession if the crying is handled properly.

Whatever the cause of the crying, the same tactic for handling it is recommended. First, assume that the crying is genuine. In that circumstance, it is appropriate to immediately go into the persuasion mode using themes such as "It is okay to cry. I might cry, too, if I had on my mind what is on yours. It is just your heart, mind, and body telling you need to get this thing out in the open and deal with it. Let's listen to that voice inside and talk about this thing now." Now is the time to throw into the mix minimization and projection scenarios.

If the crying reflects true remorse and the interviewer uses this scenario, a confession may be at hand. If the crying is a ruse to test the officer, the suspect will realize by the investigator's pitch that it is not working and quickly stop crying.

The emotional side of crying raises the issue of whether an officer should ever touch a suspect as part of his persuasion strategy. I took a confession from an attractive woman using the theme that she was not a bad person but that she was caught in a set of circumstances that made her steal, and that she had regretted the theft from the moment it occurred. The female suspect began to cry, agreed to all of the propositions, and confessed. Then, she immediately asked me to give her a hug because she really needed some reassurance at that moment. While an officer might identify with a remorseful suspect's inner needs, it would be unprofessional to comply with her request. In that case, the suspect was provided additional verbal reassurances of her general good nature.

Touching an interviewee is not recommended, particularly given this era's focus on political correctness and sensitivities. Even with a witness present, an accusation of improper conduct is difficult to defeat and likely will remain a stain on an officer's career. Nonetheless, if an investigator thought it would enhance an opportunity to move an interview forward, touching should be done in precise ways. Touching works best with an emotional inter-viewee and when timed to a sensitive juncture in the interview. Touching can be a powerful closer. Touching a male or female should be restricted to the shoulder, the side of a knee (males only), the hand, or the forearm, but never any part of the body that could indicate sexual innuendo, including the face. An interviewer may decide that such a touch might nudge the person just enough to change the balance on an issue, but before touching he should test his theory that the interview subject is receptive to the touch. This is tested by making a broad gesture with his arms, and as he approaches the interviewee, the officer must be visually fixated on him. If he notices the subject freeze or give the slightest flinch, he can continue with his seemingly natural gesture and not touch the person.

Planting the Seeds of Confession

For more details on the topic of the seeds of confession, review Chapter 7 regarding verbal strategies. I have found it to be a successful tactic on a wide variety of felony cases, even with previously convicted subjects. Sometimes investigations do not provide an interviewer with a smoking gun or similar hard evidence with which to confront a suspect. I have used this technique successfully in cases with little or no evidence with which to drive a suspect away from his steadfast denials. Sometimes it is effective to plant seeds by itemizing investigative procedures that are to be attempted or are being explored, but whose results are not known at the time. Even if the results are already known, a suspect will not be aware of that information.

The concept is to hold out as possible any number of investigative proce-dures that a subject could take as a threat to being detected as the offender. This is more effective when the possibilities are discussed conversationally and one at a time. Returning to the topic of what is yet to happen investi-gatively can be picked up again and again to include adding new thoughts to the list. This tactic combines several verbal tactics outlined here and in Chapter 7. Verbal strategies that may be joined with the planting-seeds tactic include building up to the question, the use of soft words, the good cop/bad cop scenario, and the technique of procuring attention.

As often occurs, suspects hear or assume words which they construe as being favorable to them. An officer is not responsible for the offener's wishful thinking. Sometimes the seeds may be planted within a "what-if" or dangle scenario. The concept is for the offender to know all the possible sources of damaging evidence that may come to light and that he may interpret as a threat to his freedom. Those pieces of the investigation are theoretically applied to his set of circumstances via a scenario beginning with, "What if I were to find…." The mention of those investigative procedures is presented without the certainty of incriminating evidence being discovered (Inbau, Reid, and Buckley, 1986; Inbau et al., 2004). A broad list of possibilities for investigative avenues may be cited. As a reminder, the suspect knows precisely how the crime went down, so you may hit on a factor that, unknown to you, will worry him. The mistakes or oversights often made by other offenders when committing a crime can be brought forward (using the mind reading technique), along with the interviewer's suggestions of possible investigative techniques that could be used. Each investigative technique or process is a seed and may trigger a reminder of errors that were actually made by the culprit.

Some of the topics that may be "planted" as seeds include the possibility of discovering an eyewitness who can place him with the victim or near the scene, the possible existence of a security camera (even in rural areas), any possible forensic evidence, evidence accidentally overlooked or left behind, the family's attitude about the recovery of the victim's remains, and how the prosecutor approaches cases.

Case 9.8

While interviewing an individual who did not test well on intelligence tests but functioned well living on his own, I took time on a couple of occasions to explain Locard's theory of trace evidence, which forms the basis for all forensic testing (Moenssens, Moses, and Inbau, 1973). The scenario presented was how trace evidence is left behind by an individual, or picked up by an individual as he passes through the crime scene. The story was amplified by mentioning the advances in science for examining such trace evidence and the certainty of this investigative technique. After completing the scenario for the second time, the suspect looked at the author and said, "You found it, didn't you?" Having no idea what he was referring to, the author presented a positive demeanor and said, "Certainly, but you will earn credit by mentioning it yourself." The suspect's response was, "You found it, my driver's license. I lost it when I dumped her body."

Case 9.9

This case was briefly discussed in Chapter 7, but a more thorough examination may make the technique more clear. As part of a planned strategy, it was calculated that the suspect might decline to be interviewed about the abduction and homicide. In those circumstances, if the suspect declined to talk about the case but did not invoke his Miranda rights, three agents would engage him in a generalized conversation. By design, they were occasionally to drop in a few seeds. Knowing that he was previously convicted for a rape that included an anal assault, a brief mention of DNA and cleanup mistakes often made by offenders ensued. No reference to anal rape was made, just to the possible presence of blood. An example was presented of how a fine mist of blood often follows hitting someone in the nose. The example included the gesture of a fist hitting an open palm (nose). To add to the description, an agent suggested that often offenders try to clean up their scenes but always miss something minor such as a very fine drop of blood. An example was used of how such a fine mist might deposit a small drop under the seam or roll of a seat cover. Later this topic was picked up again, and an example was added regarding how little blood is now required to determine a person's identity because of the giant strides made in DNA science. A finger was held up to represent a tiny needle. The example mentioned was that all that was required to determine someone's identity was a drop so small that it could be balanced on the tip of that needle. A brief reminder followed about how some criminals forget to thoroughly clean up their crime scene.

Other examples about microscopes for hair comparison and the position the prosecutor may take were interspersed through the conversations until the suspect declared that he wanted to return to his cell. He provided a complete confession two days later without a single question being asked. The "seeds" had weighed heavily on his mind since the initial contact. He believed that it was better to settle the matter then and there than to prolong it and have positions harden. The seeds had the "feel of evidence" to him.

In American culture, security cameras are everywhere. Many are so powerful that they encompass areas greater than required by the homeowner or company using them. The cameras are so plentiful and noted so frequently in news stories and TV crime shows that their presence is assumed, accepted, and dismissed from thought. One of the seeds to be planted is that security cameras are a natural feature of the American landscape. They are everywhere. They may be described as existing or as being sought out as part of the ongoing investigation. The seed is built up by describing the clarity provided by the camera, the number of cameras in the area, and the coverage they afford well beyond what is needed. Case examples, real or made up, can be introduced depicting how miraculously a case was solved by the offender being caught on a video recorded great distances from the actual crime scene. If the criminal is at all concerned about how careful he was in committing the crime, he may become worried about explaining his image on the film. The pitch to the suspect may include the advantage of coming forward on his own before his picture is found so that he may earn credit for standing up and taking responsibility for his actions. A suspect who is involved in the crime may respond that he is doubtful that the cameras will have his picture; however, his denial will not be as absolute as in, "You can't find me on the film because I was not there." The telling point of all dangle questions like the video camera ploy is how the subject asserts his rejection of any possibility of the dangle ploy affecting him, that is, being identified by a witness, his fingerprint being found at the crime scene, and so on.

Case 9.10

When the initial suspect in a murder was shown fingerprints supposedly lifted from the crime scene, he assumed that they were his and made serious alterations to his story. When the officer had him trapped, he admitted his guilt but identified his friend as being the primary participant (Suspect 2). Suspect 2 was interviewed on the basis of the first suspect's identification. When he was informed that his fingerprints had been found in the victim's room, he rejected that as not being possible because he had never been in the room. A second dangle ploy was attempted in which Suspect 2 was told that a security camera had recently been installed, and that he was filmed at the entrance of the victim's room. At this assertion, he became adamant that he could not be on film because he was not there. He offered to view the film to show the detective his error and to show that it was not him being photographed. Those denials are typical of how an innocent party will react to a dangle ploy.

Third-Person Scenarios

It is helpful to find a tool to start a suspect on the path of reasoning along the same line as the interrogator. Third-person scenarios fit the bill as they encourage him to tell a story with supposed immunity. First, be certain that the interviewee is listening and following what is being said. This may be accomplished by prefacing the question with his first name, building up the question, or gently tapping his knee.

Then, to achieve the goal of speaking in the third person, some ground rules are explained before beginning the tactic. The suspect is told that there is a way he may speak without any guilt attached to anything he says. The suspect may be reminded of the game "Simon says," in which the players are to follow directions only when the request is asked using a specific phrase. Similar to that game, the suspect is informed that if any statement is made by him when first saying, "What if I were to tell you ...?" it cannot be used against them because they really did not say it. The crook is free from having admitted anything at all because he said *"What if* I told you."

This tactic is useful when a suspect has heard the arguments, themes, and RPMs (rationalizations, projections, and minimizations) without continuing to raise strong denials but is yet to make an incriminating statement. It is highly difficult for a person to continue speaking in the third person. Most will fall quickly to the first person without realizing they have done so and continue to speak as if the statements are protected.

Another use of the third-person technique is to entice reluctant suspects to identify what they can give the prosecutor should he desire to offer any consideration or leniency. Clearly state that you do not have the authority to make any deals but are willing to act as a conduit to the prosecutor. Ask, "What can I tell the prosecutor on your behalf?" At this point, introduce the third-person technique. Further, tell him that you will relay exactly what he wants you to and see if there is any interest in his information. It is advisable to provide an example of what he may say: "See, if you were to say, 'What if I could provide … ,' what consideration would be given?'"

It is practical to have a prosecutor who can be readily reached so any arrangement can be made on the spot.

The likelihood of success with this technique drops significantly once the contact is terminated and the atmosphere grows cold; there is time for second thoughts, or the offender has an opportunity to consult with an attorney or confederate. The drop off in success occurs even if the officer has secured a promise of continuing the interview at a fixed time. Strike while the iron is hot.

Case 9.11

Richard Grissom Jr. is now a convicted serial murderer who a police officer and I interviewed about the disappearance of three young women. Well into the interview, the third-person scenario was utilized without immediate success. However, hours later when I escorted him to a holding cell pending his appearance before a magistrate, Grissom said in substance, "You tell that prosecutor I can give him everything." He was asked if "everything" meant telling about the abduction and murder of the women and the location of their bodies. He agreed those items, and others, were covered in the term *everything.* Note that he did not insert any mitigating phrase in front of his statement. He was convicted of all three murders.

Case 9.12

After a stepfather suspected of having killed his stepdaughter had failed to show up for a polygraph test offered by the state police, I was asked to polygraph him. Two features of this interview were interesting and revealing. First, the suspect showed up for the interview more than an hour early. Also, the suspect said he was a "trucker" when asked about his employment. It was known that he drove a step van for local deliveries, but this distortion was heard without comment. In his mind, he saw himself as a trucker, or a tough guy.

Case analysis disclosed the likely scenario for the problem between the stepfather and his new stepdaughter was his demand to force her to be accountable to him for her curfew and with whom she associated. Although he denied it, I always suspected the stepfather had a sexual interest in his attractive stepdaughter, based in part on his belief she was sexually active with others. During the confrontational phase of the contact, the third-person scenario was employed. He was repeatedly asked to tell his story. As is natural, he often forgot to invoke the introductory phrase. When this happened, additional questions were put to him, and he answered them in the first person. Eventually, he was asked if he was ready to put his confession in writing as he had repeatedly told the story in the first person. He dramatically slapped the polygraph charts and announced that he was sticking to his story. The stepfather was asked to mentally review his statements that were made in the first person, and he took a moment. Then, sheepishly, said he would sign the confession.

The "strike while the iron is hot" came into play when the stepfather in the early part of the interview continued to state that he loved his wife, the victim's mother. At one point he said he wanted to leave and speak with his wife, but that he would immediately return and finish the interview. He said he wanted to tell his wife first. There was something in the way this message was delivered that caused great concern on my part. First, if he left he would not return. Second, what did he want to tell his wife before telling the authorities? I immediately suspected a murder-suicide plot was unfolding and changed gears in the interview. The man was reminded of his repeated statements of love and affection for his wife and was told "Look, if you really care for her you can't just walk up to her and say your daughter is dead. If you give me just a little hint of what she will be told about her daughter, to soften the blow for her, I will give her that hint for her sake." He responded by saying the daughter would never return. This was leveraged to get more "hints," which included that she was dead, that she was in water, and that her body would not be found for weeks.

As he signed his confession and was taken into custody by local authorities, he also provided consent to search his vehicle. Inside his truck they located a shotgun and box of shells that he had purchased that day just prior to reporting for the interview.

Role Reversal

Role reversal has been mentioned before but not in detail. It is derived from an old parable "stand in my shoes and see what I see." Role reversal is integral to the reasoning phase of interviewing, particularly in the confrontation stage. As with any other element calling for processing critical thoughts, the interest and attention of the subject must be secured first. Most of the emotion from the confrontation should be dissipated by having allowed the person to make a denial before using this technique. Or, a point may be chosen when the emotions are under control. Not reaching either emotional state will interfere with rational processing. Role reversal requires the interviewer to present the strengths of the investigation or weaknesses of the subject. He then asks the offender to take a step back and see how someone removed from the case would view those facts.

In whose shoes do you ask the suspect to stand? Just about anyone can be used for the example. The "shoes" may belong to his spouse, children, employer, or someone else he admires. I preferred to use my supervisor, the prosecutor, members of the jury, or occasionally to offer up my own "shoes." The options are presented to the subject and he is encouraged to adopt the perspective of a rational or neutral party. For instance: "Look, Tom, let's review what is known at this point. Most of these things have already been talked about here today, but while I run them down, think about how someone else will see them. Look carefully at what direction this information points. Then ask yourself if you understand why you are sitting in that chair today and why I am sitting opposite you." The "someone else" should be named and his qualities and integrity itemized. An alternative approach may be as follows:

Tom, I have been in this game for many years and have been through lots of trials. I can tell you without a doubt that the court system is not perfect, but it is pretty damn good. Sure, mistakes are made because it is made up of people. I have watched juries being picked and said to myself, "I would not want that person on my jury." But something almost magical happens when those 12 people come together and they reason as one person. I am sometimes truly amazed, but they get it right almost every time. They can read people and how they tell their story and decide if they are truthful. Together, they will find the holes in the stories. Now, picture your jury sitting over here in the corner. How will they see you when they have heard [enumerate strong points and who will tell them] or when you take the stand and tell them the nonsense you have been telling me? But, why would you want to go that far? Why not get the best deal you can before you spend all of your family's money on an attorney and make the prosecutor mad on top of that? Do it right and don't wait for the jury to expose you to their harsh judgment. In this case, who is going to believe you?

Reading Minds

Can you read minds? Despite your quick response, the correct answer is, "Yes!" Think about this: If I could tell what you are thinking, would it undermine your confidence? Having read in this book about conducting analysis in criminal matters, studying the victim's lifestyle, recognizing the thought process of the criminally inclined, and the methods employed by rapists, an investigator can quickly imagine how that person would handle all parts of his crime. His experience with other criminals involved in similar crimes, or crime in general, should equip the investigator with the knowledge of how the criminal world deals with crime, co-conspirators, the ugly nature of their crimes, their fears, and their vulnerabilities. Those are among the messages you can send to a suspect that will unconsciously cause him to feel like you are reading his mind, that you are inside his consciousness, and that you understand him, flaws and all. By using the mind-reading technique, the interviewer places himself inside the suspect's psyche. When a suspect believes you are superior to him and that you know how he has thought about crime, how he has thought about this crime with this particular victim, and what he is thinking on the spot about how to best defend himself, he is more likely than not to believe he can trust you with his secrets.

He is more ready to accept you as a confidante when you have softened the crime and his culpability through themes, RPMs, reasoning, and by telling him how he views his situation. By reading their minds, the investigator can accomplish what Holmes (1995) described as taking the wind out of their sails. This analogy means that, like a sailboat without wind in its sails, the suspect whose mind you are reading has the feeling that he is dead in the water.

The reading of minds technique is especially powerful if the officer never mentions the suspect's name while describing what he knows about criminals. Allow the suspect to make the connection between the officer's experience and knowledge base and his own internal guidance system. It is better for him suddenly to realize that while you are not mentioning him directly, you are actually talking about him. This tactic is most powerful when delivered lightly, with a feather touch that dances across the offender's psysche. Do not use a sledgehammer to drive home the same messages.

Good Cop/Bad Cop

The good cop/bad cop scenario is a tried-and-true technique police have been using for more than 100 years. It continues to be effective, even when the person is an experienced criminal. It works even when the criminal knows that the tactic is being used.

Case 9.13

While assisting a local police department on the highest-profile case they had ever had, I was requested to interview a suspect. The investigation involved a mother, her daughter, and her daughter's friend. All three mysteriously disappeared from a residence after a graduation ceremony. The interview plan called for a good cop/bad cop ploy at some point late in the interview. When it came into play, the subject was quick to point out that he knew what was happening. His comment was ignored, and the ploy continued to unfold. Several minutes after he had labeled the technique, the subject related that the three bodies had been placed in a well, and a trucker whose first name was known was involved in the disappearance.

The original design of the good cop/bad cop plan called for two officers to play off each other by presenting opposing versions of a crime. One officer would offer a soft version that was more favorable to the suspect, while the second officer would present a much harsher version of what had happened and the suspect's role in those acts. I prefer to use only one officer, the lead interviewer, and to portray the prosecutor as the bad cop. This variation seems to work better. Also, the prosecutor will probably never enter the interview room, so there is little chance of mixing up the "scripts." The variations of story lines are unlimited. An example of the good cop's role could be found by portraying the events as being "an accident" or a story line suggesting that the victim precipitated the events that led to the assault and murder. This approach is contrasted by a harshly stated position that casts the suspect as one who thoroughly planned the entire string of events, who enjoyed the murder, and who would do it again. Without taking a break, the contrasting version is again presented, perhaps with some minor changes, and the subject is asked which is closer to the real story, the harsh version that draws on a negative image of the suspect or the more generous story that treats the acts as unfortunate but understandable. The good cop position makes generous use of RPMs. Reid and associates package this ploy as one of their nine steps of interrogation under the label "Alternative Question."

The good cop/bad cop technique may be combined with several other tactics, such as planting seeds or role reversal. One of the strongest recommendations for this technique is that it allows the officer who is playing "good cop" to confront the ugly nature of a crime without getting his hands dirty or losing his bond with the subject. The bad version is not his, and he sees some good qualities of the subject or more favorable circumstances in the crime.

The good cop/bad cop technique allows the interviewer to confront without a confrontation.

Polygraph Question

Some jurisdictions have attempted to protect legitimate victims by making it unlawful to give them polygraph examinations to determine if their complaint is truthful. I am unaware of any jurisdiction that has forbidden the asking of questions about the polygraph technique. To err on the safe side, an officer should seek legal advice within his department or from the prosecutor who has to defend his actions in court. Dangle and bait questions are also addressed in Chapter 7. By asking the polygraph bait question, the interviewer is forcing the interviewee to deal with the issue of lying: "My boss is a real stickler on this type of inquiry. So if he were to ask you to take a polygraph, would you do it (even though he can't require you to)?" Most people, truthful or deceptive, will agree to take the test. The immediate follow-up question from the officer is, "When asked on the test about the criminal acts, how will you do?" The value of this pair of questions is that the deceptive suspect is likely to immediately start making excuses why he cannot take the test.

Case 9.14

The FBI was investigating an unexplained death in a federal penitentiary. An elderly inmate with a very thin, lightweight build had been found hanging in his shower. The pathologist reported that the elderly inmate could not have hanged himself as his weight was insufficient to cause the deep furrows in his neck. His cell partner came under immediate suspicion. The cell partner was a hardened criminal and a member of a white supremacist gang and was clearly a very strong individual. I was requested to assist in the investigation, and as I prepared to conduct the polygraph, asked, "How are you going to do on this test?" The response was, "I am not going to do worth a damn because I killed the … ." The remainder of the test was cancelled. The same approach could be used in a structured interview without actually using a polygraph.

Bury Personal Beliefs

Anyone who claims not to have bias is only fooling himself. Whatever the bias, it must not leak into the interview forum. My one-time partner hated child molesters. Many in policing likely share a strong distaste for that vile criminality. My partner's approach was to defer those interviews to someone else. That was an approach that worked for him, but not everyone in policing has that luxury. The secret for interviewing someone who scores low on a list of admirable attributes is to focus on the interview process and the goals of the interview. If the person can be demonstrated to be a child abuser, then focus on taking him off the street and placing him somewhere he cannot reach another child. The interview that contains elements that trigger a strong emotional feeling within the interviewer require strong adherence to an interview plan loaded with techniques designed to steer away from the problem. Offender characteristics are not justifications for an officer becoming upset and making the interview personal. Avoiding demeanor slips will not be easy, but the professional officer can master it. A professional interviewer must learn to keep his personal feelings out of the interview process.

Listening as a Tactic

Interviewing may be divided into two portions of equal importance. One phase is the interview phase, and the other is the interrogation phase. In the interview phase, the interviewer strives to cause the interviewee to provide more information. His role in interviewing is to lessen his speaking parts by following Sapir's 5%/95% rule (1987, 1992a). See Chapter 7 for a more detailed explanation of that rule.

When the interview moves to the interrogation phase, the officer remains charged with carefully listening, but he has the added burden of being responsible for doing most of the talking. Once he has outlined the case against the person and allowed a suspect to make his denials, the officer's job is to make use of the themes, RPMs, and reasoning lines, speaking in a neutral tone. The key to doing an effective job is to know when to listen and when to talk.

In both the interview and interrogation phases, an officer must also listen for evidence of an uncooperative interviewee by listening carefully for the use of linguistic codes. Lack of cooperation can be found in how a question is answered. When an officer makes a statement requiring an answer, a straightforward answer signals a cooperative person. If the same clear statement is made and the person responds with a question, he is signaling resistance to the thrust of the interview.

Resistance may also be read as a clue to an attempt to conceal information. The stalling created by the return question gains more time for the suspect to consider what information he will give up and what part of the statement will be edited. Per Sapir (1987, 1992a), note should be taken of any question asked by a subject at any point during the interview. Every question signals the sensitivity of the question to the subject and is for the interviewee a decision point for deciding whether to conceal data. The interviewer should take a brief mental break and assess why the person could not answer that question and why the question would be a topic sensitive to him.

Linguistic Codes

Linguistics means the study of language, while a *code* refers to disguises. So, the use of linguistic codes means to speak using words whose true meaning may not be known. Active and intense listening may well turn up linguistic codes chosen by the interviewee. When a person has used the "question answered with a question," or any other technique, to buy time, he may be editing his answer with words specifically chosen to conceal additional data. One way to conceal is to use a precise term whose meaning may not be known by anyone other than the speaker. The selected term may be chosen in the belief that the officer will assume he knows what it means but is only being used to cover the editing of data. If the interviewer does not isolate his attention on such phrasing and follow up with illuminating questions, the true meaning of a statement may never be known. The lyrics to the song "Seems it Never Rains in Southern California" contain the phrase "don't tell them how you found me." Contemplate what that sentence would mean if it were to be used in an interview. By the phrase "how you found me," is the speaker talking about the method of finding him or the condition in which he was when found?

In an interview setting, the above phrase is an example of linguistic code. Such codes are used universally under the assumption that the speaker knows what is meant, as does the listener. In interviewing and interrogating, one cannot make the assumption that both the speaker and listener have the same interpretation of a phrase. An interviewer must be attuned to the use of linguistic codes and always clarify the exact meaning of each rather than assume the interviewee knows what is meant.

In a homicide interview, a subject might make a statement and quickly follow it by saying, "You know what I mean." He may not be challenged regarding what exactly he was referring to when he used that phrase. It is usually preferable to take notice of the phrases that may be linguistic codes, allow the person to tell his story, and then go back over the data with the codes to ensure clarity in the statements.

Material edited from a statement may be covered over with the use of linguistic codes. Linguistic codes are the left-behind traces of what has been edited can be explored to reveal what was edited, altered, or outright omitted, but only if the code is noted and follow-up questions are pursued.

Answering a Question with a Question

Careful listening by the interviewer will identify the subject's use of a question to answer a question as a stalling tactic that represents resistance to providing answers on a particular issue. Why is there a need to stall? Stalling is most often characteristic of a person who is being deceptive or who is troubled enough by the sensitivity of the question to want to avoid the topic. The stall may be used to gain time to formulate a response consistent with previous answers and to compare his answer with questions expected to be asked down the road. The interviewer must separate out whether the person is being deceptive or is uncomfortable with discussing the topic. It may be that the person is not involved in the crime but has information around the subject matter and would rather not provide it. Sapir (1992a, 1998) instructed that any time a question is used as part of an answer to a clearly stated question, the person is signaling that the question has hit on sensitive information, and he needs to stall to fabricate or edit his statement.

Nonresponsive Interview Subject

A subject may balk at answering certain interview questions, sometimes by not saying anything or responding with a question of his own. Either nonresponse indicates resistance. If the question asked is clear and there is no need for the subject to ask for clarification, it is best for the officer not to respond but to restate the question and pause for an answer. Should the subject still not provide an answer, in accordance with Sapir's (1987, 1992a) SCAN (scientific content analysis) program, the officer may say, "Why is it difficult for you to answer this question?" This is a polite question, but it is also a firm question requiring an answer. The officer's response psychologically suggests that the inability to answer is indicative of someone who has something to hide from the police.

Forbidden Phrases

As instructed by Sapir (1987), a police interviewer must never assist in an interview by supplying the wording of an answer. He should always avoid completing a sentence for the interviewee when the interviewee appears to be stuck for words. An officer should not provide an excuse as to why the other person should not take a question seriously or not answer the question at all. Such interjection defeats the interviewing process and alters the reality of a suspect's answers. It is not rude to remain passive and silent when a person stumbles for words. It is unprofessional to provide an answer, relieving the subject of responsibility to put his statements into his own words.

Therefore, it is out of bounds for an interviewer to say, "I know this is a hard question," "You may not know the answer," or "This won't be easy for you." This is providing forgiveness in advance and giving the person an excuse to avoid providing an answer. The guilty will immediately latch on to such phrases and repeat them back, completely dodging the issue (Sapir 1987, 1992a).

Real-Time Evaluations: Did the Subject Answer the Question?

Reid and Sapir teach a firm stance regarding nonanswers often provided by those trying to cloud the issues or skip answering tough questions. If a simple and clear question is put to someone in a criminal inquiry, the person should be able to answer it. It is not acceptable to allow a person to slide when asked a direct question, such as "Did you do it?" or "Are you somehow involved in this matter?" When the response is, "I would not do something like that," "I am not that desperate," or "I have no reason to do that, I am making good money," the question simply has been avoided. Who would want to avoid answering that type of question? The answer is the person involved in the crime. By not answering the question, the subject has, in fact, answered the question. If the answer is not a clear and an unequivocal "No," the person has by default said "Yes." I endorse Sapir's doctrine that the answer, "Listen, I am telling you I didn't do it," is not a denial. He did not simply say, "I didn't do it."

Any time an answer does not match the question, the interviewer should take special note of that area of questioning. Particular attention should be paid to answers that are out of sync with the question. For example, the question "What time did you arrive home to find your daughter missing?" receives an answer, "I was late getting back; some time after noon would be my guess. But I was no longer angry with her by then." A portion of the answer is out of context with the question and may point to a reason the child is missing. At a minimum, there is an obligation to clear up the mystery of information provided outside the context of the question. In such a situation, the individual is signaling that the additional data are a concern to him and are on his mind. The linguistic code here must be explored and broken. The officer has to decide whether to broach the "anger" issue immediately or to wait to see if that topic surfaces elsewhere. Holding back on the follow-up is recommended because jumping into the topic flags it and places the person on alert to avoid any further mention of anger.

Conclusion

The tactics approved by the courts for police interviews are many, and they multiply when one is combined with another. The interview plan calls for an outline of those tactics chosen based on the analysis of the crime, the understanding of how the victim's lifestyle played a role in selection as the victim, and the vulnerabilities of a suspect based on the targeted suspect interview. Many choices must be made before the difficult task of interviewing commences, and those choices will most likely determine the outcome of the inquiry.

Bibliography

Abrams, Stan. *Complete Polygraph Handbook*. Lexington, MA: Lexington Books, 1989.

Caplan, Gerald M. Questioning Miranda. *Vanderbilt Law Review* 38(6) (November 1985): 1417–1476.

Cassell, Paul G. Balanced Approaches to the False Confession Problem: A Brief Comment on Ofshe, Leo, and Alschuler. *Denver University Law Review* 74 (1997): 1123–1143.

Deaver, Jeffrey. *The Sleeping Doll*. New York: Simon and Schuster, 2007.

de Becker, Gavin. *The Gift of Fear*. Boston: Little, Brown, 1997.

Ekman, Paul. *Emotions Revealed*. New York: Holt, 2003.

Gudjonsson, Gisli. *The Psychology of Interrogation, Confessions and Testimony*. Chichester, UK: Wiley, 1992.

Hare, Robert D. *Without Conscience*. New York: Guilford Press, 1999.

Hazelwood, Robert R., and Ann W. Burgess. *Practical Aspects of Rape Investigation: A Multidisciplinary Approach*. 4th ed. Boca Raton, FL: CRC Press, 2009.

Hess, John E. *Interviewing and Interrogation for Law Enforcement*. Cincinnati, OH: Anderson, 1997.

Holmes, Warren D. Interrogation. *Polygraph* 24(4) (1995): 237–258.

Holmes, Warren D. *Criminal Interrogation*. Springfield, IL: Thomas, 2002.

Inbau, Fred E., John E. Reid, and Joseph P. Buckley. *Criminal Interrogation and Confessions*. 3rd ed. Baltimore, MD: Williams and Wilkins, 1986.

Inbau, Fred E., John E. Reid, Joseph P. Buckley, and Brian C. Jayne. *Criminal Interrogations and Confessions*. 4th ed. Sudbury, MA: Jones and Bartlett, 2004.

Jayne, Brian C., and Joseph P. Buckley. Interrogation Alert! Will Your Next Confessions Be Suppressed? *The Investigator* (Winter 1998): Special Edition.

Leo, R. A., and R. J. Ofshe. The consequences of False Confession; Deprivations of Liberty and Miscarriages of Justice in the Age of Psychological Interrogation. *Annual Meeting of the Law and Society Association Meeting at St. Louis, Missouri, May 30, 1997*. Law & Society Associaton, 1997. 1–71.

McManus, Barry L. *Liar*. Leesburg, VA: Global Traveler, 2008.

Moenssens, Andre A., Ray E. Moses, and Fred E. Inbau. *Scientific Evidence in Criminal Cases*. Mineola, NY: Foundation Press, 1973.

Napier, Michael R. Interviewing the Rapist. In *Practical Aspects of Rape Investigation: A Multidisciplinary Approach*, 123–137. Boca Raton, FL: CRC Press, 2009.

Napier, Michael R., and Susan H. Adams. Magic Words to Obtain Confessions. *FBI Law Enforcement Bulletin* 67(10) (October 1998): 1–6.

Napier, Michael R., and Susan Adams. Criminal Confessions: Overcoming the Challenge. *FBI Law Enforcement Bulletin* (November 2002): 9–15.

Napier, Michael R., and Kenneth P. Baker. Criminal Personality Profiling. In *Forensic Science: An Introduction to Scientific and Investigative Techniques*, edited by Stuart H. James and Jon J. Nordby, 531–550. Boca Raton, FL: CRC Press, 2002.

Napier, Michael R., and Kenneth P. Baker. Criminal Personality Profiling. In *Forensic Science: An Introduction to Scientific and Investigative Techniques*, edited by Stuart H. James and Jon J. Nordby, 615–636. Boca Raton, FL: CRC Press, 2005.

Ofshe, R. J., and R. A. Leo. The Decision to Confess Falsely: Rational Choice and Irrational Action. *Denver University Law Review* 74 (979) (1997a): 1051–1122.

Ofshe, R. J., and R. A. Leo. Social Psychology of Police Interrogation: Theory and Classification of True and False Confessions. *Studies in Law, Policies and Society* 16 (1997b): 189–251.

Rabon, D. *Investigative Discourse Analysis*. Durham, NC: Carolina Academic Press, 2003.

Samenow, Stanton. *Inside the Criminal Mind*. New York: Times Books, 1984.

Sapir, Avinoam. *The LSI Course on Scientific Content Analysis*. Phoenix, AZ: Laboratory for Scientific Interrogation, 1987.

Sapir, Avinoam. *The LSI Annual Advanced Workshop on Scientific Content Analysis*. Phoenix, AZ: Laboratory for Scientific Interrogation, 1992a.

Sapir, Avinoam, *LSI Scientific Content Analysis Newsletter Anthology*. Phoenix, Arizona: Laboratory for Scientific Interrogation, 1992b.

Sapir, Avinoam. *LSI Advanced Workshop on Scientific Content Analysis*. Phoenix, AZ: Laboratory for Scientific Interrogation, 1998.

Shuy, Roger W. *The Language of Confession, Interrogation and Deception*. Thousand Oaks, CA: Sage, 1998.

Vessel, D. Conducting Successful Interrogations. Ott, J., Ed. *FBI Law Enforcement Journal* 67(10) (October 1998): 11–15.

Yeschke, Charles L. *The Art of Investigative Interviewing*. Boston: Butterworth-Heinemann, 1997.

Zulawski, David E., and Douglas E. Wicklander. *Practical Aspects of Interview and Interrogation*. 2nd ed. Boca Raton, FL: CRC Press, 2002.

Interview of the Rape Victim and Rapist Typologies

10

MICHAEL R. NAPIER

Contents

Case 10.1

In a small Midwest city, the home of a state university, a young female coed disappeared from a birthday party without notifying her many companions that she was ill. For reasons never determined, she only confided in a male coworker, who was, unknown to her, a convicted rapist who had been released on parole after serving 10 years. Her mistake ended with her rape and murder. There was no evidence to assist authorities in undertaking an investigation. The best lead was a witness who said he saw the victim and the rapist leave the party at the same time, but he did not see them leave "together" or to go in the same direction.

Realizing he was likely to become the focus of the ensuing investigation, the rapist fled, and a warrant was issued for his arrest on a parole violation. This case became a high-profile matter and was featured on *America's Most Wanted* TV show. The rapist saw the TV show and turned himself in to the police in Florida.

Prior to his arrest, another woman from the same community contacted authorities and identified the rapist as the man who had raped her a few days before the coed's disappearance. I requested the state investigative agency to interview his latest victim and to use the questionnaire located in the Appendix. They were also asked to locate and interview the prior victim whose rape had resulted in the offender's prison sentence. Once completed, a review of both questionnaires revealed extensive similarities from both rapes even though separated by 10 years.

The review also provided a clear picture of this offender both as a person and as a rapist, and provided many usable pieces of information that would assist in his interrogation. Of particular note was both victims' description of how his demeanor changed during the rapes. Both reported a drastic change in demeanor in the rapist once he had ejaculated. At that point, he became upset, apologetic, and pleading. He used a con ruse to plead that the rape not be reported, claimed he had never done anything like that in the past, and profusely apologized to the victims.

When I interviewed this suspect, strategic use was made of the details from the questionnaires. Specifically, his behaviors as provided by the victims were described to him without any indication that the information was really about him (mind reading technique). His name was never attached to the described behaviors, but instead they were attributed to what I had learned about offenders from dealing with many rapes over the years. When his change in demeanor was described as being behavior observed about other offenders, his face was closely observed. At that point, his face drained of all color. It was clear that he was experiencing the sensation of the interviewer being inside his psyche and "reading his mind." This process, along with other tactics, wreaked havoc with his confidence and ability to defend himself from the allegations. He thought the interviewer knew him too well to be able to get through the interview without a confession.

Initial Investigative Steps

This chapter focuses on handling rape investigations, commencing with the interview of the surviving victim, and includes the typing of rapists based on the information secured from the victim.* Victim debriefing is only the first part of an investigator's preparation for a suspect interview or interrogation. The next logical step is to utilize the data from the victim, the physical crime scene, and any forensics available to place the rapist in the most fitting rape type category. Once the essential victim debriefing has taken place, the astute investigator will use the data from the victim to determine the type of rapist he is investigating.

Would any competent investigator undertake an investigation and suspect interview without first processing the crime scene? Of course not. The victim's knowledge, impressions of the rape, along with her body, are crime scenes in

---

* This chapter is based on my experiences, which were shaped through lectures provided by the Behavioral Science Unit (BSU) of the Federal Bureau of Investigation (FBI), principally by Robert R. Hazelwood, as well as many personal conversations with him. I am proud to claim Roy as a friend, mentor, and partner. His publications in professional journals and books on these topics also serve as a factual basis for the information here. Every professional working sex crimes of any type should possess and be familiar with *Practical Aspects of Rape Investigations*, co-edited with Ann Wopart Burgess. This book is currently in its fourth edition (2009).

a rape investigation. The most viable information that can be obtained about the rapist is imprinted on the victim's psyche and will not be eradicated for many years to come, if ever. She will likely experience night terrors, flashbacks, and many other aspects of the post-traumatic stress syndrome.

The sex crimes investigator has a choice to make regarding whether he does a generic interview of the victim or enters into a behaviorally directed interview. A thorough interview of the victim goes beyond obtaining the offender's description and establishing the statutory requirements for prosecution (e.g., penetration against her will). The proper foundation for a rape investigation must begin with the physical crime scene combined with a behavioral-oriented interview of the victim.

Using Rapist Typologies

Human behavior cannot be placed in neat pigeonholes. However, rapist typologies are highly utilitarian for a knowledgeable investigator. The known behaviors that fit the FBI research-based descriptions provide a good guide for focusing the early planning of the investigation, including emphasis on which potential suspects are the most viable.

What is the importance of behaviors captured by the behavioral interview of the victim?* It is a behavioral principle that people attempt to act in a manner in which they are most comfortable and to avoid conduct that makes them uncomfortable. A reliable behavioral corollary that flows from this principle is that offenders behave in their everyday activities along the same lines as they do in their criminal acts (e.g., if they are abusive and degrading with the victim, they will generally treat nonvictim females similarly). It is also evident that offenders reveal some of their hidden personality, proclivities, and insight into their identity through the manner in which they act with the victim.

Therefore, what is gleaned from the victim debriefing is revealing regarding the man, and the rapist, when the victim describes his:

Verbal and sexual strategies
Physical strategy of minimal force or uncalled-for physical injuries
Approach method
Techniques for maintaining control of the victim
Possession or absence of a weapon
Myriad other actions contained in the questionnaire

A few explanations are in order to emphasize the benefits inherent in conducting the interview geared to discovering the offender's behaviors. One of the

---

* See Hazelwood's "Behavior-Oriented Interview of Rape Victims: A Key to Profiling," in the Appendix. It accompanies the sexual assault victim's interview questionnaire.

major concerns of a rapist is how he will gain control of a victim without being identified or injured. Hence his approach plan is significant to him in practical ways, but the plan must also be psychologically comforting and in keeping with his comfort realm. Only three choices are at his disposal. He may approach the victim with a simple or elaborate con or story to gain her confidence to place her more at ease before turning aggressive. He may confront her with immediate violence, rendering her unable to resist, or he may lay in wait for her behind a bush or inside her residence using the cover of darkness to employ his surprise approach characterized by his reduced violence.

The first option will be used by a rapist who is verbally skilled and secure in his ability to deal face to face with a female. The second option is the blitz assault will be played out by an angry rapist who is not concerned about injuring the victim by his immediate use of brutal and injurious force. He is likely in a state of anger arousal with women in general. The last option, the surprise method, is for the man who is not angry with women, is not looking for an opportunity to harm them, and does not have the strength of character to engage them in verbal exchanges.*

These, and several other traits, are readily accessed by asking the victim the recommended behavioral questions, as presented in the Appendix. Almost without exception, the rapists' verbal strategy, injury-causing physical behavior, and his level of sexual violence will be consistent one with another. For example, if he is inquisitive of the victim, is nonprofane in his direction to her, and exhibits verbal concerns for her comfort, he generally will be reluctant to physically injure her, and his sexual demands will be less rough.

For the interview to be worthwhile, the officer needs to patiently work with the victim to obtain information on each verbal utterance, physically injurious act, and sexual demand with precision and in sequence. The best data in each category are those that the officer is comfortable with placing in quotation marks. For example, it is noteworthy for the victim to simply indicate that she was threatened, but it is more useful to determine if the rapist said, "I will hurt you if you do that again" or "If you do that again, I will hurt you." They are the same nine words, but they represent entirely different rapists. One has "hurt" out of his mouth more quickly; therefore, "hurt" is more on his mind.

To further explain the worth of this concept, it should be understood that behaviors do not happen in isolation but rather as a sequence of events. If the victim is cautioned that she will be harmed if she repeats an act of resistance, the sequence of events leading up to, and following, that caution complete the picture. Why did the offender feel it necessary to caution her (rather than punish her), and if she repeated her resistance, did he again caution her, or did he do as promised and harm her? The implementation of this

---

* See the article by Hazelwood and the assault victim's interview questionnaire in the Appendix for more questions that reveal offender behaviors.

verbal tactic is not random. It reveals the rapist's comfort with violence, his motivation for the rape, his ability to handle stress, and other traits that are useful in the offender-specific interview plan.

Rape Victim Interview Reminders

To be successful and productive in interviewing the victim, an officer must remember that she is a victim of violence, that she likely did not know if she was going to survive the encounter, and that her sense of autonomy has been denied to her by the actions of the offender. In an effort to restore her sense of control over her environment, it is best to extend the courtesy of asking, "Is it okay if I get you ... a coffee or a soft drink?"

She may be at a loss in dealing with the emotions of the ordeal, and likely she will be reluctant to relive the experience via a detailed interview. Although today's society is less judgmental about rape victims, there remains a self-imposed sense of blame and guilt by the rape victim. Her other emotions will likely be in a jumble. She may be numb, attempt to mask all emotions, or inappropriately respond to questions that are reasonable from the police perspective. Yet, she is being requested to relate the most intimate details of her rape to a stranger. These reactions should be expected, anticipated, and received without judgment. It is conceivable that the victim will continue to experience the aura and presence of the offender long after the assault and carry that sensation into the police contact.

This may be so obvious that it should go without being stated: An officer's number one priority for the victim interview should be to ensure that it is conducted with privacy. I mention this because I have witnessed this delicate interview conducted at an investigator's desk in the middle of a squad room populated by other victims and offenders. I have observed firsthand victims standing in plain view as the officer dictates the questions and answers from the interview to a secretary/typist whose primary job is to greet and screen everyone entering the Crimes Against Persons Unit.

The second priority of the investigator should be to react only with empathy and support for the victim and to avoid any display or tone of voice that could be construed as judgmental. When questioning the victim's resistance, the sex crimes investigator must accept "passive resistance" as legitimate behavior and give credence to the terror the victim experienced. Careful phrasing is necessary on many questions likely to be posed to the victim. It is not necessary to use harsh terms such as "the rape" or "the assault," as the victim will certainly know what he is speaking about when the phrase "the thing that happened" is used. Along the same line of consideration for the victim, the question, "Did you resist?" is judgmental and should be replaced by inquiring whether she ever considered it safe to resist or flee.

To diminish the injured party's reaction to highly personal questions about her victimization, an officer is well advised to forewarn her early in the questioning that at some point questions will be asked that she would likely rather not answer. She should be told that the questions will be personal and involve intimate details of the rape, but she should also be reassured that they are vital to conducting a thorough interview and apprehending the culprit. The time lag between this warning and the actual questioning will allow her to prepare psychologically and will remove some of the emotions from the questions and answers.

As anyone would expect, a victim will remain in a fearful state following the rape and probably will not want to return immediately to her residence if that is where the assault occurred. Most likely, the offender promised to return if she reported the rape and reinforced his threat by building into his statement some personal information, such as her name or place of employment. It will be of no benefit to the victim to tell her that only rarely do rapists recontact a victim, because his presence and warning loom large in her perspective. The professional officer will be prepared to reassure the victim regarding her future safety. He can do several things to assist her, easing her concerns and worries. He may request increased patrols in her area and have the officer patrolling pause or park in front of her house for a time or perhaps use his cell phone to call her, advise her of his presence, and inquire about her welfare or whether she requires any attention from him.

The thoughtful investigator will also have business cards and toll-free numbers of victim counseling services, women's shelters, victim's advocates, and victim witness coordinators. These should be provided as a courtesy and without the victim having to solicit them.

Roy Hazelwood has related in personal conversations that it is appropriate to say "Thank you" to the victim as part of closing the interview. Such a statement indicates sensitivity to the victim's trauma and recognition of what she endured in her testimonial reenactment of the rape and its circumstances. Remember, a primary goal of interviewing the victim is to minimize her trauma and secure her future cooperation with the criminal justice system. The closing of the interview should include a listing of what she may expect in the future from the police, the prosecutor, and others involved in the criminal justice system.

Analytical Product

Once critical data about the offender's behavior are obtained, he may be placed in a rapist typology category. A decision regarding the category should be made without haste, and attention must be provided to all the data available. Table 10.1 is a guide to placing rapists in the proper category. It is revealing to

Table 10.1   Summary Chart of Stranger-to-Stranger Rapist Traits and Characteristics

Behavior	Power Reassurance	Power Assertive	Anger Retaliatory	Sexual Sadist
Motivation	To prove to himself, his masculinity, or ability to have a female relationship; to obtain sense of power by taking power from victim	Confident of sexual prowess; needs to express or demonstrate it to victim as he is a male and entitled to do as he wants	He seeks revenge for real or imagined wrongs created by women with whom he is openly angry; he needs to vent anger directed to a symbolic woman.	To receive victim's emotional and physical response to torture; response sexually arousing
Key personality feature	Low self-esteem and lack of personal confidence	Arrogance/ "macho"; described as "a man's man"	He has a constant angry demeanor	Leads two lives: normal and bizarre
Victim selection	Targeted via continuous nocturnal surveillance; targets based on personalized victim traits, favored location, and victim living arrangements, either alone or with small child	Opportunity: selects personalized victim traits beginning with available and vulnerable; victim wrong place at wrong time; often meets same day	Opportunity is involved: victim is in the wrong place at the wrong time; some symbolism may be involved	Opportunity: victim wrong place at wrong time; may be known to rapist, possibly through casual contact, but are usually female and strangers
Method of approach	Surprise method, often via entry into residence during night; generally no forced entry; typically strikes during hours of darkness.	Con method; uses verbal skills to entice and impress victim	Blitz method is used; assault is immediate and brutal	Initially uses con method, changing to violence once in his control

Table 10.1   Summary Chart of Stranger-to-Stranger Rapist Traits and Characteristics (Continued)

Behavior	Power Reassurance	Power Assertive	Anger Retaliatory	Sexual Sadist
Violence level	Minimal force used; relies on verbal control and presence of weapon; may slap to get victim's attention or to have victim follow his requests; prefers compromise and lack of violence, but will defend himself up to and including committing murder.	Moderate-to-brutal force used even if no resistance; uses personal weapons of hands and feet, victim likely to be hurt	Brutal-to-excessive force is used, and victim may require medical attention; violence against a woman fulfills his emotional needs. His anger builds and may be triggered by anything.	Excessive level due to torture; likely has kill or torture kit; may experiment with different tortures; most violent of all rapists; victim likely to die
Verbal strategy	Generally not talkative; inquisitive, personal, caring, concerned, nonprofane, reassuring, and complimentary comments	High profanity content; expresses male superiority to female; con aspects developed in fantasy	He does little talking, perhaps just utterances, but this will be profane, derogatory about women. He is not there to talk.	Smooth talker with con; once under his control becomes instructive, imparts rules, and speaks unemotionally; likely to record his contacts
Physical strategy	Relies on presence or referral to weapon for control; will defend self if victim is aggressive	Will do whatever is necessary to accomplish rape	Punishment is intentional. There is no regard for victim's injuries.	Uses devices to torture victim, who will require extensive medical care if she survives
Sexual strategy	Masculinity reassured usually with one sex act: vaginal sex; will compromise or negotiate if victim balks at sex act	Wants sexual contact purely for his benefit; will commit multiple sexual assaults with each victim	He uses sexual body parts to hurt, degrade, and punish. He will beat and rape until anger is vented.	May have no sexual contact with victim; may experiment with victim or may masturbate, leaving semen on victim's clothing

Table 10.1 Summary Chart of Stranger-to-Stranger Rapist Traits and Characteristics (Continued)

Behavior	Power Reassurance	Power Assertive	Anger Retaliatory	Sexual Sadist
Possible sexual dysfunction	If present, likely erectile dysfunction or premature ejaculation due to low esteem and performance anxiety	If he has one, most likely retarded ejaculation	If he has one, most likely it is retarded ejaculation due to anger in life.	If he has one, invariably is retarded ejaculation due to pervasive anger
Victim traits	Targets victim in his own age range	Targets victim in his own age range	He targets a victim in his own age range or somewhat older.	May be male victim but typically female and of any age
Rapist view of victim	Does not want or intend to harm, punish, degrade victim; fantasizes consenting relationship with victim who is special to him; concerned with potential to harm victim; does not like what he is doing	Victim exists for his uses/ gratification; may rape even if she would consent or does not resist; victim equivalent of trash, throw her away when done	Injury of victim is of no concern except that it is intentional and brutal. The assault lasts until anger is vented.	Master/slave relationship; do as told or will punish
Comfort zone	Generally small but size adjusted by type of community; does not stray too far from familiar; enlarges as his rapes are "successful"; typically walks to victim but may use bicycle or public transportation	Personal confidence makes zone large and varied; assaults more distant from his personal spaces; will not rape in victim's residence unless she takes him	He is capable of having a large comfort zone, but does not travel great distances to rape.	Personal confidence makes zone large and varied; enjoys driving and looking for potential victims; safe, secluded location for planned torture

Table 10.1   Summary Chart of Stranger-to-Stranger Rapist Traits and Characteristics (Continued)

Behavior	Power Reassurance	Power Assertive	Anger Retaliatory	Sexual Sadist
Victim's clothes removal	Asks victim to remove to fulfill fantasy of consent; will remove if she refuses	Rips and tears clothes	He rips and tears clothes sufficiently for rape.	To facilitate torture and terror may use knife to cut off clothes
Weapon purpose	To intimidate and control; may or may not have any weapon; may show and then conceal if weapon present; reluctant to use	Typically uses personal weapons of hands and feet	Typically, he uses personal weapons.	To traumatize to get emotional response and pleading; uses tools and devices for torture
Ritualistic or impulsive	Extensive use of fantasy in which rituals and paraphilias are likely developed; engages in acts unnecessary to rape	Fantasy minimal except as focused on his con style; little or no ritual	He has intrusive and violent thoughts that are undeveloped; he is highly impulsive and spontaneous.	High fantasy levels and ritualistic with paraphilias

Note: See Appendix for a glossary of definitions, the original Behavior-Oriented Interview of Rape Victims, and its corresponding victim's questionnaire.

note the descriptive names for each typology as they were carefully chosen to convey images of the rapist, such as his motivation and violence level.

Bibliography

Groth, A. Nicholas, and H. Jean Birnbaum. *Men Who Rape, the Psychology of the Offender.* New York: Plenum Press, 1990.

Hare, Robert D. *Without Conscience.* New York: Guilford Press, 1999.

Hazelwood, Robert R., and Ann W. Burgess. *Practical Aspects of Rape Investigation: A Multidisciplinary Approach.* New York: Elsevier Science, 1987.

Hazelwood, Robert R., and Ann W. Burgess. *Practical Aspects of Rape Investigation: A Multidisciplinary Approach.* 2nd ed. New York: CRC Press, 1995.

Hazelwood, Robert R., and Ann W. Burgess. *Practical Aspects of Rape Investigation: A Multidisciplinary Approach.* 3rd ed. Boca Raton, FL: CRC Press, 2001.

Hazelwood, Robert R., and Ann W. Burgess. *Practical Aspects of Rape Investigation: A Multidisciplinary Approach.* 4th ed. Boca Raton, FL: CRC Press, 2009.

Hazelwood, Robert R., and Janet I. Warren. The Sexually Violent Offender: Impulsive or Ritualistic. In *Practical Aspects of Rape Investigation: A Multidisciplinary Approach*, edited by Robert R. Hazelwood and Ann W. Burgess, 97–112. Boca Raton, FL: CRC Press, 2001.

McDowell, Charles P., and Neil S. Hibler. False Allegations. In *Practical Aspects of Rape Investigation: A Multidisciplinary Approach*, edited by Robert R. Hazelwood and Ann W. Burgess, 275–298. New York: Elsevier Science, 1987.

Napier, Michael R. Interviewing the Rapist. In *Practical Aspects of Rape Investigation: A Multidisciplinary Approach*, Hazelwood, R.R. and Burgess, A.W., Eds. 123–137. Boca Raton, FL: CRC Press, 2009.

Napier, Michael R., and Kenneth P. Baker. Criminal Personality Profiling. In *Forensic Science: An Introduction to Scientific and Investigative Techniques*, edited by Stuart H. James and Jon J. Nordby, 531–550. Boca Raton, FL: CRC Press, 2002.

Napier, Michael R., and Kenneth P. Baker. Criminal Personality Profiling. In *Forensic Science: An Introduction to Scientific and Investigative Techniques*, edited by Stuart H. James and Jon J. Nordby, 615–636. Boca Raton, FL: CRC Press, 2005.

Napier, Michael R., and Robert R. Hazelwood. Homicide Investigation: The Significance of Victimology. *National Academy Associate* 5(5) (September/October 2003) 14–32.

Targeted Subject Interview
Interviewing the Rapist*

11

MICHAEL R. NAPIER

Contents

Case 11.1

"I was awakened by a nudging of my shoulder. The first thing I saw was a knife blade directly in front of my eyes. In the darkness of my bedroom, illuminated only by my alarm clock light, I heard a male voice saying, 'Don't make me use this.' That was the last time I saw the knife, but I knew he had it.

"I could see the outline of his features when he leaned down to speak. He was a white male about my age. He was clean shaven and smelled of an aftershave I did not recognize.

"As he placed a pillowcase over my head, he referred to me by my name and said, 'Doris, do everything I tell you, and I won't hurt you. This won't

---

* This chapter was originally published in 2009 in *Practical Aspects of Rape Investigation*, edited by Robert R. Hazelwood and Ann W. Burgess, and was revised for this chapter.

be anything that you haven't done before, and I know you are alone. I am sure you deserved the manager of the month award from the bank.'

"I tried to get up, but he pushed me down and sat on my chest. He said, 'I told you I will hurt you if I have to. Now be nice like you are with your boyfriend. We are going to start with me up your backside.' I struggled harder and told him I would not do that because it would be painful. He said, 'Okay, okay. But you will go down on me first.' As he removed my panties he remarked 'You're looking fine.'

"He then patted my cheek and rolled over on his back, pushing my face into his crotch. He was semilimp. He forced me to perform oral sex until he became erect. Then he quickly rolled me back over and briefly penetrated my vagina until he ejaculated. He asked me if I was 'satisfied' and said, 'That is probably as good as you ever get, right?'

"He told me he would know if I called the police, and that he had a secret hiding place from which he would be watching me. He reminded me he knew where I worked, and that I usually came home alone at about 8:30. He said he would come back and get me if I did anything before counting slowly to 100."

The dialogue in Case 11.1 is a combination of several real-life rape victim statements. It also depicts the core behaviors (verbal, physical, sexual) of rapists, and understanding them is essential to comprehending offender motivation and analyzing the crime. The behaviors of a specific offender are best identified through a behavior-oriented interview of the victim. This type of interview is highly valued by investigators because it provides useful investigative information, such as rapist type, his unconsciously disclosed motivation, and the presence or absence of his fantasy acted out by the rape. For further explanation, see the reprinted article "The Behavior-Oriented Interview of the Rape Victims: The Key to Profiling" and its accompanying sexual assault questionnaire, which are located in the appendix.

A victim's behavior-oriented interview statements provide a reliable road map of how to approach the rapist in an interview and obtain admissions or a confession. Once the victim has been interviewed, the officer is encouraged to closely read and dissect the statement, noting each of the core behaviors. This rapist was clearly a power reassurance rapist. This type of rapist is responsible for a large percentage of reported and unreported rapes.

Targeted Subject Interview

Optimizing the opportunity to obtain admissions or confessions is a goal of every law enforcement interview plan. Trusting an interview to luck or good fortune is not advisable when the safety and welfare of a community have been placed in your hands. Besides considering and implementing all the techniques, tactics, and strategies, how can the interview or interrogation be placed on the best footing for success? One answer stands above all others: Target the individual suspect's vulnerabilities and weaknesses using the targeted subject interview (TSI). This sounds great, but how is that done? Using the guides provided here and in chapters on additional criminal violations, an officer should be able to place most crime features into a known typology. Analysis of the behaviors found in the typology is based on meticulous observation of the crime scene and will reveal those known and likely chinks in his armor.

Any additional information gathered about the particular suspect should be combined and incorporated into the interview plan. From the knowledge of the type of offender, an interview plan may be developed to take advantage of most suspect behavior traits, weaknesses, and vulnerabilities. Not all criminal behavior has been broken down into typologies, but a clever and inventive investigator may take the technique and adapt it to a particular situation.

Is it difficult to dissect the behavior of a bank robber, seeking out his likely motive, criminal sophistication, control over himself, and so on by examining his approach to the robbery? Banks and other institutions have a victimology just as individuals do, and it may be factored into the analysis. Once this type of breakdown has occurred, the officer can select the techniques he will include in his interview plan. The TSI may be utilized and incorporated into any type of interview, whether of a witness, victim, or a suspect. The practical aspect of this technique is developed further in the following text. Some of the interviewing techniques introduced in this chapter are dealt with in greater detail in Chapter 7 and eliminated here to avoid redundancy.

Developing the Interview Plan

The reader is encouraged to reread Case 11.1 and look for the verbal, physical (injurious), and sexual behaviors of the rapist. As stated, recognizing and isolating these behaviors will assist in planning an early interview of a rape suspect (Table 11.1).

The officer should note for his interview plan the following behaviors: complimentary wording, willingness to negotiate and lack of force, solicitation of compliment, reluctance to use rough or violent behavior, conditional erection, pat on cheek as may occur in a consensual relationship.

Conducting an interview of a rapist is a difficult and complex matter. Several considerations must be dealt with simultaneously to keep the process on the planned course. The interviewer must keep in mind all case data, the cast of characters, the suspect's role in the crime, all appropriate legal

Table 11.1   Behaviors of a Rapist

Verbal Behavior	Physical (Injurious) Behavior	Sexual Behavior
"Doris … I won't hurt you"	No injurious force	Wanted anal sex
"Be nice like with your boyfriend"	Nudged her shoulder	Negotiated oral sex
Negotiated sex acts	Pushed her back down	Was semi-erect
"You're looking fine"	Patted her on the cheek	Became erect after oral sex
"Are you satisfied?"		
"As good as you ever get, right?"		
Knew where she worked		
"Don't make me use this" (knife)		

considerations, his interview plan, the question just asked, the answer given, his evaluation of the answer just given in the context of the verbal and nonverbal response, and the question to ask next. The logical and well-constructed interview plan aids in simplifying this difficult process.

Every interview should be a planned event. Interviews are built from a carefully laid foundation designed during the planning. Case 11.1 provides the outline of a basic interview plan. The rapist has unwittingly disclosed his motive, fears, concerns, and interview vulnerabilities. He has also revealed a glimpse into his fantasy. Utilizing the described behavior, the detective will have several valid and reliable clues regarding how to conduct the interview.

An analysis of the case informs the investigator that he is dealing with a power reassurance rapist. He should keep in mind that the characteristics attributed to this type of rapist will not apply to all such rapists in this category.

When planning the interview, this information (as with all unproven information) should be presented to a suspect only by reference, using flexible phrasing, such as *probably* or *may be*. By so doing, the investigator protects his credibility even if the information is found to be incorrect. If proper terminology is used during the interview, even generalized information (based on perceived rapist type) will not have a negative impact on the interview process.

Traits of Successful Interviewers

Study a truly talented interviewer and you will observe that he has a number of highly specialized personal qualities. The first essential trait of an accomplished interviewer is that victims, witnesses, and even suspects sense that the officer *feels* the words he speaks. The extent to which they are at ease with the officer determines the level of trust they place in him and therefore determines whether they share their secrets. Such trust lays the foundation for obtaining information that the victim, witness, and certainly the suspect may initially be reluctant to provide. For additional data on interviewer traits see Chapter 4, section titled "Setting the Stage for Success."

It is imperative that victims and witnesses see an empathetic and professional person in front of them. With suspects, the interviewer must genuinely project a high degree of neutrality and impartiality prior to any necessary confrontation—all directed toward obtaining an admission or confession (Holmes, 1995).

As happens in the professional interview setting, the interviewing officer may question the credibility of a victim or witness. He may also have suspicions about the guilt of a suspect. The interviewer must guard against leakage of any bias or skepticism until sufficient evidence is identified to justify that position. To allow one's suspicions to become prematurely known by the interviewee will almost certainly lead to antagonism and distrust. This problem most often surfaces in the interview of witnesses, especially if they could be suspects because of their relationship to the victim (parents of a missing child, the significant other of a missing adult).

Question Formulation

No constitutional mandate exists regarding the style of questions utilized in interviewing a sexually violent suspect. The courts, however, tend to take a dim view of statements elicited by closed-ended questions that contain crime-specific information, such as "Tell me more about the white man who left the crime scene in the red Ford Thunderbird." If that type of information was later "parroted" back to the interviewer, it might appear to corroborate a confession. Such contamination usually occurs when closed-ended questions are used early in the interview process. Open-ended questions introduced by phrases such as "Describe for me … ," "Tell me about … ," "Explain how … ," and so on guard against contaminating the interview. Once the contamination error has been made, it cannot be undone.

The overall goal of an interview is to obtain information. Ideally, the initial questions should be short and the answers long. The recommended approach is to begin the criminal interview with open-ended questions, allowing the subject to answer without interruption.

If it is necessary to utilize a direct or closed-ended question, that should be reserved for the end of the questioning phrase. As much as possible, the phrasing of a closed-ended question should avoid any crime details not previously furnished by the interview suspect. The skilled use of open-ended questions is one of the primary tools of the professional interviewer and is one of the best practices for protecting the interview product.

Tools of the Profession

As a general rule, the interview should be a straightforward process. Neither the interviewer nor the interview process benefits from complicated ploys, intricate props, or elaborate tricks. There is no need for questioning to become complicated, and such attempts usually fail because they are transparent to the interviewee.

Reading Minds

How would you be affected if another person could accurately tell you what you were thinking? What if the topic of your thoughts could impact the quality of your life if known to others? For example, what would be the effect if the boss could "read your mind" and knew your true thoughts on his management style? One of the most powerful interview techniques available is called *reading minds*. The term is not to be applied literally; however, when properly done, the interview subject feels as though the officer *is* plainly reading his mind. Holmes (1995) referred to this tactic as "taking the wind out of their sails." That metaphor is well understood to mean the person would be "dead in the water" without any wind.

The destruction of the suspect's confidence in his ability to defeat police interviewing is one of the primary goals of an interviewer. If the mind-reading tactic is properly presented, the suspect will feel the interviewer is taking a walk through his psyche by telling him what he has thought, is now thinking, how he viewed the victim, and the cause of his behavior. To accomplish this with a sexually violent suspect, there are five rules to follow.

First, the interviewer's terminology must be somewhat vague and qualified. He must avoid concrete statements, such as, "You sat around and in daydreams planned this rape from start to finish." A more appropriate statement would be, "Tom, in all my 20 years of talking with people in your situation, nearly everyone has said that these thoughts just came to them over and over until they formed what appeared to be a good plan." This allows the suspect to hear and interpret the words as he wants. If any statement is too rigid or even a little off the mark, the suspect will hold to the discrepancy no matter how small, and the interviewer will be discredited. From that point, what he says will lack validity. An example of proper wording for the prior case would be as follows: "Tom, in looking at this case one detective concluded that you had no intent to harm Doris," or "You put the knife down, and this was possibly done because you didn't want to use it to harm her." These statements are ambiguous, and also illustrate the good cop/bad cop technique, allowing the officer to make some points while providing for the possibility of error.

Closely aligned to the first rule is the nearly universal principle that criminal interviewers should scrupulously avoid using harsh or highly charged terminology, particularly with "inadequate" personalities such as the power reassurance rapist. Conversely, when the officer refers to "that thing that happened last Thursday in the park," the suspect will clearly know the incident for which he is being questioned.

Next, the item or thought being dangled in front of the suspect should not be offered in a blunt manner. It should be made as the culmination of a few lead-in remarks. For example, "Tom, I have an important thought on this case. It is important and affects you because … ." This allows the officer to get the suspect's attention, and it also allows the suspect to track the question's impact and relationship to himself.

It is recommended that the interviewer subtly present his expertise and reputation when beginning his mind-reading statement. Power and status are added to his message when he begins in a manner such as:

> I have been in this business for 25 years and have been involved in several hundred cases similar to this one. I always try to talk with the men after they make their statements to learn what was really on their mind. One of the things that I have heard time and time again in these situations is that they never had a thought of hurting the woman. In fact, they went out of their way to avoid doing anything that might hurt her. When they tell me that, I always mention it in my report because I believe they deserve credit for having concern for the lady and being a man about it.

Finally, it is extremely critical that the interviewer not mention the suspect's name when reciting what he knows about criminal behavior or criminal mentality.

Planting Ideas

Using a similar presentation format, the interviewer may provide investigative concepts for the offender to consider so that he may personally determine if they pose a threat to his being identified or linked to a crime. For example, it may become necessary to interview a suspect early in an investigation armed only with circumstantial evidence. This calls for great care because any allegation of guilt unsupported by evidence may doom the interview. If the unsupported allegation reduces the subject's respect for the officer, it may also damage any chance for rapport in future contacts—even those in which there may be evidence supporting the offender's guilt.

Rather than alleging irrefutable guilt, the interviewer can speak to the suspect in terms of what evidence is *likely to be developed*. It has been my experience that a suspect will visualize how each piece of *possible evidence* would be a threat to his well-being. This technique has been especially effective with suspects having a prior criminal past. See Chapters 7 and 9 for more details on these techniques.

Case 11.2

State authorities requested me to develop an interview plan for confronting a suspect. The plan had backup contingencies in the event he refused to participate in a classic interview. After he was provided his Miranda rights, he was asked if the victim had ever been in his truck. He stated she had never been in his truck, and that he did not want to talk about the victim or the investigation. He did not invoke his Miranda rights. The suspect was then, per the interview plan, given the option of returning to his cell or having some time outside, where he could smoke and have a soft drink. He chose to remain out of the cell, likely realizing that he was going to spend many years behind bars.

Over the course of the next hour or so, the investigators remained with the suspect and casually spoke of various ways *this case could unfold, including various types of evidence that might be recovered and could incriminate the suspect.* There was conversation about the amount of blood required for DNA testing, what it would mean if a single strand of the victim's hair was found in his recovered truck, and how crime scene processing worked. The second phase of the interview plan had two tactics. The first was to introduce the good cop/bad cop scenario, using the local prosecutor as the foil. The second tactic was to discuss the role the victim's mother played in using the media to demand the recovery of her daughter. Eventually, the convicted rapist said he wanted to return to his cell, and the interview ceased.

On contact 2 days later, the offender was pumped up and could not wait to state that he wanted to confess. My assessment of why the rapist was willing and almost eager to confess was his recognition of various "threats" he found in the investigator's description of how evidence would be collected and used against him.

Theme Development

The absolute heart of effective suspect interviewing is the extensive use of themes. Themes have a variety of sources, and the most effective themes contain examples of human behavior that can be almost universally recognized. Themes are used after a subject denies his involvement in a crime. Themes contain psychological wording which seems to mitigate a subject's culpability. See Chapter 7 and the Appendix for theme examples.

As an interviewing technique, themes are most often combined with other themes containing similar ideas. The themes may appeal to the suspect for any number of reasons but largely because they treat the suspect as a vulnerable human being with problems that can be resolved with help from the interviewer. Themes also contain the same excuses the suspect used to justify his criminal deeds to himself.

Sometimes, the rape suspect will diminish his culpability using soft words as substitutes for more accurate descriptions of his behavior, thus making his role in the criminal act less repugnant. For example, one rapist used the phrase "when we were together" rather than "when I raped her." This is called *minimization*.

The aim of a theme is to make it as easy as possible for a rape suspect to admit to a "lesser or diminished" level of guilt, and by doing so he agrees to some degree of participation in the crime and contact with the victim. His admission has altered the situation morally but not legally.

Offender-Specific Tactics

Targeted Subject Interviews

There are professional tools that can be geared specifically to offenders.

When planning the interview strategy, the offender traits and vulnerabilities of the suspect must be taken into account. As part of the interview plan, the interviewer should document all *sensitive* techniques (i.e., interview strategies suggesting the victim is at fault or that the offender was entitled to attack, etc.) and place their use in perspective. Any such tactics should be noted in the investigative file in advance of the TSI and explained as a technique to obtain a confession. The officer should state that such techniques are not a statement of responsibility on the victim's part or that the rape is justified in any way. The offender bears complete responsibility for his criminal acts.

It is much more effective to tailor the interview approach to fit a specific type of sexual offender rather than trying to use one approach for all sex offenders. To assist in that process, the traits of four rapist types are examined next, and suggested interview strategies are provided.

Power Reassurance Rapist

The power reassurance rapist is most likely a serial rapist and in my experience accounts for more victims than any other rapist type. Therefore it is recommended that the investigator make only the sexual assault with the strongest evidence the sole focus of the initial interview. Once the offender has confessed to one rape, the interviewer can turn to the offender's other cases for resolution.

This type of rapist selects victims through surveillance and is a cautious rapist—one who must be geographically comfortable within the attack environment. Consequently, it is inadvisable to bluff him about the environment of the rape and its surrounding area. He will likely know the area much better than the investigator.

The interviewer should keep in mind that the motive driving this rapist is the reassurance of his masculinity. Typically, he is inadequate and has a low opinion of his personal qualities. As a rapist, he seeks power over a female and fulfills a need to *have a sexual relationship with a woman*. His many inadequacies will be evident when the behavior-oriented interview format is used. It would be counterproductive to remind him (in any way) of his shortfalls as a man or as a person. Additional specific suggestions can be seen in Table 11.2.

It must be noted that this type of rapist shares several personality traits with individuals who could give a false confession to escape police attention and pressure. For example, this type of rapist has inadequate personality features (e.g., personally devaluing himself; withdrawing from others, including those who could bolster him by providing a support mechanism), lacks those qualities that allow him to assert himself and reduce the impact of stressful situations such as intense police questioning, internalizes regret or guilt for all the rapes he committed (even if they are not the subject of their current questioning), and so on. Consequently, unless there is firm evidence linking a particular person with the crime, the interviewer must exercise caution. Although the interview subject may possess the characteristics associated with a power reassurance rapist (see below)—and may even give a confession—he may not be responsible for the crimes.

The Power Assertive Rapist

The power assertive rapist is the most likely to enter the police interview room as a suspect. He is verbally, physically, and sexually aggressive with the victim, and as mentioned elsewhere, this rapist is confident of his sexual prowess. Unlike the power reassurance rapist, this man has no doubts about his masculinity. In his assaults, he is asserting his masculinity because he believes that as a man he is entitled to do so. This man views himself as a role model of manhood and virility, and others who know him superficially would agree with that assessment.

He acts impulsively and may have met the victim the same day of the sexual assault. However, this type is also frequently observed in stranger-to-stranger offenses. In either case, once he has captured the victim, he employs a moderate or higher level of violence and sexually treats the victim as an object to be used.

Table 11.2   Power Reassurance Rapist Interview Techniques

Trait	Techniques	Examples
Low self-esteem Unsure of manhood Ashamed of his crime	Build rapport sufficient for suspect to function given his low-self-esteem by pacing the interview	*At the outset*, refer to him as Mister (Smith). Ask him before using his first name. Use examples of good or decent things he has done, even if exaggeration is required.
No intent to physically harm Does not consider the rape as harm, which is likely the strongest trait benefiting the interviewer	Mind reading, minimization	Build up his self-esteem. He likely made diligent efforts not to harm the victim. Give him credit for purposefully not hurting the victim. Compliment him on how he had control over the victim and did not do other acts as some rapists have done. Assure him that sooner or later he will encounter a situation that goes bad, and he will hurt or kill a victim. Read his mind by telling him "horror" stories of victims being seriously hurt or murdered.
Brings and considers the weapon as control technique	Minimization, mind reading, projection	Repeat his belief that he would never have used the weapon and would have left before using the weapon; he only had it to maintain control and keep her from hurting him.
Security conscious, planner, surveillance Average or better intelligence	Building his confidence	Because he is a loner and may be socially awkward, do not assume he is mentally challenged or slow.
Poor interpersonal skills	Rapport building; a relaxed, friendly, slow start to the interview Likely suspicious, on guard for insincerity; do not expect lengthy verbal exchanges	Conduct lengthy discussion of the circumstances of his daily life, how he spends his time, who he knows, and the like. When introducing the subject of the interview, use soft terms such as "the thing that happened last Tuesday" versus "the rape."
Sexual incompetence	Minimization	Do not mention any sexual dysfunctions, the need for masturbation, and so on.

(continued)

Table 11.2 Power Reassurance Rapist Interview Techniques (Continued)

Trait	Techniques	Examples
Rich fantasy life; preselects victims	Rationalization, minimization, mind reading	After denial, describe how most people in his position have *intrusive thoughts* that cause them to act. They almost always are drawn to a particular woman because of her personal qualities, the type he desires in all his relationships.
Young adult victims Same age range of offender	Rationalization, minimization, mind reading	Deal with the assault by indicating that it has grown out of proportion in offender's mind. Remind him that he did not assault an elderly grandmother or a small child, and nothing happened that she had not done before. Combine technique with other examples of offender behavior that minimize his acts.
"Unselfish or gentlemanly qualities" • Low force level • Did not verbally abuse her or use vulgar language • Did not physically abuse her • Normal sex • Desires to please her	Planting seeds, mind reading, minimization, projection, good cop/bad cop	State that he treated her gently, as a lady or wife, like her boyfriend or lover would. Indicate that he went out of his way to do so. He did not even call her names, except as a compliment. The only *pressure* applied was because of the way she acted. He even involved her in the type of sex she liked just to make her happy. The interviewer is aware that the prosecutor or supervisor believes that he did terrible things, but the interviewer has seen all the facts and understands all the efforts the suspect made to be nice and treat the victim well. Likely, he even stopped some acts when the victim asked him to stop (negotiated with victim).
Minimal force level used	Mind reading, minimization, projection	In the interviewer's vast experience, he has been told of suspects' real concerns and how they did everything possible not to harm the victim as long as she did not harm them.

Table 11.2 Power Reassurance Rapist Interview Techniques (Continued)

Trait	Techniques	Examples
Fantasizes as consenting contact	Minimization, projection, mind reading	This woman is the kind who the suspect would like to have met some other way, in another situation. She really liked him; she even took off her own clothes and made no real objections.
	Closers • Hard evidence • DNA • Video from area	If the "hit-with-evidence" approach is used early, this type of rapist may withdraw from the interview and be unwilling to discuss other crimes. Save these "blunt" tactics as a last resort.

In date or acquaintance rape situations, the initial goal of the interviewer is to obtain the offender's agreement that a sexual encounter with the victim occurred. The interview should then proceed by allowing the physical evidence of torn clothing and physical injuries to tell the story of nonconsent and rape.

In Table 11.3, a differentiation is made between the date/acquaintance and stranger rapist. If the information is applicable to the date/acquaintance and stranger rape, the term *both* is utilized.

The Anger Retaliatory Rapist

The anger retaliatory offender is angry at women for real or imagined wrongs and wants to punish and degrade them. Those who know him understand that he has a violent temper, which he is sometimes able to keep in check, and that he hates women, blaming them for all his troubles and failures. His attacks are impulsive and essentially dependent on when he becomes emotionally overloaded—he may attack at any time and at any place. He selects victims of opportunity who happen to cross his path, and the fact they are women is sufficient criteria for this angry offender.

Circumstantial evidence of his propensity to rage against women generally will be available from associates and coworkers. Because this man, if he has an arrest record, it typically is a diverse arrest history, he is streetwise; therefore the overall strategy of an interview is simply to place him near or with the victim at the time of the assault. The main tools available to the officer are minimization of his acts and projecting responsibility for the event onto the woman. A workable theme might be that with today's attitudes, women have it easy and get jobs that men need to support their families. If the man is receptive, the officer can explain that the best way for him to handle this is to get his opinion of women on the record.

Table 11.3   Power Assertive Rapist Interview Techniques

Trait	Techniques	Examples
Has high opinion of himself	The officer subtly controls the interview. Begin by directing the suspect to a particular chair. The rapist believes he is smarter than the officer. The interview should be arranged without an ending time constraint.	Both: If caught in lie(s), do not initially challenge him. Collect all lies and misstatements. Confront him with them collectively so they will take on the "*feel* of evidence."
Enjoys deferential treatment he receives from other males	The interviewer should impress him with competency and authority of an interviewing officer.	Both: Upon arrival, acknowledge his presence, but make him wait several minutes before he is taken to interview room. Once the interview has begun, have a planned interruption causing a delay in the process. Another officer, within the hearing of suspect praises the interviewing officer.
Sense of entitlement The right of a male	Minimize the crime and project blame onto the victim.	Both: Indicate officer is dealing with still *another* female complaint.
Views women as objects, inferior	During the interview, use projection, minimization, and mind reading; build up questions and officer's experience; plant seeds; use the good cop/bad cop technique.	Date/acquaintance: Encourage him to adopt minimized version of event. She did not know what she wanted, first she was attracted to him because … ; she encouraged him, then she cooled down; men can't change that fast. It was not the suspect's fault that she drank so much and was out of control. Stranger: It is likely she is making the claim because of the need to explain what happened to her boyfriend.
Acts impulsively	Interviewer should use minimization.	Date/acquaintance: He is smart enough to stay away from this kind in the future. She rushed him and encouraged him, and he did not think about how she would handle the situation.

Table 11.3   Power Assertive Rapist Interview Techniques (Continued)

Trait	Techniques	Examples
Has sense of entitlement	Interviewer should use minimization, projection, reading minds.	Both: Indicate that another team is reviewing the victim's statement for errors, lies. Her story is likely not a true reflection of actual events. Date/acquaintance: She came on to him or agreed to sex then changed her mind. A man can't turn his sex drive on and off at the drop of hat.
Man's man	Use rationalization here.	Date/acquaintance: He acted as any real man would with an aggressive, suggestive woman.
Physical violence	Interviewer should use projection.	Both: Blame the victim for any injuries and state that she likely became aggressive and attacked him, and he only defended himself. Date/acquaintance: Nothing would have happened if she had only been in control of herself. It would likely have been worse if he was not a gentleman and a man able to control her.
	Make use of closers. • Interviewer will request he undergo polygraph examination. • If he agrees, quickly ask how he will do when asked questions specific to the victim's statement.	An indicator of lying is if he agrees to do it *sometime*. If lying, he will make excuses why he cannot be polygraphed or *hypnotized*.
Useful with any rapist type	Use a test of commitment.	

The Anger Excitation Rapist

The anger excitation rapist is more commonly referred to as a *sexual sadist*. Of all the rapists, this man will be best prepared to deal with a police interview. It is probable that he will not consent to an interview but will invoke his 5th Amendment rights and demand an attorney, possibly by name. However, the detective should be prepared for him to agree to an interview—his purpose being not to provide information but rather to obtain information. He considers himself superior to the police and will use the interview setting to explore the evidence against him.

Do not allow the focus of the inquiry to become diffused by accusing him of multiple assaults. When the subject is believed to be responsible for multiple crimes, it is recommended that the crime with the best evidence be the focus of the interview. Questions should be phrased in a manner that does not provide information to the offender. Questions of this type are discussed in the section on question formulation and in Chapter 7.

Such offenders are typically narcissistic, and the officer's status must be projected as detective or higher, thus playing to the criminal's perceived superiority. His narcissism also creates an inability to withstand criticism, and the officer may subtly criticize an aspect of the crime through questions such as: "The victim said that she fought you in every room of her apartment. Why weren't you able to control her?" Chapter 9 has techniques for controlling interviews.

He may be lured into bragging about his cleverness and cunning. However, if this does happen, it will only be after he is convinced that there is substantial evidence against him. I was taught always to begin by stroking the ego; after a long interrogation without results, then challenge the ego since the challenge will impair any relationship the suspect has with the interrogator.

Case 11.3

Dennis Rader, the self-named BTK (for bind, torture, and kill) serial killer, was an infamous sexually sadistic offender in the Midwest. He escaped detection and apprehension for over 3 decades. Fortunately for society, his narcissism created an inner need for recognition of his perceived brilliance. It also created a need to engage the police and further demonstrate his criminal mastery; this is what led to his downfall.

When Rader was arrested, he was confronted by his nemesis, Lt. Kenny Landwehr, commander of the Homicide Unit, Wichita, Kansas, Police Department. Lt. Landwehr and FBI agent Robert Morton showed Rader a computer disk that he had mailed to the police and explained the process that had been used to identify him as BTK.

He was asked to provide the date of a message he had mailed to the media and the police. If Rader provided the date, it would help to confirm that Rader was BTK. As his hand hovered over a calendar, Rader asked if they had DNA evidence to prove he was BTK, and it was explained that he had been linked to the crimes by DNA. Rader then said, "I am BTK." This response by BTK exemplifies the sexual sadist's need to be convinced by evidence that he has been caught and his criminal career is at an end.

Bibliography

Criminal Interview of Dennis Rader, aka BTK. Wichita, KS: Wichita Police Department, 2006.

Deaver, Jeffrey. *The Sleeping Doll*. New York: Simon and Schuster, 2007.

Depue, Roger L., and Joyce M. Depue. To Dream, Perchance to Kill. *Security Management* (June 1999): 66–69.

Gudjonsson, Gisli. *The Psychology of Interrogation, Confessions and Testimony*. Chichester, UK: Wiley, 1992.

Hazelwood, Robert R., and Ann W. Burgess. *Practical Aspects of Rape Investigation: A Multidisciplinary Approach*. 3rd ed. Boca Raton, FL: CRC Press, 2001.

Hazelwood, Robert R., and Ann W. Burgess. *Practical Aspects of Rape Investigation: A Multidisciplinary Approach*. 4th ed. Boca Raton, FL: CRC Press, 2009.

Hazelwood, Robert R., and Michael R. Napier. Crime Scene Staging and Its Detection. *Journal of Offender Therapy and Comparative Criminology* 48(6) (December 2004): 744–759.

Hess, John E. *Interviewing and Interrogation for Law Enforcement*. Cincinnati, OH: Anderson, 1997.

Holmes, Warren D. Interrogation. *Polygraph* 24(4) (1995): 237–258.

Holmes, Warren D. *Criminal Interrogation*. Springfield, IL: Thomas, 2002.

Inbau, Fred E., John E. Reid, and Joseph P. Buckley. *Criminal Interrogation and Confessions*. 3rd ed. Baltimore, MD: Williams and Wilkins, 1986.

Inbau, Fred E., John E. Reid, Joseph P. Buckley, and Brian C. Jayne. *Criminal Interrogations and Confessions*. 4th ed. Sudbury, MA: Jones and Bartlett, 2004.

Jayne, Brian C., and Joseph P. Buckley. Interrogation Alert! Will Your Next Confessions Be Suppressed? *The Investigator* (Winter 1998): Special Edition.

Michaud, Stephen G., and Robert R. Hazelwood. *The Evil Men Do*. New York: St. Martin's Press, 1998.

Napier, Michael R., and Susan H. Adams. Magic Words to Obtain Confessions. *FBI Law Enforcement Bulletin* 67(10) (October 1998).

Napier, Michael R., and Kenneth P. Baker. Criminal Personality Profiling. In *Forensic Science: An Introduction to Scientific and Investigative Techniques*, edited by Stuart H. James and Jon J. Nordby, 531–550. Boca Raton, FL: CRC Press, 2002.

Napier, Michael R., and Robert R. Hazelwood. Homicide Investigation: The Significance of Victimology. *National Academy Associate* 5(5) (September/October 2003): 14–32.

Rabon, D. *Investigative Discourse Analysis*. Durham, NC: Carolina Academic Press, 2003.

Sapir, Avinoam. *LSI Advanced Workshop on Scientific Content Analysis*. Phoenix, AZ: Laboratory for Scientific Interrogation, 1998.

Shuy, Roger W. *The Language of Confession, Interrogation and Deception*. Thousand Oaks, CA: Sage, 1998.

Vessel, D. Conducting Successful Interrogations. *FBI Law Enforcement Journal* 67(10) (October 1998): 11–15.

Yeschke, Charles L. *The Art of Investigative Interviewing*. Boston: Butterworth-Heinemann, 1997.

Zulawski, David E., and Douglas E. Wicklander. *Practical Aspects of Interview and Interrogation*. 2nd ed. Boca Raton, FL: CRC Press, 2002.

Recognizing and Investigating False Allegations of Rape

12

MICHAEL R. NAPIER

Contents

Overview

No officer should be quick to dismiss as false any rape allegation. When a report of rape is believed to be false, a great deal is at stake: everything from not catching a violent rapist, to causing mistrust for future victims' reports, to damaging the image and status of the police department.

The indicators of a potential false allegation of sexual assault and the descriptions of pseudovictims are presented as a guide on how this somewhat counterintuitive phenomenon plays out in police investigations. I have followed closely the issue of reporting false rape allegations for many years and have relied on the work, lectures, and private conversations of Roy Hazelwood for much of my academic background in that area of investigations. Hazelwood and his coeditor Ann Burgess have included a chapter on this topic in their prior editions of *Practical Aspects of Rape Investigations* (Hazelwood and Burgess, 1987, 2001b, 2009). A great deal of the following material is rightly credited to them. I have had the added benefit of having consulted on many cases that were believed to contain false allegations and have seen them through to resolution. I continue to learn from my law enforcement students when I instruct on this topic.

When investigating rape cases that are thought to be founded on totally erroneous reporting by a victim there are several possible "costs" when pursuing the case. Two are important. First, the financial cost to the police department in terms of the manpower allocated to resolve the issues can be significant. Second, in some cases false reports can generate antagonism and very real anger within the investigative agency. I have consulted on a case that was correctly handled but had quite unusual results. It was a tragic case that concluded in the death of a young man. The department's assessment of the false allegation was vindicated by a thorough investigation. However, later when the undersheriff who had handled the case was running for sheriff, his investigation became the central focus in the election. He lost the election even though he professionally and competently handled the case.

When serious investigative warning signs are raised because of indicators observed by an officer, a second examination of the facts needs to be instituted. Every angle in the inquiry must be examined, with serious efforts made to prove that the allegation is valid and to scrutinize the known facts to determine if there is something wrong with the report. Conclusions should be held in abeyance until the results are known. The justification for labeling a report as false occurs when finding a significant pattern of indicators which are found to meet the criteria of known markers for false allegations. Even then, it is wise to seek an independent opinion.

Known markers for false allegations are provided in this chapter. A pattern of those markers will lend credence to the false allegation label. Many of the markers involve inconsistencies. The contradictions will be found via analysis of these four portions of the investigation:

1. Variations in the details within a victim's statement, or between statements. However, some variations are normal and to be expected based on the victim's trauma at the time of her interview and subsequent to that.
2. Inconsistencies between the victim's statement and the crime scene (i.e., claim of struggle in an area without grass but no mud stains on clothing).
3. Differences between the victim's story and forensic testing.
4. Injuries that are not in keeping with the struggle as related by the victim.

Cautions

Throughout this book the role and influence of an officer's attitude and demeanor in conducting investigations and interviews have been stressed. Nowhere is guarding against those types of slipups more in demand than in the interview of a victim. Any "leakage" signaling doubt or distrust of the victim's report is likely to generate verbal and nonverbal reactions by the victim. The downward spiral of doubt and reaction can lead to misreading her report and wrongfully filing it away as "unfounded." The victim's distrust of an interviewer, whether or not it is founded, is the victim's absolute reality. Once the bond between officer and victim is broken, the victim likely will never trust that detective again and will be skeptical of all others as well.

One difficulty in handling a false reporting investigation is that there are no absolute indicators that the report is fabricated. Most of the markers pointing in the direction of a false allegation are occurrences that happen with regularity in valid reports. There are land mines everywhere that must be carefully negotiated by the assigned officer. That adds to the burden of locating a compounding of markers that form a pattern justifying serious doubt about the report.

Victim Traits and Characteristics

There are few limitations on the type of person who may cast him or herself as a pseudovictim. False allegations occur in nearly every age, race, economic group, and geographic location. The core of personality is our self-concept, or our self-esteem. It is the record of how we view ourselves when we examine our internal mirror. Most people look in that mirror and consider themselves to be "okay," not necessarily perfect, but without serious flaws. A person who would make a false allegation is likely to have low self-esteem. He or she magnifies all his or her flaws, many of which are truly small and not noticed by anyone else.

Along with the low self appraisal, the pseudovictim probably has consistent difficulties navigating the usual trials and tribulations of everyday life. If additional stressors are placed on top of those that are straining a person's ability to keep her balance, the observable result is a person whose coping mechanism is overwhelmed. When the dust has settled in a confirmed false allegation case, the officer will probably be able to locate the pseudovictim's prior attempts to get her life on track through less drastic and dramatic means. However, when those efforts have failed, the pseudovictim is liable to find herself unable to suitably control her life. She may describe her day-to-day existence as having "gone astray" or "off the track," or that her world is upside down.

Having possibly progressed through milder attempts to gain solid footing in her world only to find additional failures, she may now be primed for claiming to have been victimized in the most personal manner possible outside of being murdered. Officers working investigations into crimes against persons should stop for a moment and consider the depth of desperation a person must feel to voluntarily but falsely claim such an intimate and degrading experience. One explanation for this behavior is that the individual has a goal that she believes will be met by becoming a pseudovictim.

It is not always recognized that positive developments in a life can be as stressful as negative developments. For example, a man may be overjoyed to receive a major promotion with substantial pay and benefit increases. The price for accepting the promotion is to move from a smaller community where his family is established and comfortable. He must trade all of the features of his current lifestyle and that of his family and make a move to a larger city which has a much different set of demands and routine. This "good news" can add considerable stress to all concerned. If some member of the family is only succeeding day to day in keeping her life balanced, they may be overwhelmed and seek a way to compensate for the new stressors.

Motivation and Manipulation

What could motivate a person to voluntarily take on the burden of being a victim of one of the most despicable crimes committed by one person on another? Some of what is happening with a pseudovictim most likely occurs on a level of consciousness just below awareness. Other features of the self-victimization are just as likely to be calculated as part of a process of satisfying personal *needs* created by a systemically diseased psyche. To fulfill those inner needs, the pseudovictim invents her "victimization" in search of a goal. The goal may be to cover a failure or a perceived failure or to force a new action. Some of the "failures" can be as simple as being late for a curfew, fear of pregnancy from a consensual relationship, or being involved in an accident in the spouse's vehicle. Attempting to reach either goal is indicative of manipulation, not only of the criminal justice system but also likely of someone with whom they are closely associated.

Case 13.1

I was asked by a police agency to review a case they believed to contain a false allegation of rape. The woman was married to a Marine and had been pushing him to relocate to another state that she favored and to change his schedule so he was home more in the evenings. She had been unsuccessful. One night she claimed that a group of black men raped her. She understood that her husband had a particular bias against black men. Her story raised several flags, including the manner in which she claimed to have resisted and then blacked out. When she made her complaint to the police, they were suspicious. My analytical conclusion weighed in heavily on the side of the claim being made up. After unsuccessfully attempting to obtain an admission that the charges were trumped up, the case lingered for a while and then was dropped.

As a result of the incident, her husband sought and was granted a transfer to a location deeper in the southeast United States. A few months later, the police department at the new location made inquiries to the police at the first location about whether they knew the victim. The inquiry was the result of a claim of rape that explicitly duplicated the story she told in her original complaint. The changes she sought did not solve her internal strife, which most likely included serious marital problems. Her manipulation was successful, but the results left much to be desired by the pseudovictim.

I become especially concerned when I read a victim's police interview that reports the husband or boyfriend was present during the inquiry. Who would willingly inflict on a loved one the need to sit and listen to a story about another's intimate violation of her body? It would appear that his presence in the interview reflected her choice of who she wanted to manipulate.

Case 13.2

A local campus of a major university encountered a financial crisis that necessitated terminating several faculty members. A man and wife were employed in the same department; however, she had seniority/tenure over her husband. She was retained, but he was terminated. He left the area to find other employment. The budget problems were eventually corrected, and his employment slot was available on his return. After she advised him that he could return to his old job, he did not return. Shortly thereafter, she reportedly attended a music concert on campus, and while she was walking home alone, she was accosted, dragged into bushes, and raped. Her husband returned immediately.

Under close and astute questioning, she admitted making up the story in an effort to get her husband to return. Her goal was achieved, but at a price. She manipulated the criminal justice and medical systems to secure her personal goals.

One of the prevailing goals for making false reports is the desire for attention, usually from a particular source. The attention is desired to fulfill a deficit in daily life. This "need" can be a powerful motivator.

Prior Attempts

Sometimes the final police involvement with a pseudovictim occurs after a series of smaller, less serious complaints.

Case 13.3

A female in her mid- to late thirties was employed in an emergency medical services (EMS) capacity in a town. She worked closely with the city police and ambulance crews. She lived within the county sheriff's jurisdiction. She began making complaints about nuisances, including peepers and prowlers. Her statements were taken and given serious attention. Her calls to the department escalated to reports of attempted break-ins and the poisoning of animals. On one occasion, she claimed to return home to find the light out in her garage where the animals were kept. She stated that those lights were never turned out. She entered the garage and was accosted, and a ligature was placed around her neck and tightened until she lost consciousness. She had abrasions and red marks to confirm the assault. She also found a dead animal that had been hung by its neck and graffiti spray painted on the garage walls.

The sheriff's department took all of her claims as serious matters and conducted thorough investigations. A deputy was assigned to stay in her house during the nighttime hours. She reported that threatening messages were scratched into the paint on her vehicle. The gist of the message was that she had allowed someone to die and would now have to pay a price for that.

The sheriff became concerned about the possible sexual conduct of the woman and his deputy, and his worries were escalated when he determined that no one had died on any EMS response she made. The deputy admitted to having been seduced and was removed from his assignment. The female was confronted with the suspicion that she had made several false reports. She denied each accusation.

The police and ambulance crews she worked with in the city sided with her, while the deputies believed she had made false allegations. The relationship between the agencies was severely strained. The woman became angered with the sheriff's department and ordered that they stay away from her residence. On the final night of this saga, she called the sheriff's department and demanded that they stay clear of her property. A unit was dispatched to her residence to observe the situation. Immediately after the call, a fireman from the city department informed the sheriff's department that he had been invited to the female's residence. He was urged to stay away.

Without the knowledge of the sheriff's department, she had called her former husband earlier in the day and asked him to come to her residence and to bring a friend because she feared someone was going to attack her. On their arrival, she positioned them in a specific area and gave them a walkie-talkie. The area of their position did not allow them to view any of what followed.

The young fireman arrived first, was dressed in new jeans, and gave the appearance of expecting dating activity to occur. Just as the sheriff's deputy arrived, the young fireman staggered into the yard and collapsed, having been hit with a shotgun blast. His final words were, in effect: "Don't go in there, that bitch is crazy." The crime scene details did not corroborate her claim that she was attacked by the fireman threatening her with a knife. She would eventually plead guilty and serve a brief prison sentence. On her release, a local minister took up her cause and in the election campaign was instrumental in getting the incumbent undersheriff defeated when he campaigned for the job of sheriff.

There are several teaching points to this episode. This is a rare example of a false victimization claim that ended, after escalating claims, in violence. However, it portrays an example of how needs were not being met, the result of which was an escalation in her outcry. It also demonstrates how loyalty for a victim and her claims is not always based on knowledge of the facts but on personal relationships. The divisiveness within and between agencies can be disruptive. Also, even when confronted with strong indicators of manipulation and false reporting, some pseudovictims will not admit their acts.

Escalation in other cases may involve harassing or hang-up telephone calls, obscene telephone calls, breaking and entering, report of panty thefts, obscene or threatening notes left on windshields, vandalism, or similar nuisance crimes.

Most reports of false allegations involve low-end claims such as telephone calls, notes left, etc. As the reports are examined, most are found to be valid false allegations of sexual assault. Rarely, an officer may find a case in which a victim had self-inflicted wounds or self-mutilation, or high-end violence as in the case reported.

Prevalence

There is no known agency that keeps statistics on the number of false allegations made to the police. While doing research on this topic with Roy Hazelwood, we elected to personally contact 20 then present or former members of the law enforcement community who were known to be at the top of their field in experience and expertise. They represented every level of law enforcement agencies from the East Coast to the West Coast and some jurisdictions in between. Two Canadian provinces were represented in the survey. All were queried with the same questions about allegations of nonfatal rape. They were asked to estimate from memory certain areas of their experience and to answer questions from their investigative perceptions.

Collectively they had 560 years of police experience and involvement in an estimated 33,360 violent crimes, which tallied out to an average per officer of 1,682. They had been involved collectively in just under 500 false allegations of nonfatal sexual assault, which is obviously a very small percentage of all their criminal investigative experience. We did not enter our own experiences into the survey, but our experiences closely mirrored those of the group surveyed. The final calculation for false reporting in nonfatal sexual assault reports was about 3% of all their sexual assault cases.

All pseudovictims in the case histories were white females, and 65% were between the ages of 21 and 30 years. The age category of between 31 and 45 years accounted for 25% of all pseudovictims. The remaining 10% were recalled to be in the age range of 15 to 20 years old. It is probable that this last category has grown considerably in recent years.

Characteristics of a False Report

As already noted, an officer should not be too quick to label a report as "unfounded," and care should be taken to recognize that no single marker of false allegations can justify declaring a report as false. Such labeling requires that the analytical results have developed a pattern of inconsistencies, remembering that each marker is likely found in legitimate and valid claims.

It is well established that rape is a crime that is grossly underreported, so a delay in reporting a rape is not a standout feature. That said, experience has indicated that late reporting of this type of violent act can be a flag of concern. It is not the nonreporting that is the real marker, but the disturbing feature is not reporting when there have been abundant opportunities to do so. A second feature of concern is when the false victim reports the incident first to a non-law-enforcement party. The second party usually will react to the report by insisting that the pseudovictim involve the police. False reports of rape often occur in a close conjunction to a similar event that has been widely reported in the media. Also, many victims will have a prior history of making false allegations or a knowledge of such occurrences.

There are a few patterns in the actual reporting of a false rape incident. The pseudovictim will make a statement containing either great detail or she may give only a vague accounting of the incident. Her story may be told without appropriate emotion, or conversely, she may be overly dramatic. The vague story is contrived to create little detail to track, while the elaborate story and delivery are likely the result of rehearsals. A theme of a victim distancing herself from her allegation may occur as the investigation progresses. The distancing may present itself in the form of noninvolvement in the process or indifference to the police inquiries. Should a suspect be developed, she will be hesitant to assist in furthering the investigation and unwilling to identify the person in a photo spread.

The recounting of the alleged assault will probably provide little in the way of investigative threads that the police may follow. If the details are vague or minimal, the victim may note that she passed out or closed her eyes for a long period of time. Her description of the assailant will have him as "average" in each descriptive category. She may have known his name at one point, or she may recall that he was a "friend of a friend," but no names can be recalled. Another missing thread is her inability to recall the exact location of the attack.

When the interviewing officer attempts to penetrate this veil of nonfacts, he may find the pseudovictim attempting to steer the interview to "safe" areas, away from details of assault or assailant. Safe areas in which she will engage the officer would involve her injuries, the overwhelming size or number of the assailants, or her inability to escape despite great and desperate attempts to escape or defend herself. She may employ the psychological defense mechanism of "self-handicapping," by which she uses some personal condition present at the time to explain why she failed to ward off the offender, such as "If I had not just gotten over the flu …" or "… would have gotten away if I had not tripped this week and sprained my ankle."

Reporting of Injuries

The nature, type, and location of any reported injuries should be closely examined and evaluated by the detective. Some of the characteristics of wounding usually found in conjunction with false allegations are described next. As soon as possible after the report of the attack the investigating officer should examine the victim and take fingernail scrapings. If there is any DNA material found, it can be used to substantiate or discredit her story.

Be alert to whether the injuries are minor or superficial and specifically whether they involve sensitive or painful areas. If the wounds are self-inflicted, they will usually be within the alleged victim's personal reach and will likely contain indications of hesitation. It is not easy to hurt yourself.

Because the harm results from the pseudovictim's own efforts. she may report them with an indifferent attitude and brush off statements of concern about the pain from the damage. Another feature of the injuries is that they are the source of attention, likely one of the overarching goals for the false report.

Collective experience has found that "carved" message injuries are highly unlikely in legitimate situations. Also fitting this feature are "cut-and-paste" notes, either before or after the alleged incident, which are unusual in actual rape events.

Conducting the Investigation

Quality investigations of false allegations begin where all solid investigations start: with a well-grounded investigator. Such investigators have developed an open and inquiring mindset, always searching for indicators no matter in which direction they point. A quality investigator is thorough and does not leap to conclusions but lets the case facts play out to the end. This requires a great deal of patience. Such persistence pays dividends for his department and future victims whose allegations are true.

A portion of each rape allegation should include questions concerning the stability of the victim's lifestyle, particularly in search of any recent upsets in her life. The pseudovictim is likely to have issues within her life or among her closest associates. It is also advisable to probe for past experiences that may be seen as false allegations on similar, or perhaps smaller, complaints. As noted above, a false allegation often follows media attention to an investigation into a false complaint.

Interviewing a Suspected Pseudovictim

Because of the dedication a pseudovictim has to setting her life on the right course along with the depth of her need for obtaining her goals, she has invested a lot in the false allegation. That makes it doubly difficult to obtain an admission or confession from her.

Case 13.4

A mother of two young children contacted the police with a claim that someone entered her house and hung stuffed animals over the beds of her children. She claimed that the stuffed animals had a heart shape on the chest in red marker and a pen was stabbed into that spot. She complained that this was a direct threat to the safety of her children. The police conducted a thorough investigation but could neither validate nor disprove her story. Because of the nature of the allegations, the chief assigned manpower from his Crimes Against Persons Unit and supplemented this with officers from the Homicide Investigations Unit. Some members of each squad sided with the mother, insisting that her claims were valid. Some disagreed just as adamantly.

The Federal Bureau of Investigation (FBI) offered to assist by providing two experts in the disciplines of Münchausen syndrome and Münchausen syndrome by proxy and their role in false allegations. The two experts formed contradictory opinions. In the continuing investigation, the FBI also provided a pole-mounted camera that captured the mother carrying the stuffed animals and hanging them outside the residence. Even when confronted with this evidence, she refused to admit to fabricating her story. As this investigation went on for months and many of her family members were consulted about the alleged victim, it was not until the videotape was made that her father volunteered that it was strange that this was happening to her as something similar had occurred when she was in college. The appearance of the stuffed animals ceased, but it was learned that a few years later she began taking her children to emergency rooms because they were vomiting and dehydrating.

As is true with all interviews of victims, witnesses, and suspects, the officer should strive to keep the contact from becoming personal or an assault on the person. The interview should focus on the criminal act and not on the character of the interviewee. There are four methods for placing the contact within this atmosphere. The first method has been discussed several places in this book, and it has to do with the projected attitude and demeanor of the interviewer, which may unintentionally communicate dislike, distrust, or hostility. The officer's attitude and demeanor should be, and be seen as, neutral.

To protect the primary investigator's status with the victim, the confrontational interview should be handled by someone disassociated from the rape inquiry. It is not necessary to choose a female, but I have seen this technique work well. Whether a male or female, the interviewer needs the ability to project empathy, understanding, along with tact and firmness. The goal is to create a calm, reasoned, professional, unbiased confrontation. The resolution of the situation will most likely come by challenging the false allegation, not the victim. The interviewer's objections to the report should be derived solely from the inconsistencies in the victim's statements, highlighting their disparity from all of the findings of the investigation. By using rationalizations, projections, and minimizations (RPMs), especially projections and minimizations, the officer will lay the groundwork for a face-saving scenario that also repudiates the false allegations. Without providing an "out" for the victim, the interviewer is making it more difficult to obtain admissions.

Only with coordination within the chain of command and with the agreement of the prosecutor, it may be effective to relate that what is sought by the officer is any indication by the pseudovictim of the false nature of the allegation. Additional prosecution for the criminal violation of having made a false police report is not being sought. Depending on the extent of publicity the case has garnered, it may be helpful also to promise that her statement will not be publicized.

As mentioned, requesting the victim to undergo a polygraph can be highly effective in these situations. See the polygraph question in Chapter 9. The phrasing of the request should place responsibility for the request on the officer's supervisor. Should the complainant agree to the polygraph, she should be asked the follow-up question regarding how she will do when questioned about the truthfulness of her statement. It is at this point that the deceiver will begin to backpedal and make excuses about why she cannot take the test.

The incidence of a pseudovictim making her final appeal to the media with allegations of police insensitivity, unprofessional conduct, and incompetence is low, but the officers involved in apparent false allegation situations should be mindful of such a possibility. When some victims are cornered, they will protect their self-esteem with extreme measures.

Bibliography

Hazelwood, Robert R., and Ann W. Burgess. *Practical Aspects of Rape Investigation: A Multidisciplinary Approach.* New York: Elsevier Science, 1987.

Hazelwood, Robert R., and Ann W. Burgess. False Rape Allegations. In *Practical Aspects of Rape Investigation: A Multidisciplinary Approach*, 3rd ed. edited by Robert R. Hazelwood and Ann W. Burgess, 177–195. Boca Raton, FL: CRC Press, 2001a.

Hazelwood, Robert R., and Ann W. Burgess. *Practical Aspects of Rape Investigation: A Multidisciplinary Approach.* 3rd ed. Boca Raton, FL: CRC Press, 2001b.

Hazelwood, Robert R., and Ann W. Burgess. False Rape Allegations. In *Practical Aspects of Rape Investigation: A Multidisciplinary Approach*, edited by Robert R. Hazelwood and Ann W. Burgess, 181–198. Boca Raton, FL: CRC Press, 2009a.

Hazelwood, Robert R., and Ann W. Burgess. *Practical Aspects of Rape Investigation: A Multidisciplinary Approach.* 4th ed. Boca Raton, FL: CRC Press, 2009b.

McDowell, Charles P., and Neil S. Hibler. False Allegations. In *Practical Aspects of Rape Investigation: A Multidisciplinary Approach*, edited by Robert R. Hazelwood and Ann W. Burgess, 275–298. New York: Elsevier Science, 1987.

Napier, Michael R., and Kenneth P. Baker. Criminal Personality Profiling. In *Forensic Science: An Introduction to Scientific and Investigative Techniques*, edited by Stuart H. James and Jon J. Nordby, 531–550. Boca Raton, FL: CRC Press, 2003.

Napier, Michael R., and Kenneth P. Baker. Criminal Personality Profiling. In *Forensic Science: An Introduction to Scientific and Investigative Techniques*, edited by Stuart H. James and Jon J. Nordby, 615–636. Boca Raton, FL: CRC Press, 2005.

Using Statement Analysis in Rape Investigations

13

PETER SMERICK

Contents

Introduction

Many investigations of alleged sexual assault begin with a victim dialing 911. On receipt of the call, uniformed police officers and emergency medical personnel are dispatched to the victim's location. If the victim is coherent, the first officer at the scene will conduct a brief interview to ascertain what happened to her and whether she is able to describe her attacker. One detective may be dispatched to the hospital to gain additional information from the victim there; simultaneously, a team of investigators and crime scene technicians conducts a crime scene search. Investigators are assigned to the case, and at some point, after the victim has been treated at the hospital, a lengthy interview may be conducted.

Every detective is faced with the same dilemma when investigating an allegation of sexual assault. Is the alleged victim telling the truth about the incident, or is it a fabricated story? If physical evidence, especially the semen and saliva of the assailant, are discovered, the victim's story is generally believed. When forensic evidence is not available, however, the investigator has to rely on his or her skills as an interviewer to find the truth.

Many experienced investigators are confident that they are capable of determining the truthfulness of statements provided to them because of their

195

ability to "read" an individual's verbal and nonverbal behavior. Although investigators have been taught to be objective and to keep an open mind, an investigator's thought process is frequently influenced by his or her perception regarding how an authentic rape victim should behave. Often, an investigator may believe that a real rape victim should be hysterical, crying, and unable to control her emotions; conversely, the victim should be quiet, emotionless, and in a state of shock. In reality, the range of emotions expressed by a victim of sexual assault can include silence, laughter, apparent indifference, anger, or a methodical, by-the-numbers recitation of the incident.

The consequences of an incorrect assessment by the detective are profound. If the victim's story is not believed and she was sexually assaulted, her needs for assistance may not be adequately met, and a sex offender will be free to strike again. Conversely, if the victim's allegation is believed and her story turns out to be fabricated, an investigator has wasted valuable time pursuing a nonexistent offender or has possibly stigmatized an innocent person.

Most interviews of rape victims focus on fulfilling the legal obligation of establishing that the elements constituting a criminal act did occur. The format consists of the investigator asking questions and the victim providing answers. This fact-based approach, while establishing that forced sexual intercourse or sodomy may have occurred, has often proven to be unreliable when attempting to ascertain the truthfulness of a victim's statement; that is, some people lie more convincingly than other people tell the truth. As an FBI Agent I was afforded the opportunity to take training in statement analysis directly from the man who originated Scientific Content Analysis, Avinoam Sapir. His program is extensive and complex. It is also highly integrated with each piece incorporating and expanding the next. By comingling what I learned from Sapir into the knowledge base utilized by the FBI's Behavioral Science Unit I have accumulated an extensive data base and a proven skill level in evaluating spoken or written messages. Nonetheless, Sapir's instructions, my personal conversations with him, and my personal notes from the course have greatly influenced much of what appears below. Part of my assignments with the FBI involved providing an analysis of communications with questioned authorship and discovering the true meaning of specific communications involving extortions, kidnap/ransom notes, anonymous voice messages, texts, and faxes. As it turns out the FBI's experience and my personal experience closely parallel the message delivered by Sapir. I note also that I took training from the Central Intelligence Agency (CIA) in this subject matter when they presented at the FBI Academy circa 1998.

An investigator's ability to detect deception can be enhanced by the application of the findings of the FBI, the CIA, and Avinoam Sapir (1992a, 1992b). When he was working toward his master's degree in criminology, Sapir conducted extensive research in the communications field that analyzed the "linguistic code" used by people when they provide information verbally or in writing. This is the same application and practice used by the FBI and myself in particular. Sapir's work complimented the FBI process and stimulated me in my search for the true meaning of communications. Based on this research, Sapir developed a program he called scientific content analysis (SCAN), which revolutionized the way that investigators gain information from individuals they interview.

Sapir's methodology, and that of the FBI, deviated from traditional interviewing techniques relying instead on gleaning information from the interviewee's *own words* rather than relying solely on the investigator's written report. This means, of course, that the interview subject must have a basic understanding of English grammar and proper sentence structure.

Sapir (1992a, 1992b, 1998) emphasized that the SCAN technique relied on the officer's ability to *understand* the subject's answers as incorporated throughout his presentations and workbooks. Sapir believed that the interview process might teach a person how to lie to the investigator. After each question, the person being interviewed can analyze the investigator's questions to determine what type of information he or she believed the investigator wants to hear.

We automatically assume that when we converse with someone, we understand what he or she is saying, but what we as listeners fail to do is appreciate what the person really means when he or she uses certain words. A classic example of this concept can be attributed to former President Bill Clinton, who made remarks at a 1998 White House press conference regarding his relationship with Monica Lewinsky. At the conclusion of the televised press conference, President Clinton said:

> Now, I have to go back to work on my State of the Union speech and I worked on it until pretty late last night. But I want to say one thing to the American people. I want you to listen to me, I'm going to say this again: *"I did not have sexual relations with that woman, Miss Lewinsky."* I never told anybody to lie, not a single time, never. These allegations are false, and I need time to get back to work for the American people. Thank you. [Italics added]

President Clinton did not lie when he said, "I did not have sexual relations with that woman, Miss Lewinsky." In the minds of most adults, a sexual relationship may mean two people acting together to provide sexual pleasure and gratification to their partner. In the mind of Bill Clinton, however, since Monica Lewinsky was providing him with sexual gratification and he was not reciprocating, it was not a sexual relationship. It is imperative that the investigator understand what a person means when they use a certain word or phrase.

There would be a difference in a relationship if a man described a woman as being my girlfriend, a girlfriend, the girlfriend.

While providing useful tools for investigators, it is my personal under-standing, belief, and experience that one drawback to Sapir's program is the caveat that SCAN is most effective **prior** to conducting an interview. This requirement runs counter to every instinct of an investigator who has been trained to ask questions, and it may be impossible to attain a "pure" state-ment from a sexual assault victim since she probably has been questioned at the crime scene and at the hospital.

Nonetheless, it is still recommended that sex crime investigators utilize SCAN prior to conducting an extensive interview of the rape victim. The victim should be asked to describe her ordeal **in her own words** by writing or typing a report or speaking into a tape recorder.

The benefits of using this approach are that the victim is not being influ-enced or coerced in any way by the investigating officer, and that she chooses the words to use in her statement (Sapir, 1992a, 1992b, 1998). The facts of the incident as provided by the victim can be compared with the physical and behavioral evidence discovered at the crime scene to identify possible con-tradictions in the story. As an example, Sapir (1992a, 1998) suggested that the victim should be instructed to tell the investigator everything that happened to her from the time she woke up in the morning until the time she went to sleep on the day of the assault. This is an open-ended question that allows the victim to begin her statement anywhere she wants, provide as much informa-tion as she desires, and to end the statement wherever she desires. She must commit herself to a story told in her own words.

General Principles and Methodology of Statement Analysis

Prior to analyzing a statement for information and indications of deception, an investigator should keep in mind the following beliefs identified as signifi-cant by Sapir (1992a, 1992b, 1998) and found to be reliable in my extensive experience:

1. Everyone wants to give information, and everyone wants to be believed. For instance, you are in the kitchen washing the dishes and hear a loud crash in the family room. You rush into the room and observe your son and daughter standing over your antique lamp in pieces on the floor. Do the children remain silent? Do they ask for an attorney? No, they want to explain what happened and probably blame each other for the incident. There is no logical explanation for why people want to talk—they just do.
2. A person cannot tell everything that happened to him. Life is not like a Rocky movie in which every punch and counterpunch in each round of the fight is rehearsed and the actors remember precisely

the sequence of every movement. When a person is physically or sexually assaulted, the victim is mentally in a fight-or-flight mode because of the rush of adrenaline. When the victim tells her story, the events may not be in precise order.

Be wary of any victim's statement that is short, factual, and with a function for every detail of the story. Most deceptive stories are governed by logic. *Truthful statements usually contain a great deal of extraneous information that seemingly may have little or nothing to do with the incident. An investigator may think the information is not relevant; therefore, the victim must be lying. While the out-of-sequence data may not make sense to the interviewer, there is a connection in the victim's mind.*

In addition, a victim or witness will engage in an "editing" process, providing the investigator with only the information he or she thinks is important for the detective to know. According to Sapir, the majority of people do not lie (completely fabricating events); they simply do not tell everything that happened.

3. In any story told by a victim, there should be a balance between what happened to the victim *prior* to the incident, what happened *during* the incident, and what happened *after* the incident. Every story has a beginning, a middle, and an end. However, the amount of space in a statement devoted to each category can be instrumental in determining if the statement is true or false. According to Sapir, no more than 20% of the statement should be devoted to what happened *prior* to the incident. At least 50% of the statement should be devoted to what happened *during* the sexual assault, and no more than 30% of the statement should be devoted to what happened *after* the attack occurred. No truthful statement should end immediately after the assault is over since the victim should describe what happened to her after the assailant left. The rape would be considered as "starting" after a weapon or use of force was mentioned in the statement. The rape would be considered as "ending" after the offender left the victim.

Be wary of any statement that devotes an inordinate amount of space to what happened prior to the incident. If the sexual assault actually occurred, the victim should be providing a considerable amount of detail about the incident as it happened to her. An easy way to determine if the statement is proportionally balanced is to number every line of text in the statement. Underline the last line that describes events that occurred prior to the sexual assault, and underline the last line describing what happened during the sexual assault. The majority of the space in a truthful statement should be devoted to the event itself because something significant happened to the victim.

This concept was helpful when analyzing a 16-page, typed statement provided by a white male incarcerated at a correctional institution in Texas, who claimed that he had been anally raped by four unidentified black inmates in the prison chapel. The statement consisted of 14½ pages devoted to what happened to him prior to the incident, a half page about the sexual assault itself, and one page explaining what happened to him after the assault—the statement was unbalanced. An investigation revealed that the inmate had fabricated the story to obtain a transfer to a prison closer to his home.

During the analysis of the victim's prepared statement, pay attention to how long the victim believed the assault took and compare that amount of time with the activities she described. In some instances, the victim may claim that the offender attacked her for over an hour and yet describe activities that would have taken a considerably shorter period of time. Keep in mind that the accuracy of a victim's recollection of time is affected by the fear and stress she was under at the time of the assault. In addition, a victim who has been given a date rape drug may not be able to write a detailed statement at all.

Analytical Procedures

After a statement is prepared by a rape suspect or rape victim, the statement should be photocopied. Underline or highlight any points of interest on the photocopy. Do not make any marks or changes on the original document.

The investigator should realize that one does not need a degree in forensic linguistics or English to conduct this type of examination, but a basic understanding of the rules and methodology outlined next is required. As taught and published by Sapir (1992a, 1992b, 1998) and validated in my examination of hundreds of communications, the investigator needs to be mindful of the following points, which are also contained in my instruction to law enforcement personnel:

1. In sexual assault cases, statements written by a victim, witness, or suspect should be in the first-person singular, past tense. Example: "I was raped by a white guy." Not: "I am being raped by a white guy." *The use of past tense is normal because the subject is relating an incident that has already occurred. While the occasional use of present tense is acceptable since the victim is reliving the assault, the overwhelming majority of the statement should be in the past tense. Underline all of the verbs in the statement.*
2. Lack of the pronoun "I" in the statement might indicate deception or a desire to detach oneself from the situation. Example: "Went to the bedroom." "Saw a good-looking guy lying on the bed."

3. Lack of "I" in a statement prepared by a rape suspect may represent a denial of responsibility for what took place. Example: "Never touched her." "Would never do such a thing."

   This is considered passive language that indicates the subject is distancing himself from the incident. Also, be concerned if the writer uses "I" in short sentences since this may indicate tension.

   The use or nonuse of "I" is a significant point for the interviewing officer to consider. After reviewing the statement written by the victim or suspect, the interviewer should direct follow-up questions to those sentences in which "I" is absent. By placing circles around all of the "I's" in a statement, it will become apparent where the subject is distancing himself from the statement or possibly denying responsibility for what took place.

4. Use of "I" means one person, while the use of "we" indicates more than one person. Example: "He had sexual intercourse with me." Versus: "We had sexual intercourse." A shift from "I" or "he" to "we" in a rape victim's statement may reveal personal involvement.

5. "We" is not usually found in the statements of a rape victim describing what happened during the actual sexual assault but may be found in the description of events prior to and after the rape, especially in date rape situations. Example: "My boyfriend and I went on a picnic. We walked into the woods until we found a secluded spot. He wanted to have sex with me, but I wasn't in the mood. He pulled down my pants, and he raped me. After he was done with me, we walked back to his car. I broke up with him after that." An indication that the sexual activity was consensual would have been the phrase "we had sex," rather than "he raped me."

6. "We" can also be viewed as an indicator of the degree of closeness between people.

   Example:

   A. We went to the dance.
   B. My wife and I went to the dance.
   C. I went to the dance with my wife.
   D. I went to the dance with the wife.

   In Example D, the writer uses the phrase "the wife" instead of "my wife," which is a further indicator of a lack of physical or psychological closeness in a relationship.

7. "We" can also provide insight regarding the interaction between friends and associates. Example: "I met four of my college friends at Charlie's, a neighborhood bar. We had four or five beers and listened to the band. I stayed until after midnight and danced with some girls. I left alone." Although the subject was physically at the bar with four friends, the only time he was actually in the presence of his friends

was when they had four or five beers together. Other than that time, the subject was elsewhere.

8. Be alert for words classified as "unnecessary connectors." Examples are "later," "shortly thereafter," "sometime later," "afterward," "after," "when," "the next thing I remember," and "because." When these adverbs are positioned close to a description of the sexual assault, the writer may be intentionally leaving out important information. *Example: "I really don't understand what the problem is. I talked to the girl for a while, and we seemed to hit it off. We walked into the backyard to get some fresh air. Afterward, I came back inside because it was getting cold. I don't know what happened to that girl."*
   The information that has been omitted will be found between the words "fresh air" and "Afterward." These unnecessary connectors will enable the investigator to read between the lines and gather additional information and intelligence about what really happened at a scene. The writer did not lie; he just did not tell the whole story. Highlight every unnecessary connector.

9. There are phrases to watch for that may indicate that the writer is attempting to conceal critical details, suggesting that he or she is not committed to the statement. Example: "I think ...," "I thought ...," "I believe ...," "I seem to recall ... ." When a subject makes a statement about an incident that happened a year ago, these phrases may be acceptable. If the event occurred 2 days ago, the subject's memory of the event should be intact.

10. Did the subject answer the question? Example: *Question*: "Did you rape that woman?" *Answer*: "How dare you ask me that question! I am a respected member of the community. I go to church every Sunday. I would never even think of doing such a thing." When he or she avoids answering a simple yes or no question, the subject may be providing more information than he or she realizes.

Statement Analysis

Exercise 1

The following statement was prepared by Allison, a 28-year-old white female:

I left my basement apartment located at 134 Lawrence Lane at approximately 8:15 a.m., Friday morning, July 14. I am a sales clerk at Brooks Department store. I hate my job but it pays my bills. On the way to work, I got gas for my car at an Exxon Gas Station and bought a pack of cigarettes. I also bought a cup of coffee and a doughnut.

I was scheduled to work from 9:00 a.m. to 5:00 p.m. although I have a habit of getting to work slightly early. It was a boring day at work. Around 5:10 p.m. I left work and drove straight home. I parked my car in its assigned space at my apartment complex. As I was getting out of my car, I thought I saw someone in the trees near my apartment building. I stopped and looked in that direction, saw no-one and thought I was imagining things. I entered my apartment, changed clothes, made some macaroni and cheese for dinner and watched the evening news.

Around 9:00 p.m., I showered and put on a halter top and shorts. Shortly thereafter, I drove over to Paddock's Sports Bar & Grill on Deluth Street to see if any of my friends were there. No one was there that I knew, so I had a couple of glasses of white wine (Chardonnay) and listened to the band. I didn't dance with any of the guys although several good-looking guys hit on me. I told them that I wasn't interested in "hooking up" because my boyfriend recently broke up with me and I was through with men for awhile. I left the bar around 10:00 p.m. and went straight home.

I parked my car in the usual spot, checked to make sure no one was loitering about, and got out of my car. I wonder if I gave the cocktail waitress a big enough tip, she sure earned her pay listening to me bitch about men. I went inside my apartment, turned on the lights, and I think I locked the door behind me. I changed into my nightgown and brushed my teeth. I may have left my sliding door open for some fresh air. Air conditioning is too expensive for me. I turned out all of the lights (except for the night light in my bedroom), and went to sleep.

Think it was about 11:30 p.m. that I woke up and feel something on my face. I can hardly breathe. When I pull the pillow away, I see someone over me. Believe he is a white guy, big, muscular, and he smells of alcohol. Try to scream but feel a hand go over my mouth and another over my eyes. Hear myself say: "No!" I think he took his hand off my mouth and I remember saying: "Please don't hurt me." He says: "Don't scream, and I won't hurt you!"

I am very quiet and don't say a word. I remember being terrified. He spreads my legs (I am not wearing panties). I am very nervous and feel myself shaking.

He gets on top of me and tries to penetrate me but can't because I am dry. He rolls off me and fingers me for a few minutes. Afterwards, he gets on top of me again and we have sexual intercourse. I don't remember if he came or not. He gets off me now, pulls up his pants, and leaves.

I think he left through the front door. I immediately called my boyfriend but he didn't answer his cell phone. I then called the police.

Analysis of Allison's Statement

Of 42 total lines of text, approximately 28 lines pertain to events that happened prior to the sexual assault, 12 lines were devoted to the assault itself, and 2 lines deal with what happened after the attack. The entire one-page statement is unbalanced and indicative of deception.

Whether the overall statement is true or false, it should be noted that the first part of any statement is probably true since the victim is setting the stage for what follows, and there is generally no reason to lie about these events. Allison began her story at 8:15 a.m., but could have chosen any time.

False allegations of rape do not normally occur in a vacuum. There are usually stressors that occur in a victim's life compelling her to fabricate a story. These stressors may include a need for attention, revenge, or in some cases, an effort to resurrect or save a failing relationship. Subconsciously, Allison may have revealed the reason behind her story of being raped by stating that her boyfriend had recently left her. At the end of her statement, she said she called her "boyfriend," not her "former boyfriend," which suggests that she was hoping this incident would cause him to come to her rescue.

When describing the actual sexual assault, Allison's narrative is brief and logical, but she relates it predominantly in the present tense. There were occasions when she distanced herself from the story by eliminating "I," and there were several short sentences containing "I." In addition, when the offender penetrated her, she said that "we have sexual intercourse."

This statement has many indicators suggesting that it is a false allegation.

Exercise 2

The following statement was prepared by Kim, a 26-year-old white female:

I went to bed at 3:00 a.m., Sunday morning, May 10. I had been reading a book in bed prior to falling asleep. I was awakened by the sound of my bedroom window closing. When I looked toward the window there was a guy standing there by a plant, naked. I asked him what he was doing there. He said shut up lady and I won't hurt you. I asked him again what he was doing there and he said think of someone you hated the most and that's who sent him there. He came over to my bed and he had a knife and said shut up, don't make a sound and I won't hurt you. He was on the bed and told me to take my panties and gown off and just laid there. He asked me if I was on birth control and I said no, then he said I can't come inside you. He moved me to the center of the bed. He got on top of me and proceeded to do his thing.

After about 10 minutes he told me to turn over and I said no. He said if you just turn over and cooperate, I'll be out of here in about 30 minutes. I wouldn't turn over so he said if I can't come inside you, then you have to make me come. Then I laid there. He asked me where Courtney was. I asked him how he knew my daughter. I told him I was going through a divorce and that I was the only one taking care of my daughter. He asked if I liked kissing girls. I said no. He slapped me and called me a liar. He said he saw pictures of me kissing a girl. I told him that was my sister. Wait, when I didn't turn over the first time he told me he had some friends outside who are waiting their turn with me. He started having intercourse with me. He made me put my arms around him and tried to make me put my tongue in his mouth and I wouldn't. He laid on his back and he tried to make me perform oral sex. I told him I didn't know how to do it. He took my hair and pushed me down. He said if I bit him, he would kill me. He told me to get on my knees in front of him and I said no, he took my hair and said get on your knees and that's when I saw the knife lying on the bed next to him.

So, I grabbed the knife and I told him you are raping me with a butter knife. I went to the end of the bed and he slammed me down on my right side trying to get the knife from me. I started screaming and screaming and that's when he started punching my face. He punched me in the lip and I felt my lip burst. I said I thought you said you weren't going to hurt me.

He said don't do anything stupid and that's when he pulled the cord out of the phone. He started backing down the hallway and I followed him into the living room and that's where he got his clothes near the loveseat. He put his jeans on, I didn't see any underwear. He had a light colored shirt and no shoes. He opened the door and told me he would be back. I locked the front door and went back to the bedroom to make sure the window was locked. I put a robe on and went back in the living room made sure the sliding doors were locked. I called 911.

I also want to add that before he asked me to perform oral sex I asked him if he knew what day it was and he said no. I told him it was Mother's Day and asked him if he had a mother, because he was doing this to somebody's mother. He got mad. He was a white male about 5'7", real slim and trim, and he didn't have any hair on his chest. He was probably in his late teens or early twenties. He was muscular for his age and he had a complete tan from his waist to his thigh. The police arrived and took me to the hospital. I have never seen this guy before.

Analysis of Kim's Statement

Kim could have started her story the evening before the attack but chose instead to start her statement when she heard the bedroom window closing.

Kim's statement consists of 45 lines of text. Six lines pertain to what happened to her prior to the incident, 28 lines describe what happened during the assault, and 11 lines of text focus on what happened after the incident. Based on Sapir's formula for truthfulness, the statement is balanced correctly. The majority of the statement deals with the main issue, the sexual assault.

It should be noted that the victim consistently used "I," and the verbs were in the past tense. Her story was not in chronological order and contained miscellaneous, out-of-sequence information that did not pertain to the rape itself.

This statement has many indicators suggesting that it is a true statement.

Summary

The SCAN technique, as developed by Sapir, is a useful tool for gathering information from a person's own words and in some cases can aid in detecting deception. SCAN is not foolproof and is just one of many tools an investigator can use to determine the truth.

This chapter focuses on the use of SCAN in sex crime investigations. Other factors may have to be taken into consideration when using the SCAN technique to analyze other types of cases.

SCAN cannot be used on statements written by a detective after he or she has conducted an interview with the subject because the language in the statement may not accurately represent what the subject said. Another limitation involves the difficulty of obtaining a "pure" description of events from the victim before she has been formally interviewed by law enforcement.

The most important lesson to be learned, however, would be for every investigator to allow a victim, witness, or suspect to prepare his or her own statement before being questioned by detectives.

Bibliography

Sapir, Avinoam. *L.S.I. Advanced Workshop on Scientific Content Analysis.* Phoenix: Laboratory for Scientific Interrogation, 1998.

Sapir, Avinoam, *The L.S.I. Annual Advanced Workshop on Scientific Conent Analysis.* Phoenix, Arizona: Laboratory for Scientific Interrogation, 1992a.

Sapir, Avinoam, *L.S.I. Scientific Content Analysis Newsletter Anthology.* Phoenix, Arizona: Laboratory for Scientific Interrogation, 1992b.

Is the Caller the Killer? Analyzing 911 Homicide Calls*

14

TRACY HARPSTER AND SUSAN H. ADAMS

Contents

Truth will come to light, murder cannot be hid long.

William Shakespeare

Dispatcher: 911, what's your emergency?
Caller: Yes, I have an emergency, someone is … ah, injured here.
Dispatcher: How did they get injured?
Caller: I don't know, there is blood all over the floor, I just came upstairs.

In this case, the 911 caller's wife was fatally shot in the head in their home. This chapter provides a structured method for analyzing such a call and examines this specific call in depth to gain insight for conducting a

---

* Portions of this chapter were reprinted with permission from the *Law Enforcement Bulletin*. Adams, Susan H. and Harpster, Tracy, 2008. 911 Homicide Calls and Statement Analysis: Is the Caller the Killer? *Law Enforcement Bulletin* (June 2008): 22–31.

thorough interview of the caller. The 911 calls provide invaluable clues to investigators because the caller, in fact, may have committed the crime. It is not unusual for homicide offenders to contact 911 without revealing their involvement in the murder. A homicide study in Washington state revealed that 19% of 911 homicide calls were made by the offender posing as an innocent witness (Keppel, n.d.).

Homicide calls are unique. They originate from distressed callers confronted with urgent life-and-death situations. These initial contacts can contain the most valuable statements of the entire case for they are the statements least contaminated by suspects' attempts to conceal the truth, attorneys' advice to remain silent, or investigators' leading questions (Sandoval, 2003).

Statements solicited by police officers are contaminated by both the interviewer and the environment in which the interview occurs (Shuy, 1998). The physical and psychological demeanor of the officer asking the questions directly influences statements. For example, close-ended, leading questions fired at a suspect by an overly aggressive officer usually result in obtaining minimal information. The physical environment of the interview inherently affects the individual's statement as well. Most citizens are anxious and intimidated when arriving at a law enforcement agency and providing a statement to an investigator in the unfamiliar, sterile police interview room. In addition, an interview conducted in the individual's home often subjects the statement to noise distractions and interruptions from other household members.

The purest and least-contaminated statements made to law enforcement are the initial comments made by callers to the 911 police dispatcher. During these emergency verbal exchanges, the 911 dispatcher is trained to initiate the conversation by asking the open-ended question "911, what is your emergency?" The burden shifts to the caller to verbally solicit assistance for the emergent event, and neither the interviewer nor the setting of the interview contaminates the caller's initial comments. In an emergency involving a murder, the 911 caller's pure statement can be a critical element in assisting law enforcement during the subsequent homicide investigation. The dispatcher simply asks, "What is your emergency?" and the caller responds with insightful, uncontaminated verbal and vocal clues.

Fortunately, all 911 calls are recorded. Therefore, investigators have access to a recording, a transcript, and thus important evidence. They can examine the tone of voice and each word in the text of the call. An analysis of the calls can provide investigators with immediate insight to help identify the offender. Some cases, lacking direct physical evidence or eyewitnesses, can still be solved by analyzing 911 callers' statements to the dispatcher and exploring these statements during the subsequent interview with the caller.

We analyzed 100 homicide calls* from adjudicated cases to examine the differences between innocent and guilty callers. Innocent individuals made 50 of the calls, and guilty persons who either committed the homicide or arranged for another person to do so made the other half.

Specific differences appeared that helped distinguish innocent callers from guilty ones during an examination of the answers to the following three questions: (1) What was the call about? (2) Who was the call about? and (3) How was the call made?

What Was the Call About?

The call can be analyzed several ways, discussed next.

Request for Help

When analyzing a 911 homicide call, the investigator's primary question should be, "Was the caller requesting assistance?" If not, why not? Was the individual simply reporting a crime? Almost twice as many innocent callers (67%) in this study asked for help for the victim than did guilty callers (34%).

Relevance of Information

During the dispatchers' questioning, few of the guilty 911 callers actually lied unless forced to do so. Most of them deceived by omission rather than commission. Instead of offering the complete truth, such as "I did it," many provided rambling information instead of concise points; confusing, rather than clear, details; and extraneous information instead of relevant facts. People who provide more information than necessary may be attempting to convince someone of a deceptive story rather than simply conveying truthful information (Rabon, 1996). Extraneous information, although appearing irrelevant to the dispatchers' questions, frequently provides important insight. In this regard, investigators must listen carefully to the complete call because the caller may have provided information that reveals vital clues to the homicide. Consider the following exchange:

---

* The callers for this study represented 19 states and had the following characteristics: 56% were male and 44% were female; 69% were Caucasian and 31% were African American. Their ages ranged from 19 to 68 years. Victims ranged in age from newborn to 69; 67% were male and 33% were female; 64% were Caucasian, 30% were African American, 1% was Hispanic, and 5% represented other ethnicities.

Dispatcher: How old is your son?

Guilty caller: He's only six, he's like eaten an apple and he's burpin' it up, he's not, not, it's like a seizure type, we got in a, yeah, we got in a car wreck 2 months ago.

In this 911 call, there was no plea for help, and the mother of the dying child communicated unsolicited, unexpected, extraneous information to the dispatcher by mentioning "we got in a car wreck 2 months ago." There was no clear connection to the child having difficulty breathing and a car accident 2 months ago (the caller did not state that since the car accident the child had difficulty breathing). Therefore, this would be an example of the *extraneous indicator*. The subsequent investigation revealed that the child's father severely beat his son in the mother's presence, and the victim died before the medics arrived.

Of the 911 homicide callers, 44% included extraneous information in their call. Of those, 96% were guilty of the offense, and only 4% were innocent. Extraneous information was the strongest indicator of guilt in the study.

Innocent callers, instead of adding extraneous information, were more likely to focus on the objective—getting medical assistance for the victim as soon as possible. According to the four maxims of communication, people should provide accurate, concise, clear, and relevant information (Grice, 1989); most innocent callers in the study did so to obtain immediate medical assistance. The following exchange illustrates an innocent 911 caller providing accurate, clear, and relevant information regarding a homicide.

Dispatcher: What is your emergency?

Innocent caller: I'm at the East End Bar. Please, there's been gunfire. People are running out of the building. We need help as soon as possible.

Attitude Toward the Victim

Blame or insults directed toward a dying victim in 911 calls indicate strained relationships. As an example, a father called 911 to report that his 4-year-old daughter was in serious medical distress.

Dispatcher: Do you know what's wrong with your daughter?

Guilty caller: Not a clue.

Dispatcher: Has she taken any medications?

Guilty caller: Maybe. She's very, very sneaky. She threw a huge temper tantrum earlier. She might have taken something.

As his daughter lay dying, the father unexpectedly insulted her with the description "very, very sneaky" and referred to her "huge temper tantrum." The investigation revealed that the girl disobeyed the caller by taking a sip of her sister's (his biological daughter's) drink. As punishment, the caller tied the victim's hands behind her back and forced her to drink 64 ounces of water. She died of *hyponatremia*, a dangerously low sodium concentration in the blood, caused by rapid ingestion of the water. He later was convicted of her murder.

Similarly, individuals should not blame dying victims for the predicament. For illustration, a woman called 911 to report that her husband had been shot.

Dispatcher: Was this accidental or on purpose?
Guilty caller: We were having a domestic fight, and he threw me on the bed and grabbed my purse so I couldn't leave.

Instead of answering the dispatcher's question, the wife blamed her husband for his fatal injury, suggesting that he was responsible for his death because he threw her on the bed and stopped her from leaving. The subsequent investigation revealed that the woman intentionally shot and killed him; she was convicted of his murder.

Five percent of the callers in the study insulted or blamed the victim, and all were guilty of the homicide. No innocent callers did so; they simply sought help: "A kid fell down the steps. He's bleeding real bad. Hurry!"

In the preceding example, the innocent caller not only sought help for the victim, but also focused on the victim's condition ("He's bleeding real bad."). In contrast, guilty callers focused on the condition of the scene: "There's blood all over the carpet." "Her brains are on the couch." All callers in this study who included such blood and brains comments pertaining to the scene were found to be guilty of the homicide.

Accuracy of Facts

Innocent callers in this study were much more likely than guilty ones to correct erroneous information when additional details revealed discrepancies.

Dispatcher: 911, what is your emergency?
Innocent caller: There's a man been shot down the hall of my apartment.
Dispatcher: Can you check and see if he has a pulse?
Innocent caller: OK. [The caller checks on the victim.]
Innocent caller: I thought it was a man, but it's a lady. It's a lady, and I didn't feel a pulse.

The caller was innocent, did not know the victim, and had assumed that the person was male. After learning additional information, he corrected the previous inaccuracy about the victim's gender. Innocent 911 callers also remained more consistent regarding facts.

Several guilty callers provided information that conflicted with previously provided details and failed to resolve the discrepancy. For example, a mother contacted 911 to report that her baby was not breathing.

Dispatcher: How long has your baby not been breathing?
Guilty caller: Just now. She's been fine for the last few hours.
Dispatcher: Has she been sick lately?
Guilty caller: No, we were just sleeping, and the phone woke me up.

The caller advised the dispatcher that her baby had "been fine for the last few hours." However, she later added a conflicting statement indicating that the phone just woke her. How could she have known her child's condition? The mother was charged and convicted of killing her daughter. Twenty-eight percent of the 911 homicide callers gave conflicting facts and failed to correct them; all were guilty of the offense. Six percent of the callers corrected themselves when they learned additional information, and all of these were innocent.

Who Was the Call About?

This section deals with who the call was about: topic, focus, and attitude of caller.

Topic of the Call

When contacting 911, innocent individuals remained focused on the victim. For example, one caller urgently stated, "This guy's hurt real bad. Tell them to hurry!" Why would individuals call the emergency line and focus on themselves, instead reporting a problem without asking the dispatcher for assistance for the person who needs it? The following dialogue occurred when a father called 911 concerning his son:

Dispatcher: 911. What is your emergency?
Guilty caller: I have an unconscious child who is breathing very shallowly.

In this case, the father took personal possession of a problem ("I have") and referred to his problem (his dying son) as "an unconscious child." When the paramedics arrived at the residence, the child already had died. The father had assaulted his son, causing cerebral hemorrhaging. Twelve percent of the 911 callers in the study took personal possession of the problem. All were guilty of the homicide.

Focus of the Help

When individuals call 911 because someone is in critical condition, they logically ask for help for the victim, even if the callers themselves need assistance. However, when callers request help only for themselves and not the victim, homicide investigators should realize that the caller could, in fact, be the killer. As an example, a young man called 911 to report that his father had been shot:

Dispatcher: What happened to your father?
Guilty caller: Say something to me! Help me!

In this example, the caller wanted help for himself and never asked for help for his father. The investigation revealed that the son shot his sleeping parent. The man died of the wound, and the son was convicted of the crime. Seven percent of the callers in the study requested help for themselves and not for the victim. All were guilty of the homicides.

Conversely, 41% of callers requested help for the victim alone; 68% of these were innocent, and 32% were guilty. The following call serves as an example of an innocent individual demanding assistance for a victim:

Dispatcher: What's your cell phone number?
Innocent caller: Just get to 829 Euclid!
Dispatcher: The officers are going to be coming in a minute.
Innocent caller: They have to come now!!!!

Attitude Toward the Victim's Death

People can survive horrific injuries, such as gunshot wounds to the head and stab wounds to the heart. Therefore, a 911 caller should demand help for the victim even if survival appears doubtful. The caller should not accept the victim's death before the person's actual condition becomes known. For instance, patrol officers who have informed a citizen that a family member has been killed in a traffic crash know that people often respond with denial because of their inability to immediately process such shocking information. The surviving family members cannot accept the fact that their loved one is dead, and they want every lifesaving measure attempted, even demanding medical help for individuals in full rigor. The following quotation is from an innocent witness trying desperately to save a life: "He don't have a pulse. He don't have nothing! Just please send somebody."

However, a caller stating that a victim is dead without absolute proof (e.g., decapitation) should raise serious questions. An example illustrates this point:

Dispatcher: 911, what is your emergency?
Guilty caller: I just heard a gunshot in the apartment next door, and I went over. My neighbor is dead!

In this case, the caller immediately declared the mortality of the victim. The subsequent investigation revealed that the caller had been romantically interested in his neighbor. He later confessed that he killed the victim because she refused to date him. In the homicides in which mortality was not obvious, 23% of the callers accepted the death of the victim. Of this total, all were guilty of the homicide.

How Was the Call Made?

Next, we discuss how the call was made.

Voice Modulation

Investigators gain a distinct advantage when analyzing 911 calls because they can hear the caller's voice rather than relying solely on a written transcript. How someone delivers a message can offer as much insight as the message itself. Did the caller use voice modulation with loud volume, fast speed, varied pitch, and emotional tones? Or, did the caller lack voice modulation by communicating in a low, slow, even, and unemotional manner? Emergency situations demand urgency, and previous studies of homicide statements have shown that the presence of emotion indicates the likelihood of veracity (Adams, 2002).

Most often in this study, when making genuine demands for medical assistance for critically injured victims, callers displayed varied voice modulation rather than an even-paced, emotionless, and robotic tone. Yet, the absence of voice modulation was even more informative than its presence. Only 4% of innocent callers had no voice modulation, while 35% of guilty callers lacked voice modulation.

Urgency of the Call

When individuals call 911 to obtain medical assistance in a grave medical emergency, they logically will make an urgent demand for help. A study of arson emergency calls in London supported this claim (Olsson, 2004).

The following exchange occurred after an innocent witness observed a drive-by shooting:

Dispatcher: 911. What is your emergency?
Innocent caller: I need an ambulance at 78 North Central Street! Hurry up!
Dispatcher: What's the phone number you are calling from?
Innocent caller: Just get to 78 North Central!
Dispatcher: What's your phone number, sir?
Innocent caller: She's shot in the head! I don't know! Just send somebody!

The caller demanded an immediate response from medical personnel. This contrasted with callers who patiently and politely used such words as "please," "thank you," or "pardon me."

A woman who murdered her spouse called 911 to report that an unknown assailant had shot her and her husband. The opening dialogue in the call is an example of the words of a guilty caller:

Dispatcher: 911. What's your emergency?
Guilty caller: Hi, I've been shot, and my husband has been shot.

The wife used the unexpected friendly greeting "Hi" with the dispatcher while her husband, who had been shot in the head, lay dead on the floor. The wife should have remained focused on demanding immediate medical assistance for her spouse. The investigation revealed that the woman intentionally shot and killed her husband and superficially wounded herself.

In contrast, an example of an urgent demand for help involved an innocent mother who discovered that her infant had died during the night, and she screamed the following question to the dispatcher:

Dispatcher: Is the baby breathing?
Innocent caller: What the [expletive] is taking them [paramedics] so long?

In this case, the mother did not care about politeness and civility. She focused only on obtaining immediate medical assistance for her baby. The investigation revealed that the infant had accidentally wedged his head between the mattress and the crib and suffocated during the night. He had been deceased for several hours and was blue and cold to the touch before his mother discovered his condition. However, she refused to accept the death of her child and was demanding and rude to the dispatcher in an effort to get immediate help. Thirty-seven percent of the callers in the study made urgent and demanding pleas for help, and each was innocent. This finding was the strongest indicator of innocence in the study. Conversely, 22% of the callers were patient and polite, and all were guilty of the homicides.

When an individual calls 911 to obtain medical assistance in a grave medical emergency, the plea for help should be made in the most expedient fashion. The faster the 911 caller can communicate pertinent information, the faster the dispatcher can send help for the victim. A caller who does not use contractions in the opening communication illustrates a lack of urgency and is actually delaying police and medical assistance by that behavior. Seven percent of guilty 911 callers failed to use contractions during the opening exchange with the dispatcher, and all were guilty of the murder. No innocent callers failed to use contractions during their emergency calls.

The following call illustrates the *lack of contractions indicator*:

Guilty caller: My wife has been shot.
Dispatcher: Do you know who did it?
Guilty caller: No, I do not.

Level of Cooperation

If focused on obtaining assistance, 911 callers cooperate by answering questions concerning the crime. In this study, innocent individuals did so more frequently than guilty callers, who resisted full cooperation by not responding to the dispatchers' inquiries concerning the criminal act, failing to perform cardiopulmonary resuscitation (CPR) as instructed, repeating words, and providing unclear responses.

A caller reported that his girlfriend needed medical help. The dispatcher asked a question to gain more information, but the individual did not cooperate.

Dispatcher: Did something happen to her? Was this more than just an argument?
Guilty caller: That's all I'm trying to report.

In this case, the caller resisted providing any further details regarding the condition of the girlfriend. Officers located the dead girl in her apartment, and the boyfriend was convicted of the offense.

Similarly, a guilty parent called to report a stabbing incident. The individual subsequently resisted answering the dispatcher's questions.

Guilty caller: They just stabbed me and my kids, my little boys!

Dispatcher: Who did?
Guilty caller: My little boy is dying!
Dispatcher: Who did this?
Guilty caller: They killed our babies.

Such resistance to cooperation existed in 26% of the calls. All were made by guilty callers.

Guilty callers also resisted cooperation through repetition. People who do not tell the truth tend to repeat words or phrases (DePaulo and Morris, 2005). Through repetition, a guilty person can gain time to think of a reasonable answer to an unanticipated question or may avoid answering altogether. An example of repetition occurred in the following communication after a 911 caller reported an assault by an unknown assailant who allegedly had also shot her husband.

Dispatcher: Ma'am, do you know what he was wearing?
Guilty caller: Oh God, um … um … oh God, oh God, oh my God … oh my
          God.

The woman, calm enough to answer other questions, repeated the phrase "Oh God" and never answered this question. If cooperative, she at least should have attempted to answer the question or explain why she could not do so. In this case, the caller killed her husband and blamed the homicide on a fictitious assailant. Fifteen percent of the 911 homicide callers in the study included repetition during the call. All were guilty of the crimes.

When a 911 caller unexpectedly responds to a dispatcher's relevant question with such comments as "Huh?," "What?," or "Do what?" it reveals a disconnect in the thought process known as the *huh factor* (Harpster, 2006). These responses indicate that callers are caught completely off guard and are not tracking their own answers (unless, of course, excessive background noise prevents them from clearly hearing the dispatcher's questions). For example, a caller reported that his wife suffered a serious accident:

Dispatcher: 911, what is your emergency?
Guilty caller: I just came home, and my wife has fallen down the stairs. She's
          hurt bad, and she's not breathing!
Dispatcher: How many stairs did she fall down?
Guilty caller: Huh?

When the dispatcher asked a relevant question regarding the accident, the caller, who had assaulted and killed his wife, could not immediately answer because he had not tracked his own fabricated story. Had the victim actually fallen down stairs, the caller should have known whether she fell down a few stairs or a whole flight and would not have been confused by this unanticipated question. The huh factor was present in 12% of the homicide calls. All but one of these callers were guilty.

Innocent callers attempted to convey information to the dispatcher clearly and accurately. However, when asked specific questions by the dispatcher, guilty callers frequently used vague terms (i.e., somebody, someone, something, kind of, think, probably, maybe) to describe their loved one or circumstances surrounding the homicide of their loved one. This unexpected equivocation during a 911 emergency call is an example of the *equivocation indicator*, as the following exchange illustrates:

Dispatcher: 911, what's your emergency?
Caller: Ahh, some peoples from ahh, from Vegas, they, they killed my fiancée.

The caller referred to the alleged suspects with the vague term "some peoples." However, he obviously had additional information about the alleged suspects because he knew they were from Vegas. Yet, during the call, he volunteered no additional information about the "killers" (gender, race, number of people, descriptions, or how he knew they were from Vegas). In the study, the equivocation indicator was present in 66% of the guilty calls. In contrast, the equivocation indicator was present in only 8% of the innocent calls.

Investigators should ask whether the caller continues with one thought process or uses self-interruptions and changes the direction of the topic. In calls containing self-interruptions, the first topic can reveal important clues. In the following example, the husband began to state that his house had been burglarized but changed the topic midsentence.

Dispatcher: 911, what is your emergency?
Guilty caller: There's been a burg ... my wife has been killed, I think!

The critical condition of the caller's wife should have been the primary topic, yet he began with the less-critical subject, burglary. The investigation revealed that the caller arranged for an accomplice to burglarize his own residence and traumatize his wife. Thirty percent of the callers in this study used self-interruptions, and all were guilty. This was the second-strongest correlation with guilt in the study.

Case 14.1

The following transcript is from a death investigation initiated when a man called to report an emergency involving his wife. The reader can analyze the transcript using the indicators of guilt and innocence explained in the text and score the results on the COPS (Considering Offender Probability in Statements) scale that follows:

Dispatcher: 911, what's your emergency?
Caller: Yes, I have an emergency, someone is … ah, injured here.
Dispatcher: How did they get injured?
Caller: I don't know, there is blood all over the floor, I just came upstairs.
Dispatcher: Who … You say there is blood all over the floor?
Caller: Yes.
Dispatcher: Is it your roommate that is hurt or what?
Caller: I'm sorry, it is my wife.
Dispatcher: It's your wife? You don't know what happened to her?
Caller: No, I just came up out of …
Dispatcher: Is she breathing?
Caller: There's blood all over the floor.
Dispatcher: Is she breathing?
Caller: Hold on …

   [Nine-second pause; one can hear the communications technician typing in the background.]

Caller: I think, I think she shot herself.
Dispatcher: Okay, listen to me, listen to me, I'm going to transfer you over to a medic, don't hang up.
Caller: All right.

   [Call being transferred to fire department dispatcher.]

FD: Fire dispatch.
Caller: Hello.
FD: Hello, fire department.
Caller: All right, I'm at 5945 Northern Pine Street …
FD: Yes.
Caller: and I think my wife shot herself.
FD: You think she did?
Caller: Yes.
FD: Okay, is she there with you?
Caller: She's on the floor here, I just came upstairs and I think she's dead. Oh my God.
FD: Okay, all right. Did you tell the police this too?
Caller: I just now came upstairs.
FD: Okay, we've got medics on the way, okay?
Caller: All right.
FD: All right they're on the way

Caller: Bye.
FD: Bye.

---

911 COPS Scale

Considering Offender Probability in Statements
Place check marks at the appropriate end of each scale for any descriptor that applies.

Innocent Callers			Guilty Callers
WHAT is the call about?			
Request for Help	( )	( )	No Request for Help
Relevant Information	( )	( )	Extraneous Information
Concern for Victim	( )	( )	Insulting/Blaming Victim
Correction of Facts	( )	( )	Conflicting Facts
No Equivocation	( )	( )	Equivocation
WHO is the call about?			
Help Requested for Victim	( )	( )	Help Requested for Caller
Help Requested Immediately	( )	( )	Help Requested Later in Call
Focus on Victim's Survival	( )	( )	Focus on Caller's Problem
No Acceptance of Victim's Death	( )	( )	Acceptance of Victim's Death
HOW is the call made?			
Voice Modulation	( )	( )	No Voice Modulation
Urgency	( )	( )	No Urgency
Cooperation with Dispatcher	( )	( )	Resistance to Answer
No Self-interruptions	( )	( )	Self-interruptions
No Blood/Brains Reference	( )	( )	Blood/Brains Comment
Rudely Demanding	( )	( )	Polite and Patient
		( )	Repetition
The absence of Repetition, Lack of		( )	Lack of Contractions
Contractions and the Huh Factor does		( )	"Huh" Factor
not necessarily indicate innocence			

Source: Harpster and Adams ©.

Case Study 14.1 Analysis

The following transcript includes a full analysis of the 911 call in Case 14.1:

Dispatcher: 911, what's your emergency?
Caller: Yes, I have an emergency.

The caller responds to the dispatcher's open-ended, introductory question by commenting "Yes, *I have an emergency,*" simply repeating the dispatcher's word. This also illustrates the focus on the caller's problem indicator. The caller fails to immediately ask for specific help (medic, police) for his wife and is an example of no request for help. In fact, the caller never asks for help during the entire phone call.

Caller: Someone is … ah, injured here.

The term *someone* is an unexpected, distancing, and vague reference to the caller's wife and is an example of the equivocation indicator. The caller continues by pausing and choosing the term *injured* to refer to his wife's critical physical condition. The term *injured* is an adequate description when commenting on a sprained ankle; however, it is unexpected and purposely vague in this instance. The caller's failure to use a contraction (someone's) in this sentence is an example of the lack of contractions indicator.

Dispatcher: How did they get injured?
Caller: I don't know, there is blood all over the floor, I just came upstairs.

The comment "there is *blood all over the floor*" is an example of the blood and brains indicator. The caller adds the comment, "I just came upstairs," which reveals that the caller may be minimizing his involvement in the offense. It is interesting to note that the husband claimed to have no knowledge ("I don't know") on how his wife became "injured," although later in the call he stated that she had been shot. At this point in the call, it would be logical for the husband to have explained why he had come upstairs (i.e., "I was sleeping and I heard a gunshot"). However, the caller omitted a comment on the gunshot or why he was alerted to come upstairs.

Dispatcher: Who … You say there is blood all over the floor?
Caller: Yes.
Dispatcher: Is it your roommate that is hurt or what?
Caller: I'm sorry, it is my wife.

The dispatcher had no idea that the victim was actually the caller's wife and asked, "Is it your roommate that is hurt or what?" The dispatcher's specific question forced the caller to clarify, and he replied "*I'm sorry*, it is my wife." His polite and apologetic comment, "I'm sorry," at a time when his primary concern should be demanding assistance for his wife is an example of the polite and patient indicator. The caller continued the sentence by failing to use a contraction when he commented: "*It is* my wife." This is the second example of the lack of contractions indicator.

Dispatcher: It's your wife? You don't know what happened to her?

The dispatcher's follow-up question, "It's your wife?" contrasts with that of the caller because, in a hurry to get information, she appropriately used the contraction "It's" when speaking of the victim.

Caller: No, I just came up out of ...
Dispatcher: Is she breathing?
Caller: There's blood all over the floor.

After the pertinent question, "Is she breathing?" the caller replied, "There's *blood* all over the floor." His response was his second use of the blood and brains indicator. A closer look at his response indicates that the caller never answered the dispatcher's question regarding whether the victim was breathing. The husband's failure to address the pertinent question is an example of the resistance to answer indicator.

Dispatcher: Is she breathing?
Caller: Hold on ...

[Nine-second pause; one can hear the communications technician typing in the background.]

Caller: I think, I think she shot herself.

The dispatcher was forced to immediately repeat the same question and after a 9-second pause, the caller replied, "I *think*, I *think* she shot herself." Again, the caller failed to answer the dispatcher's question concerning his wife's breathing; this is another example of resistance to answer. In addition, the caller's use of the term *think* when commenting about his wife shooting herself is the second example of the equivocation indicator. Why does the caller think his wife shot herself? If the victim had an observable bullet wound, if the caller heard the gunshot, or if a pistol was laying near the victim, the caller should have made the appropriate comment by this point of the call.

Dispatcher: Okay, listen to me, listen to me, I'm going to transfer you over to a medic, don't hang up.
Caller: All right.

[Call being transferred to fire department dispatcher.]

FD: Fire dispatch.
Caller: Hello.
FD: Hello, fire department.

Caller: All right, I'm at 5945 Northern Pine Street ...
FD: Yes.
Caller: ... and I think my wife shot herself.

After being transferred to the fire dispatch, the caller again advised the dispatcher "... and I *think* my wife shot herself." Again, the term *think* is vague and equivocal and is the third time the caller has used the equivocation indicator.

FD: You think she did?
Caller: Yes.
FD: Okay, is she there with you?
Caller: She's on the floor here, I just came upstairs and I think she's dead.
      Oh my God.

In the last segment of the last sentence here, the caller accepted the death of his wife by commenting "and I think she's *dead*. Oh my God." This is an example of the acceptance of death indicator.

FD: Okay, all right. Did you tell the police this too?
Caller: I just now came upstairs.

The caller attempted to minimize his involvement in the situation, and he did not answer the dispatcher's question, an example of resistance to answer.

FD: Okay, we've got medics on the way, okay?
Caller: All right.

The husband patiently and politely replied "*all right.*" One would expect that a husband would be urgent and demanding in his attempt to make sure that help for his critically injured wife arrived promptly. However, the caller lacked the urgent tone and demanding nature characteristic of innocent callers; therefore, this is a polite and patient indicator.

FD: All right they're on the way.
Caller: Bye.
FD: Bye.

After the dispatcher advised the caller that "they're on the way," the caller responded with a simple and polite "*Bye.*" The caller closed with an inappropriately polite term as his loved one was dying on the floor beside him. This is the third example of the patient and polite indicator. It is unexpected that the caller would end the conversation with the dispatcher in such a quick, abrupt fashion. Had he chosen to stay on the line he could have assisted his wife by making certain that the medics did not have difficulty getting to the right address, or he might have received help from the dispatcher in performing CPR on the victim. Clearly, he was not focused on his wife's survival.

The husband was robotic, monotonic, and detached when communicating with the dispatcher. Although his wife was dying while he communicated with the dispatcher, his voice lacked inflection or emotion. This was unexpected behavior in an extremely stressful situation and is an example of no voice modulation. Throughout the call, the caller displayed no indication that his wife's critical injuries were of an urgent nature. His voice remained slow, and he expressed no need for the medics to hurry, thus illustrating the no urgency indicator.

After scoring the COPS scale, the form should appear as follows:

9-1-1 COPS Scale

Considering Offender Probability in Statements
Place check marks at the appropriate end of each scale for any descriptor that applies.

Innocent Callers			Guilty Callers
WHAT is the call about?			
Request for Help	( )	(√)	No Request for Help
Relevant Information	( )	( )	Extraneous Information
Concern for Victim	( )	( )	Insulting/Blaming Victim
Correction of Facts	( )	( )	Conflicting Facts
No Equivocation	( )	(√√√)	Equivocation
WHO is the call about?			
Help Requested for Victim	( )	( )	Help Requested for Caller
Help Requested Immediately	( )	( )	Help Requested Later in Call
Focus on Victim's Survival	( )	(√)	Focus on Caller's Problem
No Acceptance of Victim's Death	( )	(√)	Acceptance of Victim's Death
HOW is the call made?			
Voice Modulation	( )	(√)	No Voice Modulation
Urgency	( )	(√)	No Urgency
Cooperation with Dispatcher	( )	(√√√)	Resistance to Answer
No Self-interruptions	( )	( )	Self-interruptions
No Blood/Brains Reference	( )	(√√)	Blood/Brains Comment
Rudely Demanding	( )	(√√√)	Polite and Patient
		( )	Repetition
The absence of Repetition, Lack of Contractions and the Huh Factor does not necessarily indicate innocence.		(√√)	Lack of Contractions
		( )	"Huh" Factor

Source: Harpster and Adams ©.

Seventeen checks appear on the guilty side of the COPS scale and none on the innocent side. This indicates the likelihood that the caller may be the offender. In this case study, the caller was indeed guilty of killing his wife and was convicted of the homicide.

Conclusion

By examining 911 homicide calls, investigating officers can gain vital clues. It is suggested that homicide investigators obtain a copy of the 911 tape as soon as possible and personally transcribe it to minimize errors. During the careful process of repeated listening to the call, to obtain an accurate transcription, the investigator can glean critical insight that otherwise might be missed.

While listening to the call and analyzing the transcript, the investigator should ask three critical questions:

1. What was the call about?
2. Who was the call about?
3. How was the call made?

The answers to these three questions can provide clues to offender probability. If the data recorded on the COPS scale indicate the likelihood of the 911 homicide caller's guilt, investigators can use the insight developed through analysis to plan a strategy for successfully interviewing the individual and conducting the subsequent investigation.

References

Adams, S. 2002. Communication Under Stress: Indicators of Veracity and Deception in Written Narratives. Ph.D. dissertation, Virginia Polytechnic Institute and State University.

DePaulo, B. M., and W. L. Morris. 2004. Discerning Lies from Truths: Behavioural Cues to Deception and the Indirect Pathway of Intuition. In *The Detection of Deception in Forensic Contexts*, edited by P. A. Granhag and L. Stromwoll. Cambridge, UK: Cambridge University Press, pp. 15–40.

Grice, P. 1989. *Studies in the Way of Words*. Cambridge, MA: Harvard University Press.

Harpster, T. 2006. The Nature of 911 Homicide Calls: Using 911 Homicide Calls to Identify Indicators of Innocence and Guilt. Master's thesis, University of Cincinnati.

Keppel, R. n.d. Unpublished research study on the percentage of homicide calls made by offenders. Seattle University.

Olsson, J. 2004. *Forensic Linguistics: An Introduction to Language, Crime and Law*. London: Continuum International.

Rabon, D. 1996. *Investigative Discourse Analysis*. Durham, NC: Carolina Academic Press.

Sandoval, V. 2003. Strategies to Avoid Interview Contamination. *FBI Law Enforcement Bulletin* October, 1–12.

Shuy, R. 1998. *The Language of Confession, Interrogation and Deception*. Thousand Oaks, CA: Sage.

Analyzing Homicide Cases Preparatory to Suspect Interviews

15

MICHAEL R. NAPIER

Contents

Introduction

The purpose of this chapter is to provide a foundation, along with other parts of this book, for analyzing homicide cases in preparation for interviews and possible interrogations. No attempt is made to explore all the facets of investigating homicides and homicide crime scenes.

The Behavioral Science Unit (BSU) and National Center for the Analysis of Violent Crime (NCAVC) founded their analytical process on the substantiated concept that a person's personality strongly influences his behavior. In the commission of a crime, the offender will leave behavioral traces at the crime scene and in his interaction with the victim. An investigator trained in examining crime scenes can separate the behaviors and make reasonable deductions about the traits of the offender. When those traits are combined with the additional research conducted by FBI agents in face-to-face interviews with rapists, murderers, arsonists, and child molesters, a crime scene reconstruction is possible in which the three core behaviors are sequenced. This process defines the criminal investigative analysis methodology used so successfully over many years in countless crimes submitted to the FBI for analysis.

Offender Behavioral Patterns

From extensive interviews, the FBI found two distinct patterns that separated homicide offenders. They elected to label those patterns with simple terms: organized offender and disorganized offender. Take just a moment or two and think of some words that are synonymous with each offender type.

Organized Offender	Disorganized Offender
Controlled	Uncontrolled acts
Orderly	Spontaneous
Planned	Unplanned, poor plan
Thought out	Messy
Done with purpose	Chaotic
Methodical	Impulsive
Systematic	Random

From thorough processing of a crime scene, the analytical details can form the impression of which offender type was involved. As mentioned in Chapter 5, one of the factors that should be clear in evaluating a scene is the extent that the offender had control over himself and the victim. An organized offender, one who fantasized and planned his crime, will exhibit considerable control. Conversely, one who is disorganized because he has not fantasized or thought through his criminal behavior will exhibit poor planning in the commission of his crimes.

Consult Chapter 5 to be refreshed on the three-step process for using criminal investigative analysis. The process is briefly explained in Table 15.1, using details from a crime scene.

These few analytical points are certainly not all-inclusive and are only a shorthand to illustrate the process. They point to common factors in

Table 15.1   Process for Criminal Investigative Analysis

Behavioral Act	Why Done	Analysis of the Act
Crime spans four rooms as evidenced by blood spatter	Attempts to control victim	Check victimology regarding assertiveness; no or poor plan for controlling victim
Knife removed from block in kitchen; small amount of victim's blood on it	Use as offensive or defensive weapon	If viewed as defensive weapon, had no control over victim
Victim shot with .38 pistol not from residence	Use personal weapon to kill victim	Knife as defensive weapon; could not subdue victim even with presence of gun
Victim wealthy, nothing taken	Victim chosen for robbing or chosen for who she was	Panic after killing; came to kill victim; came for purpose other than robbery
Victim raped postmortem	Could not control her alive; feared rejection if alive Rape intended as motive	Poor plan; loner, socially and sexually inept; if rape intended, did not know victim well; inadequate personally

the right column and should cause an officer to consider a disorganized offender who acted impulsively, left a chaotic and messy crime scene, panicked, and fled.

Table 15.2 illustrates some of the features of organized and disorganized offenders. Because analysis is not like a cookbook, some of these items have serious exceptions.

The same process and typology apply to homicides and sexual homicides. A sexual homicide is a homicide in which the offender exhibited a sexual interest in a victim. The sexual interest may be indicated by the victim being naked or undressed, sexual parts of the anatomy being uncovered, body posed in a sexual manner, evidence of intercourse or masturbation, or insertion of a foreign object.

When there is no clear motive or a crime seems random, a valid place to begin is to consider a sexual angle to the crime. An offender may not have had the opportunity to finalize his crime plan in the course of the crime, so the sexual interest may not be evident.

Targeted Subject Interviewing for Homicide Suspects

Examining the chart for character and then comparing its features to your actual crime scene will reveal behaviors that are indicative of the suspect's vulnerabilities and weaknesses. Those features may then be incorporated into an interview plan targeting a specific individual. Other data known about a specific individual should be included in the overall strategy. Some sample tactics are discussed briefly next and do not represent every interview technique that may be extracted from a particular crime. Consider whether these apply to a particular crime and supplement any omission based on that crime.

Organized Homicide Offender

The organized type homicide offender often believes he is more clever than the police. His confidence may be lessened if some staging of the interview occurs in the form of efforts to build up the status of the interviewer. Those tactics are discussed in Chapter 9. Because of his thinking his crime through prior to acting, he may need to be impressed with actual evidence developed from the scene or subsequent interviews. If evidence is in short supply, the planting-seeds mind-reading techniques and use of dangle or bait questions may generate concerns on his part or a belief that additional evidence implicating him exists. Role reversal and timing the confrontation concerning any lies made to the officer

Table 15.2 Features of Organized and Disorganized Offenders

Crime Scene Data	Organized	Disorganized
Weapon choice[a]: Was it one of opportunity? Was it special to offender?	Special to offender	From scene
Body location[b]: Did offender move it or leave the body where the victim died?	More likely to move body	More likely to leave or leave it where victim fell
Control over victim: Little or great?	Expect great control	Usually little control
Sexual contact: Was sexual contact while victim was dead or alive?	Most often while alive	
May engage in necrophilia	Usually when dead or unconscious	
Social competence: Was offender competent, successful, or shy/underdeveloped?	Most often competent Can meet and mix	Usually shy, loner, isolated
Sexual competency: Was competency little or significant?	Competent Likely has had several partners	Incompetent Little or no experience Curious about anatomy May be a voyeur
Evidence of penis penetration: Was penetration likely or unlikely?	Likely	Maybe, not likely May be semen at scene but not in victim
Evidence at scene: Was there a lot or a little evidence?	Little or none depending on extent of fantasy planning	Likely lots No plan for cleanup
Offender's comfort zone: Did offender have a large or small comfort zone?	Large and varied	Small, adjusted for geographic features
Trophy or souvenir: Did offender take a trophy or souvenir?	Trophy	Souvenir

[a] Weapon of choice or opportunity: In some locales, many men carry a knife in a scabbard on their belt all the time. Because it was the weapon used does not make it a favorite, but its usage may only signify that it was handy. The use of a knife from the victim's residence usually indicates a weapon choice based on availability, but a large knife can be found in every house.

[b] Body moved: Organized offenders may move a body to delay discovery, to revisit the body, or to pose the body to shock. Disorganized offenders may move a body so it is more likely to be found, suggesting a personal connection between the offender and the victim.

may also take on the weight of evidence. Depending on his degree of psychopathy, he may be persuaded to protect himself if he had a partner. An officer may reason with a suspect and demonstrate the practicality of cooperating. People with psychopathic traits lack loyalty to anyone but themselves. The use of rationalizations, projections, and minimizations (RPMs), especially projections and minimizations, are usually effective with the organized offender.

Disorganized Homicide Offender

Because of personality traits, as evidenced in the commission of his crime, the best approach to the disorganized type of homicide offender is more relaxed, empathetic, and understanding. This offender is most likely more emotional, anxious, and stressed; therefore the use of emotional themes or dangle or bait questions should be effective. The mind-reading and planting-seeds techniques suit his vulnerabilities and may cause him to make admissions. The use of RPMs, especially minimizations, usually has a favorable impact because of personal uncertainties. Make several efforts to find his good qualities and remind him of them, even if it is necessary to stretch the imagination to locate them.

Bibliography

Douglas, John E., and Alan E. Burgess. Criminal Profiling: A Viable Investigative Tool Against Violent Crime. *FBI Law Enforcement Bulletin* 55(12) (December 1986): 9–13.

Douglas, John E., Ann W. Burgess, Allen G. Burgess, and Robert K. Ressler. *Crime Classification Manual.* 2nd ed. San Francisco: Jossey-Bass, 2006.

Douglas, John E., Robert K. Ressler, Ann W. Burgess, and Carol R. Hartman. Criminal Profiling from Crime Scene Analysis. *Behavioral Science and the Law* 4(4) (1986): 401–421.

Hazelwood, Robert R., and John E. Douglas. The Lust Murderer. *FBI Law Enforcement Bulletin* (49) (April 1980): 18–22.

Hazelwood, Robert R., and Stephen Michaud. *Dark Dreams.* New York: Martin's Press, 2000.

Hazelwood, Robert R., and Michael R. Napier. Crime Scene Staging and Its Detection. *Journal of Offender Therapy and Comparative Criminology* 48(6) (December 2004): 744–759.

Manhunt in the Heartland. Produced by Pie Town Productions. Learning Channel, 2000.

Michaud, Stephen G., and Robert R. Hazelwood. *The Evil Men Do.* New York: St. Martin's Press, 1998.

Napier, Michael R., and Kenneth P. Baker. Criminal Personality Profiling. In *Forensic Science: An Introduction to Scientific and Investigative Techniques*, edited by Stuart H. James and Jon J. Nordby, 531–550. Boca Raton, FL: CRC Press, 2002.

Napier, Michael R., and Kenneth P. Baker. Criminal Personality Profiling . In *Forensic Science: An Introduction to Scientific and Investigative Techniques*, edited by Stuart H. James and Jon J. Nordby, 615–636. Boca Raton, FL: CRC Press, 2005.

Napier, Michael R., and Robert R. Hazelwood. Homicide Investigation: The Significance of Victimology. *National Academy Associate* 5(5) (September/October 2003): 14–32.

Ressler, Robert K., and Ann W. Burgess. Violent Crime. Edited by Thomas J. Deacon. *FBI Law Enforcement Bulletin* 54(8) (August 1985): 18–25.

Ressler, Robert K., Ann W. Burgess, and John E. Douglas. *Sexual Homicide; Patterns and Motives.* Lexington, MA: Lexington Books, 1988.

Ressler, Robert K., John E. Douglas, A. Nicholas Groth, and Ann W. Burgess. Offender Profiles: A Multidisciplinary Approach. *FBI's Law Enforcement Journal* 49(9) (September 1980): 16–20.

Child Molesters and Pedophiles

16

MICHAEL R. NAPIER

Contents

Introduction

Probably because we all regard the topic of child molestation as repugnant, it is a subject we find confusing. Entire books are written on that subject alone, yet it remains largely misunderstood. This chapter is intended as a summary about child molesters from a law enforcement perspective. It also briefly incorporates portions of the information provided by Kenneth V. Lanning, a leading authority on the subject of child sexual victimization. The chapter contains two tables on molesters that are intended to allow some comparison between types of molesters. Both tables contain information based on Lanning's extensive experience in this area but are presented here only as thumbnail sketches. It is from those tables, and Figure 3.1 in Chapter 3 (regarding the offender's use of criminal fantasy), that most of the following discussion originates.

Anyone seeking a true comprehension of the types, methodologies, and motivations of child molesters must read and digest Lanning's work. His latest work places child molesters on a continuum, emphasizing that the categories of situational and preferential molesters are not an "either/or" proposition. Instead, Lanning explains how they move along a continuum of behaviors involving child molestation. To advance the understanding of deviant individuals who molest children, he states: "One of the best indicators of the continuing lack of understanding of the nature of pedophilia is that the media and society still view as a contradiction the fact that someone could be a caring, dedicated teacher (e.g., clergy member, coach, doctor, children's volunteer) and sexually victimize a child in his care" (Lanning, 2001a, p. 17).

A child molester is anyone who molests a child, as defined by pertinent statutes, particularly with regard to age of consent. The appearance of innocence or physical development do not govern the definition of a child. With

233

that in mind, prosecutors are faced with an uphill battle when the "child" is physically developed and appears to be more adult than child. The definition of a "child" is established by law and not by physical or emotional development. This issue also affects prosecution when the trial finally is scheduled and the victim no longer appears as he or she did when being molested.

The term "pedophile" is often misused. Properly, it is a diagnostic term which may be given only by a qualified psychologist or psychiatrist. However, it has entered our language and is often utilized in law enforcement and by lay persons to describe child molesters in general. That is improper usage of the word.

A pedophile is sometimes properly referred to as a preferential child molester as is the case in this chapter. Those terms are used interchangeably to mean a person who "prefers" to have sex with a legally described child. They are distinguished from other child molesters in that their fantasies, erotic images, and sexual preferences are focused on a child. One can be a pedophile without ever molesting. That person would have all the desires, drives, and fantasies of a child molester but has never acted on them. Not all child molesters are pedophiles.

Further distinction is made by noting that a child molester is anyone who molests a child, including a pedophile or preferential child molester. Not every child molester meets the criteria to be called a pedophile or preferential child molester.

Lanning (1987, 2001a,b) divided child molesters (not pedophiles) into two broad categories: situational sex offender and preferential sex offender, with both categories then refined into more specific typologies. The characteristics and traits of those categories are briefly depicted in the thumbnail charts.

Targeted Subject Interviewing for Child Molesters

The concept of TSI, or targeted subject interviewing, is promoted as one of the most effective methods for interviewing suspects and subjects of specific crimes. Identifying and interpreting behavior is an essential component of the TSI process. Utilizing offender behaviors that are imprinted at the crime scene and in their interactions with victims, an experienced detective can readily place the offender in the proper classification. In an interview an officer may make mention of the behaviors attributed to a particular child molester type or subtype even if those behaviors are not included in the report of the victim and are not known to have occurred. Caution must be used when pitching a suspect with unreported behaviors such as those generally found in a child molester type or subtype, and any mention of the unreported behaviors should not be stateded as *absolute fact*. They may be mentioned during the interview in a casual or offhand manner by an officer recounting what he has learned from his vast experience or what other offenders have related to him. Some will hit the mark. This softer approach is included in the mind-reading and planting-seeds approaches. See Chapters 7 and 8 for how a variety of tactics, such as good cop/bad cop or mind reading, which can use the information from typologies.

Take note of the traits of each type and subtype of child molester in Figures 16.1 and 16.2 and review them for indicators of offender vulnerability based

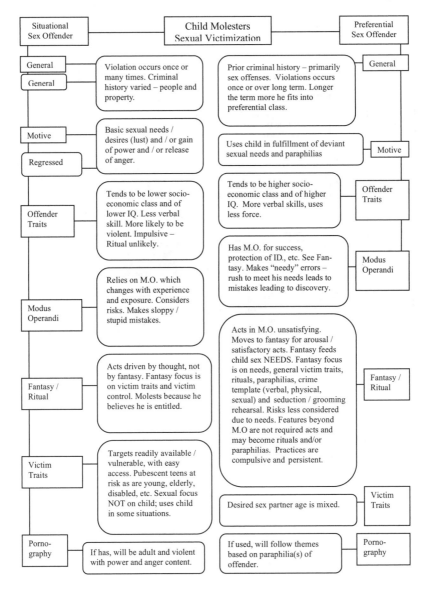

Figure 16.1 Situational and preferential child molesters.

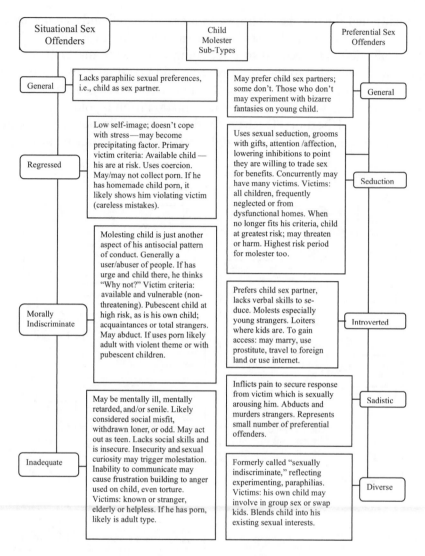

Figure 16.2 Child molester sub-typologies.

on their behaviors and thought processing. Then marry those indicators of vulnerability to any of several tactics and build them into the sales pitch and reasoning portions of the interview and interrogation process. Also, review Figure 3.1 in Chapter 3 regarding fantasy, modus operandi (MO), ritual, and paraphilia.

One example of how this process may work would be to note (assuming this fits the case being investigated) that the behaviors and interaction with the victim indicate a high fantasy content, rituals, or paraphilias. This knowledge may then be incorporated into how rationalizations, projections, and minimizations (RPMs) are presented (i.e., those unconscious mental

Table 16.1 Characteristics and Interview Vulnerabilities: Situational Sex Offender

Characteristic	Offender Characteristics	Interview Relevance
Intelligence	Tends to be less intelligent	Speak in common terms; you may need to use street terms. Do not be judgmental, be empathetic. Emphasize that his is a human failure, not one of character. Say good things about him.
Economic and social status	Tends to be in lower economic and social strata	Project blame to economy, stresses of providing for a family. Minimize by saying the rich do the same things and get away with it.
Needs satisfied	Tends to service basic sex needs or nonsexual needs of power or anger	He prefers sex with adults, so project blame on regular sex partner for absence, refusal, not meeting needs, and so on. If victim is pubescent, rationalize by indicating that she was physically able for intercourse and needed to be shown facts of life by someone who cared. Use reading-minds technique. Minimize injuries.
Tends to be opportunistic and impulsive	Acts are thought driven; tends to consider risks	Emphasize impulsiveness, giving in to inborn needs, that he would not do it again and this is a once-in-a-lifetime mistake. Focus on a single incident for initial admission. Let him assume you are investigating a single incident; choose the incident with the best evidence.
Type of mistakes	Tends to make sloppy mistakes	This subject is best not mentioned early, but it does indicate a tendency to buy into good ideas presented via RPMs.
Pornography	If he collects, tends to be violent, reflecting power and anger	Use mind reading to indicate interviewer's experience with others who prefer adults. Justify by indicating that he uses adult porn but he let his weakness get the best of him.
MO or rituals	Relies primarily on MO	Use reading—minds technique and minimize. "It is not like he sat around dreaming of violating child."
Paraphilias	Not likely	Rationalize by indicating that he is not like a preferential sex offender, who has perverted, degenerate behaviors.
Force and violence	More likely to use force or violence to obtain compliance; may kill child	Minimize the situation: he did not really hurt the child, there was no permanent injury. Urge him to keep this matter in the correct perspective, that is, it is not as if he killed or maimed the child, there were no broken bones, the child still has eyesight, and so on.

Table 16.2   Characteristics and Interview Vulnerabilities: Preferential Sex Offender

Characteristic	Offender Characteristics	Interview Relevance
Intelligence	Tends to be more intelligent	He may be impressed with deference shown interviewer by others who refer to him as "Sir" and treat him with respect. Have subordinate escort him to the interview site. Along the way, the subordinate gives friendly information about the interviewer and his reputation for thoroughness, fairness, and understanding.
Economic and social status	Tends to be of higher economic strata and social status	He has a lot on the line. Several themes and approaches in Chapter 7 will work well. One theme to consider is that at this point in time, there is some privacy in what is known, but *when* the case is finished many negative stories will appear in the newspapers and in open court. Now is the best time to straighten out the matter.
Needs satisfied	Tends to be servicing deviant sexual needs—paraphilias	Minimize responsibility; rationalize by indicating that so many others are similarly involved. Use mind reading to plant seeds that he has needs based on his paraphilias, compulsions, and so on. Emphasize his is a human failure, not one of character.
Paraphilic behaviors Tends to make "needy" mistakes	Tends to be fantasy driven	They seek validation by example of others, tell BTK (bind, torture, kill; Dennis Rader) story about how fantasy controlled him (Chapter 3) and he could not stop himself. Contrast his gentleness with BTK's murder and torture. He could not stop at that point because of intrusive thoughts.
Pornography use Narcissistic	Tends to be with themes following paraphilias; will photograph self in sexual acts with victim	If possible, approach with a search warrant in hand but not disclosed. Seek cooperation. Use mind reading to show you are aware of his needs and tendencies to keep porn and erotica. Explain how others have become victims of paraphilias.
MO or rituals	Relies on MO and rituals	Use information to build into planting-seeds and reading-minds techniques. Indicate his loss of control and how "intrusive" thoughts took him over the brink.

Table 16.2   Characteristics and Interview Vulnerabilities: Preferential Sex Offender (Continued)

Characteristic	Offender Characteristics	Interview Relevance
Paraphilias	Highly likely	The situation is a compulsion problem, which takes over. It was not him acting but a twist of mind. After admissions, use mind reading built around collecting pictures and erotica, validation by others, trolling for victims. Tell him how these "problems" cause behaviors or practices to be repetitious and predictable.
Force and violence	May use force or violence for compliance; pedophile seduces	Minimize likely psychological damage to child. Stress how there is no permanent physical injury and how he intentionally avoided it; he was only nice to the kids.
Seeks validation	Highly important to pedophile	Use mind reading to describe acts of others and the rationale for these acts. He cruises the Internet searching and finding validation and individuals doing the same things.
Use of computers	Likely central processing unit (CPU) not erased; is record keeper	See pornography section. Use mind reading.

processes are compulsive, intrusive, and so strong that the offender could not resist the urges).

Another example would be to use the descriptors in the two child molester figures to construct an approach for a situational sex offender–regressed subtype by noting his lack of self-esteem and ability to cope with stress. This subtype may be approached in an empathetic manner similar to how the power reassurance rapist is approached as outlined in Chapter 11.

Comments on Cyberpedophiles (Cyberpeds)

Technology has changed the behavior of pedophiles. Computers and the Internet have made it easier to access others who are similarly engaged and therefore validate their acts, while affording them access to more sources of erotica and greater storage capacities. They can easily store, transfer, and even create child pornography.

One of the traits of pedophiles is their sharply honed ability to relate to children. They often use superior listening skills, know the latest lingo and music, and are aware of the latest fashion and toy trends for victims in their age preference. Cyberspace has not altered those types of behavior but has facilitated the opportunities to contact, seduce, and lure more children.

In my estimation, pubescent children have four common areas of interest. First is desire for independence from their parents. Another is their borderline child/adult quandaries, which lead to internal and external conflicts, protests, and rebellion. They have exaggerated concerns about what their friends are doing and whether they are "normal" in comparison. There is a tremendous amount of competition and peer pressure. Last, but certainly not least, is their interest in sex, sex, and sex, which may be subdivided into their sexual development and body image in comparison to their peers and questions and concerns about sexual contact. These are all areas into which the anonymous cyberped will tap and through which they provide empathy and a listening post for a potential victim's venting. It also provides the opportunity for cyberpeds to keep a long list of children on the string while cultivating each with attention, time, and gifts. They often trade photographs, some of which are sexually explicit, made easy by the prevalence of cell phone cameras. These are the same practices they used precomputer and pre-Internet. The leopard has not changed his spots. He still goes where kids can be found, but now they have less parental supervision and guidance. Other than an additional need for how these technologies work, the interview of this new predator follows basically the same rules as before. One difference is that now the cyberped does not need as many interpersonal skills because he is communicating from a distance.

Bibliography

First, Michael B., and Robert L. Halon. Use of DSM Paraphilia Diagnoses in Sexually Violent Predator Commitment Cases. *Journal of the American Academy of Psychiatry and the Law Online* 36(4) (2008): 443–454. http://www.jaapl.org/cgi/content/full/36/4/443 (accessed May 16, 2009).

Lanning, Kenneth V. Child Molesters, A Behavioral Analysis for Law Enforcement. In *Practical Aspects of Rape Investigation: A Multidisciplinary Approach*, edited by Robert R. Hazelwood and Ann W. Burgess, 201–256. New York: Elsevier Science, 1987.

Lanning, Kenneth V. *Child Molesters: A Behavioral Perspective*. 4th ed. National Center for Missing and Exploited Children, Washington, DC: 2001a.

Lanning, Kenneth V. Child Molesters and Cyber Pedophiles: A Behavioral Perspective. In *Practical Aspects of Rape Investigation: A Multidisciplinary Approach*, edited by Robert R. Hazelwood and Ann W. Burgess, 199–220. Boca Raton, FL: CRC Press, 2001b.

Lanning, Kenneth V. Cyber Pedophiles: A Behavioral Perspective. In *Practical Aspects of Rape Investigation: A Multidisciplinary Approach*, edited by Robert R. Hazelwood and Ann W. Burgess, 381–407. Boca Raton, FL: CRC Press, 2009.

WebMD Medical Reference. Paraphilias. WebMD. October 2003. http://www.medicinenet.com/paraphilia/article.htm (accessed May 16, 2009).

Interpersonal Stalking
Characteristics of
Predators and Prey

17

MICHAEL R. NAPIER AND R. STEPHEN MARDIGIAN

Contents

What Is Stalking?

Stalking is a sometimes "passive" or silent violent crime but is often a prelude to a physically violent and potentially deadly crime. Three stalking types are presented to illustrate certain distinctions that separate different classes of stalkers.

Stalking—that word has an ominous sound to it, as well it should. It implies dark, stealthy, harmful, and defenseless acts that often end in violence, injury, and death, particularly when it occurs in the family setting or when the stalker is mentally ill. In recent years, stalking has reemerged in our vocabulary and has invaded the lives of many with the added prefix *cyber*. Sometimes it involves new endeavors by sexual deviants, who are labeled cyberpedophiles.

Stalk is a verb defined as "to pursue quarry or prey stealthily." It also means repeated harassing behaviors intended to intimidate, control, or terrorize the victim. A stalker is generally "obsessed" with his* target. Stalking is the act of following, viewing, communicating with, or moving threateningly or menacingly toward another person. Stalking is motivated by interpersonal aggression rather than by material gain or sex (Douglas et al., 2006). Stalking usually involves a constellation of behaviors over an undefined period. To appreciate the events, they must be viewed individually and then collectively.

Individual incentive (i.e., "What's in it for me?") is presented when each stalker classification is discussed. The drive that originates within the mind of the stalker will be individualized to meet his particular needs but will have the universal components of power, fixation, and obsession. Stalking is a goal-oriented behavior. Commonly, the attempt to obtain and exercise power to attain a goal, or the abuse of power, is present in each of the stalker types. Stalkers are typically dedicated to obtaining their goals, and some will go to extreme lengths to meet them.

In striving for their objective, stalkers sometimes take extraordinary risk and take their behaviors to extremes that expose them to injury, identification, or capture. While not always present, the investigator should anticipate the extremes of dedication and risk taking.

Stalkers share tactics that range from sending gifts, flowers, and amorous letters to sending dead flowers and making intimidating threats, gestures, and physical assault.

There are some misconceptions about stalking because what is *now deemed illegal* is usually a cluster of behaviors that, when standing alone, are not illegal. In many jurisdictions, the offense of stalking merits a charge no more serious than a misdemeanor and is investigated accordingly. That penalty designation is changing in some areas, and the elements of the current laws now require a series of acts that would cause fear in the mind of a reasonable person.

Advice to Victims

Police are often placed in a difficult position of being solicited for safety advice by victims of stalkers. They understand that "standardized" advice may be as dangerous as the threat posed by the stalker. There is no advice that can guarantee the victim's well-being. Police may be asked for advice at a time

* For simplicity, the male pronoun is most often used, although stalkers can be females as well.

when the situation is in flux and the stalker may not have revealed his true nature. The officer is not in a position to know the capabilities of the victim when it comes to controlling her emotions, being assertive, or verbalizing her fears, resentment, and concerns to a known stalker. Any advice provided by the police carries the potential of leading to safety, or conversely, to injury or even death of the victim. The officer's best guide is to know the potential of violence of the stalker (i.e., his past history of violence). Some general suggestions for safety are presented in the Appendix.

The officer investigating a stalking event should maintain an open mind regarding the victim's complaint, her sometimes crumbling composure, and her emotional, explosive, or hysterical demeanor, which occasionally ends with her projecting her fear and frustration onto the officer.

The Victim's Point of View

Victim's View of Stalking

The stalking victim today often finds herself in the same position formerly reserved for rape victims. Great strides have been made in American culture regarding how rape victims are viewed. In the not-too-distant past, women who had suffered the most vile and personal violation of their body and psyche were openly condemned as "wanting it" or "deserving it" and generally held accountable for being a victim. Those times are largely behind us.

However, the victim of stalking is expected to make all the adjustments to secure privacy and safety. In a stalking situation, it is more often than not the victim who must relocate, seek new employment, register her children in new schools, get new telephone numbers, and make new friends, all while and fearing that the stalker will again find her. "In extreme cases, targets (victims) of stalkers have joined the military, quit their jobs, changed their names, and moved to other parts of the country" (Smerick, 2007).

Also, the victim is placed in the circumstance of being the evidence collector to prove the accuracy of her contention concerning the stalker. She is the one expected to know what is significant, to preserve it, and to document how it came into play during the stalking event.

Victims often find themselves in a continuing struggle filled with great concern, terror, sometimes physical confrontations, fear, apprehension, and ever-increasing frustration with the criminal justice system. No matter how they adjust their lives, they face uncertainty for their personal safety and that of their children, other family members, and new relationships. These victims find themselves trapped in this environment without the hope of a place to turn for sound, immediate, and effective assistance.

Victim's Dealings with a Stalker

A victim truly has few options available if law enforcement fails to adequately handle complaints. She may choose to act as though she has not been stalked, or she may choose to confront the stalker when that is possible. She also could have someone else confront the follower and deliver the message to leave her alone. The best alternative is to contact knowledgeable and well-trained authorities and rely on their earnest efforts, including the confrontation of the stalker. When non-law-enforcement friends or family members undertake the role of "protector," they may cast themselves as the obstacle the stalker must overcome to fulfill their goals. This position is fraught with danger.

Fortunately, publicly and privately funded victim counseling and advocacy associations are available in many locations to lend a hand and a place of temporary refuge. Many of these agencies have led the way in providing multidisciplinary training for law enforcement, Sexual Assualt Nurse Examiners (SANE) nurses, jurists, victim/witness units, and other social service agencies. Up-to-date investigators generally have at their fingertips a list of those resources, including contact personnel, addresses, and telephone numbers.

How Well Is Your Department Handling Domestic Violence Stalking?

An effective tool used by many law enforcement agencies in the United States is the "fatality review" process (Websdale, 2003). With this review system, representatives of several community organizations come together to review all the circumstances leading up to a death believed to be a domestic violence-related murder. These fatalities often have had stalking as a precursor. The community agencies usually include prosecutors, law enforcement officers, and social agencies specializing in assisting women caught in the web of domestic violence. They gather all known and relevant information lifestyle data concerning the victim, including social and economic functioning. Most importantly, the review focuses on events leading up to the death of the victim believed to be caused by domestic violence. These studies include the examination of the role that social policies play in the environment that brought about a compromise in the safety and welfare of the victim and her children. An answer is sought regarding to what extent society failed the victim. When these exercises are undertaken with an open mind, progress can be made in determining how these members of society slipped through the social and legal cracks.

Typologies

Typologies are a form of shorthand and deliver a quantity of information in a small space. One drawback to using typologies is that they may be viewed as definitive or absolute (Sapp and Mahaffey-Sapp, 1995). To appreciate the value of stalking typologies, certain topics need to be understood. Typologies may also be called categories, slots, pigeonholes, and so on. Typologies may be divided into groupings with very trait-specific descriptions, or into broader classes with less specificity, depending on the intended use of the typing. Generally, those engaging in clinical usage require more details, traits, and descriptors, so an appropriate diagnosis and treatment plan may be instituted. Individual experts will use differing criteria and will "slice the pie" into various numbers of typologies.

Diagnosis and treatment are not the goals of law enforcement. Their goal is to comprehend the illicit behavior and plan for all eventualities, including interview techniques geared to offender-specific traits (targeted subject interviewing, TSI). Therefore, for law enforcement usage, broader and more general information is suitable.

Three broad categories are used in this book for the purpose of assisting in designing interview strategies. Just as there are different types of stalkers, there are varied types of stalking. They are discussed later in this chapter.

When an investigation has been properly conducted, the investigator will have a long list of the stalker's behaviors to study. The analysis of these behaviors, in the hands of an officer versed in the study of stalking behavior, will reveal many secrets to the investigator. In most cases, the offender behaviors will clearly indicate the motivation for stalking, the extent of his rational planning, the likely relationship with the victim, and most importantly, the extent of his dedication to achieving his goals.

Victimology

The study of the victim is called *victimology* (Napier and Hazelwood, 2003). As noted by Lt. Kenny Landwehr, victimology is the second most important investigative skill outside of collecting, testing, and evaluating physical evidence (*Manhunt in the Heartland*, 2000). The study of the victim should begin immediately on institution of the stalking investigation, with bits and pieces added beginning with the first contact with the victim and witnesses and from each interview of friends, associates, and coworkers.

No bona fide investigation of a violent crime better demonstrates an officer's investigative skill than the immediate inquiry into all known aspects of the victim's lifestyle. How the victim went about all aspects of life will illustrate how likely she was to become a victim of a violent crime, her assertiveness, the degree of her security precautions, the likelihood of being immediately harmed, and likely her past history, if any, with the stalker.

Stalking and Psychopathy

In a study of stalkers conducted by Reavis, Allen, and Meloy (2008), psychopathic traits were present but generally of a different type than in stalkers who were labeled as psychopaths. Psychopathy is indicative of a tendency for a lack of genuine affection, trust, loyalty, and violence. This study indicated that stalkers and psychopaths have differing attachment and affection problems. Stalkers generally have disturbances in their attachment process, whereas the psychopathic personality has attachment difficulties with individuals and society across the board. The psychopath's lack of a positive bonding ability is deeply ingrained in their personality and behavior and present at least from adolescence. Because there were fewer followers who qualified as psychopaths does not truly lessen the dangerousness assessment of stalkers. For a more detailed discussion on psychopathy and psychopaths please see Chapter 3.

Investigative Suggestions

Table 17.1 provides investigative suggestions.

The Three Stalker Types

There are three stalker types: domestic, organized (nondomestic), and delusional, and they are discussed below.

The Domestic Stalker

This is the most prevalent type of stalker, and the victim is most likely to be harmed by this type, or to be driven to suicide. Domestic stalking acts are usually carried out by a person who is legally sane. This type of stalker is most likely to act out physically against the victim or to intentionally damage or vandalize the victim's personal property.

Between 1,000 and 1,600 American women are murdered each year by their intimate partners (Websdale, 2003). From 1976 through 2005, homicides

Table 17.1 Investigative Suggestions

Initial Contact

Listen openly, without judgment or bias.	Make cassette tape of pertinent portion of 911 tape.
Take notes to demonstrate interest and to document details.	Photograph or gather any evidence of assault, breaking and entering, violence.
Be reassuring, listen attentively. Attend to record keeping.	Reassure her that you will arrange for increased patrolling in her area.
Ignore emotional outburst, even if directed at you, remembering that she is fearful for her safety and that of her children.	Arrange for increased patrolling and request slow drive-bys, visibly stopping in front of her residence.
If victim is injured during this incident or a prior incident, obtain written consent for release of any necessary medical records.	Randomly, have patrol officer call her while in her area just to remind her of his presence.
Obtain a photo of stalker if known and distribute it to patrol officers.	Thoroughly interview any witnesses; conduct brief area canvass.
Provide the victim with all available contact numbers, including victim witness officers, women's shelters, women's advocacy groups, 800 numbers for any related agencies, and the like.	Reassure victim that her complaint is being taken as a serious matter. Remind her that police assistance is available via 911 should she see the stalker or **reasonably** feel the need for an emergency response.
Educate the victim regarding expected course of events and what may be expected of her.	Encourage the victim to follow through on her complaint.

On Recontact

Synopsize and review investigative information from initial contact.	Determine if any new contacts have occurred. Collect any evidence retained by the victim (i.e., journals).
Determine if any new details or memories have surfaced.	Bring her up to date on investigation undertaken, file reviews, NCIC checks, and so on.
Advise victim of any plans to interview or otherwise confront the stalker if identity is known.	Forewarn victim of timing of contact of stalker and advise her of measures she can take.
Provide security awareness briefing.	Ask if she wants employer or neighbors contacted to be on alert for suspicious activity.
Educate the victim regarding expected course of events and what may be expected of her.	Encourage the victim to follow through on her complaint.

(continued)

Table 17.1   Investigative Suggestions (Continued)

On Arrest	
Advise the victim of the arrest. Determine if the victim wants a restraining order issued as part of initial court proceedings.	Arrange for jailer to block calls from the facility to the victim so stalker cannot further intimidate or threaten victim or attempt to get her not to follow through.
Work with the agency preparing information for the judge, inform it of the victim's fears, concerns, and any physical injuries or damage done to property.	Provide same information to the prosecuting attorney. Request the highest possible bond.
Encourage prosecutor to play 911 tape if it is dramatic or involves threats, motivation statements, upset children reacting to situation, or acts of violence.	Focus investigation on behaviors of the stalker, not on the victim's statements. Obtain evidence to prove case even if victim backs out.

committed by male intimate partners accounted for a full 30% of all female murder victims in the United States. Sapp and Mahaffey-Sapp (1995) cited a slightly higher rate; they indicated fully one-third of all women killed are murdered by their husbands or boyfriends. Female stalking victims outnumber males by a two-to-one margin (Websdale, 2003). Females are most likely to be stalked by a present or former intimate partner who seeks dominance and control over them, which leads to confrontations and sometimes death (Catalano, 2007). It is estimated that a significant number of the 6,000 women who commit suicide did so after periods of abuse by their married or commonlaw spouses (Websdale, 2003). A female may also be a domestic stalker but is in the minority of this type of stalking offender.

The domestic stalker may originate his stalking from a discreet distance without the victim's knowledge of his activities. The stalking often begins prior to the initial ending of the relationship. This kind of stalking often begins with surveillance of the victim to keep track of her activities. The purpose of this type of stalking is usually to regain or continue the intimate relationship, and to dominate and control his victim.

The stalker's motivation of domination is probably a continuation of his routine domestic activities, which likely caused most of the original troubles in his relationship with his former partner. When speaking with the victim of this type of stalking, she will often describe being smothered within their relationship. Her present or former partner kept tabs on her in everything she did, from choosing her daily attire to the times she leaves for and returns from work. He attempted to control every aspect of her life down to who she socialized with or spoke with on the home phone. He has acted through their entire association with a sense of "entitlement," demanding total dominion over her and her life. Interestingly, he will describe their relationship in terms of *his being mistreated.*

The domestic stalker has an advantage over other stalking offenders in that he already knows many details of the victim's life and lifestyle. There are two locations significant to this stalker. First, he knows where the victim lives; second, he knows where the victim is employed. Either location can be a likely assault location or death scene. The most likely scenario leading to violence is when the stalker confronts the victim face to face and is rejected. That contact may escalate from a simple meeting, to a firm rejection, and then spiral into a full quarrel with physical contact, sometimes leading to a deadly assault. Rage is often found in situations involving the domestic stalker. The stalker of an intimate partner is likely to bring a weapon when contacting his partner or former partner.

Restraining orders have a mixed history with the domestic stalker and others but provide a chargeable violation that may have an effect in the short term. On occasion, the domestic stalker will abduct the victim for the purpose of having some private time with her in an attempt to persuade her to continue or recommence their relationship. The abduction raises the level of danger for the victim, as she is separated from any type of help and must make convincing decisions regarding their future association.

The domestic stalker may adopt the mindset: "If I can't have her, then nobody will." This thought process represents dangerousness at its extreme. The stalker who feels this way is prepared not only to kill the victim but also to deal violently with anyone who stands in the way of his goal of continuing or reestablishing the partnership.

All sworn officers should be well versed in the likelihood that in escalated situations that culminate in the death of the victim there is a consistent possibility of a scenario playing out of murder/suicide or *murder/suicide by cop*. Suicide by cop involves a situation in which an officer is confronted with an armed individual who acts in a threatening or menacing way toward the officer or a third party. The armed individual's goal is to provoke the officer into shooting and killing him. The officer perceives the need to defend himself or the third party. On occasion, the armed individual intended to commit suicide, perhaps after committing murder, but at the last moment could not complete the suicide or decides it is better to be killed by the officer.

The Organized (Nondomestic) Stalker

The organized stalker is most often *not mentally ill* but may have a diagnosable personality disorder—most commonly, antisocial personality disorder. He may have other mental or personality disorders as well. This type of stalking is just another element of his usual antisocial behavior. The organized stalker should be considered a predator with an ability to detect weakness in his victims.

He and the victim are usually strangers. The victim's prior knowledge of the stalker may be nonexistent or so casual that she is virtually unaware of his existence. He may be a coworker, neighbor, or someone with whom she has coincidentally crossed paths. He is organized in the approach to his chosen victim, who is usually a female. Initially, he may have some infatuation with the victim. At some point, he may declare his presence or his interest in the victim, and that will be the victim's first inkling that he exists in her world.

His clandestine and early endeavors often are filled with adoration, infatuation, love, praise, and complimentary gestures. There is no particular set timing for this phase, and it is sometimes skipped by some nondomestic stalkers.

His behavior will likely include a search for information about the victim, which he will use to gain an advantage over her. His knowledge of her will be provided to her in ways that will frighten and intimidate the victim. He will gather details of her activities and feed them back to her. The information may include comments she made privately to friends, the clothes she wore, places she went, and the names of others who were involved socially with her. He obtains these tidbits by covert stalking and provides them with the intention of frightening her. At some point, she will, however, become aware of his presence and interest in her as he moves from the anonymous shadows to overt behaviors. His negative approach to a victim may begin with harassing or obscene calls or letters or papers left at the victim's residence or on her vehicle.

Delusional Stalker

The mentally ill stalker is the least frequently encountered but the one that usually gathers the most media attention. In this type of stalking, the victim may be male or female, as may the stalker. The delusional stalker will have a thought disorder and may be diagnosed as a schizophrenic. His thinking will be disorganized and irrational regarding the victim. The victim may be anyone on whom the stalker fixates and who becomes entwined in his thought pattern. He may truly believe that his victim returns his affection. He may also believe that she communicates with him in secret ways, such as giving him a special look or mentally transmitting endearing terms to him. If he or his family have sought psychological treatment for him previously, he probably is "off his medicine." He often lives alone, as his family has found his behavior and mental problems to be more than they can handle. Therefore, he often will have no personal support mechanism to help guide his life. If the delusional stalker attacks his victim, the assault will likely be up close and personal.

The Erotomaniac

A subcategory of the delusional stalker involves erotomania. The erotomaniac stalks those whose attention and affection in real life he could never gain, often a person who he considers to be in a socioeconomic stratum above him. Not all of his victims are public figures or hold glamorous jobs. Usually the victim is someone in a position of perceived higher rank such as a supervisor, but may be a total stranger who is fixated upon. Whoever the chosen target, the stalker continuously obsesses about the target and his affiliation with him or her. Some of his behaviors will track along the same lines of being off his medications and with no social support mechanism.

The erotomaniac's obsessional infatuation with the victim may originate from simply having seen the victim one time. For instance, in the case of Arthur Jackson, he saw his victim in a single movie. Jackson became obsessed with actress Theresa Saldana from that exposure. Saldana rose to fame as the female lead in the television series *The Commish*. Jackson saw her in a movie in a theater in Scotland, where he lived, and he traveled extensively until he could locate her. He moved from adoration to dedicated rage, which ended in her attempted murder in a daring and public attack. Before she could reach the hospital, it is estimated that she was stabbed and slashed so extensively that she had lost a full gallon of blood (Curtis, 1995). David Mark Chapman's assault on John Lennon followed a similar path. These assaults followed extensive stalking and surveillance, another earmark for this type of stalker. They also indicate the extent to which a stalker will take his dedication to finding and destroying a victim.

Characteristically, the interest of the stalker is a one-way avenue, as his presence is unknown to his victim. Nonetheless, he has chosen his victim and has fixated on her, and his fantasy-driven plans are known only to him. He rehearses his relationship with the victim in a "fantasy-based idealized romantic love or spiritual union of a person rather than sexual attraction" (Douglas et al., 2006, p. 151).

The erotomaniac stalker has a discernable mental illness in which he is psychotic and losing contact with reality through his delusions or hallucinations. A part of the delusion is the belief that the victim has an intense interest in him (or her) and secretly discloses that interest in communications to the stalker through small, quick gestures, such as an incidental eye contact or a smile directed at another person. A religious overtone may be included that involves the stalker receiving orders from some sort of deity. It is not unusual for the stalker to live alone, so taking of medications is unsupervised and often missed.

Should they seek psychiatric treatment, which is doubtful, the likelihood of being successful is dim. Two of the key features of the erotomaniac stalker are the intensity of his obsession and the extreme length to which he will go to reach his mission.

Weakness and Vulnerability

Assisting in the interviewing of all stalking suspects is the evidence gathered by the victim regarding harassing and threatening telephone calls and notes, recording of events, including license plate identification, and records of public confrontations can be helpful to the investigator. If handled properly, these pieces of evidence can prove to be convincing.

The Domestic Stalker

The best approach to the domestic stalker is to play to his obsession in controlling the victim, to justify his belief of entitlement, and to indicate the unreliable and unpredictable nature of women. Cast him as a victim. Your initial goal is to get admission to as many of his acts as possible. The officer is seeking a connection to the stalker's covert and overt behavior by playing to the underlying understandability of his problems in the relationship. Never should an officer indicate that he would do the same thing in the same circumstances. The pitch is that he can understand how someone could do those things. Empathize with his beliefs that the victim is the problem, and that she does not recognize him as the man he is. He may ultimately respond to the rational approach that his life is truly not lost, and that he can move on. This agreement may be a setup to get the officer off his back. The mind-reading, planting-seeds, and dangle/bait question approaches stand a good likelihood of working. Since his contacts may be in a public venue, he cannot be sure that no one has overheard his threats and accusations and seen his nonverbal threatening gestures, which validate his former partner's accusations.

Given the overall level of danger because of the context of the domestic situation, the potential threat of this stalker must be kept in mind. The interview is better conducted at the station house, and the stalker should be electronically searched with a wand if that has not been done on entering the police department. Do not lose sight of the potential for suicide by cop, which the stalker may feel will be punishment for his victim because she objected to or rejected his emotional overtures.

The Organized Stalker

The best location for the interview with the organized stalker is the police station. This interview is similar to the standard criminal contact for admissions or confessions. The subject may have a criminal background with prior police interviewing. He has a dislike and distrust for women in general, and this may be played as reasonable given today's preferential treatment of women. Let him feel that his behaviors are understandable, and perhaps many others would agree with them. See the caution in the preceding section about the officer not indicating that he would act the same way. With this type of stalker, the more evidence that can be related to him the better. He will be swayed with physical evidence. Therefore the mind-reading and planting-seeds techniques and dangle or bait questions surrounding potential evidence can be powerful persuaders. Remember the power of catching an offender in lies and presenting them as evidence. In this case, his early denials may be attacked through the itemized techniques that would indicate he did in fact lie. He may be swayed by a pitch that he committeed the acts but meant no harm, and had actually sent live flowers and nice notes.

The Delusional Stalker

It is a difficult assignment to interview someone who is overtly mentally ill unless his delusions or hallucinations are medically under control. If he is in a state in which his conditions are active and not medicated, any admissions obtained are likely to be challenged as unreliable. Do not take on the role of psychologist or psychiatrist, because he likely has a difficult time with those who try to force him to take medications that he believes makes him sluggish, irritable, anxious, or nauseous. An open statement of empathy for those effects may be helpful absent statements that he would regard as condescending, for instance, "You are better off taking your meds."

Conclusion

The term "stalker" encompasses a wide variety of intimidating behaviors. While stalkers have some common features and motivations, the three types discussed in this chapter are noted to have several highly distinctive behaviors that need to be fully recognized. There is a great deal that officers can do to assist stalking victims by giving them the full attention the crime requires and providing them every measure of safety that is available. Because so many stalking incidents accompany domestic violence situations, a crime problem generally with a low priority, often such criminal acts are left unaddressed with the victim and her children still exposed to danger. A group effort is needed and should involved several agencies beyond the police and the prosecutor.

Acknowledgment

Special thanks to Terry Reardon, Academy Group, for her editing advice.

Bibliography

Catalano, Shannon. *Intimate Partner Violence in the U.S.* Washington, DC: U.S. Department of Justice, Bureau of Justice Statistics, 2007.

Coleman, F. L. Stalking Behavior and the Cycle of Domestic Violence. *Journal of Interpersonal Violence* 12(3) (1997): 420–432.

Creating an Effective Stalking Protocol. Executive Summary. Washington, DC: U.S. Department of Justice, National Center for Victims of Crime, 2002.

Curtis, Bill (producer). *Stalkers: Deadly Obsession.* 1995.

de Becker, Gavin. *The Gift of Fear.* Boston: Little, Brown, 1997.

de Becker, G. *Protecting the Gift.* New York: Dial Press, 1999.

Domestic Violence, Stalking and Antistalking Legislation; Annual Report to Congress. Washington, DC: National Institute of Justice, 1996.

Douglas, John E., Ann W. Burgess, Allen G. Burgess, and Robert K. Ressler. *Crime Classification Manual.* 2nd ed. San Francisco: Jossey–Bass, 2006.

Helpful Guide for Stalking Victims. Washington, DC: U.S. Department of Justice, National Victims Center, 1994.

Legislators Talking the Terror of Stalking. *USA Today* (July 21, 1992): 9A.

Manhunt in the Heartland. Produced by Pie Town Productions. Learning Channel, 2000.

Meloy, J. Reid. *The Psychology of Stalking.* San Diego, CA: Academic Press, 1998.

Napier, Michael R., and Robert R. Hazelwood. Homicide Investigation: The Significance of Victimology. Edited by Ashley Sutton. *National Academy Associate* 5(5): (September/October 2003): 14–32.

Napier, Michael R., and Stephen R. Mardigian. *Protecting Stalking Victims.* Manassas, VA: Academy Group, 2008.

Reavis, James A., Elizabeth K. Allen, and J. Reid Meloy. Psychopathy in a Mixed Gender Sample of Adult Stalkers. *Journal of Forensic Science* 53(5) (2008): 1214–1217.

San Diego Stalking Strike Force. *Training Manual on Stalking.* 1996.

Sapp, Allen D., and Carla C. Mahaffey-Sapp. A Motive-Based Offender Analysis of Stalkers. *FBI's Negotiator Notes* (1995).

Sapp, Allen D., and Carla C. Mahaffey-Sapp. A Preliminary Analysis and Typology of Stalkers. *Platte Valley Review.* 27(2) Kearney: University of Nebraska, Spring 1999.

Smerick, Peter A. Strategies for Dealing with Stalkers. In *Psychologie du harclement criminal,* edited by M. St. Yves and M, Tanguay. Quebec, Canada: Yvon Blais, 2007.

Soukhanov, Anne H., and Kaethe Ellis. *Webster's II New Riverside University Dictionary.* Boston: Houghton Mifflin, 1994.

Tjaden, Patricia. *The Crime of Stalking: How Big Is the Problem?* Washington, DC: U.S. Department of Justice, National Institute of Justice, 1997.

Tjaden, Patricia, and Nancy Thoennes. *Stalking: Its Role in Serious Domestic Violence Cases, Executive Summary.* University of Colorado at Colorado Springs, 2001.

Websdale, Neil. Reviewing Domestic Violence Deaths. *National Institute of Justice Journal,* November 2003.

Williams, W. L., J. Lane, and M. A. Zona. Stalking: Successful Intervention Strategies. *The Police Chief* (February 1996): 24–26.

Wright, James A., Allen G. Burgess, Ann W. Burgess, A. T. Laszlo, Gregg O. McCrary, and John E. Douglas. A Typology of Interpersonal Stalking. *Journal of Interpersonal Violence* 11(4) (1996): 487–502.

Training Manual on Stalking. San Diego, California: San Diego Stalking Strike Force, 1996.

Cultural Considerations for Interviewing 18

BARRY L. MCMANUS

Contents

Culture is the collective programming of the mind which distinguishes the members of one human group from another.

Geert Hofstede (1997, p. 51)

Introduction

The situation: A foreign operative from a Middle Eastern group is in your custody and is charged with helping al Qaeda build or develop a nuclear weapon. You are charged with interviewing this subject.

During the elicitation phase of the interview, the subject readily admits that he has talked to bin Laden and al-Zawahiri about their struggle against the West and the great chance that a change is coming. They spoke, according to this subject, about building a bomb.

You wonder why someone who hates you so much, and truly believes you are an infidel, would so readily tell you so many revealing details. In addition, when the interview started the subject delivered a detailed lesson in American history and discussion about why you, an African American (also a minority in his eyes) would be questioning and interrogating him for a confession. It does not take long to realize that this subject is someone well versed in his culture and the culture of the West. This interview could readily become quite difficult if you cannot demonstrate your own intelligent grasp of the topics dear to the subject.

Thus, it is important to comprehend the range of the opposition's beliefs, traditions, values, and religion. With such knowledge, the interviewer may be able to establish rapport and perhaps achieve the goal of eliciting actionable information.

One other benefit accrues when one is comfortable with knowledge of the opposition's culture: One may relax enough actually to listen to the subject during the course of the interview, possibly determining the subject's flaws and vulnerabilities (which are common to all human beings).

It has been 8 years since the United States was attacked by 19 al Qaeda terrorist conspirators who entered the United States for the specific purpose of carrying out a suicide mission. Until recently, little solid research has been done to guide the thought processes of interviewers or interrogators as they conduct interviews with or interrogations of this type of operative.

I have been successfully extracting confessions and eliciting significant information throughout my years with the Central Intelligence Agency (CIA) through the deliberate practice of seeking threads of information. I have viewed the world through an intelligence community lens, but I am still able to translate this knowledge and experience into an application for law enforcement. The subjects, targets, and operatives I have interviewed cover a wide spectrum ethnically, politically, and psychologically. One thing they had in common was involvement with hostile intelligence services, political organizations, or terrorist organizations.

There is a difference between seeking information and interviewing for confessions. Understanding this difference requires that the interviewer bring to the situation a diverse background in elicitation and interrogation. *Elicitation*, like so many terms in this field, has a variety of meanings. Generally, however, it is the application of reasonable behavioral science principles to draw out information during the course of discussions. Interrogation is a targeted and formal interview of subjects to gain specific information. The successful application of elicitation techniques requires considerable practice.

It also involves a lifelong study of cultures and the knowledge that seeking information, not just getting confessions, is the goal. Being able to convince someone to provide information requires the interviewer to communicate effectively with the person being interviewed. Communicating cross culturally requires the interviewer to understand who he or she is interviewing.

For example, the Arab culture is a culture of relationships, hospitality, conspiracies, and revenge. Therefore interaction with an Arab subject would best be supported by application of principles that place the subject at ease within his cultural climate. In this application, a conversation with someone from the Middle East would start with "small talk" or a social exchange. Generally, that is a way to break the ice with the subject. In most cases, the offering of drinks would also be appropriate if the circumstances allow for it. An Arab who is Muslim would usually abide by Islamic restrictions on his behavior and social duties as dictated in the Koran. My experience has been that some interviewers or interrogators are unfamiliar with Islam or the Koran. It would be useful for a person seeking information from a Muslim Arab to read the Koran to gain insight and understanding of his mindset.

Today, we actively continue to seek answers and solutions in situations like the one presented to prevent another attack. Identifying the threat and being able to obtain information to deter or stop the threat are critical. I have spent years traveling extensively abroad and hundreds of hours instructing and guiding men and women through courses in elicitation, interviewing, and interrogation with a Middle Eastern and Arab context. Natasha Crundwell, a friend and confidant, is a communications specialist and shared the following with me in 2008; her words have always remained part of my description of culture:

> We are actively engaged in learning our culture from the moment we are born. Our core values and beliefs are deeply embedded in our social makeup and define our responses to any given situation. We often refer to our comfort level as being like a "fish in water" or when uncomfortable as being like a "fish out of water!" The proverbial "water" is our cultural context which we learn from birth without realizing we are going through a learning process and indoctrination in our core values.

Americans are often bombarded with contradictory advice on how to behave and respond in a global society, and anyone promising a silver bullet or magic formula on how to behave would certainly be oversimplifying the complexity and issues involved in human interaction. There are few hard and fast rules in engaging people from various cultures. There are, however, multiple guidelines and directions one can take to improve understanding between various cultures. One such example is that of the Middle East and the Arab culture.

Cultural Consideration and the Role of the Interviewer in the Middle East

I have always believed that people are more alike than different; it is just those differences that we must understand (McManus, 2008). In the United States, we have status according to what we do; our actions can earn us more respect, authority, and power. Therefore, we tend to identify ourselves by our achievements rather than by our family (Nydell, 1996).

In the Middle East, status is gained by being born into the right family (Nydell, 1996). In general, it has been my experience as an observer that upward social mobility remains limited in the Middle East. Therefore, Arabs, for example, are conscious of their status and will go to extremes to protect it, which then maintains respect, authority, and power both for themselves and for their families (Nydell, 1996). Their belief about status, as reflected by Islam, is generally along the lines that if God or Allah did not want you to be important, you would not have been born into a family of status or importance. And, if you are born into status, you must protect your status from all challengers the rest of your life. If you fail, you lose some of your status, and your family also loses. While *status* is not perfectly defined and is quite subjective, it is nevertheless real to the holder of status. Thus it can be challenged in a number of ways; some are well known by custom, some more in the perception of the individual holding the status. For example, status may be lost by being insulted or criticized in public without a successful challenge to the criticism. Social mobility regardless of birth status is beginning to appear, to a degree, in the Middle East, but that occurrence is still new and suffers setbacks from generations of individuals who have labored under the original conventions (Nydell, 1996).

What Is Culture?

Culture is a set of learned beliefs, values and behaviors; a way of life shared by the members of a society.

Society for American Archaeology: Teaching Archaeology n.d., p. 28

As an investigator, intelligence collector, or business analyst working in an international setting, you must understand the cultures of the world. Whether dealing with the history and culture of Latin America, the Oriental concept of the self based on Buddhism, Confucianism, and Feudalism, or the study of Islam, success truly depends on taking the time to study.

Negotiating with a Middle Easterner is not an exact, predictable science. It is a complex art form involving many unknowns and uncertainties, and it is always wise to have a variant strategy or approach. I also attempt in the following passages to note general tendencies of individuals from this part of the world and focus on the traits of Middle Easterners, Arabs, and southwestern Asians who are involved in deviant and criminal behavior. There is no foolproof recipe; there is always the possibility of unpredictable behavior.

Interview with a Middle Easterner

There are a lot of misperceptions in America and the West toward the Arab world, and vice versa. America looks at the Arab world as backward and violent, and in the Arab world America is seen as aggressive and arrogant. For a person like me, who knows America as well as I do and loves America so well and is from the Arab world, I find myself in sort of a limbo. I go back home and find myself defending America. I come to America and find myself defending the Arab world.

The Kuwaiti Ambassador to the United States

The *Middle East* is usually defined as an area consisting of 21 separate countries. These countries vary widely mainly due to their vastly different cultures (McManus, 2008). One common thread between the countries is the religion of Islam. Initially, most feel that Muslim Arabs, for example, are difficult to understand, and that their behavior patterns are not logical. In fact, to the contrary, Arab behavior is quite comprehensible and predictable if their cultural patterns are understood (Nydell, 1996).

It becomes important for interviewers to be aware of these cultural patterns and distinguish them from individual traits. For example, in the Arab culture, the Koran is the most read, recited, memorized, debated, analyzed, and venerated book in the annals of history (Nydell, 1996). In the Middle East, while over 90% of all Arabs are Muslims, only 25% of the Muslim community is Arab. This requires not only knowledge of Islam, but also independent information concerning each culture in which it is practiced. There are some doctrines of Islam that Muslims incorporate regardless of culture. Their adoption, however, can vary in intensity because of the culture; that is, most feel that their religion (Islam) and culture are superior to any other religion or culture.

Some aspects of various cultures that are shaped by Islam produce behavior in personal interactions that may be confusing to the West. Set forth next are some cultural issues that might trouble uninformed individuals who contact Islamic cultures. For example:

Q: How does a Middle Easterner exercise a sense of personal responsibility?

A: There is no sense of personal responsibility as practiced in the American culture. For example, if you say to a Middle Easterner, "You lost it," he will say, "I didn't." This answer is partly to protect himself against the accusation, but it also encompasses an issue of philosophy, that is, if something was lost, it was meant to be lost as part of Allah's plan, but he, personally, did not "cause" it to happen (McManus, 2008).

Q: What about something as simple as a handshake? How would you greet a Middle Eastern male?

A: Generally, if you watch two Middle Easterners meeting, they may shake hands with both hands extended to the other person. Then, both hands may move to the person's shoulders, followed by a brief or enthusiastic hug, depending on how well you know the other person (McManus, 1996).

Q: Why shake both hands?

A: Always use both hands because this shows your intentions are peaceful, and that there is no dagger in either hand (McManus, 2008).

Q: What about the strength of the handshake? In America, a firm handshake shows strength of character.

A: I would say it depends. I would use less strength than when shaking hands in the United States or you may come across as hostile or crude (McManus, 1996).

Q: What is helpful to establish rapport between the American and Middle East cultures?

A: It is always nice to mention some of the contributions of the Middle East to the Western culture. Such contributions would include astronomy as well as geometry, the Arabic numbering system, and the basic mathematics and sciences used in today's technology (McManus, 1996).

In general, in any contact with Arabs, it is never appropriate to display impatience or undue haste because these traits are normally interpreted as evidence of insincerity or lack of self-control. Conversation is opened with small talk and pleasantries, centered on the health and well-being of the participants and their respective families. Avoid any direct questions about female relatives. Stay away from political and religious subjects.

Avoid patronizing Arabs. Do not talk down to someone if he does not speak English well. Be as clear and concise as possible in your speech by speaking slowly. Avoid using slang. It is also best to avoid a direct argument. Once an Arab has made a decision, it is unlikely that he or she will immediately change his or her mind. It is better to drop the argument and approach the problem from a different direction.

Unlike Americans, Arabs do not accept or give criticism directly. It is also especially rude to contradict a person of status or a superior in rank or age. It becomes the interviewer to develop the art of tact when addressing issues of concern or disagreement rather than trying to confront, accuse, or prove an Arab wrong with facts—which is surely not a good idea. Arabs understand and appreciate tact because it protects public image, avoids insult, and allows a face-saving gesture. Arabs are adept at reinterpreting facts to suit themselves, particularly when defending their dignity. Avoid placing any personal blame or connotations of blame or incompetence on an Arab. Always try to provide an Arab a way out and project the blame elsewhere.

The True Believer

The key to the highly motivated true believer is to get him or her to talk about anything at first before we fine tune our discussions to get those answers we know are critical.

Meloy, 2004

There are ways of eliciting information from the highly motivated true believers, some more effective than others. These individuals are motivated by deeply held beliefs, one of which is that he or she serves as an agent of his or her God. They may also intend silence as an attempt to demean the interviewer as an "unbeliever." The true believer draws his sustenance from internal beliefs and images. Typically, they do not consciously need external sources of gratification (money, power, or sex). The true believer generally practices self-discipline and may not necessarily exhibit many emotions during an interview. What is known is that the true believer responds best if the interviewer shows genuine interest and sincerity (Meloy, 2004).

As we try to understand the dedicated jihadist or motivated believer, let us look at how the rapport elicitation process should work.

Case 18.1

A citizen of a neighboring country, which was also a country of interest to the United States, was applying for a work visa. This subject had been previously refused admission as an intended immigrant because he had no valid visa. In the initial interview, the subject was advised that I was aware of the previous problems he encountered while attempting to enter the United States. I believed that the key in this interview was to avoid using charged words like *illegal* and *crimes* and to impart to him that we understand and sympathize with his attempts to better his chances for success in the United States. We then talked about his family and what his short- and long-term plans might be. Based on our small talk, it was clear that the subject was well educated and had already established a successful business enterprise in a neighboring city. From talking with (**not to**) the subject, it was apparent that he was part of the progressive movement in the country of his birth. We elicited enough information to learn his perspective of his country affairs to take the relationship that we had established in the interview to the next level. During the continuation of the conversation, the subject was asked if he had knowledge of or had been asked to do anything contrary to his upbringing and beliefs.

Surprisingly, he replied "Yes" and went on to recount several incidents. A sampling of these incidents included his having been asked to help individuals (including one identifiable U.S. citizen) to enter his country of birth and then help these individuals to continue on to another "country of interest." The subject was asked if it would be possible for us to introduce him to another associate regarding the aforementioned incidents and if he would also agree to cooperate with us in the future. He agreed to both.

A Contrast: Interviewing the Latin American

Latin America is an area made up of 24 separate countries. Latin American cultures vary among the countries. The cultural differences between Ecuador and Argentina alone are as diverse as those between France and China. The ethnic and social differences make it difficult to generalize about the Latin American area. Nevertheless, along with the variety in Latin American culture there are also similarities (McManus, 2008). Latin America is a homogeneous culture in that relationships and family are important. Spanish in general is the native language.

There are also a great number of similarities between the Hispanic and Middle Eastern cultures. Although there are no steadfast rules, there are some general guidelines for understanding Latin American culture that may be helpful in establishing rapport. For example, hospitality is one of the cornerstones of the Latin culture. At a minimum, it is common courtesy in Latin America to say "Hello," to shake hands, and to ask about one's family. Anything less is an insult and provokes a deep emotional reaction; it is difficult to communicate effectively with clenched teeth (McManus, 2008).

With regard to body language, most North Americans stand at arm's length when talking face to face, while the Latin American stands much closer. It is a common complaint among Latin Americans that North Americans are cold; they keep you at arm's length and do not want to get close (McManus, 2008).

Similar to the Arab and Middle Eastern culture, Latin Americans of the same sex touch more than North Americans of the same sex do. Young women will hold hands while walking. Men hug in greeting, while a woman commonly greets another woman with a light kiss on the cheek and always a handshake (McManus, 2008). In the Latin American culture, handshaking is softer than in the United States. The firm, frank handshake is a hostile greeting in Latin America, while a soft handshake misleads Americans into thinking the person is a little less than honest and sincere (McManus, 2008).

Voice inflection, gestures, and emotion are important in any discussion for the Latin American, while Americans tend to consider softer voice, fewer tones, fewer gestures, and less emotion as the sign of a poised individual. The expressiveness and emotion in talking are tied to the Latin concept on individuality and "machismo" (McManus, 2008). Machismo is widely known in the United States but little understood. Usually, North Americans connect machismo to sex alone. In Latin America, it is more the "essence" of being masculine. The basic male outlook is involved, whether the man is tall, short, skinny, ugly, or handsome. A macho man is confident. He is considered a good talker, both eloquent and witty (McManus, 2008).

As for eye contact, there is no general rule, although some Latin Americans are taught that it is respectful to look down, to lower their eyes, when with someone in authority. To most North Americans, this may look "shifty," but most do not realize a cultural pattern of respect is operating (McManus, 2008).

In the end, the Latin American cultures, like the Arab and other Middle Eastern cultures, are still in transition even though still largely traditional cultures in which personal relationships are the key to all functions. The "survival network" is still strong. People take priority over institutions and paper laws and regulations. Generally, the only way to get things accomplished is through a "friend" or a "friend of a friend" (McManus, 2008).

The following example is presented to demonstrate how rapport might be gained in an interview:

Case 18.2

During a crime scene investigation of a massive head-on collision along the Mexican and U.S. border, a Hispanic male was being interviewed as a witness. He was asked to describe what he saw that led up to this incident. During the initial interview with a uniformed officer, the subject volunteered that he was a naturalized U.S. citizen and was returning from a medical conference at the University of Monterrey in Monterrey, Mexico. During a follow-up discussion with an investigator at the local station, the subject stated that he was a postdoctoral research assistant at Texas A&M University at College Station, Texas. When asked about his area of study, the subject stated that he was working in the virology program (virology is the study of viruses and their role in disease), but that he was a veterinary researcher who specialized in animal husbandry. During further conversation, the subject advised that he was married to an Egyptian citizen, whom he met while both were studying at Texas A&M. After a short courtship, they were married in Cairo, Egypt. After 6 years of marriage, the subject stated his wife was recently naturalized as a U.S. citizen.

The subject explained that a Texas A&M research assistant drove down to attend the conference at the University in Monterrey. The research assistant flew back at the end of the conference and left the car for the subject. The subject stated that he attended the 3-day conference at the University of Monterrey and then drove to Laredo, Texas. The subject provided vague answers about activities during the rest of his time in Mexico. He consented to further inspection of his belongings, and he consented to a search of his vehicle. During the inspection, officers found scientific literature related to genetic engineering and avian influenza (bird flu). In addition, there was Arabic literature with known jihad symbols.

The subject was asked to explain his interest in the area of avian flu. He indicated that he had particular interests in exploring the avian flu and the spread of livestock diseases. He stated that his objectives were to (1) deepen his knowledge of communicable diseases among animals and how they are spread and (2) assess state-of-the-art advances in biotechnology and recent research efforts of scientists through networking and attendance at seminars. Because of the rapport we developed through the elicitation process, he volunteered that his intent was to assemble biological agents to attack the United States. His wife's father and brother were pressuring him to be part of the jihad. He was extremely uncomfortable about the politics of jihad yet wanted to appease his wife's father and brother. He also was seeking assistance from those who would listen and understand his cultural dilemma.

Understanding culture and using that knowledge to establish rapport and elicit information can lead to a more productive interview. In the end, I encourage interviewers and interrogators to talk *with* the subject and not *to* him, and to be well informed about the cultures and politics of the countries of interest.

At this point, a word of caution: The material presented assumes the contact with a foreign national who may have information of value. It does not dwell on a situation with that foreign national being a hostile individual already situated in the United States. If the individual is suspected of being a foreign operative, the approach ideas will still apply, but the personal safety of the contacting agents should never be far from conscious thought. If the individual is already sold on his cause, he may also have a desire for martyrdom.

The contact could present an opportunity to carry out this wish, perhaps on a smaller scale than originally fantasized. To the subject, his own death may be a small price to pay for taking with him an officer or two.

Some Basic Data Necessary for Elicitation and Interviewing

Tenets Shared by Muslims and Christians

What most Muslims believe about God is readily agreed on by most Christians and Jews.

God created the entire world and all of its inhabitants and physical features.

God has imparted his rules and guidance for how people are to live life.

There is only one God to be worshiped, replacing any and all other previously worshiped items (i.e., idols, money, pleasures, and power).

God will judge all people at the end of time.

Those who fulfill the divine command of Allah will enter heaven.

Some Basic Beliefs

Everything and anything that happens occurs because it is God's will, and Muslims often invoke the phrase *inshallah*, meaning something will happen "if God wills it" (Clark, 2003). This may present an obstacle to an interviewer when attempting to get a Muslim to take personal responsibility for something that he has done because he may believe that he was not in control and what happened is what was God's desire.

Quran (Qur'an, Koran, Coran, Alkoran) is the Islamic holy scripture and is followed by many as a literal recitation of Allah's words. Muslims believe that the Quran is specifically the word of God. The Quran is the only book many Islamists ever possess. It is read as a text that provides the rules, laws, and philosophy of Allah. The details of the Quran were provided to Muhammad by the angel Gabriel over a 22-year span. He orally relayed this scripture to his followers, and it was haphazardly recorded. The Quran was written some 19 years after Muhammad's death by those who knew him. The Quran is only part of an original book that is maintained in Heaven. The original transcript is a recording of all previous history plus a recording of what is yet to occur. Therefore, all that will happen is already foretold and is God's will. The Quran is "the pristine truth and is immutable" and is infallible (Sabini, 1994).

God's revelations to Moses, David, and Jesus come from the same heavenly book as the Quran but are incomplete and were corrupted. Because of the corruption, God sent Muhammad with a pure and complete record (Clark, 2003).

Modern Historical Perspective

Toward the end of the eighteenth and into the nineteenth centuries, most of today's Muslim land was controlled by European nations. Independence from that colonization came during the last half of the twentieth century, making their nationhood a recent historical event.

Islam's Rank in the World and the United States

Muslims are becoming the second largest religious group in the United States; therefore, understanding their culture is a practical imperative (Clark, 2003). Islam ranks as one of the major religions of the world and is followed by about 25% of the entire world's population. At least some of the perceived anger and hostility associated with Islam stems from their overwhelming possession of the world's oil reserves and contact with the West that goes hand in hand with petroleum commerce. One of the conflicts with Islam's unchanged and unchanging core religious, civic, and political beliefs is today's "Western influence" and materialism, represented primarily by the United States. Islam is compelled to deal with this conflict in order to operate in the modern world. Some of the fundamentalists, especially those in Iran, have responded by enforcing a revival of the rigid and authoritarian rules of the male-dominated society. That type of extreme movement is often loud and gathers widespread attention but represents a truly small portion of the entire Islamic population. Individuals in mainstream Islam far outnumber the radicals, whose numbers, and concomitant threat to those who do not agree with them, appear to be growing.

Islam, the Quran, Violence, and Coexisting

Muslims are commanded by God to bring all people into Islam, but the dictate is not to be accomplished by force of arms. Dating back to at least 616, BCE, Muslims have espoused the avoidance of bloodshed. The Quran makes a special note of Christianity and Judaism and does not classify their adherents as nonbelievers (Clark, 2003).

Allah, God, Muhammad, and Christ

Allah is the supreme being in the Islamic religion, which, like Christianity, is monotheistic. Allah is considered the exact same God as worshiped by Christians and Jews. Muslims reject the concept of the Holy Trinity. There is only God, and he has no equal. Christ is a **man** and **not** the son of God but is a **revered** Islamic prophet.

Muslim (or Moslem) also refers to a person who submits to God. Muslims should never be referred to as Muhammadans as they do not worship Muhammad; they worship God. This is in contrast to Christianity's worshiping Christ. Muhammad is a prophet, but also a man, not to be worshiped or used for intercession with God. Islam's God is a personal god and communication is directly with him. Muslims believe that God is as close as the vein in their neck (Clark, 2003). Muhammad was not intent on founding a new religion but was bringing forth God's word to correct and complete the message delivered by his forerunner, Christ.

Muhammad is the last in the line of prophets. As the basis of faith, Muhammad brought directly from Allah his words and instructions, which are recorded in the Quran. Religious tolerance was a belief and practice of Muhammad. He believed that the Quran was God's revelations to him, which were God's final word. He also believed that the portions of the Old Testament called the Torah by the Jews and parts of the New Testament were divinely inspired. He referred his followers to those scriptures for instructions about Islam. He called Jews and Christians the "People of the Book" and offered them relative freedom to worship under his protection.

The Meaning of Islam

Islam is the name for a Muslim's submission to the will of God (Allah). This is the defining attitude and practice of members following Islamic beliefs. Islam embodies or defines a way of life, including legal and moral standards and rules applicable to every aspect of life for a follower. As further explanation, the separation of church and state, a fundamental principle for America, is a totally foreign idea in Islam. All aspects of everyday life are comingled and governed under Islam's umbrella. Islam dictates all aspects of human society, including political and cultural considerations (Clark, 2003).

Divisions of Islam

Muslim means a practitioner of Islam. *Islam* refers to the Muslim religion and the areas of the world where that religion is practiced. The overall division of Islam is twofold. The Sunnis comprise the overwhelming majority of Islamists. It is estimated that nearly 90% of all believers are in the Sunni grouping. They follow the fundamental beliefs and practices of Islam. The Shi'a is a minority within Islam comprising 10% to 15% of the believers. Shi'i and Shi'ite are derivates. The Shi'a has divided into many sects who oppose the Sunnis and each other. The split into sects came about because of a political question regarding who is the rightful heir to Muhammad (Clark, 2003).

Heaven and Hell

One point of contrast with Christianity is the Islamic belief of heaven and hell. They believe both exist, but being cast into either population is held in abeyance until the Last Day (Judgment Day). Until that time, the soul remains in the grave receiving a preview of what is to come.

Role of Protector

When interacting with someone of the Islamic faith, it is a good practice to avoid asking specific questions about his wife or any other female family member. Likewise, if attempting to establish rapport, questions about other relatives should be framed in terms explaining why the question is pertinent to the inquiry. At least part of the rationale for this restriction is that in the Middle East a man is the guardian of his immediate and extended family. He is their protector, and anything done by any member of the family reflects on every member of the family. It is considered proper in the Middle East culture, specifically the Muslim population, to make a broad inquiry concerning his "family" without specifying any individual member. While American custom permits a direct or blunt approach to asking questions, in the Middle East that is contrary to their custom.

Rapport Building and Muslims

As indicated, a period of cordiality and friendly conversation should precede broaching a discussion of serious matters. In the rapport-building period, aggressive behavior, suggested or implied threats, and direct confrontation will not be well received. Before jumping into the primary topic, ask questions of a general nature to show interest in him as a person and as a Middle Eastern man. The interviewer should come prepared to be patient and to make a display of sincerity. The art of questioning someone from the Middle East is to take the conversational approach, which improves the opportunity to obtain information. A reasonable approach to developing rapport may be to begin with asking questions that flatter his achievements and travels. Such banter assists in lowering the barriers to being interviewed. When an interviewer is sufficiently versed, he is well advised to include references to the many contributions made to civilization by the Middle Easterner's ancestors. The impact of Muslims on the development of the world's current culture is profound. From Islam came many of the foundational pieces for the European Renaissance or rebirth. Their culture has had a strong impact on architecture, literature (especially poetry), philosophy, and reason. In addition, the writing and rewriting of the Quran had an impact on the development of calligraphy and art, as well as the appreciation for and preservation of all types of knowledge. The sciences, mathematics, chemistry, and medicine were areas of specialization arising from Islam.

Use of presumptive questions is sometimes helpful in gaining information. A presumptive question is the type that contains phrases that suggest the answer is already known. By using this technique, you are only asking for confirmation or affirmation, for example: "What was Mohammed's role in the cruise ship attack?" or "Tell me what happened on Friday."

Direct Questions Involving Islam

It would be considered rude to make inquiries about a Middle Easterner's religion unless it is pertinent to the purpose of the interview. Even in those circumstances, it is better to establish rapport before asking those types of questions. He is the protector of his religion, just as he is of his family. There is substantial risk of losing rapport when discussing either topic.

Islamic Law

At the peak of Islamic thought is the Law, which is considered to be of divine origin and was transmitted from Allah through Muhammad. There is no distinction between religious and secular application. The Law is detailed to establish the proper standards for every aspect of a Muslim's life.

Sunna refers to the traditions of Mohammad. Those behaviors and actions are the recorded recollections of the sayings and deeds of Muhammad. As recorded, it is called the Hadith. It is ranked second only to the Quran as the source of belief and practices. Those who adhere closely to the Sunna are called Sunni or Sunnite and are considered an orthodox group.

Muslims' Contributions to Civilization

Muslims' preserved and translated ancient Greek works deal with several subjects that would have been otherwise lost during the Dark Ages but were preserved to fuel the Renaissance era. Those contributions include advances in medicine, mathematics and algebra, philosophy, astronomy, and architecture.

Bibliography

Clark, Malcolm. *Islam for Dummies.* Hoboken, NJ: Wiley, 2003.

Hofstede, Geert. *Culture and Organizations: Software of the Mind, Interculltural Cooperation and Its Importance for Survival.* New York: McGraw-Hill, 1997.

McManus, Barry L. *Liar.* Leesburg, VA: Global Traveler, 2008.

Meloy, J R. Indirect Personality Assessment of the Violent True Believer. *Journal of Personality Assessment* 82 (2004): 138–146.

Nydell, Margaret K. *Understanding Arabs.* Boston, MA: Intercultural Press, 1996.
Sabini, John. *Islam: A Primer.* Rev. ed. Washington, DC: Middle East Editorial Associates, 1994.
Society for Amerian Archaeology: Teaching Archaeology. http://www.saa.org/jportals/o/saa/publications (accessed March 8, 2010).

Legal Perspectives on Interviewing

19

JOHN C. HALL

Contents

Introduction

The objective of this chapter is to identify the legal rules of universal application throughout the United States that affect the lawful acquisition of self-incriminating statements in criminal prosecutions. It is not intended to be a legal treatise with case citations and detailed discussions of court decisions; in fact, the only case mentioned by name is *Miranda v. Arizona* because that case title has become synonymous with the legal rule it spawned. It is hoped that the information contained in this chapter will serve as a practical guide to investigators in ways to apply the constitutional rules to best advantage in the course of their investigations. Even though court cases are not cited, the legal principles discussed are found in case law.

The focus of this chapter is on relevant federal constitutional provisions, the only legal rules that are binding on all law enforcement officers within the United States. Although the states may have stricter rules that apply to state and local officers within their jurisdictions, they are not applicable to federal law enforcement officers. Only the federal constitutional rules constrain *all* law enforcement officers at every level of government.

The Significance of Government Action

The Bill of Rights in the U.S. Constitution was originally designed to restrain the power of the newly created central government and did not apply to the states. One consequence of this fact was that state and local law enforcement officers were bound only by the law in their respective jurisdiction and could legally acquire evidence in ways not permitted to their federal counterparts. Since that evidence was not the product of any federal constitutional violation, it could be admitted as evidence in federal criminal prosecutions. This practice became known as the *silver platter doctrine* since state and local officers could present evidence to their federal counterparts on a silver platter.

This picture dramatically changed in the twentieth century as the U.S. Supreme Court increasingly applied portions of the Bill of Rights to the states through the 14th Amendment "due process" clause. Before long, most of the provisions of the Bill of Rights—and particularly those relating to police powers—were as binding on the states as on the federal government.

This revolution in constitutional interpretation effectively put an end to the silver platter doctrine in its original form since state and local officers were now governed by the same rules that governed their federal counterparts. However, the doctrine should still apply to private investigators or other private persons who are not acting in concert with or under the direction or control of government agents.

The Relevant Constitutional Provisions

The provisions of the U.S. Constitution that govern the admissibility of self-incriminating statements in federal and state courts are

1. The Fourth Amendment prohibition against unreasonable searches and seizures
2. The Fifth Amendment prohibition against compelled self-incrimination and the requirement of due process
3. The Miranda rule requirements for an advice of rights and waiver prior to custodial interrogation
4. The Sixth Amendment right to the assistance of counsel in all criminal prosecutions

The nature and scope of these constitutional protections, their proper applications, and their relevance to the acquisition of information from criminal suspects by law enforcement officers are discussed in detail next.

The Fourth Amendment

> The right of the people to be secure in their persons, houses, papers, and effects, against unreasonable … seizures, shall not be violated...

In 1914, the U.S. Supreme Court ruled that evidence obtained by federal law enforcement officers as the result of an unreasonable search or seizure may be excluded from use in federal criminal prosecutions. In 1961, the Court expanded application of this "exclusionary rule" to the states. As a consequence, any evidence, whether physical or testimonial (statements), obtained in violation of the Fourth Amendment is subject to exclusion. This led to the development of the "poisonous tree" doctrine, by which any evidence derived from tainted evidence is also subject to exclusion. For example, if law enforcement officers make an unconstitutional arrest, evidence obtained in a search incident to that arrest may be subject to exclusion at trial; the same is true of statements taken from the arrestee as well as any physical evidence recovered by virtue of the statements. It is comparable to a chain reaction.

To avoid the consequences of the exclusionary rule, it is incumbent on law enforcement officers to understand the different types of Fourth Amendment seizures and the legal rules that govern them.

A Fourth Amendment seizure occurs whenever law enforcement officers intentionally deprive a person of his freedom of movement. Thus, all arrests are seizures, but not all seizures are arrests. A second type of seizure is the investigative detention, often referred to as a *temporary detention*. The distinctions between an arrest and an investigative detention are several and significant.

An *arrest* is a complete seizure of a person for the ultimate purpose of charging him with a crime. The arrestee, and the area within his immediate control, may be thoroughly searched for weapons, evidence, or means of escape; he may be handcuffed and transported to a police station or other government facility, at which time he may be fingerprinted, photographed, "booked," and interrogated before being locked in a cell. Eventually, he will be taken before a magistrate. There can be variations on this theme, depending on the circumstances and the needs of the case. But, the point is that an arrest is a highly intrusive action by the government and must be supported by the constitutional standard of "probable cause."

The investigative detention is a significantly less intrusive seizure. As with an arrest, an investigative detention is a *forcible* seizure, which means that the suspect is not free to leave for the moment, and officers are justified to use the reasonable force necessary to maintain the detention. However, it is different in several respects:

1. An investigative detention does not require probable cause but only a reasonable suspicion that "criminal activity is afoot."
2. Officers may conduct a limited frisk *only* for weapons and *only* when there is a reasonable suspicion that the detainee is armed.
3. An investigative detention does not permit removal of the detainee to a different location without consent or a clear investigative or safety purpose.
4. For reasons that will become apparent, an arrest is "custody" for purposes of the Miranda rule, but an investigative detention is not.

Understanding these distinctions will lessen the risks that officers might unintentionally convert a lawful investigative detention into an unlawful arrest. When that occurs, any evidence acquired as a result, including statements, may be lost.

The Fifth Amendment

No person ... shall be compelled in any criminal case to be a witness against himself, nor be deprived of life, liberty, or property without due process of law.

Both portions of the Fifth Amendment quoted above—forbidding compelled self-incrimination and requiring due process—have been deemed by the U.S. Supreme Court as relevant to the admissibility of confessions in court. If there was a distinction between the two protections in the past, they have essentially merged in recent decades into the concept that any self-incriminating statements must be given voluntarily. However, due process—interpreted by the Supreme Court as "fundamental fairness" or avoiding "actions that shock the conscience"—remains a potentially broader concept and invites courts to condemn law enforcement practices that are not clearly prohibited by other portions of the Constitution. It is difficult to offer guidance regarding how one may avoid this problem; after all, what shocks the conscience of one court may not have the same effect on another. As a practical matter, if investigators make good faith efforts to ensure that statements are voluntarily given, the risks of shocking anyone's conscience seems remote. A useful point to ponder when considering creative interrogation techniques is their potential impact on a jury. Even if a judge does not consider it necessary to suppress a statement, a jury may express its own disapproval with an acquittal.

The Fifth Amendment protection against compelled self-incrimination was originally intended to prevent a criminal defendant from being compelled to take the witness stand at his trial. In modern times, it has been expanded to cover incriminating statements acquired by the government before trial.

Since this Fifth Amendment prohibition is limited to compelled self-incrimination, it obviously does not apply to either volunteered statements or compelled statements that are not self-incriminating.

Voluntariness

The Fifth Amendment standard of "voluntariness," like the Fourth Amendment standard of "reasonableness," "is not capable of precise definition or mechanical application." Both standards are defined by the "totality of the circumstances." This can be somewhat frustrating to those who like bright-line rules but gratifying to those who appreciate the flexibility afforded law enforcement officers in matching their wits with criminal suspects.

Given the standard of voluntariness, the goal of law enforcement officers must be to avoid any technique that suggests "compulsion" or "coercion." While it is not possible to provide a laundry list of do's and don'ts, it is possible to identify the typical things that courts have focused on to determine whether a statement was the product of coercion:

1. Physical torture or abuse or threats thereof. These are the clearest examples of coercion and surely do not require extensive examples to make the point. The best that can be said is that they do not seem to occur much these days.
2. Deprivation of necessities. Depriving an in-custody person of food, water, sleep, bathroom privileges, etc., will cause courts to view statements extracted through these tactics as coerced.
3. Promises of favor or leniency. Promises can "encourage" a person to confess to a crime and are not generally viewed as coercive. However, they may be viewed as either coercive or as violations of due process if they are likely to induce an innocent person to admit to something he did not do. For example, a promise not to charge a family member in return for a confession would probably not be viewed kindly by the courts.
4. Regarding deception, trickery, and lies, law enforcement officers frequently use some form of deception during interrogations, and courts are seldom offended. Caution: It is *never* permissible to deceive a person into waiving constitutional rights. The proper use of this technique is to encourage truthfulness from a person who is already willing to answer questions. Here are some notable examples of cases in which officers have used deception, even lies—or what Winston Churchill might call "terminological inexactitude"—resulting in confessions from the suspects:
   a. Officers told a burglary suspect that his fingerprints had been recovered from the crime scene.

    b. Officers told a suspect that his partner in crime had already talked and placed the blame on him.

    c. Officers told a suspect that witnesses had identified him from a photo display.

    d. Officers told a suspected rapist that his "ass print" had been removed from an automobile where the crime had been committed, and that it could be used to identify him as the rapist.

    e. When a burglary suspect agreed to submit to a "lie detector test," officers sat him down by a large machine, put what appeared to be a hubcap on his head, and asked if he had committed the burglary. When the suspect said "No," an officer punched a button, and the machine ejected a sheet of paper bearing the printed words "You're lying."

    f. Officers confronted a bank robbery suspect with a bank surveillance photo taken during the robbery depicting the robber wearing a mask and told the suspect that the image of the mask could be removed from the photo by the FBI laboratory.

Deception is an acceptable tactic for encouraging truthfulness but must not be of the type to cause an innocent person to confess to a crime he did not commit. In considering a particular kind of deception, officers should always be mindful of the risk that courts would view that tactic as one that shocks the conscience, thus violating the due process clause as well.

The Miranda Rule

The Miranda rule is a creation of the U.S. Supreme Court designed to enforce the Fifth Amendment protection against compelled self-incrimination. Understanding the underlying rationale of the rule is helpful in understanding its proper application.

The Miranda rule is based on the presumption that "custodial interrogation" creates an inherently coercive atmosphere. If the decision had ended with that presumption, no statements acquired as the product of postarrest questions by law enforcement officers would be admissible in court. However, the Court decided that the inherently coercive atmosphere could be dispelled if the officers advise the in-custody suspect of certain rights and obtain a voluntary waiver of those rights before beginning any interrogation.

From an understanding of the Court's rationale, we can readily determine *when* the Miranda rule applies; it is (a) when the suspect is in **custody** and (b) before **interrogation** begins.

Custody

Custody can be simply defined as *arrest*. It is not sufficient that a person has been "seized" or is "not free to leave"; as we have discussed, there are varying degrees of Fourth Amendment seizures, and not all of them rise to the level of an arrest.

The features of a typical arrest are readily recognizable: Officers announce the arrest; the arrestee is then handcuffed, searched, and transported to a police station or other government facility. However, an arrest can occur even if one or more of these features is absent. Whenever a person is subjected to the same kind and degree of control as a typical arrest, even though an arrest was neither announced nor intended, courts have concluded that the "functional equivalent" of an arrest has occurred. The test is not a subjective one. A suspect may think he is in custody simply because he has been approached by the police. Officers may think a person is not under arrest simply because they have not told him that he was. The relevant test is objective: whether a reasonable person at the time and in the same circumstances would believe that he is under arrest.

One fairly recent Supreme Court decision amply illustrates this point. A police officer went to a suspect's home to question him about his involvement in a particular crime. Although the officer possessed a warrant for the suspect's arrest, he made no mention of it to the suspect but proceeded with interrogation. There was no advice of rights given or waiver obtained. After the suspect provided an incriminating statement, the officer executed the arrest warrant. In response to the argument that the suspect was in custody from the beginning because the officer went to the residence with the intent to arrest him, the Court held that an officer's unannounced intention to make an arrest at the conclusion of the interrogation did not amount to an arrest.

Law enforcement officers often labor under the misperception that an immediate advice of right at the moment of arrest, even though not necessary, is a wise precaution against later problems. This is somewhat puzzling because officers seldom seek a "waiver" of the rights at that time, and the advice of rights without a waiver is meaningless. Nevertheless, the primary concern appears to be that the arrestee will say something important while under arrest and without having been given Miranda warnings. The question is often asked: "What if you don't give the advice of rights at the time of the arrest and he starts blurting out incriminating statements?" The answer is simple: Never interfere with a person's First Amendment freedom of speech and make good notes. Officers are permitted to ask clarifying questions, such as "What are you talking about?" but no significant questioning beyond that should be considered without full compliance with *Miranda*.

Once an arrest has been made, the first condition for applying the Miranda rule has been met, but only the first. There is not now, and there has never been, a requirement to advise a person of his rights at the moment of arrest.

Having, it is hoped, established that an arrest, by itself, does not trigger the Miranda rule, we proceed to the second essential ingredient—interrogation.

Interrogation

Interrogation is defined as either direct questions or any words or actions by known law enforcement officers that are intended to elicit self-incriminating responses from the arrestee. It is not the style of the question (e.g., casual, conversational, confrontational, accusatory, etc.) but the intent that is relevant to the definition.

A thorough understanding of this definition is critical to the proper application of *Miranda*. Particularly important is the requirement that the arrestee must *know* that he is being questioned by law enforcement officers. Without that knowledge, the presumption of "inherent coercion" is absent. Accordingly, using surreptitious techniques, such as cell-mate informants or undercover officers, does not fall within the definition of interrogation.

The Miranda Advice of Rights

Although we have already noted that the Miranda rule applies only when a person is under arrest and about to be interrogated, the continuing confusion on this point justifies some further emphasis. It might be helpful to identify some of the erroneous notions regarding the timing of the advice of rights that have persisted over the years and that have never been a part of the law:

1. At the moment of arrest
2. Whenever a person is deprived of his freedom of movement
3. Whenever the focus of the investigation is on the person being questioned
4. Whenever the questioning of a person reaches the accusatory stage
5. Whenever there is "station-house" questioning (i.e., the suspect is being questioned at the police station)
6. All of the above

Which of the above is correct? The answer is that none is correct.

Since the Miranda advice of rights is not required until the suspect is under arrest and about to be interrogated, it is important to note that law enforcement officers generally control the timing of both of the *Miranda* preconditions. As the Supreme Court observed in one celebrated case, there is no constitutional right to be arrested or to be arrested at a particular time. Likewise, there is no constitutional right to be interrogated or to be interrogated at a particular time. Both issues are left to the officers' discretion. In some instances, officers may deem it necessary or wise to proceed with interrogation immediately after an arrest. In others, they may determine that it is best to delay for a variety of reasons. Each situation is unique.

Consider this scenario:

1. An officer investigating a burglary attempted to contact a suspect at his home. When there was no response, he left a business card with a note requesting a call.
2. Later, the suspect telephonically contacted the officer, who offered to return to the suspect's residence to discuss something with him.
3. Instead, the suspect volunteered to drive himself to the police station.
4. When the suspect arrived at the station, the officer thanked him for coming and told him he was not under arrest.
5. When questioned, the suspect denied any involvement in the burglary.
6. The officer then told the suspect (falsely) that his fingerprints were recovered from the burglary scene.
7. The suspect then confessed to the crime.
8. The officer advised the suspect of his Miranda rights.
9. The suspect signed a written confession.
10. The officer allowed the suspect to leave.
11. Based on the suspect's confession, a warrant for his arrest was obtained, and he was arrested.

Based on what we know about the Miranda rule, at what point during this scenario was it necessary for the officer to provide an advice of rights and obtain a waiver? The answer is at no time since the suspect was never in custody while he was being interrogated at the station. He came to the station voluntarily; the officer told him that he was not under arrest; when the suspect confessed to the crime and signed a written statement, he was allowed to leave. The officer exercised his discretion, followed a scheme that produced a confession, and correctly applied the law. Even though the suspect confessed and the officer could have arrested him on the spot, he chose not to do so until he had obtained a warrant. The fact that the suspect was allowed to leave the station made it easy for the courts, including the Supreme Court, to determine that he was not in custody.

Note that the officer dispelled any notion the suspect might have had about his custodial status by telling him that he was not under arrest; he then avoided any later ambiguity by allowing him to leave. The officer exercised discretion and controlled events, and his decision to provide Miranda warnings after the confession but before the signed statement was of no legal consequence whatsoever. Fortunately, it had no practical consequences either; it was unnecessary and could have discouraged the suspect from providing the signed statement.

Lest one think that this scenario was fabricated for the purpose of making a point or that it reflects some recent changes in the law, it should be noted that these facts and the conclusions were taken from a Supreme Court case decided in 1977. There was nothing in the Court's opinion that was not already suggested by the *Miranda* decision 11 years earlier.

Once the decision has been made to interrogate the arrestee, *Miranda* requires the advice of rights and a waiver before that interrogation begins. Although the content of the advice of rights is well known, the burden is on law enforcement officers to ensure that the arrestee is aware of them. Essentially, there are two rights: the right to remain silent and the right to have an attorney present during questioning. In addition to the two rights, there are two explanatory statements advising the arrestee that anything he says may be used against him in court, and if he cannot afford an attorney, one can be appointed for him to be present during interrogation.

Ironically, the Fifth Amendment, on which the Miranda rule is based, contains no explicit reference to a "right to remain silent." The Fifth Amendment protection is against compelled self-incrimination. For that reason, even after an arrestee has asserted his right to silence and to counsel, officers may ask questions that do not fall within the definition of "self-incriminating statements." Examples are questions relating to another person's involvement in criminal activity or routine booking questions. Properly framed booking questions sometimes elicit incriminating responses, even though that was not intended, and those statements are admissible in court.

There is no requirement that the advice of rights be given in specific words or phrases; it is essential to provide the substance of them in language that the arrestee can understand. Many law enforcement agencies use printed forms for this purpose because they ensure that the required information is communicated to the arrestee, and they provide a written record for use in court. If a printed form is used, it is a good practice to allow the arrestee to read it as well as to have an officer read it aloud to him. To ensure that the arrestee can read, it is advisable to have him read some portion—preferably some portion that he is unlikely to have memorized—to establish that he is literate. The use of a printed form does not preclude the interrogating officers from being flexible in tailoring the advice of rights to the situation and to the arrestee. It may be presented in a formal or a conversational style as the officer deems most suitable to the occasion and the arrestee.

The Waiver

Once the advice of rights has been given to an arrestee, it is essential to obtain a "knowing, intelligent, and voluntary waiver" of those rights before interrogation can commence. The *knowing* and *intelligent* portions of this requirement are presumably satisfied by an effective advice of rights. The burden is then on the police to establish that those rights are waived voluntarily. If a printed form is used, it is a good practice to ask the arrestee to sign the form. While a written signature is not legally mandated, it carries a great deal of weight in court. Officers should check any signature proffered by the arrestee to ensure that it is his true name. More than a few waivers have been signed by "Napoleon," "Hannibal," or "Alexander the Great."

Arrestees may express a willingness to waive their rights but decline to sign the waiver. Apparently, the reluctance to sign one's name is based on the erroneous assumption that an oral waiver does not count. Of course it does, but it does not have the same weight as a signature. One possible solution is for the interrogating officer to make a written notation on the form to the effect that the arrestee verbally agrees to waive his rights but prefers not to sign the waiver form; ask the arrestee to read the notation aloud to confirm its accuracy and then ask him to sign the notation to confirm that those are his words. This is perfectly legal since the arrestee is not being "tricked" into waiving his rights; he already did that verbally, and he is voluntarily confirming his decision in writing.

Another technique that should be considered is to request a waiver of each right individually as it is presented. For example, after the arrestee is given his right to remain silent, ask if he is willing to waive that right. If the answer is affirmative, ask if he is willing to sign a waiver to that effect. If this procedure is used, it is convenient to have a form that provides a signature line after the end of each of the rights. Then, proceed to the next in the same manner. It is hoped that the fact that he has already waived the right to remain silent will make him more likely to waive the right to an attorney. This next point is extremely important: If he declines to waive the right to remain silent, there is no necessity or advantage to continue. It is best to discontinue the advice of rights and await a later opportunity to try again. As we will see, the possibility of a later opportunity may depend on this "incremental waiver" approach.

To fully understand the advantage to this approach, it is necessary to note the distinction between an assertion of the right to silence and the right to an attorney. The Supreme Court has held that if an arrestee *asserts the right to remain silent, no further attempts at interrogation may occur at that time.* However, officers are permitted to return after a reasonable lapse of time (e.g., a few hours) and try again. It is conceivable that the arrestee will have reconsidered his position and changed his mind. On the other hand, if the arrestee *asserts the right to an attorney, no further attempts at interrogation may occur until an attorney is present or unless the arrestee initiates the second contact with the officers.* The effect of an assertion of this right means that as long as the arrestee remains in custody, no attempts may be made by any officers—including those from other agencies—to interrogate him. Because of the distinct consequences of the assertion of either the right to remain silent or the right to an attorney, it is important to properly record the arrestee's responses to an advice of rights and to communicate them to any other officers who may desire to interrogate him.

Public Safety: An Exception to the Miranda Rule

The exception to the Miranda rule for public safety can best be understood by briefly reviewing the facts from which it emerged. A suspect believed to have committed a violent crime with a firearm just moments before was pursued on foot by police officers and finally arrested in a nearby grocery store. When an immediate search failed to locate the firearm, one of the officers asked the suspect where he had put it. The suspect responded that it was in the store and assisted the officers in retrieving it. Technically, this would appear to be a clear violation of *Miranda*: There was custody (arrest) and interrogation (a question regarding the arrestee's involvement in a crime) but no advice of rights and waiver. However, the Supreme Court concluded that the need to protect the public from an imminent danger outweighed the need to comply with *Miranda*. The Court viewed the purpose of the officer's question as intended primarily to protect the public from a known danger; the fact that it may also have elicited an incriminating response and led to the recovery of evidence was secondary.

It is not yet clear how far the courts will go in applying this "public safety" exception to the Miranda rule. Officers should be aware of it and understand that they are unlikely to be placed in the situation of having to choose between preserving lives or preserving evidence. Given a reasonable perception of danger to the public, they may be able to do both.

The Sixth Amendment: Right to Counsel

> In all criminal prosecutions, the accused shall enjoy the right ... to have the assistance of counsel for his defense.

The explicit language of the Sixth Amendment guarantees the right to the assistance of counsel for the defense during any criminal prosecutions. The language, and the history, suggests that the protection was intended as a "trial" right. However, in 1964 the Supreme Court ruled that a "criminal prosecution" does not begin at trial; it begins when a person has been either formally charged or taken before a magistrate for his first appearance regarding a specific crime. From that point forward, the accused has the right to be represented by counsel at any "critical stage of the prosecution"—that is, whenever he is confronted with the forces of government attempting to deliberately elicit evidence concerning the specific crime for which he is being prosecuted. That right to counsel must be voluntarily waived by the defendant before such deliberate elicitation can occur.

The same procedures for obtaining a waiver of Miranda rights will also serve to waive the Sixth Amendment right to counsel. As with *Miranda*, an assertion of the right to counsel precludes any attempts at interrogation until the attorney is present unless the defendant initiates the contact with law enforcement. It should be noted that a defendant's request of a court to have counsel appointed to represent him during the criminal prosecution is not the same as an "assertion" of the right to have an attorney present during police questioning. Accordingly, unless the defendant has asserted the latter right, law enforcement officers may approach him to determine if he is willing to waive his Sixth Amendment right and answer questions.

The Sixth Amendment right to counsel is distinct from the Miranda rule in several particulars: (1) *Miranda* applies only when there is "custodial interrogation," while the Sixth Amendment right to counsel applies to the "deliberate elicitation of statements" from a person against whom a "criminal prosecution" has begun. The Sixth Amendment applies whether or not the accused is in custody; (2) *Miranda* applies to interrogation of an arrestee concerning any criminal activity, while the Sixth Amendment right to counsel applies only to the government's efforts to elicit evidence concerning the specific crime with which the defendant has been charged; and (3) *Miranda* applies only when information is elicited from an arrestee by a known law enforcement officer, while the Sixth Amendment prohibits deliberate elicitation of statements from the defendant by the government through any means (e.g., informants, undercover officers, etc.).

In many cases, both *Miranda* and the Sixth Amendment right to counsel will apply (e.g., if the subject has been arrested *following* a formal charge). Because the subject is in custody, no interrogation can occur without a waiver of Miranda rights, and as noted, a valid waiver of Miranda rights serves to waive the Sixth Amendment right to counsel as well. A complication is more apt to arise when the subject has been formally charged but is not in custody, either because he has not yet been arrested or because he has been released on bond. Officers seeking to question the subject about the crime with which he is charged may not know that while *Miranda* does not apply, the Sixth Amendment right to counsel does. Without a valid waiver of the Sixth Amendment right to counsel, any statements obtained concerning the specific crime with which the defendant has been charged are subject to exclusion.

Appendix A

Glossary

A glossary for sexual violence and criminal investigative analysis (CIA) was first developed by supervisory special agents Robert R. Hazelwood and John Douglas, now retired, for the Behavioral Science Unit (BSU) of the Federal Bureau of Investigation (FBI) at the FBI Academy. The defining of those new and sometimes complex terms facilitated learning the analysis and profiling process. For similar reasons a select set of terms have been chosen to assist the interviewer in blending CIA sexual violence data into a successful interview and interrogation process. The glossary is intended as a quick reference for the terminology that is more fully developed in various chapters.

Anger Retaliatory Rapist: The anger retaliatory rapist is motivated by a need to strike back and get even, and chooses women as his target. He uses his sexual anatomy to implement his nonsexual motivation. Power, another nonsexual motive, is most likely part of his overall drive. He is highly aggressive, exhibits no concern for the victim, and uses excessive force on the victim, who may require extensive medical attention. His crimes are opportunistic in that the victims happen to be at or near his location when his anger becomes overwhelming and explosive.

Bait Question: *See* Dangle Question

Behavior: Refers to the acts of an offender or of the offender and a victim that are left imprinted on a crime scene or obtained from a behavioral-oriented interview of a surviving rape victim. These acts may be observed with a trained eye. On analysis, the behaviors will reveal the personality of the offender, his motive, and many traits and characteristics of the offender. Behaviors reflect personality, as the mind controls behavior.

Behavior-Oriented Interview of Victim Questionnaire: Type of interview aid that allows a victim to describe the behaviors of a rapist and her corresponding behaviors. The officer using the questionnaire and doing the interview must carefully guard his attitude and demeanor and ask questions without judgment. The sum of the information provided reveals behaviors reflective of motive, noncriminal lifestyle of the offender, and more. When combined with rapist typology and research information, the data will assist in formulating an interview plan for a targeted subject interview (TSI).

Closed-Ended Questions: Questions that may be answered simply with a yes or no, often containing descriptors of crime details that may be adopted by a suspect, parroted back, seeming to validate a false confession. Closed-ended questions tend to give away investigative knowledge and direct the interviewee to limit his information input. They are more appropriately used after clarification has been obtained using open-ended questions. They are employed after obtaining a version of events to which the interviewee is committed.

Comfort Zone: Refers to the geographical area within which an offender is calm and at ease. In sex crimes committed by the power reassurance rapist or the disorganized offender, this area usually translates into an area that is within walking distance (1½ miles) of where he lives, works, or regularly frequents. The size of the zone for those offenders must be adjusted for population density and geographic features (i.e., in more rural areas, the zone may be larger). For offenders with more personal confidence, their zone is larger.

Core Behaviors: The sex offender has three forms of behavior to build his modus operandi (MO) and ritualistic crime behaviors. The behaviors are verbal (what offender says or demands the victim to say); physical (intentional injurious force used during sexual assault); and sexual (type and sequence of sexual acts in which a victim is forced to participate). How an offender implements each category of behavior reveals his motivation for a sexual assault and the degree to which the behaviors are fantasy driven and demonstrate his criminal sophistication.

Criminal Behavior versus Noncriminal Behavior: In committing a crime, an offender uses the type and level of behavior with which he is comfortable, and is compatible with his personality. Those behaviors closely parallel his general behavioral framework in his noncrime situations. For example, if a rapist is abusive, vulgar, and demeaning, he will act in a similar manner with women he encounters in his noncrime life.

Criminal Investigative Analysis: An umbrella term encompassing several processes or conclusions. CIA can be mistakenly used to refer to criminal personality profiling, but profiling is only one of the analytical products. Criminal investigative analysis can result in an indirect personality assessment, equivocal death analysis, investigative suggestions, trial strategy, characteristics and traits (profile) of unidentified offenders, interview strategy, and a threat assessment. Criminal investigative analysis utilizes the analysis of all known crime scene data and useful investigative efforts conducted to the date of the analysis.

Properly used, CIA involves three analytical steps considering all of the core behaviors individually. An experienced analyst may be skilled enough to process the three steps mentally. The pencil-and-paper process consists of dividing a sheet of paper into three columns and labeling each. Column 1 is "Individual Behavioral Act"; Column 2 is "Why Was This Behavior Done?," and Column 3 is "What Type of Person Would Do This?"

In Column 1, each piece of known behavior is examined separately from other pieces. Directly from the item in Column 1, a multi-item list is made of each possible explanation for the act, which is recorded in Column 2. In Column 3, each item in Column 2 is connected to a type of person who would behave in that manner. Column 3 should utilize lay terminology and brief descriptive phrases (i.e., out of control, undisciplined, messy, organized, etc.). When completed, the descriptors in Column 3 should contain a pattern of related terms that will reflect on the person, motivation, criminal sophistication, relationship with the victim, amount of time spent in the crime scene, levels of control of the victim, and so on.

Dangle Question: This type of question is also known as a bait question. The concept is to provide a carefully worded question, usually based on a "what-if" premise, to see if an interviewee will alter or change any part of his story, for example, "What if I find a witness who can place you near the crime scene?"

Erotica: Any item, photograph, behavioral act, or literature that an individual finds sexually arousing is considered erotica. Others may find the same item ordinary and not arousing. It is the individual's personal assessment of the item that causes it to be stimulating to him. Valuing the items as erotic is individualistic and developed in the person's fantasies.

False Allegation: A term used to describe a false claim by a pseudovictim of having been sexually assaulted or stalked or having received threatening or obscene notes or telephone calls.

Fantasy: A criminal concept for offenders for whom MO features of not getting caught, successfully escaping, and completing the crimes are no longer stimulating or satisfying. In that situation, an offender may search for alternative fulfilling behaviors. By definition, these new behaviors will go beyond the three features of MO. The search occurs by way of daydreams, also known as fantasies. Within the fantasy structure, the offender will orchestrate and sequence the core behaviors of verbal, injurious physical, and sexual strategies. Fantasy is a mental rehearsal of his contemplated crime or a template of what he wants to accomplish. The extent of that search is limited only by the imagination and intelligence of the offender. As part of developing his fantasized behaviors, he will also attempt to work out methods to not leave evidence for the police.

Force Levels: A rapist has four levels of force that he may apply when gaining and maintaining control of the victim. Each of the levels is indicative of the rapist's motivation and his intensity of anger and hatred of women. The four levels are as follows: (1) minimal force with little or no physical violence except a mild slapping to intimidate or gain a victim's attention or compliance (power reassurance); (2) moderate force; the victim is painfully and repeatedly slapped or struck even when not resisting. Most often, the victim requires no medical attention (power assertive). (3) Excessive force is found in cases in which the victim is seriously beaten, resulting in bruises and lacerations sufficient to require medical attention and possible hospitalization (anger retaliatory). (4) The victim is subjected to extreme violence that causes severe injuries necessitating extensive hospitalization or ends with her death (sexual sadism).

Good Cop/Bad Cop: This is a tried-and-true interview technique with opposing points of view being presented about the offender, his motivation, and his crime behaviors. It may be played out with two officers being present to confront him with their alternating harsh and mild views of his crime behaviors. It is just as effective when only one officer is present who presents the harsh view held by someone else, such as his supervisor or the prosecutor, and then contrasts those condemnations with his milder, more appealing view of the same topics.

High-Risk Crime: A crime committed at a time or location that posed a great threat of discovery to the offender. This category of crime is normally attributed to the "disorganized" criminal personality. Use of alcohol or other drugs will greatly enhance the risk potential of the offender by lowering his or her inhibitions.

High-Risk Victim: The victim is a person who, because of occupation, sexual history, lifestyle, or a given set of circumstances, would be highly vulnerable to a violent crime. Such victims make the crime analysis a very difficult undertaking because their lifestyle opens them to possible victimization by a large number of criminal types.

Hypnosis Question: The concept for both the polygraph and hypnosis questions is to provide an opportunity for a suspect to prove his truthfulness or innocence by either taking a polygraph test or undergoing hypnosis. There are two keys to using both techniques. First, the idea for the need to use either technique is attributed to the interviewer's supervisor. By blaming the supervisor for the requirement to be hypnotized or polygraphed, there is less chance of creating a breach between the interviewer and interviewee. Second, the primary question is to be immediately followed up with a question inquiring as to how the interviewee will do in either situation when he is asked about the criminal issue.

Impulsive Offender: Sexual offenders may be either impulsive or ritualistic. Impulsive offenders are driven by basic, simple, and underdeveloped criminal thoughts, as opposed to ritualistic offenders whose behaviors are considered, developed, and expanded in the fantasy process. The impulsive sex offender employs an M.O. process which is driven by simple thoughts, not by a better developed fantasy driven course of action about the criminal behaviors to be used. Because MO is a learned behavior, the impulsive sex offender is likely to change the way in which he implements the features of his MO. For a complete understanding of impulsive and ritualistic offenders a cluster of terms such as M.O., ritualism, paraphilia, and fantasy development must be understood collectively.

Indirect Personality Assessment (IPA): An assessment of an individual based on information provided by people who know him or her. No data are gathered by directly communicating with the subject. The questions are categorized to deal with all facets of the subject's lifestyle, history, rearing environment, parental relationships, and so on. This technique has many applications, including utilization in preparing for interviews, for assessing his reaction to a stressful event and his propensity to use violence, how to best cross-examine him, and other similar situations.

Interview Plan: The plan is made in preparation for conducting an interview or interrogation. It becomes the expected structure of the contact, including questions that are anticipated, techniques and strategies to be employed, and a list of pertinent data connected to the interview. The interview plan ensures that certain points are covered, establishes a comfortable pattern for the interviewer, paces the interview, allows for verbal and nonverbal responses to be measured, and so on. The plan is a central piece in the targeted subject interview.

Low-Risk Victim: A person who is at a low risk of becoming a victim of a violent crime has certain personality and lifestyle traits. Their victimology (sexual habits, lifestyle, pastimes, etc.) does not suggest that he or she is a likely candidate to become the victim of a violent attack. A person's risk level may increase because of who they associate with and the locations they visit. Should this person become a victim of a violent crime, this suggests that the offender targeted the victim, took advantage of the vulnerability of the person, or was personally associated with the person.

Methods of Approach to Victim: An offender only has three methods for approaching a victim: (1) the con approach, by which he lulls the victim with a story or trick before becoming aggressive; (2) the blitz, by which the offender takes control of the victim by an immediate and disabling assault; and (3) the surprise method, by which the offender lies in wait for the victim from a position of concealment or enters her residence, usually under the cover of darkness.

MO (Method of Operation; Modus Operandi): Learned behavior that is ever changing. It is developed over a period of time, and its principal functions are to protect the offender's security and safety, ensure success, and facilitate escape. When attempting to link one case to another it is noted that in sex crimes the offender's M.O. is valid for only 3 to 4 months as it is a learned behavior and therefore subject to alteration.

Moderate-Risk Victim: Such persons would normally not be expected to become the victim of a violent crime, but because of the environment, who they are with, or what they were doing at the time of confrontation, the risk of becoming a victim of a violent attack is elevated.

Motivation: A basic understanding of motive is reflected in the question, "What's in it for me?" Motive may often be determined by an examination of the behaviors left at a crime scene or through the interview of the victim in cases of rape.

Normal and Natural Occurrences: Generally, events occur and are reported in accordance with what would be expected as "natural and normal." This is one accurate measuring device for credibility and believability of the statements of victims, witnesses, and suspects.

Nuisance Sexual Offense: These are nonfelony sexual crimes such as window peeping (peeping tom), exhibitionism (flashing), telephone scatology (obscene phone calls), obscene notes, and frottage (rubbing against another).

Open-Ended Questions: This style of question is the preferred question type as it (1) forces a person to provide information; (2) does not contaminate the interview product; (3) gives a subject the opportunity to lie, which often benefits the interviewer. The open-ended question begins with phrases such as "Tell me ... "; "Describe ... "; and "Explain how ... ."

Paraphilia: Formerly termed *sexual deviation*, paraphilias are characterized by intense sexual urges or fantasies generally involving (1) inanimate objects, (2) suffering or humiliation of self or another, or (3) children or other nonconsenting partners. They may or may not be harmful to the individual or others. The most common paraphilias are exhibitionism, fetishism, frotteurism, pedophilia, sexual masochism, sexual sadism, transvestic fetishism, and voyeurism. A paraphile will usually be involved in two or more paraphilias.

Personality: Personality involves the behaviors of a person and is usually based initially on an evaluation and judgment of the person's exterior actions, not his or her inner values and attitudes. Personality is demonstrated in behaviors, but most people have a "secret" side of their personality that is closely held and not revealed except within the commission of a crime. Those secret behaviors may be revealed and used in the evaluation of the whole person and his personality.

Planting Ideas; Planting Seeds: Interview technique that features the investigator relating various ways an investigation may be conducted and the likely investigative or forensic results. His statements are bolstered with stories about how other investigations have been successful with these techniques being employed. The concept is for this outline of investigative techniques to provide a framework of features that a suspect may perceive as threatening to his identification as the offender or that may lead to confirming evidence identifiable with him.

Polygraph Question: With or without the intent of using a polygraph test, the officer may indicate that someone in a position of higher authority may ask the suspect to validate his story by taking a polygraph. The question is, "If my boss [state his position] thinks it is necessary, would you be willing to take a polygraph about this matter?" The question is asked directly to the suspect and includes the position of the higher-ranking officer. In my personal experience, it is rare for a suspect to decline, especially if the context of the question is that the test may be given at some nonspecific date in the future. On receiving affirmation that he will take the test, ask how he thinks the results will reflect on him when he is tested on whether he committed the crime or not. A guilty party is likely to immediately backpedal by stating reasons why he is not a good candidate for a test (i.e., he takes medicine, the tests are not valid, he would need to consult his doctor or attorney, etc.).

Power Assertive Rapist: This is one of the four types of rapists often assigned by the police. He is motivated to rape by his sense of entitlement and his confidence in his masculinity and manhood and his desire to demonstrate those abilities to the victim. He uses a somewhat elevated level of violence.

Power Reassurance Rapist: This is another of the four types of rapists often assigned by the police. This type is the most prevalent but least violent of all rapists. His most outstanding personality feature is very low self-esteem, which motivates him to rape so he may be "reassured" regarding his virility and ability to have sexual relationships with females. He needs to demonstrate his ability to himself to bolster his confidence and esteem. He engages in many fantasies in which he designs his verbal, physical, and sexual behaviors to fulfill his esteem needs.

Predator: A term usually reserved for an individual who is continually on the prowl for a situation, location, and victim that match his ideal construct for the commission of his crime. Predators are considered to have the ability to quickly evaluate a person and a location in the context of successfully deciding to act out criminally.

Pseudovictim: This is a term used for a person falsely claiming to be a victim of a rape or stalking or recipient of a threatening communication. It most commonly refers to a person falsely claiming to have been raped.

Question Buildup: This is an interviewing technique used to procure the attention of an interviewee by a brief explanation of the investigator's experience level, the history of and importance of the question, and why the question is pertinent to the person being interviewed. This method should not be overused but reserved for questions that truly have an impact on the interview.

Reading Crime Scene Behavior: Reading the scene is the basic tool for an investigator when commencing an investigation. A trained eye will take in the offender's behaviors and the mixture of his behavior with that of the victim. The investigator's goal is to extract those behaviors individually and collectively so that he may determine specific features of the offender and sequence his acts. The determination of offender traits and characteristics is based on the premises that behavior reflects personality: You are as you behave.

Reading Minds: This powerful technique is available for combining several techniques for use in appeals phase of interviewing a suspect. The essence of this technique is to relate, almost as an aside, a story which incorporates a brief buildup of the interviewer and statements pertinent to the case being investigated such as possible developments as the investigation proceeds (dangle questions). Included are statements about what the investigator has learned about offenders from similar cases. The subject's name is never mentioned as it is more powerful to allow him to conclude that the lessons learned about how offenders think (and thought at the time of the crime) and how he resolved issues. It is as if the interviewer is talking about the offender's innermost thoughts and reading his mind.

Ritualistic Offender: Rituals are the repetitive and psychosexually gratifying behaviors of a sexual offender. These practices are not to be confused with an offender's modus operandi (MO). Sexual offenders may be either impulsive or ritualistic. Ritualistic offenders are unsatisfied with their MO as they find it lacking as far as sexual arousal and gratification. With those feelings, they may enter into the use of some degree of fantasy in search of behaviors outside those necessary to commit a sexual offense. If the new behaviors are satisfying and arousing, they will be repeated over and over, becoming rituals. The offender is dependent on the presence of those rituals to find pleasure and fulfillment in his sexual offenses.

RPMs: An acronym for rationalization, projection, and minimization. All are ego defense mechanisms. These techniques initially downplay the suspect's culpability by omitting the suspect's provocative behavior, blaming others, or minimizing the suspect's conduct. It may be necessary to suggest that the suspect's criminality was an accident or the result of an unexpected turn of events, events that were perhaps provoked by the victim. The investigator's goal is to obtain an admission or to place the suspect near the scene or with the victim. From the original admission of guilt, the experienced investigator refines his techniques by using all the case facts to point out the flaws and insufficiency in the original admission and obtain a fuller, more accurate description of the suspect's criminal behavior. The practiced interviewer uses the initial admission as a wedge to open the door to additional incriminating statements.

Self-Esteem: When a person takes stock of himself, his successes, and failures, he evaluates the type of person he is and decides the extent of his pride in himself. His choices are positive, neutral, or negative. How someone values himself determines his capacity for making conversation, interacting with others, and his ability to empathize. These qualities are transported by the individual into his criminal acts and establish the manner in which he will utilize his verbal, sexual, and physical behaviors in the commission of a crime. The physical aspect selects for evaluation those physical acts that are intended to knowingly hurt, harm, or damage a victim. In rape situations, these core behaviors are indicative of motive and criminal sophistication along with other offender traits. The recognition of the crime plan surrounding the core behaviors is critical to typing rapists.

Sexual Bondage: A technique for physical or emotional binding of self (masochistic) or another (sadistic) for sexual excitement. It may be demonstrated by restriction of the senses (using blindfolds, gags, hoods) or by the restriction of movement of the limbs. Sexual bondage is manifested by any of four characteristics (symmetry, unnecessary bindings, variety of positions, or extreme care in the placement of the bindings [neatness]).

Sexual Disorders: There are only two official sexual disorders. One revolves around different types of organ dysfunction and is commonly associated with males but affects women also. A major difference is that the male is unable to perform sexually, but the female can still function. The second disorder is called a *paraphilia*, which originates in fantasy as this is where the individual turns when usual and ordinary sexual practices are not fulfilling. Paraphilias are deviant sexual practices condemned by society. Because they are fulfilling to a particular individual they will have become a regular practice and designated as rituals. Therefore, paraphilias are regular and deviant practices.

Sexual Ritualism: Acts committed by the offender that are unnecessary to the accomplishment of the crime. Such acts are repeated by the offender over a series of crimes. The acts are performed to increase his or her psychosexual gratification. Ritualism should not be confused with modus operandi. For a fuller understanding of sexual ritualism see also the definitions of M.O., paraphilia, ritualistic offender, and fantasy development.

Sexual Sadist Rapist: This is the rapist who derives sexual excitement and arousal from the physical, emotional, and sexual suffering of victims he tortures with implements and tools. His excitement is not derived from the torture but from the victim's response to the torture and the victim's pleas and submission.

Souvenir: This refers to a personal item belonging to the victim of a violent crime that is taken by the offender. Items most commonly taken include an article of jewelry or clothing, photograph, or driver's license. The item taken from the victim is a reminder of a pleasurable encounter and may be used for masturbatory fantasies. The offender taking an item as a souvenir is typically an inadequate person who is likely to keep it for a long period of time or give it away to a significant other in his life. *See also* Trophy.

Staged Scene: This is a crime scene in which someone (most often the offender) arranges the scene or commits certain acts to have the scene convey a motivational intent different from the original motive or to mislead investigators regarding the logical suspect.

Targeted Subject Interview (TSI): This form of interviewing is a highly specific and most effective interview format. It may also be called Offender-Specific Interviewing. The interview utilizes the deduced weaknesses and vulnerabilities of an offender as determined by a "read" of the crime scene, details from victim and/or witness interviews, and early investigative results. The most effective are built around the weaknesses and vulnerabilities. TSI may be combined with any interview techniques, tactics, or strategies.

Test of Commitment: A test of commitment is comprised of several questions designed to determine if a victim, witness, or suspect is standing by his version of events because they are truthful statements.

Themes: Themes are stories, sometimes called *arguments* or *pitches,* used to convince a suspect that his criminal behavior was not as aberrant, offensive, or as brutal as it appeared. Often, the themes utilize RPMs to make convincing statements about a suspect's minor involvement in a crime or to project guilt or responsibility onto others.

Threshold Diagnosis: This term describes an impulsively provided opinion about a case without having access to all pertinent facts or prior to having analyzed case materials. This tendency is very dangerous and leads to narrowed point of view, poor judgment, and improper focus on the wrong suspect.

Triggering Cue: This refers to a part of an offender's preoffense behavior. The cue will usually involve a personal setback or stressor that precipitates his criminal acting out. The offender's stimulation may be in his interpersonal relationships, financial dealings, or family/spousal relationships or affect his emotional composure.

Trophy: A trophy is a personal item belonging to the victim of a violent crime that is taken by the responsible offender. Most commonly taken items include an article of jewelry or clothing, a driver's license, or a photograph. The item represents a victory or conquest to the criminal and may be used for masturbatory fantasies. The offender who takes a trophy is typically an aggressive individual who is unlikely to retain the item and may dispose of it or give it to a significant other in his life. *See also* Souvenir.

Typologies: The typing or classifying of offenders is an attempt to divide those individuals into groupings using preselected criteria such as motivation or type of victim selected, etc. Typologies create a shorthand understood by professionals who study offenders. Some typologies are very exacting and may have many divisions of types. A finely tuned typology of this type is preferred by clinicians, who use the types for diagnosis and treatment. Other professions are equally well served by few, broader types sufficient for their understanding of an offender to aid in investigating and interviewing.

Victimology: A behavioral study of the victim of a violent crime. Included are behaviors that have an impact on the analysis of the crime (most frequently homicide but is appropriate in rape investigations). The analyst examines the victim's personality characteristics, reputation, strengths and weaknesses, occupation, hobbies, lifestyle, drug and alcohol usage, choice of associates, sexual history, habits, and pastimes to form an opinion regarding the individual's risk of becoming the victim of a violent crime.

Victim Risk: The degree to which the victim's history or circumstances contributed to the likelihood that he or she would become a victim. A
victim's risk category may change dramatically due to faulty decision
making or a judgmental error on his or her part.

Victim Type Selection (Targeted, Opportunistic): There are two victim
types. One is a person who is selected and targeted by an offender.
This victim is referred to as a *targeted victim*. The other is a victim
by reason of a chance encounter or crossing paths with an offender.
This victim is labeled a *victim of opportunity*. Some victims are first
victims of opportunity who are then subjected to further scrutiny by
an offender, becoming a targeted victim.

Wordsmithing: This is a talent for properly constructing a syntax that utilizes words that are sufficiently appealing and meaningful to a victim,
witness, or suspect to enable them to communicate the information
sought by an interviewer.

Appendix B

The Significance of Victimology*

Michael R. Napier and Robert R. Hazelwood

Police officers responded to a noise complaint in an expensive apartment building and were directed to a third floor residence. The apartment door, which had a peephole, was slightly ajar, and the chain lock was dangling from the door. On entering the foyer, the police were confronted with blood on the floor and walls. They also noticed blood and signs of a struggle in the kitchen, living room, and bedroom. In the bedroom, the victim, a 29-year-old Caucasian female, was found lying on her stomach and nude from the waist down. She had been stabbed in excess of 30 times, manually strangled, and beaten severely in the face, head, and body with blunt force. The injuries to the head and body had most likely been caused by shoes or boots. She had defense wounds to her hands and forearms and had been forcefully penetrated vaginally and anally, but there was no evidence of seminal fluids. A bloody dildo was lying on the bedroom floor. Preliminary investigation determined that the victim was Christine Jurgens (a pseudonym) and that she was single, lived alone, and was an attorney. Her purse had been taken from the scene, but no knives were missing. It is believed that the killer brought the murder weapon with him.

What happened in the apartment? What was the motive for the crime? Who was responsible?

Every homicide investigator asks these questions when confronted with a death scene. The answers may lie in the answer to a fourth question: Who was Christine Jurgens? All we know thus far is that she was a 29-year-old single white female who was an attorney and lived alone in an upscale apart-

* The original version of this article was first printed in 2003 as Napier, Michael R., and Robert R. Hazelwood, Homicide Investigation: The Significance of Victimology. Edited by Ashley Sutton. *National Academy Associate* (FBI National Academy Associates) V, no. 5 (Sepember/October 2003): 14–32.

ment building, but we really do not know *who* she was (victimology), and that may be the most important question in death cases.

For the purposes of this discussion, *victimology* is defined as the collection and study of all significant information about the victim in a death investigation. Such information will include answers to the following questions: What were the characteristics and traits of Ms. Jurgens? What were her hobbies, her habits, her sexual interests, her lifestyle, her reputation, and her pastimes? Who were her associates? Did she habitually place herself in situations or locations that put her at risk of becoming the victim of a violent crime? A more comprehensive listing of information to be gathered is provided in the appendix to this article.

While such information is also critical in other criminal investigations of violence, such as sexual assault (Hazelwood and Burgess, 2001), equivocal deaths (Hazelwood and Michaud, 2001), autoerotic fatalities (Hazelwood, Dietz, and Burgess, 1982), and suicide, this discussion addresses its significance as it specifically relates to homicide investigations.

A comprehensive study of the victim's history will provide the officer with an invaluable tool that will help in focusing the investigation, conserving valuable resources, and making sense of the chaos (or orderliness) present at the crime scene. In turn, such knowledge can significantly enhance one's ability to reliably interpret the offender–victim interaction and develop a theory regarding why this particular person was selected by this particular offender at this particular time and location.

Questions, Questions, Questions

In Ms. Jurgens's case, blood was found in the foyer and hall. It is obvious that the initial attack took place in this location. Why? Was Ms. Jurgens security conscious and therefore one who would have looked through the peephole before opening the door? Or was she the type of person who would simply open the door, not knowing who was outside? If she did look through the peephole, would she only open the door to someone she recognized?

Detectives are routinely trained to identify the presence of physical and trace evidence and take steps to protect that material from contamination. In fact, many departments now have specialized units (i.e., crime scene investigation) specially trained and equipped to collect, preserve, and analyze such evidence. Less well understood are the behaviors that explain the location and patterns of that evidence. In many instances, the placement of the evidence is determined by the extent to which an offender has control over a victim, and the amount of control over a particular person is frequently determined by the personality and subsequent reactions of the victim.

Why did Ms. Jurgens become a murder victim? What was the killer's reason for selecting her?

Was she the targeted victim of a serial killer? Was she a randomly selected victim? Or, was she the victim of a killer who was personally angry at her, and if so, for what reason?

Every offender has victim selection criteria. For some, the criteria are a part of a complicated sexual fantasy; for others, they are simply a matter of randomness (i.e., victim in wrong place at wrong time), and for still others, they have to do with a motive of revenge or profit.

Ted Bundy, a sexual serial killer, most assuredly had multiple factors that he considered in the selection of a victim, but it is known that a primary criterion in his choosing a woman for victimization was what he described as "worthiness." During the last 4 days of his life, Bundy advised FBI agent (retired) Bill Hagmaier that, at the height of his criminal career, he selected "worthy victims." He explained that anyone could obtain a prostitute off the street (like the Green River killer) or a child from the ghetto (like the Atlanta child killer), but to convince an intelligent, middle-class woman (a person worthy of being chosen) to willingly walk away with a total stranger took class (personal conversation with Mr. Hagmaier).

Leonard Lake, another sexual serial killer operating in California in the 1980s, made a preoffense videotape in which he stated that the "ideal" victim was 18 to 22 years old, slim, petite, small breasted, and with shoulder-length hair. He is known to have been involved in the murder of several women. The women were not involved in activities or at locations that made them particularly susceptible to victimization.

Robert Pickton, a Canadian believed to be responsible for the deaths of several women and known as "the pig farmer," was much less discerning. He is believed to have restricted his selection process to women who were active in street prostitution and to have solicited them to return to his residence, a trailer located on a pig farm.

Jack Trawick, a confessed serial murderer, largely left the selection process to chance. He would attack whenever the urge struck him, and he was not hesitant about attacking at any time or at any location. He abducted women who were walking on the street, driving cars, or in a shopping center parking lot. His selection criteria seem to have simply been gender, availability, and vulnerability.

Then, there are killings in which the victim selection process is limited to a specific victim being targeted. In such cases, the offender is frequently driven by a motive of personal anger or profit (i.e., marital murders, kidnapers, organized crime "hits").

Was there something about the lifestyle of Ms. Jurgens that contributed to her becoming a murder victim?

The Victim Risk Factor

The victimology will provide the officer with the victim's *risk factor* for investigative consideration. The risk factor is the degree to which a person's history or circumstances contributed to her victimization. In other words, how likely was the possibility that a particular person would become the victim of a violent crime? Would she be considered a high-risk victim, a moderate-risk victim, or a low-risk victim (Hazelwood and Burgess, 2001)? The high-risk classification is assigned to those individuals whose lifestyle or employment consistently exposes them to danger. Such a person could be *expected* to become the victim of a violent crime because of who they were (i.e., prostitute, drug dealer), what they were doing at the time (i.e., hitchhiking), or where they were physically located (i.e., high-crime area) when targeted by the offender.

A low-risk classification would be assigned a person whose personal, professional, and social lives did not normally expose them to the threat of violent crime (i.e., a stay-at-home mom who was raped and murdered in her subdivision home at 2 p.m.). It is not expected that such a person would become the victim of a violent crime. In our experience, such victims have been specifically targeted by the offender.

A moderate-risk classification is assigned a person who, while generally of good reputation, has an escalated possibility of becoming a victim because of working hours or environment or because of circumstances beyond the person's control (i.e., car breaking down on the interstate).

From what we know at this point in the discussion, it would seem that Ms. Jurgens was a low-risk victim who led an enviable life. She was well educated, an attorney, obviously successful, and enjoying the luxuries of life when she was killed in her apartment. However, as is the case with most people, there may have been a part of her life that was not known to those around her. Only an extensive investigation into her life would determine whether this was true in her case.

And Even More Questions

Why were signs of a struggle evident in the kitchen, living room, and bedroom? Was Christine Jurgens the type of person who was assertive (even aggressive), and was she physically fit? If so, *might* this account for why she fought even though her assailant was armed with a knife? On the other hand, if she was verbally and physically passive, it would seem that there must be another reason that she fought so fiercely.

Why was she stabbed in excess of 30 times? The scene documented that the struggle continued into several of the apartment's rooms. Was that the reason for the multiple stab wounds (i.e., the offender was trying to subdue the victim or to stop her from screaming)? Or, was it because he wanted to ensure that she was dead? Or, a third possibility, was it because the offender was personally angry at her, and the multiple stabs were simply an expression of that rage? Then, if that was the case, what was the basis for that savage anger?

Ms. Jurgens was beaten and kicked in the head and body after she was on the floor. Did the killer simply want to quiet her moans, or was it again an expression of anger? There are so many questions to be answered and many more to follow.

The Motive and Suspects

From an initial assessment of the crime scene, many thoughts will flow, but none is more important than a theory of motive. When the motive has been established, many of the questions that have already been asked will be answered. Again, the investigator must turn to the victimology to provide him with working theories regarding the motive. Of equal importance, the victimology will assist the officer in helping him to eliminate false theories of motive. If the investigator were to learn that the victim was a compulsive gambler and was in debt for more than $300,000, those facts would certainly suggest a viable motive and could quite possibly provide a specific list of suspects. However, if it was learned that Ms. Jurgens was a heavy user of cocaine, that would suggest a different set of potential motives and another list of suspects. Conversely, if she were not engaged in any type of illegal activity but was simply a successful criminal defense attorney, the detective would have yet another set of theories and possible suspects.

Of course, any time a female is the victim of a homicide, consideration must be given to the possibility of a sexual crime. To whom did the bloody foreign object (dildo) belong? The victim? If so, it became a weapon of opportunity, and its use may very well have been an impulsively committed act by the killer, or equally possible, it could have been an intentional act specifically designed to mislead the investigator by staging the crime as a sexual offense. If, on the other hand, the killer brought the dildo, then it becomes a premeditated act, one that identifies still another group of suspects (i.e., sex offenders).

Interview or Interrogation Strategies

When the investigation produces a viable suspect, it is the responsibility of the investigator to be fully prepared for the interview of that person. It should go without saying that the interviewer must be very knowledgeable of the suspect in any major case and certainly in a case involving homicide. However, because of a variety of reasons, the first reaction to the identification of a possible subject is frequently to bring him in for interview.

Any experienced investigator could not seriously disagree with the statement that a working understanding of what happened (i.e., sequence and specific locations of behaviors) at the death scene would contribute significantly to the interview. Any experienced officer could not seriously disagree that knowing how and why the victim was selected or knowing what the criminal motive was and how that motive is linked to the suspect would also make a valuable contribution to the interview. It all necessarily begins with the development of a comprehensive understanding of victimology.

Victim's Residence

While the scene is being searched, the investigator should make it a priority to look for any items that could potentially provide him with information about the victim. Valuable investigative leads pertaining to the victim's associates may be elicited from such sources as diaries, journals, name and phone directories, and E-mail address books. Information about the victim's sexual lifestyle may be found through the presence of sexual devices, literature, videotapes, condoms, and lubricating jelly in the bedside table and again E-mail. Additional sources at the scene would include information on the hard drive of a computer (i.e., Web site selections), electronic manager device, bankbooks, phone records, and calendars.

This by no means exhausts the potential sources of information about the victim that may be found at her residence, but it does provide suggested places to begin.

Friends, Family, and Associates

Because the victimology essentially provides the investigator with a blueprint for leads to be followed in the conduct of the investigation, the collection and processing of the victim's history and lifestyle should begin with the first interviews. In the facts presented thus far in the hypothetical case example, some potentially valuable sources of information about the victim follow logically (i.e., neighbors and coworkers). Thereafter, it should be automatic procedure to make the victim's personality, lifestyle, and habits central areas of inquiry with each person questioned. We can practically guarantee that every neighbor and coworker knows *something* about the victim that will help the investigator move ever closer to the persons who have even more useful information about the deceased. This process may be visualized as the ripples caused by a stone dropping into water. By beginning with the outer ring and following each ring inward, the investigator will identify those having the most intimate knowledge of the victim.

The information being sought is, by its very nature, necessarily personal; consequently, the interviews of family and friends should be conducted individually and in a private setting. Depending on the interviewee's association with the victim, investigators can expect to encounter greater or lesser degrees of reluctance in providing lifestyle information about the victim. Some may regard such disclosures as disrespectful to the memory of the deceased, and others may view it as outright betrayal. To compensate for this reluctance, the investigator must ensure that the person being interviewed clearly understands that such questions are not intended to suggest that the victim was in any way responsible for her death, and that the information is most necessary. The investigator may choose to explain the rationale and necessity for such personal questions and that there is a common goal shared by the police and family members or friends, which is to bring closure to the matter by identifying the responsible person.

The reliability of the information provided must be assessed based on the nature of the interviewee's relationship with the victim, the frequency of their interaction, the length of their association, and the date of last contact. Each interviewee should also be asked for names of others who have the potential of providing additional significant information.

Let's Assume ...

Criminal investigators are taught throughout their careers never to assume anything. To do so, it goes, increases the potential of making an *ass* out of *u* and *me*. But for the purpose of this discussion, let us assume that since the discovery of her body, the information presented next has been developed about the hypothetical Christine Jurgens.

Characteristics and Traits

The investigation determined that Ms. Jurgens was a very intelligent person who had been dedicated to achieving success in her professional life. She was known as a "type A" personality and had worked extremely hard since graduating from law school. She had recently attained partner status in her law firm, the youngest to have achieved that position in her firm's history, and some of her contemporaries were jealous of this achievement. She was described as a very confident and assertive person who had a large number of associates, all of whom were within her own socioeconomic circle. On the other hand, she made little effort to be cordial to the secretaries, clerks, and doormen at her office building, and this resulted in their feeling that she considered herself to be their better.

She was security conscious, and she had installed a peephole and a dead-bolt lock on her apartment door as well as a security system within the residence. While her apartment building had no doorman, it was equipped with a speaker and buzzer system, and the tenants controlled who entered the building.

She was not a religious person, and she seldom visited her parents or other family members, all of whom resided in another state. She once told a colleague that she could only depend on herself, and that her family and God were part of her history, not her future.

Pastimes

Ms. Jurgens had no known pastimes other than reading and physical exercise. She had several expensive pieces of exercise equipment in her apartment. It was her habit to get up at 3 a.m.; work out and walk to a public park located one-half mile from her residence, where she would read for an hour or so and then jog for 3 miles before showering and going to work at 7 a.m. She also belonged to an upscale gym, where she had a personal trainer, and she would exercise each evening at the gym. Consequently, she was in exceptional physical condition and was noted for being very conscious of her health. She was a social drinker who was never seen intoxicated.

Lifestyle

Ms. Jurgens dated often and frequented expensive clubs and restaurants. It was learned that she was sexually active with a select number of men, all of whom were attorneys and within her own social class. Some of her sexual partners were married, and the marital status of her partners did not seem to concern the victim, but her colleagues did not consider Ms. Jurgens to be promiscuous. She refused to go out on blind dates because "I don't have to." She wore expensive clothing and jewelry, drove a luxury car, and regularly participated in business-related social functions. Her apartment was expensively furnished, and she had installed several thousand dollars worth of television and sound systems. She was apparently discrete with her guests as the apartment manager had never received any complaints from her neighbors. No one reported seeing a dildo in her residence, but several said that it would surprise them to learn that she owned one.

Autopsy

The autopsy revealed that Ms. Jurgens was 3½ months pregnant. No one admitted knowing about the pregnancy. Toxicology tests determined that there were no drugs or alcohol in her system at the time of her death.

Now What Do I Do?

These pieces of information about the upwardly mobile Ms. Jurgens would certainly throw a few twists into the investigation of her murder. We have learned that she was not the most popular person at her workplace. There were coworkers who were jealous of her, and she had antagonized those she referred to as the "little people" around her. She had a superior attitude toward her family as well. Ms. Jurgens was in excellent physical condition and habitually frequented a public park in the early morning hours. She was obviously conscious of the possibility of crime and had taken precautions to protect herself within her residence by installing a peephole, dead-bolt lock, and a security system.

She was sexually active with several men, including some who were married, and she was 3½ months pregnant at the time of her death. She exhibited her wealth by wearing expensive jewelry and clothing, driving a luxury car, and frequenting expensive restaurants. Her apartment contained several thousand dollars worth of sound and exercise equipment.

The picture has certainly expanded compared to when the police first responded to the complaint at Ms. Jurgens's apartment, and while the investigator's task of determining what took place, what the motive was, and who was responsible has seemingly become more difficult, it has in fact become more focused by providing some excellent investigative leads. The investigator knows she was security conscious and would not have opened the door to a stranger. He knows she was physically sound and assertive and would have fought strongly. He knows that she did not use alcohol or drugs and would not have associated with people who did use substances. He knows that she was 3½ months pregnant, and being an intelligent woman, she would have certainly recognized that fact very early. Yet, she chose not to terminate the pregnancy—why? As stated, there are some excellent leads *because* the investigator better understands and knows the murder victim.

Conclusion

It is recognized that investigative resources are a universally scarce commodity. However, we have consulted on thousands of homicide cases and consistently found that the early investment of investigative assets to learning the details of the victim's personality and lifestyle results in a more effective and efficient investigation. Conversely, the less that is known about the victim, the more likely the investigation will become bogged down with unanswered questions.

The gathering of information about the victim is of such importance that it should begin on the investigator's arrival at the crime scene with the questioning of witnesses and neighbors. The victim is well served when this investigative step is given priority and undertaken by each officer involved in each aspect of the investigation.

It has been our experience that the most competent and capable investigators are in the habit of reviewing and reevaluating their theories about the crime with each new piece of information because they recognize that a criminal investigation is a living entity, and it must be fed with an open mind. As you have seen in the case presented in this discussion, that habit is never more vital than when applied to the question of how the victim lived and approached life. The more that the investigator learns about the victim's quirks, preferences, taboos, habits, lifestyle, and sexuality, the greater the focus he will bring to his investigative task.

Capturing the victimology will (1) assist in the examination and interpretation of the crime scene; (2) identify potential motives; (3) allow a ranking of potential suspects; (4) assist in the questioning of witnesses; and (5) aid the investigator in formulating interview strategies of potential suspects.

Appendix A

In addition to the areas of interest briefly addressed in this discussion, the investigator may desire to inquire about some or all of the areas listed next. Depending on the circumstances of the homicide, certain aspects of the victim's lifestyle and traits may be more significant than others, and the weight given to each piece of data is dependent on the investigator's assessment of the death. As stated in the discussion, when gathering and weighting the information, the officer should consider the source of provided information, the nature and length of the relationship between the source and the victim, and the frequency of contact between the victim and the person being interviewed. Experienced investigators recognize that all human sources of information come with a bias; therefore, the more varied the pool of data sources, the more valid the final assessment. When attempting to gather information about a homicide victim, it is neither sufficient nor helpful to accept statements at face value. Some statements about the victim may initially seem to be useful but turn out to be superficial, for example, the statement "She was security conscious." Further inquiry should be made by pointedly taking the response to more depth, for instance, "Give me an example of how she impressed you as being security conscious." The following areas of inquiry regarding victimology are set forth as "talking points" for the investigator and are by no means to be considered exhaustive:

Education
Intelligence
Common sense
Hobbies
Physical condition
Employment
Reputation
Marriage(s)
Dating habits
Health
Personality traits
Assertiveness
Recent complaints about people, situations, residential environment
Habits
Pastimes
Sexuality
Security consciousness
Alcohol or drugs
Criminal activities
Usual mode of transportation
Family relationships
Memberships
Friends
Associates
Socioeconomic status

Bibliography

Hazelwood, R. R., and Burgess, A. W., *Practical Aspects of Rape Investigation: A Multidisciplinary Approach*, 3rd ed., 2001, CRC Press, Boca Raton, FL, p. 154.

Hazelwood, R. R., Dietz, P. E., and Burgess, A. W., *Autoerotic Fatalities*, 1982, Lexington Books, Lexington, MA.

Hazelwood, R. R., and Michaud, Stephen G., *Dark Dreams*, 2001, St. Martin's Press, New York, pp. 191–218.

Napier, Michael R., and Baker, Kenneth P., Criminal Personality Profiling, in *Forensic Science: An Introduction to Scientific and Investigative Techniques*, Stuart H. James and Jon J. Nordby (Editors), CRC Press, Boca Raton, FL, 2003.

Appendix C

The Behavior-Oriented Interview of Rape Victims: The Key to Profiling*

Robert R. Hazelwood

Introduction

Some years ago, a police agency submitted a rape investigation report to me and requested that I prepare a profile of the unidentified offender. A brief synopsis of that report follows:

Alicia, a 21-year-old white female was asleep in her apartment when she was suddenly awakened by a man who placed his hand over her mouth and held a knife to her throat. The intruder warned her not to scream or physically resist and told her if she complied with his demands, she would not be harmed. He forced her to remove her nightgown, kissed and fondled her, and then raped her vaginally. He left after warning the victim not to call the police. Ignoring the rapist's warning, she called the police and reported the crime. She told them that nothing had been stolen, and because a pillowcase was over her head during the assault, she could not provide a physical description of her assailant. The police noted that the rapist was with the victim for approximately 1 hour.

In need of additional information to prepare a profile, I provided the police agency with a set of questions specifically designed to elicit victim information concerning the offender's behavior during the assault. Using these questions, the victim was reinterviewed, and as a result, a nine-page single-spaced, typewritten statement was obtained. Based on the additional information, a profile was prepared that included the unidentified offender's age, race, marital status, occupational level, arrest history, socioeconomic status, occupational level, education, and certain personality characteristics.

* This material was originally published in the FBI Law Enforcement Bulletin as Hazelwood, Robert R. The Behavior-oriented Interview of Rape Victims: The Key to Profiling. *FBI Law Enforcement Bulletin* (Federal Bureau of Investigation), September 1983: 231–238.

The rapist was subsequently arrested and confessed to the assault of Alicia and five additional rapes. A comparison of the profile with the offender particulars determined that only the marital status was incorrect.

Motivation

Until I retired in 1994, I was a member of the famed Behavioral Science Unit (BSU) of the Federal Bureau of Investigation (FBI); this unit provided forensic behavioral assistance to law enforcement agencies in their investigation of violent crimes.

Rape is a unique type of crime, and I have had the opportunity to review thousands of police reports and rape victims'; statements over a period of 45 years. While essentials of the crime are typically provided in the reports, there is often a marked absence of information that would provide behavioral clues regarding the motive for the crime. As Groth, Burgess, and Holmstrom (1977) pointed out, rape is a behavior that, while using the sexual parts of the body, primarily serves nonsexual needs.

While it is recognized that a need exists to obtain, from the victim, the criminal's physical characteristics, that information is routinely solicited by the police investigators, and the behavioral information is often ignored. Consequently, I developed a set of questions for rape victims that are designed to elicit a description of the offender's behavior during the crime. Obtaining behavioral information makes it possible for the crime motivation to be identified, and it unquestionably provides the investigator with better insight into the criminal's personality.

The purpose of this discussion is to provide a method of eliciting sufficient behavioral information to allow an opinion to be formed about the characteristics and traits of the unidentified rapist. Throughout this discussion, the terms *investigator*, *interviewer*, and *analyst* are used interchangeably.

Profiling the Rapist

There are three essential steps in preparing a profile of an unidentified rapist:

1. A focused interview of the victim to document the rapist's crime behavior
2. An analysis of that behavior to identify the motive for the crime
3. The compilation of the characteristics and traits of the type of person likely to have committed the crime in the manner reported and for the motive indicated

Interviewing the victim is the most crucial step in the process and is one that detectives should accomplish. The final two steps are to be completed by individuals trained in the process of analyzing crime from a behavioral perspective.

Only the victim can provide the information necessary to initiate a criminal investigation and complete a behavioral analysis of the rape. Therefore, it becomes essential for the investigator to establish a rapport with the victim through a professional and empathetic approach. Such an approach will greatly assist the victim in overcoming feelings of fear, anger, and guilt, all of which will have been generated by the assault.

The interviewers should project an attitude of competence and experience and must not allow personal feelings to interfere with their objectivity. It must be recognized that there are three personalities present during the interview: the victim's, the criminal's, and the interviewer's. The analyst must remember to view the crime from the offender's perspective, and this will better enable the analyst to answer questions such as: What message is the rapist transmitting through the assault? Is it that he is angry and wants to punish women for real or perceived wrongs, or is it that because he has controlled the behaviors of a woman he has therefore proven that he is powerful? To be successful, the interviewers must isolate personal feelings about the crime, the criminal, and the victim. The investigator will be surprised regarding what such an objective and analytical approach reveals about the person responsible for the crime. The following case synopsis provides an excellent example of why this type of approach is necessary:

In a large metropolitan area, a series of rapes had plagued the community over a period of months. In each case, the rapist controlled his victim through threats and intimidation, and even when resisted, he had not resorted to physical violence. One evening, a hospital orderly went off duty at midnight and came on a male beating a nurse in an attempt to subdue and rape her. The orderly went to her rescue and overcame the attacker, holding him until the police arrived. Predictably, the orderly received much attention from the media and was given a citation for bravery from the city. Shortly thereafter, the orderly was arrested for the series of rapes mentioned. During interrogation, he was asked why he had rescued the nurse when he was guilty of similar crimes. He became indignant and advised the officers that they were wrong. He would never hurt a woman.

It is obvious that the less physically violent rapist who rescued the nurse from the more violent rapist equated "hurt" with physical trauma and completely ignored the emotional trauma experienced by his victim.

The determination of the motive for the crime will become clear only through a study of the crime behavior, and once the crime motivation is made known, the trained individual should be able to provide the police with an accurate listing of the offender's characteristics and traits. The basis for this assumption lies in the axiom that behavior reflects personality. The manner in which an individual behaves within various environments provides observers with insight into the type of person he or she is. What a person thinks of himself or herself, how well educated the individual is, how socially skilled the person is, and socioeconomic status are characteristics that are commonly demonstrated through behavior.

How is this possible? It is not uncommon to review two rape cases that are from different investigative jurisdictions, involve different offenders, and yet exhibit strikingly similar crime behaviors. Why is this true? A large part of the answer lies in the previously mentioned statement by Groth, Burgess, and Holmstrom (1977) "Rape is in fact serving primarily non-sexual needs." Consequently, if a similar need (i.e., power) is being met through the crime of rape, it is logical that the assaultive behavior employed to achieve the meeting of that need will also be similar.

Questioning for Behavior

The interview should be conducted in a tactful, professional, probative, and yet sensitive manner. It should be impressed on the victim that the investigator is concerned not only with the arrest and conviction of the offender but also with the victim's welfare. She has been involved in a life-threatening situation, and the importance of recognizing and acknowledging this fact cannot be overemphasized. The victim should be made to understand that, as a result of the interviewer's obtaining detailed information from her, the offender's identification and arrest may be expedited.

Note from the order of the areas to be questioned set forth here that the behavioral-oriented interview is conducted sequentially and in keeping with the crime as it unfolded. Therefore, the interview begins with determining the method used by the offender to approach the victim.

Method of Approach

When a person is confronted with a task, he or she will choose a method with which he or she feels most comfortable and most confident. Consequently, when deciding how to approach a victim, the criminal will select a method that he believes will be successful. I have identified three approaches used by rapists: con, blitz, and surprise.

Approaching the victim openly by using a trick, subterfuge, or ploy to gain close proximity to her is identified as the *con* approach. For example, the rapist may offer or request assistance or directions or even pretend to be selling something. He will initially be pleasant, friendly, and even charming. His goal is to gain the victim's confidence and negate any feelings of danger the victim may have until he is in a position to overcome resistance she might offer. Quite often, and for different reasons, he exhibits a sudden change of attitude once she is in his control. In some instances, the attitudinal change occurs because the offender believes he has to convince the victim of his seriousness, and at other times, it is merely an indication of inner hostility. This style of approach suggests that the rapist is more likely to be extroverted than introverted, is not intimidated by women, and is confident in his ability to interact with them.

The *blitz* approach is demonstrated when the offender immediately employs *injurious* force to subdue his victim. The attack may occur from the front or rear, and the victim is allowed no opportunity to physically or verbally resist. This method of approach strongly suggests feelings of hostility and anger toward women and may be indicative of his relationships with women in noncriminal environments as well as in rape situations.

In the *surprise* approach, the rapist may lay in wait for the victim in the back seat of a car, step out from behind a wall or from the woods, or capture her while she is sleeping. In such cases, he typically uses threats or the presence of a weapon to subdue his victims. This approach indicates that the victim has been targeted or preselected through surveillance or window peeping.

Offender's Control of the Victim

Once the offender has gained physical control of his victim, his task is to maintain that control. The method of control utilized by the offender *primarily* depends on his motivation (i.e., power, anger, or a combination of the two) for committing the assault. I have observed four control methods: mere presence, use of verbal threats, display of a weapon, and physical force.

Depending on the level of fear experienced by the victim, it is quite possible that all that is needed to control the victim is the presence of the offender. While this may be difficult for a person removed from the assault situation to comprehend, it may nevertheless be true. Too often investigators, prosecutors, and judges form an opinion on a victim's response based entirely on what they *believe* they would have done in a similar situation. In other words, they fail to take into account the victim's personality, the circumstances surrounding the assault, and the enormous influence of fear. Consequently, the interviewer must be careful not to convey a judgmental attitude toward the victim as this will undoubtedly inhibit her cooperation.

Some victims may be intimidated and controlled by harsh or threatening commands by the criminal or promises of physical violence if victim compliance is not forthcoming. In such cases, it is extremely important, if at all possible, for the interviewer to document the exact wording used by the rapist. Verbiage is an important behavior that will provide insight into the motive for the attack.

If a rapist displays a weapon to control the victim, it is important to determine when during the assault he presented or indicated he had a weapon. If he did have a weapon, additional questions should include the following: Did the victim see it? Was it a weapon of choice (brought to the scene) or one of opportunity (obtained at the scene)? Did he relinquish control of the weapon? Did he *intentionally* inflict any physical injury with the weapon? In what manner did he threaten the victim with the weapon?

Offender's Use of Physical Force

If the offender used physical force, it becomes a key factor in determining his motivation. The amount of physical violence is *primarily* dependent on assault motivation, although victim resistance may also play a role. The interviewer should determine the specific level of force used (see below), when it was employed, whether or not the force increased or decreased, and the rapist's attitude prior to, during, or after the force was used against the victim.

Because the use and level of physical force are so important to the behavioral analysis, the interviewer should obtain a precise description of the force involved. The analyst must understand that the victim may exaggerate her description of the force used by the rapist for understandable reasons. If she doubts that the authorities will believe her because there was little or no physical violence involved, she may feel it necessary to exaggerate. Another reason might be that she feels guilty because she did not physically resist the attacker. Another valid reason might be if the victim was never struck or spanked as a child and the rapist slapped her, she may truly *believe* that she has been beaten. Yet another possible explanation for exaggeration is if the victim is unable to distinguish between the sexual assault and the physical assault. For these reasons, I have defined four levels of physical force. These levels are designed to assist the analyst in arriving at a reliable assessment of the force employed.

At the first level—*minimal force*—there is little or no physical violence. While mild slapping may have occurred, it was clearly employed more to intimidate the victim than to punish her. No medical attention for injuries is required.

The second level of force—*moderate force*—involves the victim being slapped or struck repeatedly and in a painful manner. Again, however, the victim requires no medical attention for her injuries.

The third level—*excessive force*—is used to describe a situation in which the victim was beaten by the rapist and it resulted in bruises and lacerations. At this level of force, medical attention is required, and the victim may be hospitalized.

At the fourth and final level—*brutal force*—the victim is subjected to an extremely severe physical assault resulting in extensive hospitalization or death.

Victim Resistance

When ordered to do something, a person has two available options: to comply or to resist. *Victim resistance* is defined as any action, or lack of action, that precludes, reduces, or delays the attack. I have identified three methods of victim resistance: verbal, physical, and passive.

1. *Verbal resistance.* Verbal resistance may include screaming, pleading, refusing ("No, I won't do that"), or even an attempt to reason or negotiate with the attacker. Note that while crying is a form of verbal behavior, it is not, for the purposes of this discussion, considered to be a form of resistance.
2. *Physical resistance.* Physical resistance may include hitting, scratching, kicking, gouging, or even running away.
3. *Passive resistance.* While most interviewers are cognizant of, and record, physical or verbal resistance, they frequently overlook or disregard "passive" resistance. Passive resistance is evidenced when the victim does not physically or verbally protest but simply does not comply with the rapist's demands. An example of passive resistance would involve an offender ordering a victim to remove her clothing and the victim simply does not respond in any fashion. She does not physically or verbally resist, but she also does not comply with his demand—therefore she resisted.

If resistance occurred in any form, the analyst would be particularly interested in the offender's reaction to that resistance.

Offender's Reaction to Resistance

People react to stressful situations in a variety of ways. The manner in which an individual reacts can be quite informative to one trained in behavior.

No person would question the stress experienced by victims of crime, but few would consider that committing a rape also creates stress for most attackers. The criminal's fear of being identified, arrested, injured, ridiculed, or successfully resisted can all combine to create a great amount of stress. The question for the analyst then becomes how the unidentified rapist copes with stress. Consequently, it becomes crucial for the investigator to learn how the rapist reacted to any resistance offered by his victim.

Cases submitted to me over the years revealed five reactions rapists most commonly exhibit when confronted with victim resistance: (1) cease the demand, (2) compromise, (3) flee, (4) use threats, and (5) use physical force. In some instances when encountering victim resistance, a rapist will simply *cease his demand* for a particular act or behavior and move to another demand or phase of the attack. In other cases, the man will *compromise or negotiate* by agreeing to a victim's suggestion (e.g., "Let me do this instead") or by giving the victim alternatives to the activity originally demanded (e.g., "All right, do this then"). Occasionally, a rapist will, on encountering resistance, simply *leave* the victim. These first three reactions are particularly interesting from a behavioral perspective. They suggest that the offender had no desire to physically force the victim's compliance.

Other rapists may resort to *threats* if resistance is encountered. The interviewer should attempt to capture the exact wording of the threats from the victim, and if the victim continued to resist the attacker in spite of the threats, it is important to determine what his reaction was to that continued resistance. When *physical force* is resorted to, the interviewer must determine the specific level of force used by the offender.

Sexual Dysfunctions

The term *sexual dysfunction* may be defined as an "impairment either in the desire for sexual gratification or in the ability to achieve it" (Coleman et al., 1980). In a definitive study of 170 rapists, Groth and Burgess (1977) determined that 34% of the offender population suffered a sexual dysfunction during the assault. In another study involving 41 men responsible for 837 rapes and over 400 attempted rapes, 38% of the rapists reported a sexual dysfunction during their first rape, 39% during the middle rape, and 35% during their last rape (Hazelwood, Reboussin, and Warren, 1989). The occurrence of a sexual dysfunction coupled with an understanding of the causes of the various types of male dysfunctions can provide potentially valuable information to the analyst.

When interviewing the victim, the investigator should be alert to the possibility that she may not volunteer information about rapist dysfunctions. This may be due to the fact that she does not consider the information to be significant, that she is embarrassed by the acts she was forced to engage in to overcome the dysfunction, or that she is totally ignorant of such matters and did not recognize the impairment as a dysfunction. For this reason, it benefits the investigator to explain the various male sexual dysfunctions and their significance to the investigation. The information discussed next will assist in such situations.

Erectile Insufficiency

Previously termed *impotence*, this type of dysfunction affects the male's ability to obtain or maintain an erection sufficient for sexual intercourse. Masters and Johnson (1970) classified the two types of erectile insufficiency as *primary* and *secondary*. Males experiencing primary insufficiency have *never been able* to maintain an erection sufficient for intravaginal ejaculation. While this type is relatively rare and not generally of concern to the investigator, it is discussed in the interest of completeness. In cases of secondary insufficiency, the male is *currently unable* to obtain or maintain an erection. It is secondary impotence that is of interest to the interviewer in the context of this discussion.

Groth and Burgess (1977) compared the occurrence of erectile insufficiency among a group of rapists and a group of nonrapist male patients studied by Masters and Johnson. They found that erectile insufficiency was the most commonly experienced dysfunction among both groups of men.

Premature Ejaculation

Masters and Johnson (1970) defined *premature ejaculation* thus: "Ejaculation which occurs immediately before or immediately after penetration is termed premature ejaculation." Groth and Burgess (1977) found that this dysfunction affected 3% of the rapists in their study.

Retarded Ejaculation

Retarded ejaculation is evidenced by the male experiencing difficulty, or even failure, in his attempts to ejaculate. It is important to note that the individual *is not* controlling seminal discharge and therefore intentionally prolonging the sexual encounter, but because of his inability to ejaculate, he is denied sexual gratification. Groth and Burgess (1977) reported that 15% of the rapists in their study suffered this dysfunction. Masters and Johnson (1970) found it so rare among their patients that they did not rank it. In a study of 30 sexual sadists, Dietz, Hazelwood, and Warren (1990) found that retarded ejaculation was a commonly observed dysfunction in the crimes of the men. During face-to-face interviews of 20 former wives and girlfriends of sexually sadistic men, retarded ejaculation was also found to be a common dysfunction of the men (Hazelwood, Warren, and Dietz, 1993; Warren and Hazelwood, 2002). As Groth (1979) noted, "Failure to consider the possibility of retarded ejaculation may prejudice the victim's version of multiple and extended assaults" (p. 88).

Conditional Insufficiency

Groth and Burgess (1977) identified a fourth form of sexual dysfunction that they termed *conditional insufficiency*. In such cases, the rapist is unable to become erect until there is forced oral and manual stimulation by the victim. The serial rape data I and others collected suggest that rapist-forced methods of resolving the dysfunction may not be limited to forced oral and manual stimulation but may include *any* act or behavior demanded by the offender to resolve the issue. Such demands may include anal sex, analingus, or having the victim verbalize particular words or even dress in certain clothing such as lingerie or high heels (Hazelwood and Burgess, 2001).

Conditional Ejaculation

The final type of dysfunction I observed is one for which there has been no research. The rapist experiencing conditional ejaculation has no difficulty in obtaining or maintaining an erection but can only ejaculate after certain conditions have been met. Most often, the conditions involve particular sexual acts.

Type and Sequence of Sexual Acts

Holmstrom and Burgess (1980) suggested that documenting the kinds of sexual acts that occur during a rape helps us to better understand the offense. Ascertaining the type and sequence of sexual assault is helpful in determining the motivation underlying a rape. Obtaining this type of information may prove to be difficult because of the emotional trauma suffered by the victim and her understandable reluctance to discuss certain aspects of the crime because of fear, shame, or humiliation. Most often, however, the investigator can overcome such reluctance through a professional, patient, and empathetic approach.

While it is common for interviewers to ask about any vaginal, oral, or anal acts, they do not very often ask questions pertaining to kissing, fondling, the use of foreign objects, digital manipulation of the vagina or anus, or fetishistic, voyeuristic, or exhibitionistic acts by the offender. In a sample of 115 adult, teenage, and child rape victims, Holmstrom and Burgess (1980) reported vaginal sex as the most frequent act, but they also reported 18 other sexual behaviors. Also to be noted is the fact that repetition and sequence of acts are not commonly reported. More likely, the report will state "The victim was raped," "vaginally assaulted," or "raped repeatedly."

Forced sexual acts may have various and important sociopsychological meanings (Holmstrom and Burgess, 1980). By documenting and analyzing the sequence of the assault, it may be possible to determine whether the offender was acting out a fantasy, committing the sexual acts to punish or degrade the victim, or simply engaging in sexual experimentation. For example, if fellatio followed anal rape, the motivation of anger with a desire to punish and degrade would be strongly suggested. On the other hand, if the rapist is acting out a power-driven *fantasy* of being with a consenting sexual partner, he may engage in kissing, fondling, or cunnilingus *prior* to a vaginal rape.

Verbal Activity

"A common stereotype of the male rapist's attack is that he used physical force to attain power and control over victims. Not only do rapists use physically based strategies, but they also use a second set of strategies based on language" (Holmstrom and Burgess, 1979, p. 101). A rapist unintentionally reveals a great deal about himself and the motivation for the assault through his verbal activity with the victim. The words he speaks to the victim, his manner and tone, and what, if anything, he demands the victim say to him are critically important to understanding the unidentified offender.

Preciseness is essential. For example, a rapist who states, "I'm going to kill you if you don't do what I say," has unquestionably *threatened* the victim. However, when a rapist states, "Do what I say, and I won't hurt you," he may be *reassuring* the victim in an attempt to alleviate her fear of injury and gain her compliance without resorting to physical force. If an offender says, "I want to make love to you," he has used a passive, affectionate phrase that indicates he has no desire, or even intent, to physically injure his victim. Conversely, the rapist who states, "I'm going to fuck you," has chosen a much more aggressive style of verbiage with no affection intended and has strongly indicated hostility to the victim.

Compliments directed toward the victim, verbal politeness, expressions of concern, apologies, and any discussion of the rapist's personal life (whether fact or fiction) again suggest a fantasy of being with a consenting partner and having no intent to physically injure. On the other hand, derogatory, profane, threatening, or abusive verbiage is indicative of anger toward women and the offender's use of sexual behavior to punish and degrade. Such offenders often have an arrest history of abusive behavior toward women.

When analyzing a victim's statement, it is recommended that the investigator write down an adjective that describes each of the offender's statements. For example, an appropriate adjective for the phrase, "You're a beautiful woman," would be "complimentary." Other examples include the following:

"Shut up bitch."	Hostility
"Am I hurting you?"	Concerned
"How long have you lived here?"	Inquisitive
"I wasn't always like this."	Disclosing

Note that utilizing this method will help to overcome bias against the offender and provide the analyst with better insight into the offender's motivation and personality.

Forced Victim Verbal Activity

What a person says to his or her partner during sex can either heighten or reduce the participant's enjoyment. In a rape, the attacker may demand that the victim speak certain words or phrases that enhance the act for him. Determining what the victim was forced to say gives the analyst perception into the nonsexual needs the offender is attempting to have met through the assault. For example, a rapist who demands such phrases as "I love you," "I want you to make love to me," or "You're better than my husband" suggests a need for affirmation (power) that may be present because of self-esteem issues. The man who demands that the victim plead, cry, or scream strongly indicates the involvement of sexual sadism (anger), a paraphilic condition in which the person is psychosexually aroused by the suffering of another.

Sudden Change in Offender's Attitude

The victim should be asked whether she observed any change in the attitude of the rapist while he was with her. Did he suddenly become angry, contrite, physically abusive, or apologetic? If she reports such a change, the analyst must determine what immediately preceded the change. One of the rapists I interviewed assaulted a victim in the presence of her husband. During the assault, he had not been verbally or physically abusive toward the victim *until* her husband asked if she were okay. She responded "Yes, he is being a gentleman." At that time, the rapist began to use profanity, and he beat and burned her breasts so badly that she underwent a mastectomy of both breasts. During the interview, I asked the man why his attitude had changed so dramatically, and he answered, "Who the fuck is she to tell me I was a gentleman. I proved to her that I was no gentleman." When pressed for further explanation, the rapist stated, "She was trying to take control, and I showed her who was in control."

A sudden and unexpected behavioral change may be indicative that an emotional weak point has been touched or that the offender either experienced fear or perceived a threat of some sort. Occurrences that may cause attitudinal change can include sexual dysfunction, external disruptions (e.g., phone, knock on door), victim resistance, a lack of sufficient victim fear, being ridiculed or scorned, or even the completion of the assault.

It is important to be aware that an attitudinal change may occur verbally, physically, or sexually. Rape, as mentioned, may be a stressful event for the offender, and the investigator's knowledge of factors that created stress for the rapist is a very valuable psychological tool to possess during police interrogations. How the rapist behaviorally relates to stress can also be helpful information for the mental health professional during treatment.

Criminal Experience

In an attempt to determine the criminal experience of the rapist, the investigator would be well advised to question the victim about what actions the offender took to protect his identity, remove physical or trace evidence, and facilitate his escape.

As with any criminal activity, the more rapes an offender commits, the more proficient he *should* become in committing the crime and eluding detection. One type of behavior that provides insight into his experience level is the actions the rapist takes to protect his identity. If an offender is convicted because of a mistake (e.g., leaving semen at the scene), and after release from prison, he commits a similar crime, it is quite likely that he will take actions to correct his earlier error (i.e., by wearing a condom).

The rapist who is just beginning to assault is not likely to be familiar with modern medical or police technology and therefore will take minimal actions to protect his identity (i.e., wear a ski mask or gloves, attempt to change his voice inflection, blindfold the victim, or simply order the victim not to look at him). Such precautions are common and are consistent with a person who may not be knowledgeable of the scientific value of hair and fiber evidence or DNA applications.

Conversely, when an intelligent and experienced rapist is involved, the investigator will observe that his modus operandi suggests a knowledge and understanding of scientific and technological advances beyond what is expected of a layperson. For example, he may order the victim to shower or douche after vaginal ejaculation, force her to drink grapefruit juice after ejaculating into the victim's mouth, take any cigarette remnants containing his saliva or fingerprints, or even place bed sheets in the victim's washing machine. The experienced rapist may also take steps to delay the victim reporting his crime or to facilitate his escape, such as walking through the victim's residence to disable phones or alarm systems or to prepare escape routes for use after the assault.

As in all subjective analysis of criminal behavior, the experience level of the rapist can only be suggested by his actions and the investigator's subsequent interpretation of those actions.

Items Taken

It is expected that the police will record the theft of any item following a rape. However, I have found that it is not uncommon for the victim to fail to realize that items such as a photograph, a pair of panties, or an inexpensive earring were taken. For this reason, the victim should be asked to inventory such items. All too often, investigators fail to pay attention to theft unless it involves items of value. The analyst of criminal behavior is interested in not only *if* something was taken but also *why* it was taken.

Items taken by sexual offenders can be placed into one of three categories: (1) evidentiary, (2) valuables, and (3) personal. The offender who takes evidentiary items (i.e., items that may contain physical or trace evidence) suggests prior rape experience or possibly an arrest history for similar offenses. If valuables are taken, the analyst should give attention to the type of item the rapist took as this may indicate his age or maturity. For example, a young offender could be expected to take items such as compact disks (CDs), CD changers, or even speakers. More mature offenders might take money and jewelry as such items are much easier to dispose of, conceal, or transport.

When personal items are taken, they generally have no intrinsic value but instead serve to remind the offender of the crime and the victim. Personal items may include a driver's license, lingerie, photograph, or inexpensive piece of jewelry. Such items would be classified as either trophies or souvenirs (Hazelwood and Burgess, 2001). Investigators should be alert to the fact that the offender may return personal items to the victim. Some may do so because they want to continue feelings of power over the victim, while others may do so to convince the victim that they meant no harm and to convince her that they are not really a bad person.

Indications That Victim Was Targeted

Rapists often target or select their victims prior to committing the crime. For example, a series of rapes in which the victims were either alone or with small children would suggest that the offender knew of the victim's vulnerability through either window peeping or surveillance. Furthermore, if the offender's crime behavior suggests knowledge of the victim (e.g., where she works, what kind of car she drives, etc.), he may have been watching and gathering intelligence on her for a period of time. If the victim reports that he seemed comfortable in moving through her residence, he may have entered the residence prior to the attack. For this reason, the investigator should determine whether the victim or other residents of her neighborhood have experienced any of the following occurrences prior to the victim's assault:

1. "Hang-up" or "wrong number" phone calls
2. Residential or automobile break-in
3. Prowlers or "peeping toms"
4. Obscene notes
5. Attempted break-ins

Finally, did the victim experience a feeling that she was being watched or followed within the recent past? If so, the investigator should document when and where she experienced these feelings.

Conclusion

Rape is a criminal act that involves the sexual parts of the body but that serves nonsexual needs (i.e., power, anger, or a combination of the two) of the offender. An analysis of the offender's behavior during the crime makes it possible to determine the motivation underlying the assault and consequently to describe the characteristics and traits of the unidentified rapist. The victim is the only available source of behavioral information, and it is crucial that the investigator establish rapport with the victim through patience, empathy, and professionalism.

When analyzing the offender's behavior, it is imperative that any personal feelings the analyst may have about the crime, the criminal, and the victim be isolated and that the crime be viewed from the perspective of the offender.

The crime behavior also provides the investigator with information about the personality of the offender. It is obvious, therefore, that interviewing the rape victim using a set of questions specifically designed to elicit behavioral information would be the crucial first step in analyzing the crime. The questions set forth in this discussion were developed and refined over a period of years and have been found to be of inestimable value in understanding the personality of men who rape.

References

Coleman, J.C., et al., *Abnormal Psychology and Modern Life*, 6th ed., Scott, Foresman, Glenview, IL, 1980, p. 531.

Dietz, P.E., Hazelwood, R.R., and Warren, J.I., The Sexually Sadistic Criminal and His Offenses," *Bulletin of the American Academy of Psychiatry and the Law*, 18(2), 1990, 163–178.

Groth, A.N., *Men Who Rape*, Plenum Press, New York, 1979, p. 88.

Groth, A.N., and Burgess, A.W., Sexual Dysfunction During Rape, *New England Journal of Medicine*, 297(4), 1977, 764–766.

Groth, A.N., Burgess, A.W., and Holmstrom, L.L., Rape, Power, Anger and Sexuality, *American Journal of Psychiatry*, 134, November 1977, 1240.

Hazelwood, R.R., and Burgess, A.W. (eds.), *Practical Aspects of Rape Investigation: A Multidisciplinary Approach*, CRC Press, Boca Raton, FL, 2001, p. 125.

Hazelwood, R.R., Reboussin, R., and Warren, J.I., Serial Rape: Correlates of Increased Aggression and the Relationship of Offender Pleasure to Victim Resistance, *Journal of Interpersonal Violence*, 4(1), March 1989, 65–78.

Hazelwood, R.R., Warren, J.I., and Dietz, Park E., Compliant Victims of Sexual Sadists, *Australian Family Physician*, 22(4), April 1993.

Holmstrom, L.L., and Burgess, A.W., Rapist's Talk: Linguistic Strategies to Control the Victim, *Deviant Behavior*, 1, 1979, 101.

Holmstrom, L.L., and Burgess, A.W., Sexual Behavior of Assailants During Rape, *Archives of Sexual Behavior*, 9(5), 1980, 437.

Masters, W.H., and Johnson, V.K., *Human Sexual Inadequacy*, Little, Brown, Boston, 1970.

Warren, J.I., and Hazelwood, R.R., Relational Patterns Associated with Sexual Sadism; A Study of 20 Wives and Girlfriends, *Journal of Family Violence*, 17(1), March 2002, 75–89.

About the Author

Robert R. Hazelwood is a retired FBI supervisory special agent and served 11 years in the U.S. Army, achieving the rank of major. He holds a master's degree in counseling psychology and attended a 1-year fellowship in forensic medicine at the Armed Forces Institute of Pathology. He has published more than 45 articles, authored or coauthored 10 book chapters and five books, and is a member of the editorial review board of four professional journals. He has testified as an expert in city, county, state, and federal courts and before special committees of the U.S. House and Senate. He has lectured and consulted on violent crimes throughout the United States, Canada, Europe, and the Caribbean. He is currently senior vice president of the Academy Group Incorporated in Manassas, Virginia.

Appendix D

Sexual Assault Victim's Questionnaire

Instructions for Preparing This Questionnaire

You are asked to **be as accurate, precise, and specific as possible.** If any questions are difficult to answer or understand, attempt to complete as many of them as possible, then contact the investigator for assistance. Some questions may be sensitive. Each question provides some specific, vital information that may lead to the offender. If something should be brought to the attention of the investigator, add those comments to the end of this form.

I. Offender's Method of Approach
   A. Con: Did the offender approach you openly with a trick or ploy, such as asking directions or for any sort of assistance? Yes _____ No _____
   B. Surprise: Did the offender step from behind a tree or wait in the back seat of your car or were you awakened by offender standing by your bed? Yes _____ No _____
   C. Blitz: Did offender approach/use direct, immediate physical assault? Yes _____ No _____

II. Offender's Control Over You
   A. Mere presence: Was your emotional response and fear of the offender such that the offender's presence alone was enough to control you? Yes _____ No _____
   B. Verbal threats
      1. Write out the full text of verbal threats made. Note when they occurred. Also indicate what happened just prior to and just after the threat was made. List the threats in the order they occurred, including those that were repeated.
      2. Were any of the threats carried out? Yes _____ No _____
      3. Which threats were carried out and at which point did they occur? _____
   C. Use of a weapon
      1. Did the offender use or display a weapon? Yes _____ No _____

2. At what point did the offender display or indicate he had a weapon?
3. Did you see the weapon? Yes _____ No_____
4. Did the offender bring the weapon with him, or did he get it at or near the scene of the assault? Circle correct answer. Offender brought weapon   Offender obtained weapon at scene
5. At any time did the offender give up control of the weapon, that is, set it down or put it away? Yes _____ No _____
6. Did the offender use the weapon to injure you? Yes _____ No _____

D. Physical force
1. At what point did the offender use physical force against you? In order of occurrence, list each act of physical force. **If necessary, use an additional sheet of paper.**

Describe in detail the physical force used and resulting injury	What happened just before the use of this physical force?	What happened just after the use of this physical force?

2. Utilizing the following descriptions, **circle** the appropriate level or amount of force used by the offender.
   a. Minimal force. Little or no force used, slapping, or force used to intimidate rather than to punish or injure.
   b. Moderate force. Repeated slapping or hitting, even in the absence of your resistance.
   c. Excessive force. Offender beat, kicked, caused possible bruising to several parts of your body, inflicted cuts.
   d. Brutal force. Offender used torture, instruments, or other devices to intentionally inflict physical or emotional pain. Caused extensive hospitalization.

III. Victim's Resistance
A. Was it ever safe to resist the offender's attack? Yes _____ No _____
   Characterize your resistance, using the following definitions. Circle the best description of your resistance.
   1. Passive resistance. No physical or verbal resistance, but you did not comply with the offender's demands or instructions.
   2. Verbal resistance. Screaming, pleading, refusing, or attempting to reason, delay, or negotiate with the offender.

3. Physical resistance. Anything you did to avoid, delay, or reduce the attack, including (or attempting to do) hitting, kicking, scratching, gouging, or running.

IV. Offender's Reactions to Resistance
   A. Stopped the demand or attempted activity. Did the offender change to another demand or attempt a new type of attack when met with resistance? Yes _____ No _____
   B. Compromising/negotiating. Did offender compromise or negotiate by suggesting alternatives to his demands or allowing you to suggest alternatives? Yes _____ No _____
   C. Fleeing. Did the offender flee from the scene when you resisted? Yes _____ No _____
   D. Use of threats. Did offender make verbal threats to gain compliance? Yes _____ No _____
   E. Use of force
      1. Was force immediately used on you? Yes _____ No _____
      2. Was force used after a threat? Yes _____ No _____
      3. Was force used after your continued resistance? Yes _____ No _____

V. Offender's Sexual Dysfunction
   A. Erectile insufficiency
      1. Was the offender able throughout the attack to obtain and maintain an erection sufficient for sexual intercourse? Yes __ No _____
      2. At any time did the offender have only a partial erection? Yes __ No _____
      3. Was the offender able to become erect when there was forced oral or manual stimulation or after he forced you to say or do something? Yes _____ No _____
   B. Premature ejaculation
      1. Did offender ejaculate immediately before or on penetration? Yes _____ No _____
      2. Did the offender ejaculate very soon after penetration began? Yes _____ No _____
   C. Retarded ejaculation. Did offender have difficulty or fail to ejaculate? Yes _____ No _____
   D. Conditioned ejaculation. Did the offender ejaculate only after a particular sexual act or after he asked you to say or do something specific? Yes _____ No _____ If **yes**, what was done or said? _____

VI. Type and Sequence of Sexual Acts During the Assault
  A. Circle specific acts of offender if they occurred at any time.
     Number each regarding which occurred first, second, third, and
     so on and indicate any that were repeated.
     Kissing
     Fondling
     Manipulation of vagina by offender's finger or hand
     Manipulation of anus by offender's finger or hand
     Insertion or attempted insertion of any type of foreign object
       into your vagina or anus. Describe the object and manner in
       which the offender used it on you. What preceded and fol-
       lowed the use of the object? _____
     1. Did offender pay particular attention to any item, piece of
        clothing, or body part? Yes _____ No _____
     2. Did offender have an interest in watching a particular act
        performed? Yes _____ No _____
     3. Did the offender force mouth-to-penis contact? Yes _____ No _____
     4. Did the offender place his mouth on your vagina?
        Yes _____ No _____
     5. Did the offender place his mouth on your anus? Yes _____ No _____
     6. Did the offender tell you to place your mouth to his anus?
        Yes _____ No _____
     7. Did offender bite any body part (neck, arms, breasts, but-
        tocks, vagina)? Yes _____ No _____
     8. Did the offender urinate at any time? Yes _____ No _____
  B. Describe the sequence in which any of the acts just mentioned
     were used by the offender during his assault, including any
     repeated acts. _____

VII. Offender's Verbal Activity
  A. Write all verbal statements, including profanity or vulgar words,
     used by offender at any time. Indicate the order and manner
     in which they occurred, attitude, or tone of voice used by the
     offender. **Use quotation marks for exact or nearly exact word-
     ing of the offender**. *State what happened just before a particular
     statement was made.*

VIII. Victim's Verbal Activity
  A. What, if anything, were you told to say by the offender?
  B. Describe any actions you were instructed to do while making the
     statements. _____

IX. Sudden Change in Offender's Attitude
   A. Describe any changes in the offender's attitude during the assault. (Did he change from angry to physically abusive to apologetic?) Include any events that preceded the change in attitude._____

X. Offender's Actions to Protect Identity
   A. Describe any attempt by the offender to protect his identity, such as wearing a mask or gloves, giving you specific instructions, covering your head, and so on. If the offender wore gloves, did he take them off at any point?
   B. Fully describe any behavior that may indicate previous criminal experience and knowledge of rape investigations. For example, did he prepare an escape route, disable your phone, bring bindings or gag, wear gloves, order you to shower or bathe, take efforts to clean up the scene, attempt to destroy evidence, wash clothing and bed sheets, and so on.

XI. Did the Offender Take Any Items from You?
   A. Did offender take any items he had touched or ejaculated on or that may have been considered evidence, including cigarette butts, cans, or bottles? Yes _____ No _____
   B. Did the offender remove any items that you consider valuable? Yes _____ No _____
   C. Did the offender remove any personal items, such as photographs, driver's license, keys, lingerie, or other personal articles? Yes _____ No _____
      Describe the items indicated in these questions. _____
   D. Did the offender return any items that he initially took or indicated he was going to take? Did he prepare to take any item but leave it behind? Describe the items and the offender's behavior.

XII. Other Events Before and After the Assault
   If you answer "**yes**" to any of the next four questions, describe the events.
   A. Did you receive telephone calls, hang-up calls, or notes from unknown persons before or after the assault?
   B. Did you experience a recent burglary of your home or car?
   C. Did you have any incidents of prowlers or peeping toms prior to the assault?
   D. Did you have the feeling you were being watched or followed?
   E. Prior to the assault, if you were not living alone, describe your living arrangements, including any occasional overnight guests.

F. Prior to assault, did you reside in an apartment or similar type dwelling? Yes_____ No _____
G. If you have been the victim of a previous sexual assault or other personal assault, please describe the incident.

Appendix E

Structuring an Interview

Personal History Section

Date_____ Case #_____ Person_____ V W S
SSAN____-____-_____ Dob____/____/_____ Age____ POB __ Ht __Wt __
Marital Status M S D W E Address _____
Spse/FmrSpouse _____
Children _____ Brother/Sister _____
Atty _____ Mom/Dad—Spent Time—Know Diff ____ Pass On? ____
Education _____ Problems _____
Employment and Rate _____ Problems _____
Military Svc _____ MOS _____ Discharge _____
Problems _____
Med Hist. Opinion Current Health _____ Current _____
Ailments _____
Mental Hist. Counseling—Nervousness, Tension, Depression _____
Today—Medication _____ Sleep ____ Nrm ____ Alcohol ____ Narco/
Drugs _____
Arrest Record _____
Tell Me About Self, Sports/Leisure _____ Like Yourself/Why _____
Rate-Truthful ____% ____ % Honest ____% Who Do You Admire?_____
Ever Involved Any Criminal Situations? _____
Results Prior Invest. (Guilty, pled, convicted, confess) ____ Upsets in life last
6 mo.? ____ Year ____

Transition to Crime Specifics

Your role (connected to) this crime _____ Alibi for when this
occurred _____
How believe crime happened _____ UR reaction heard this
crime _____
Feel Re Interview_____ Discuss anyone/loved one_____ Most
likely to do _____
Why say you doer _____ Anyone absolutely not do _____ Happen
if false rept _____

Why someone do _____ Who had best chance _____ Who had talent _____
U do with this crim _____ Trust again _____ Invest Results Show About You _____
Bait/Evid. Connect Ploys Fp _____ Seen _____ Evid _____ Financial Audit Rslts _____
If supv. Take poly _____ How U do when _____
Willing to Undergo Hypnosis _____ Rslts _____ % Steal Fm Co _____ Easy Way Steal _____
How would U have done it? _____

Interview Plan

Important Topics	Names, Dates, or Players	Techniques	Evaluation	R U 5/95
/		/	/	/
/		/	/	/
/		/	/	/

Is there anything you know or have heard about this _____ that I have not asked about? Anything you know that I should know?

Appendix F

Themes, Openings, Arguments*

Themes are part of the reasoning process in which a subject is allowed or encouraged to rationalize, project, or minimize his involvement in crime. Themes must be delivered in a way that sounds, and more importantly feels, sincere. The first step in ensuring sincerity is to convert these concepts and ideas to your words and style so that they sound "natural." Themes do not guarantee a confession, but they embody what the police have been using in the interrogation room for many, many years with success. Some of the themes may not fit your personality or interrogation style but in fairness, give each more than one try before discarding it.

Themes work best when combined and repeated several times, perhaps with a slightly different slant from one use to another. Close observation of the subject will tell if he is totally rejecting any themes you are attempting to use. When that is your judgment, drop that theme and try another.

Some of these themes may fit in more than one style category.

Reasoning Style

I can write my report to this point. The prosecutor, grand jury, supervisor, and the like will ask me certain items. I am giving you a unique opportunity to determine your future. Help me write the ending to my report.

Did you ever have a rock in your shoe? The further you walked, the bigger the rock felt. When you dumped it out, it was only a small grain of sand. This situation is like that. Until we get it out on the table and examine it, it will seem like a big deal. Once we place it in perspective, it will look like what it really is ... a small matter. (This also can be minimization style.)

---

* Many years ago, the FBI invited the legendary Warren Holmes to speak with a group of agents. He discussed many aspects of interviewing and was very open, encouraging us to take what he had learned the hard way and use it to be more effective. In a private conversation, Mr. Holmes agreed to provide me a list of some of his most used themes. Some of those are included in this list. Others have been gleaned from conversations with individuals who specialized in interviews and interrogations, including the excellent instructors at the Department of Defense Polygraph Institute.

Americans judge the covering up of a lie more harshly than the first mistake. We have a capacity to understand how people make mistakes if given the opportunity. We have all tried to hide something. To do that, we have to tell another and another lie until it all falls apart. (This also can be minimization style.)

The "system" is not perfect but pretty damn close. Once normal people take the oath, they have a way of watching people and being able to tell if they are telling the truth. The judge is a professional at this and sees it day after day. How will you look when you tell this story before a judge and jury?

You are at a critical position in your life. You are at a fork in the road. You have choices to make. One will lead to a better situation for you. The choice is yours.

I have a fear. Thirty to sixty days from now, you will be sitting somewhere (jail) and ask yourself, "Where would I be if I had taken the opportunity to tell my story when I was talking to the FBI [or name your agency]?" Your story will never sound closer to the truth or have the feel of the truth than if you tell it today.

There is a degree of confidentiality in what we say today. If this goes to trial, then everyone will know all of the truth (or all of the aspects of a harsh version of events), and it will be even harder on you (and your wife, family).

You have some chips to play. Now is the time to play them. Our investigation is going forward. Everything we find out is one less chip you can get credit for. (Some use an analogy to playing stud poker and the need to play the cards that have been dealt you.)

The first step in rehabilitation is to admit that you have done something wrong. What if I am asked if I gave you a chance to tell your side … if I ever asked if you were sorry for what you did? I would have to say that I pleaded with you to tell the truth.

I have never talked to anyone who did not give me an understandable reason for what they did. I may not approve of your reasons, but I will understand them. People always believe and feel that they had to do what they did at the time.

Like I said, I can always understand the reasons, but what I can't understand or abide is a lie because it does so much damage.

(Use the analogy of intelligence vs. emotion, e.g., love, hate, anger, etc.) As long as the two are in balance, a person tends to behave with common sense. When emotion takes over, people behave in ways they usually wouldn't. Most of the time, a person can repress the emotion, but sometimes they just can't help it, like in this case.

The trouble with a situation like this is that sooner or later someone will talk, perhaps just a little. Then, there will not be one ounce of sympathy for you or your position.

I believe the reason you came to this meeting today is because deep down where you know right from wrong, you want to straighten this out. You are just searching for a way to do the right thing. You just wanted some help in getting out from under this burden.

Have you ever had someone stand up and tell you something you knew was a lie? You know how I feel now. What did you do when that happened? What did you think of that person?

Projection Style

Nothing in human events happens in isolation. Each act must be examined in context. What happens now is determined by what just happened. There was a triggering event, something that started you thinking about doing this, or someone did something that caused you to act as you did. From the moment we met, I have sensed that all is not right in your life; you seem upside down, out of whack, something has happened that caused you to act this way.

I don't think you meant things to happen as they did. I think that there is a reason (self-defense, to help family, victim is exaggerating, etc.), and if that's true, then I believe that should be known. But if you don't tell the truth, I will know that you aren't sorry. Don't throw your life away now. If you keep this up, it will snowball and get all out of shape.

Minimization Style

Did you ever have a rock in your shoe? The further you walked, the bigger the rock felt. When you dumped it out, it was only a small grain of sand. This situation is like that. Until we get it out on the table and examine it, it will seem like a big deal. Once we place it in perspective, it will look like what it really is … a small matter.

One thing about human nature is that everyone takes care of themselves. You have known that for years. Help me before your "partners" help me. Your role was surely less than theirs.

This was an impulsive act; I have examined it. You knew you were wrong as soon as you did it, but then it was too late; you could not turn back. You wish you could have turned back and would have done so if it were possible. It is a simple mistake made by many people I talk with. It was not a planned evil; you just made a human mistake.

(Review a long list of good qualities about the suspect, even if you have to make many of them up. Then offer to stand up for him and tell his [wife, girlfriend, boss, whoever is important to him] of his good qualities and that they should remember them, and that he only made this one mistake, error in judgment, acted on impulse.)

Since you did this (use this theme just after this happened), you haven't slept well, had trouble eating, you weren't the same around your friends. It is time to get this out on the table and see how manageable this problem is and get it behind you.

I know you feel bad about this situation and what happened. I suggest you take a step in the right direction, down the right path, and write a simple note to (boss, wife, victim) and simply say you are sorry for what you did, that you would change it if you could.

It is like the plumbing in a building or a boiler. At first, there is a little pressure, but you could handle that. Then after a while, the pressure built up, and in just the right situation or environment, it burst. That is exactly what happened to you. You couldn't really help yourself. You did what anybody would have done in those circumstances.

If you had been sober, in a normal state of mind, you just wouldn't have been capable of this thing. But, under the influence of (drugs, alcohol, personal loss), you were not only capable, but also vulnerable just like anyone else.

Remember (property case, theft) to keep this in perspective. The amount involved, while it seems like a lot, is not $100,000 like with some people who I talk with. Remember this is just money we are talking about; you did not run over a kid in the street and then drive away.

One good thing to your credit; at least you didn't shoot the money in your arm or up your nose.

Up to now, you have just made a foolish, natural mistake, but if you continue to cover up, it will appear as though you wanted to do it all along, you enjoyed and planned it and are now flaunting it.

You have had problems in your life, and you have made a few mistakes like everyone else. Right now, you have a chance to avoid the most serious mistake you could make.

You never intended to do this. It was the circumstances, or you did it to cover something else. The jury deserves to know any mitigating circumstances. This may be the last time you have some control over your destiny. Once you leave this room, nobody may ever again be interested in why you got caught up in this thing.

Ever since the pencil was invented, there have been erasers. We put erasers on pencils because we are human, and we make mistakes, just like the mistake you made in this matter.

Good Cop/Bad Cop Style

To my boss, it is no longer an issue of whether you did this. Only thing left to discuss is why and how you got hooked in this mess.

(Portray prosecutor, supervisor, cop, etc. as bad guy who interprets the crime in the worst possible light, i.e., he hurt people because he enjoys it, took job just for opportunity to steal, had done same thing numerous times or done more serious crimes. Indicate that is not your interpretation of events or his role, but you need facts to fight off this other group.)

Appendix G

Protecting Stalking Victims

Michael R. Napier and R. Stephen Mardigian

Every stalking situation, like any relationship between two people, has unique and distinctive dynamics. Tactics and strategies that are effective in one situation may be neither desirable nor effective in another. Any prediction regarding the dangerousness of another human being is not 100 percent reliable, even when made by specialists, because of the many variables affecting individual behavior. The following guidelines are offered as suggestions and are not intended to be viewed as a guaranteed solution.

Stalking is a crime. Stalking ranks high among situations that have the potential to turn violent. Experience has shown that early and assertive intervention may be effective and establishes the boundaries on acceptable behavior, i.e., behavior that the victim will not tolerate. Victims of stalking must make use of the resources of all available agencies, including law enforcement, prosecutors, courts, legal aid, victim services shelters, rape crisis centers, social services, women's advocacy and resource groups, and the victim units in police departments and prosecutors' offices.

Making adjustments. Being a victim of stalking does not mean that the victim is at fault, but stalking victims are often placed in the unfair but necessary position of making changes to their lives in order to counteract the aggressive and destructive potential of their abuser. Adjusting your social routines can cut the stalker's ties to you. If he knows where you go to church, where your health club is located, your hairdresser and your favorite lunch spots, he can find you. The added safety will far outweigh the inconvenience caused by these adjustments.

Who to trust. A stalker may attempt to reach you through friends and relatives. Sometimes the failure to keep a victim safe is traceable to the victim's indiscretion in providing details of their protective measures to individuals who fail to understand the serious nature of the victim's situation. When you have made adjustments to your living arrangements, such as changing your telephone number, finding another job, or moving to another address, restrict that knowledge to a close circle of family and friends. Explain to your close associates the deadly seriousness of the situation and the absolute requirement not to share those details with anyone. Impress upon them that *you* will determine who is to know the details of your new life.

Predicting Dangerousness

Intuition and the Sixth Sense: Trust your instincts about your personal safety. If you feel a situation, location, or an individual is dangerous, unpredictable, or bordering on violence, act on your instinct to protect yourself and your children. If it turns out you've over-reacted and made an error, the only true loss is likely to be a moment of inconvenience. Never hesitate to seek the assistance of law enforcement to check out or secure your home or to intervene and calm someone.

Characteristics of Violent Individuals: Some violent people progress along an escalating scale of violent behavior. The violence continuum begins with the conception of violence in thought involving simple, or sometimes elaborate, fantasies. These thoughts may escalate to violent acts. As the pattern of these behaviors evolves, it becomes more likely that the individual will engage in violent behavior. You should be concerned about the potential for violence by any individual who exhibits several of the following behaviors, traits or characteristics. While this list is not all-inclusive, a stalking victim should view a cluster of these activities as potentially alarming "**red flags**."

History of Violence: The more recent the history of violent behavior, the higher the likelihood of renewed violence.

Threats of Violence: Threats against those close to the individual or against anyone who "gets in my way."

Easily Frustrated: Easily angered or frustrated. Unable to cope with stress or bothersome things; always ready to explode. May withdraw into a sullen, brooding mood.

Misunderstood Victim: Places himself in the role of continually being misunderstood, taken advantage of, singled out or picked upon. It is never his fault.

Temper: Quick to resort to temper with aggressive, sexual, or profane expressions. Exhibits a physical demeanor meant to threaten or intimidate others in order to gain his desires.

Violent Themes: Habitually fills his personal life with activities demonstrating violent themes, such as violence-filled movies, magazines, games, or television programs, or his personal language. May act on these themes by harming your pets.

Beliefs: Holds bizarre or extreme beliefs and may associate with others who hold similar beliefs.

Drugs and Alcohol: Regularly consumes mood altering substances and becomes less able to control his emotions.

Victim Contact with the Stalker

Some stalkers are not easily deterred, but many do respond to defensive strategies utilized by the victim. Documenting evidence is imperative in building your case with law enforcement and the legal system, so be prepared to document every unexpected or frightening incident.

- Preserve as evidence any items sent to you by the stalker. Handle the items as little as possible. Also preserve recorded messages, such as telephone messages.
- Make a personal copy of all items you turn over to authorities. Label each item with the date and circumstances under which you received it.
- When it is safe to do so, take photographs of any suspicious or disturbing persons or items. When possible, videotape the people or items. A camera with a date-time feature is best. Use discretion because filming the stalker may provoke an angry response.

Journal: If you are being stalked, keep a log, journal, or diary of all occurrences that you think are related to the stalking or that seem unusual to you. Occurrences such as hang-up calls, suspicious vehicles, or someone loitering in your vicinity, and other similar incidents should be noted.
- Write down the license plate number of any suspicious vehicle.
- If something happens while you are away from home, when you are in a safe place, log the details of what you were doing at the time. These events can be sorted out later as to whether or not they are related to the stalking. Document now, disqualify later.
- If the matter should end up in court, take care to not record your personal thoughts or observations as the stalker is likely to see this activity.

Security: Make a habit of locking all windows and doors when you are home alone, when you are leaving or returning home, and before going to bed. Include second floor windows and garage doors in your security checklist.
- Notify apartment security and management of any potential problems with a stalker. In many locations, they have an obligation to take action.

- If you gave keys to the stalker in the past, change your locks and manage the control of the new keys.
- Some security enhancements such as safety chains, door stoppers, door alarms, wide-angle door viewers or peepholes, and other items are inexpensive and easy to install.
- Simple household items can heighten personal security; e.g., a broom handle or dowel rod cut to length can be used to keep sliding doors or windows from being opened.
- Quickly replace all burned out lightbulbs. If a critical area was lighted when you left but the light is out when you return, seek assistance from a neighbor or law enforcement before proceeding.
- If you live in an apartment, immediately request replacement of any defective security devices. Be persistent with management and keep notes as to requests made and management's response.
- Adapt window coverings to make it easy to see out but not in. Stand outside and see what the stalker would see, day or night.
- Identify anyone at your door before opening the door. This includes all utility personnel, repairmen, and salespeople. Reputable companies issue identification and you can call the company to verify the person's identity. If in doubt, don't let them inside.

Telephone Services: An unlisted or non-directory phone number may discourage some stalkers, but the number may be found through friends, surveillance, or other efforts.

- Find out if your telephone company offers caller ID or *69 programs.
- Use an answering device to screen calls and receive messages. Answer only "safe calls." Employers and friends will appreciate your vigilance.
- Some communications systems will block individual numbers or unidentified callers. If your stalker is in jail, request that they block your number so he cannot call you.
- In extreme cases, a "trap and trace" procedure can be instituted by the telephone company to identify all callers to your number.
- If evidence exists of an illegal wiretap, the phone company can physically inspect your lines. If a wiretap is found, notify the local FBI.

Law Enforcement: The police exist to serve the public, but they are under-staffed and pressed for time. However, this should not preclude a victim from seeking their assistance. You should avoid involving the police unnecessarily, but never be afraid to err on the side of your own safety.

- Tape emergency numbers near *each* telephone. Your cell phone will transmit 911 calls even if you are out of your carrier's network. This also creates a trail of your location. If confronted or abducted, hide your cell phone on your person.
- Most police departments will conduct neighborhood watch meetings for you and your neighbors, brief you on crime resistance procedures and inspect your residence with suggestions for improving security.
- If you believe you are being followed while driving and have a cell phone, call the police while the event is occurring. Lock all vehicle doors. Be careful to not turn into dead-end streets. Drive to a safe location such as an all-night gas station or food mart. STAY IN YOUR CAR. Call attention to your situation by continually honking your horn and flashing your lights; press the panic button on your key fob. Repeat this procedure at stop lights and intersections. Carry a camera or video camera and record the stalker when your car is stopped and it is safe to do so.
- If you spot the stalker outside your home, call the police and ask that they stop, identify, and detain the person.
- If a serious threat exists, ask the patrol supervisor to schedule a patrol car to drive by your residence frequently.

Friends and Colleagues: When a serious threat exists, establish a plan of routinely calling or being called by a friend.

- Establish an unusual password which will let the friend know that you are in immediate danger and the police should be sent to your location.

Notification: When a situation becomes aggravated, notify law enforcement, apartment complex security, your employer's security officer, building security, your supervisor at work, child care, close neighbors, friends, and family. Document these contacts.

- If possible, provide appropriate parties with the suspect's photograph and request their watchfulness. Provide any information you have regarding vehicles, weapons, work schedules, past violence, threats, etc.

Contingency Plans: Make a plan to vacate your residence if you believe the situation is likely to deteriorate. The plan should include having essentials packed in bags, an escape route laid out, and a destination selected.

Dealing with the Stalker: Situations Involving an Existing Victim–Stalker Relationship

The value to the stalker of any contact with his victim is the response his actions evoke. Therefore, your response to any unwanted attention, threats, or intimidation should be carefully controlled. **Caution always should be used when interacting with a stalker.**

1. Make the stalker aware of your wishes about the relationship.
   - Plan your approach carefully, but move quickly. It may be preferable to make your feelings known in writing. Be sure to date the correspondence and save a copy of the letter for your records. Do not use inflammatory language.
   - Use caution if you choose to tell the stalker of your feelings in person. Find a *public* place where you can have a private conversation. The location for the meeting should not be secluded or isolated. Be sure to sit where you can easily escape. Do not use inflammatory language or tone of voice.
   - In a firm, unemotional manner, clearly state that you do not desire his attention and want it to stop. Do not give any reasons as they may be taken personally by the stalker.
   - Be direct. Say "*No*" and do not give the stalker the satisfaction of any emotion. Stalkers are often reinforced when they learn their actions can elicit an emotional response.
   - Phrase your statement so there is no room for negotiation or argument about your decision. Select words which do not offer any possibility of a relationship. There should be no trace of any future opportunity for him, e.g., "I am not ready for a relationship."
   - Take personal responsibility for there being no possibility of a relationship; e.g., "I am not getting into a relationship." "This is not what I want." "A relationship is not good for me." "I am being selfish."
   - Do not praise the stalker or state that he is likely to attract someone else.
2. Cease or avoid all contact. If he calls, repeat a brief portion of your decision not to interact with him, say goodbye and hang up. Do not answer immediate call backs.
   - This is a significant step because stalkers feed on contact, *even negative contact*. A stalker may try numerous and clever ruses to attempt to "hook" you into further conversations. Don't take the hook!
3. If harassing telephone calls continue, get a second telephone line and a new non-directory telephone number. Selectively provide the new

number to family and friends with cautions about the necessity of keeping it confidential.

- Keep the first telephone line operative for a short period and utilize an answering device to screen calls. Use someone else's voice on the answering device to avoid providing the stalker with any contact.

4. Avoid using an intermediary to confront the stalker. With some stalkers, the intermediary may become an obstacle to be removed to acquire you.

- If intervention is necessary, it should be undertaken by law enforcement.

5. Carry yourself in an alert, confident, assertive, but not arrogant, manner.

- Be alert to your surroundings.
- Have your key ready when approaching your door.
- Check your vehicle before entering it. Park near, not under, a light so it illuminates the interior of your vehicle. Once inside the car, lock the doors and don't get out for any reason (bumped by another car, flyer on the windshield, etc.).

6. Because of the possibility of being followed or watched, inspect your regular routes for locations where you can turn around without being trapped. Vary your schedule and routes of travel. Do not become predictable.

- Know the location of police and fire stations.
- Avoid any remote, isolated area, dead-end or cul-de-sac streets, driveways, or parking lots with one way in/out access.
- Know the location of busy, well-lighted, late night gas stations, restaurants, convenience stores, domestic violence shelters, and other public areas where a stalker may be less inclined toward violence.
- If you are followed, do not drive to your home or workplace.
- If you see a police cruiser, honk your horn and flash your lights to attract the officer's attention.
- Keep a cell phone and charger in your car. Pre-program emergency numbers into the phone.
- In an emergency, your vehicle can provide a protective shell around you. If you have a flat tire, it may be better to drive on it and ruin the tire than to stop. If you believe you are being followed, safely make multiple turns and u-turns, if these can be made without entering an unsafe area.

7. When violated, **restraining, protective, and stay away orders** are tools that police use to establish intent by the stalker. Since police can only respond after the order is violated, these tools may or may not protect you depending upon the motivation of the stalker. They

are not foolproof and sometimes create an illusion of protection. Do not get a false sense of security from a restraining order.

- A restraining order will place an offender on notice, but should not be obtained without researching how these orders are enforced in your location.
- A restraining order provides the police a tool to arrest and charge a stalker. If violated, the order should be enforced on the spot.
- These orders are punishable upon violation depending on judicial review. Is violation of the order a misdemeanor or a felony in your jurisdiction? This may determine how the police respond to a violation.
- In some cases, a restraining order may make a situation worse. From the stalker's viewpoint, a restraining order is humiliating and a display of rejection by the object of his obsession. Some stalkers may become angry and want to get even or step up the pursuit. Other types of stalkers, such as domestic and delusional stalkers, may not adhere to restrictions placed upon them by restraining orders.

When a Stalker Confronts You

If confronted by a stalker, call 911 or ask another person to do so.

Professionals: Your best hope for a peaceful and safe resolution rests with these officers. Take a few deep breaths to steady your emotions. Separate the incident from the officer who is there for your protection.

Maintain control: When you are out of control, you are viewed as part of the problem. Take a moment and a few deep breaths, then make calm, clear, rational statements about what has occurred. Keep your statements accurate—do not overstate or dramatize. Avoid personalizing your statement with derogatory or inflammatory statements about the other party. Avoid using profanity; besides being offensive, profanity suggests loss of control.

Weapons: Immediately inform officers about the presence of, prior use of, or availability of weapons, threatened violence, or past violent acts by the stalker.

Privacy: To calm your emotions, ask to speak with the officer privately, away from the source of agitation or threat. If he refuses, it is likely because of safety considerations.

Cease contact: At the scene, cease all contact with the other party. Stop talking to the stalker, avoid physical contact, and otherwise ignore the person. Remember your long-term goals.

Expectations: Clearly state what you expect from the officers. Request an explanation of your options and the resources available to you. Ask for time frames by which certain actions can be expected to take place. If a restraining order has been violated, it should be enforced on the spot.

Follow through: If you request the officers to take an action, support that action. To start an action against the stalker and not follow through will probably worsen the situation and signal weakness and lack of resolve on your part. Call your local victim services agency to seek support.

Summary

These strategies are offered as behaviors which have the potential to protect you and safely resolve some stalking situations. Above all, do not hesitate to call the police in any threatening situation.

Bibliography

Academy Group Inc.: Dr. Richard Ault, Dr. Roger Depue, Kenneth Baker, R. Stephen Mardigian, Peter Smerick, Michael R. Napier, and Larry E. McCann.

Coleman, F. L. (1997). Stalking behavior and the cycle of domestic violence. *Journal of Interpersonal Violence*, 12(3), 420–432.

de Becker, G. (1997). *The Gift of Fear*. New York: Dell.

de Becker, G. (1999). *Protecting the Gift*. New York: Dial Press.

Domestic Violence, Stalking, and Antistalking Legislation. (1996, April). National Institute of Justice: An Annual Report to Congress Under the Violence Against Women Act.

Hazelwood, R. R., and Burgess, A. W. (2009). *Practical Aspects of Rape Investigation: A Multidisciplinary Approach*. Boca Raton, FL: CRC Press.

Meloy, J. R. (1998). *The Psychology of Stalking*. San Diego, CA: Academic Press.

National Center for Victims of Crime. (2002, April). *Creating an Effective Stalking Protocol: Executive Summary*. Washington, DC: U.S. Department of Justice.

National Victim Center. (1994). *Helpful Guide for Stalking Victims*.

San Diego Stalking Strike Force. (1996). *Training Manual on Stalking*.

Sapp, A. D., and Mahaffey-Sapp, C. (1995). A Motive-Based Offender Analysis of Stalkers. FBI's Negotiator Notes.

Sapp, A. D., and Mahaffey-Sapp, C. A preliminary analysis and typology of stalkers (personal correspondence with Allen Sapp, 5/15/09).

Legislators Talking the Terror of Stalking. (1992, July 21). *USA Today*, p. 9A.

Williams, W. L., Lane, J., and Zona, M. A. (1996, February). Stalking, Successful Intervention Strategies. *The Police Chief*, pp. 24–26.

Wright, J. A., Burgess, A. G., Burgess, A. W., Laszlo, A. T., McCrary, G. O., and Douglas, J. E. (1996). A Typology of Interpersonal Stalking. *Journal of Interpersonal Violence*, 11(4), 487–502.

Appendix H

Interview and Interrogation Strategy Checklist

Preinterview Data

Have security measures been considered (i.e., search of suspect when appropriate, seating arrangement that does not trap the officer, etc.)?

Have my partner and I worked out our individual roles in this interview?

Any suggestions that subject requires any "special care" handling?

Low intelligence?

Mental illness?

Personality weakness?

Recent bereavement?

Why is this person being interviewed?

Any evidence to link the subject to the crime?

Any case facts to make this person suspect?

What "soft words" will I use?

A.

B.

Is the interview room ready? Chairs aligned?

Norming Period

Time allotted for norming: establishing details regarding the interview subject in a nonthreatening environment.

Topics developed for the norming process.

Language Ability

Was it necessary to adjust my language to be understood?

Did the subject reply appropriately in context of the questions?

Examples of appropriate level of word usage?

Norming Period Verbal and Nonverbal Checklist

Check timing and consistency of
  Body posture
  Proximity
  Appropriate eye contact: asking and answering periods
  Continued frontal alignment
  Continued anxiety
  Question response timing
  Hesitancy or appropriate?
  Question avoidance
  Questions answered
Questions avoided

Roadblocks Identified

Family: Who
Employer: Who
Publicity
Fine
Jail
Other

Criminal Interview Period

Open-ended questions to use:
  Do they cover all periods of the crime, the alibi, other investigative
      data, laboratory results, etc.?
  Think *open-ended* follow-up questions
  Tell me about
  Describe
  Explain further how ...
  What did you do on Friday after 5:00 p.m.?
  How are you connected to this matter?
Was the story told at least once uninterrupted?

Transition Period

Behavior-stimulating questions:
  Do you know why I asked to speak with you today?
  What do you know about the (crime)?
  Do you think this was done by someone who _____ ?
  Who do you suspect would do something like this?

Who had the best opportunity to do this?

Who did you tell that you would be interviewed by the police?

What should happen to whoever did this?

Would you give the person who did this a second chance?

Would you be willing to take a polygraph exam on what you have told me?

How will you do on the polygraph exam?

Is there any reason, when we examine the CCTV pictures, that we will see you?

Transition questions developed to determine level of cooperation, truthfulness.

Am I prepared to "score" the verbal and nonverbal indicators of truthfulness or deception for a series of questions?

Do I have a plan for ensuring that some version of "Did you do it?" is covered?

Confrontational Interview Period

Theme Selection

How do I plan to make it easy for the person to tell me what happened?

How may this subject

Rationalize his role?

Project responsibility onto an object or a person?

Minimize his role or actions in this matter?

What four things may I tell this subject about why it is the time to tell everything? The themes I will use are

1.

2.

3.

4.

What is my "I can read your mind" scenario?

Are there any props that are appropriate?

Is it possible for the prop to be in my hands?

Is the prop believable?

Is a good-cop/bad-cop scenario appropriate? Who will be the bad cop?

What version of events will both portray?

Did he really answer the direct question of involvement?

Index